THE JOURNAL OF ANDREW ELLICOTT

THE

JOURNAL

OF

Andrew Ellicott

Late Commissioner on Behalf of the United States . . .
for Determining the Boundary Between the United States
and the Possessions of His Catholic Majesty . . .

by Andrew Ellicott

Americana Classics
QUADRANGLE BOOKS
Chicago

First edition published 1803, Philadelphia
This edition published 1962 by
QUADRANGLE BOOKS, INC. / CHICAGO

Library of Congress Catalog Card Number: 62-17142
Americana Classics No. 7

PREFACE.

THE following work as now handed to the public with the exception of the Appendix, was drawn up between the 14th of June 1802, and the beginning of November following. A press of business then commenced in the Land Office, which prevented not only a careful revisal of the manuscript, but even a second reading. This circumstance, added to my distance from the printer, has rendered a short preface somewhat necessary in order to make a few explanations, and include some additions.

When the journal was drawn up, it was my intention to have divided the map of the Mississippi river from the mouth of the Ohio, to the Gulf of Mexico, into two parts only; but when I came to lay it down, it appeared better to divide it into three: the map containing the third, or lower part, contains also the island of Orleans, and great part of West Florida.

The maps belonging to the Journal are all laid down by a scale of 15 miles to an inch, and may easily be annexed to each other by a little attention to the meridians, and parallels of latitude.

It is stated in the account of the Mississippi, and the settlements on it, that the Sieur la Salle was the

first

first European who descended that river to its mouth:
—This is the general opinion; it is however proper
to observe, that Father Louis Hennepin, a Franciscan
Friar, and missionary, claims the credit of having
descended the Mississippi, to the Gulf of Mexico, in
the year 1680, which is two years before it was ac-
complished by la Salle. Notwithstanding the relation
given by Father Hennepin, and the truth, and propriety of some of his remarks, I am of the opinion
that he has either been mistaken himself, or attempted
to deceive his readers. This Reverend Father by his
own account* left the Illinois on the 8th of March
1680, and arrived at the mouth of the Mississippi on
the 25th of the same month: from which it appears,
that he, and his two men, were 17 days in performing
the voyage; but from these 17 days, 7 are to be
deducted for the delays they met with from different
causes, they were therefore but 10 days actually employed in descending the river, which is scarcely possible: but the time spent in their return to the Illinois,
taken in the most favourable point of view, is too
short to give the least credibility to the relation, and
is moreover at variance with itself. On the 9th of
April we find Father Hennepin in the neighbourhood
of the Akanses, where he appears to have spent several days, for he informs us that he left them on the
24th of the same month, when he, and his men began
to make use of great precaution, to prevent being seen
by their comrades, whom they had left at the Illinois,
and who supposed they had gone to the north up the
Mississippi agreeably to the directions of la Salle,
instead of to the south. They appear by the same
narrative, to have passed their friends undiscovered,
and

* Printed in London in 1698.

and on their journey north of the Illinois river were captured by the Indians, who kept them prisoners several months; but what is still more extraordinary, Father Hennepin states that they were captured on the 12th of April the same year! at this very time they appear by his own account, to have been at the Akansas, (or Arkansas,) which they did not leave until the 24th. From Father Hennepin's own account of his voyage down, and up the Mississippi, I am inclined to believe the whole to be a fiction, and that he proceeded northerly up the river at first agreeably to the instructions of la Salle; and that he, and his two men, were captured by the Indians as stated by himself, which circumscribed his excursions, and left a chasm in his discoveries, which he afterwards thought proper to fill up with this relation.

Since the following work was put to the press, a great change has taken place in the political situation of part of the country on the Mississippi: I mean the cession of Louisiana by the Republic of France, to the United States. On the advantages to be derived to the United States from this cession, there will probably be a great variety of opinions: the security of the navigation of the Mississippi, is certainly an object of the last importance to the inhabitants of our western country, and without which it might be difficult to retain them in the union; but on the other hand, an immediate possession, and sale of the lands west of the Mississippi, might have a tendency to scatter our citizens, already too widely extended to experience all the advantages of society, civilization, the arts, sciences, and good government, and lower the price of our public lands by bringing too great a quantity to market.

It

It does not appear by the cession of Louisiana to the United States, that we obtain the whole of both sides of the Mississippi, for by consulting No. 5. of the maps, it will be seen that the island of Orleans, which lies on the east side of the Mississippi, only extends north to Manshack: from thence northerly along the east side of the river, to the southern boundary of the United States, is still held by his Catholic Majesty as a part of West Florida, and which separates the island of Orleans, from the other possessions of the United States on the east side of the river: but on the other hand, the cession of Louisiana separates the possessions of his Catholic Majesty on the Gulf of Mexico. On this subject a question of great importance, and by no means a speculative one, must naturally present itself to the mind of every person who carefully considers the situation of that country as held by the United States, and his Catholic Majesty. By the cession of Louisiana to the United States, we gain but little on the Gulf of Mexico, and are but little benefitted as a maritime people. The important, and safe harbours, in both the Floridas still remain in the possession of his Catholic Majesty. On the subject of those provinces, and their importance to the United States, I have been particular in the following work.

When we take into view the great extent of that part of our southern, and western country, the trade of which naturally flows into the Gulf of Mexico, and the small part of the coast to which we have any claim, a doubt will arise, whether it would not be for the interest of the United States to exchange that part of the cession lying west of the Mississippi, with his Catholic Majesty for the two Floridas. The possessions

sions of both nations would be rendered more compact by the exchange, and it would prevent the commerce of a large extent of our country lying between the Mississippi, and Chattahocha rivers being put in jeopardy by the future regulations, or directions, of any foreign power.

Lancaster, July
22d, 1803.

District of Pennsylvania, to wit:

BE IT REMEMBERED that on the Fifteenth day of August in the Twenty-eighth year of the Independence of the United States of America, Thomas Dobson of the said District hath deposited in this Office the Title of a Book the right whereof he claims as Proprietor in the words following to wit:

" The Journal of Andrew Ellicott, late Commissioner on behalf of
" the United States during part of the year 1796, the years 1797, 1798,
" 1799, and part of the year 1800: for determining the Boundary be-
" tween the United States and the Possessions of his Catholic Majesty
" in America, containing Occasional Remarks on the Situation, Soil,
" Rivers, Natural Productions, and Diseases of the different Countries
" on the Ohio, Mississippi, and Gulf of Mexico, with Six Maps, com-
" prehending the Ohio, the Mississippi from the mouth of the Ohio to
" the Gulf of Mexico, the whole of West Florida and part of East
" Florida.   To which is added an Appendix, containing all the Astro-
" nomical Observations made use of for determining the Boundary, with
" many others, made in different parts of the country for settling the
" geographical positions of some important points, with maps of the
" boundary on a large scale ; likewise a great number of Thermometri-
" cal Observations made at different times and places."

In conformity to the Act of the Congress of the United States, intitled " An Act for the encouragement of learning by securing the copies of Maps, Charts, and Books to the authors and proprietors of such copies during the times therein mentioned."   And also to the Act entitled " An Act supplementary to an Act entitled " An Act for the encouragement of learning by securing the copies of Maps, Charts, and Books to the authors and proprietors of such copies during the times therein mentioned."   And extending the benefits thereof to the Arts of designing, engraving, and etching, hiftorical and other prints.

GEO. BOND
Dep. Clerk of the District
of Pennsylvania.

CONTENTS

CHAPTER   I.   *From Philadelphia to the mouth of the Ohio*   1

II.   *Down the Mississippi to Natchez*   26

III.   *Events in Natchez*   41

IV.   *Some account of the Mississippi River*   118

V.   *Additional events in Natchez*   138

VI.   *From the Mississippi to the Pearl River*   177

VII.   *Winter in New Orleans*   190

VIII.   *Mobile, Pensacola, and St. Mark's*   198

IX.   *Around Florida to St. Mary's*   239

X.   *St. Mary's and the Okefinokee Swamp*   270

APPENDIX   1

FOLIO OF PLATES AND CHARTS   *following Appendix*

Plates A-F

Illustrations 1-8

JOURNAL.

CHAPTER I.

The author leaves Philadelphia—arrives at Pitts-
burgh—obtains boats, and proceeds down the Ohio
River to its mouth—some account of the river,
adjoining country, and inhabitants.

SEPTEMBER 16th, 1796, I took leave of my family about ten o'clock in the morning, and pro
ceeded to Chester and dined; then rode to Wilmington and staid all night.—Thermometer was 78° in the
afternoon.

17th, Left Wilmington at half past five in the
morning, breakfasted at Christiana, dined at Elkton,
proceeded to the Susquehannah, crossed the ferry
and lodged at Havre de Grace.—Thermometer 60° in
the morning, rose to 70°, fell to 62° in the evening.
Autumnal squalls and showers in the afternoon—
The water in the Susquehannah was 73°.

18th, Left Havre de Grace at five in the morning,
breakfasted at Hartford, dined at Baltimore, and lodged at my mother's on Potapsco.—Thermometer 57° in
the morning, rose to 68°.

B

The

The country from the Susquehannah to Potapsco, does not appear to be in a better state of cultivation, than it was twenty-six years ago. This disagreeable circumstance, is no doubt principally owing to the system of domestic slavery, which yet continues to prevail in the southern states. Early impressions made upon the mind, and habits acquired in youth, are rarely obliterated, though condemned by daily experience.

That domestic slavery is wrong in a moral point of view is evident from the ordinary principles of justice : And that it is politically wrong may be deduced from the following facts. *First,* that a tract of country cultivated by slaves, is neither so well improved, rich, or populous, as it would be if cultivated by the owners of the soil, and by freemen. *Secondly,* slaves cannot be calculated upon as adding to the strength of the community, but frequently the contrary, for reasons too obvious to detail. Notwithstanding those facts are constantly in view, they rarely produce the necessary effects upon minds early habituated to the custom of domestic slavery.

19th, Remained at my mother's.—Thermometer 55° in the morning, rose to 70° in the afternoon—Water in the river 57°.

20th, About 11 o'clock in the forenoon took leave of my mother, brothers and sisters, and rode to Reister's town and got some refreshment, then proceeded about seven miles further and stayed all night.—Thermometer 51° in the morning, rose to 71°.

21st, Set out before sunrise, rode 10 miles and took breakfast, the morning was fine, and pleasant, went on to M'Callester's town and dined. The town is handsome, and appears to be improving, which is not the case with Reister's town. The population of towns,

towns, and villages, is generally very rapid till it becomes sufficient for the commerce of the surrounding country, and afterwards increases, or decreases, with the general state of the improvement of the district, unless aided by something peculiarly favourable in its situation. Left M'Callester's town at 3 o'clock in the afternoon, and rode to Oxford, where I stayed all night.—Thermometer 53° in the morning, rose to 78°.

22d, Left Oxford before sunrise, rode twelve miles and took breakfast; and then proceeded to Shippensburgh. On the way crossed a spur of the Blue mountain, on which peaches were uncommonly plenty, and in great perfection. Dined at Shippensburgh, where I expected to meet our commissary Mr. Anderson, but found that he had not arrived.—Thermometer 63° in the morning, fell to 53° in the evening.

23d, Walked out about half an hour before sunrise and perceived a fine hoar frost.—The thermometer was 40° on the outside of my window; but when placed on the ground among the grass it fell to 35°; it was then placed on a fence-rail which was covered with frost and fell to 34°; but upon scraping together a small quantity of the frost, and applying it to the bulb, the mercury immediately fell to 32°. It has been supposed by some writers, that a hoar frost could be produced by a less degree of cold than 32°, because such frosts frequently appear when the thermometer stands 6 or 7 degrees above that point. This mistake must have arisen from supposing the degree of heat where the thermometer is suspended, and where the frost appears, to be the same; which upon experiment will be found not to be the case. After breakfast, walked out to the three large springs, being the principal sources of that fine stream

of

of water passing through the town, and found the water in each of them $51\frac{1}{2}°$.—In the afternoon the thermometer rose to 69°. The commissary not arriving, I set out about 3 in the afternoon, and rode to Strasburgh.—The water in the large spring in the town 51°.

24th, Left Strasburgh early in the morning. A very heavy hoar frost, vines, potato tops and corn leaves killed in the vallies between the mountains. Breakfasted at Dunn's, dined at Bird's and stayed all night at Wild's tavern at the foot of the Sideling Hill. Peaches in abundance along the road on the north sides of the hills. The frost the preceding night struck much more severely in the vallies, than on the mountains.—The thermometer in the morning on the outside of my window was at 35°, rose in the afternoon to 71°.

25th, Took an early breakfast, and rode to Hartley's and dined, from thence proceeded to Ward's, and stayed all night.—Thermometer 35° in the morning, rose in the afternoon to 73°.

26th, Proceeded to the foot of the Alleghany mountain and breakfasted, ascended the mountain about ten o'clock in the morning and proceeded to Stoy's town and dined, then rode to Mr. Wells's and stayed all night.—Thermometer 53° in the morning, rose to 71°, fell to 52° in the evening. The water in a good spring on the top of the mountain was 55°. The frost appeared to have fallen very partially on the mountains: in some places the vegetation was destroyed, and in others equally elevated, it was not touched.

A number of the farmers on the mountain were engaged in cutting their Buckwheat, and Oats; but Mr. Wells informed me that this was not common so

late

late in the season. The summer on the mountain, is not sufficiently long to bring Indian corn to perfection.

27th, Left Mr. Wells's before sunrise. A very heavy hoar frost: crossed the Laurel hill, and took breakfast at Freeman's tavern: crossed the Chesnut ridge, and dined at Baldrage's· proceeded from thence to Greensburgh, and stayed all night.—Thermometer 35° in the morning on the outside of my window; rose to 80° after crossing the Chesnut ridge.—The water, in a good spring at the base of the Laurel hill 58°, and in a spring on the west side of the Chesnut ridge 57°. It may appear singular, that the water which falls out of the west side of those mountains, should be the warmest that was examined on the road: whether it be owing to subterranean heat, or some other cause, is yet uncertain.—The coldest water in Greensburgh was 55°.

28th, Cloudy: left Greensburgh at seven o'clock in the morning, and rode to Col. John Irwin's and took breakfast, from thence to M'Nair's and dined. Left M'Nair's in a heavy rain, which continued till I arrived at Pittsburgh.—Thermometer 60° in the morning, rose to 68°.

The morning after my arrival at Pittsburgh I waited upon Major Craig, and found that he had two boats ready, one of them flat-bottomed, commonly called a Kentucky boat; the other a second hand keel-boat. These being insufficient he was requested to procure another, which he did in a few days, it was likewise a second hand one. After leaving Major Craig, I waited upon Col. Butler, and presented an order from the secretary of war for a military escort: he gave me assurances, that the men should be ready by the time the waters were sufficiently high to descend the river. The waggons with our stores, instruments and

and baggage arrived on the 3d of October. On the 4th, I examined the state of the instruments, and found that some of them were injured by the jolting of the waggons; repaired them on the 5th. On the 6th, found the water in the Alleghany river 68°; that in the Monongahela 64°; and a few paces within the coal-pit, the temperature of the water was 51°.

On the 16th, there was a small rise of the water, and the three boats were sent off, but had not water to proceed more than three miles. On the 20th, Gen. Wilkinson, and his family arrived, and he very politely gave his boat up to me; it was a second hand one, but the cabbin was new and spacious. The 21st and 22d, were spent in making some repairs to the boat, and on the 23d, I went on board of it, and proceeded down the river to the others, and made such a distribution of the loading, that each vessel drew about the same water.

During my stay at Pittsburgh, the fogs were very heavy, every morning except two, and on those days we had rain.—The thermometer was at no time below 48° nor above 71°.

The town of Pittsburgh continues to improve, the situation is favourable, being on a point of land formed by the confluence of the Alleghany and Monongahela rivers, from which circumstance it enjoys a considerable trade.

24th, Got under way about 10 o'clock in the forenoon, but the water was so low, that it was with difficulty we made eight miles.—The thermometer rose to 76°. The morning very foggy.

25th, Left the shore at sunrise. The large boat was stopped for want of a sufficiency of water, three times in the course of the day; but by the exertions of about thirty men, she was brought along. Fog in the morning—Thermometer rose from 53° to 71°.

26th,

26th, Got under way early in the morning. The large boat was so much injured by dragging her over the stones, that the men had to keep lading out the water all last night: proceeded with great difficulty down to a small town, opposite to the mouth of little beaver. The large boat did not arrive. Fog in the morning—Thermometer rose from 42° to 70°.

27th, The large boat arrived early in the morning, but so much injured that we had to unload her, stop the leaks and make some repairs; reloaded about 4 o'clock in the afternooon, and proceeded a short distance down the river, to get clear of the town, where some of our men got intoxicated, and behaved extremely ill. This will generally be found the case in all small, trifling villages, whose inhabitants are principally supported by selling liquor to the indiscreet and dissipated in the neighbourhood, and to the imprudent traveller. Fog in the morning—Thermometer rose from 41° to 69°.

28th, Left the shore early in the morning; the fog was so thick that when our boats were within twenty yards of each other, they could not be discovered by any of the persons on board. We made about sixteen miles this day. The water had but little motion.—Thermometer rose from 39° to 61°.

29th, Got under way very early in the morning: but little fog; the atmosphere had been so full of smoke ever since we left Pittsburgh that it was but seldom we could see across the river distinctly, but it was carried off this morning by a smart north west wind.

The buildings on the river banks, except in the towns, are generally of the poorest kind, and the inhabitants who are commonly sellers of liquor, as dirty as their cabbins, which are equally open to their children,

children, poultry and pigs. This is generally the case in new settlements; the land being fresh, produces with little labour the immediate necessaries of life, from this circumstance the habit of industry is diminished, and with it the habit of cleanliness.

Encamped in the evening opposite to the Mingo bottom which is rendered memorable for the inhuman murder of the Indians of that name, who resided on it, either by, or at the instigation of Capt. Cresup, Harman Greathouse, and a few others. This outrage was followed by a war of retaliation, which continued for many years with a cruelty scarcely to be equalled in the annals of history.

The evening became calm, and the atmosphere again loaded with smoke, occasioned by the dead leaves and grass, over a vast extent of the country being on fire, which during the night, illuminated the clouds of smoke and produced a variegated appearance beautiful beyond description. Our smoky weather in spring and autumn, is probably the effect of fires extending over the vast forests of our country.

Our people were much fatigued by dragging our boats over the shoals.—Thermometer rose from 39° to 57°.

30th, Detained till one o'clock in the afternoon by the commissary who was endeavouring to procure some meat; but being disappointed we proceeded down the river to Buffalo, where we were again disappointed. Buffalo is a decent village, and is situated on the east side of the river, just above the mouth of a rivulet of the same name. Left Buffalo in the evening, and proceeded about three miles and encamped. The morning was very smoky.—The thermometer rose from 30° to 51°.

31st,

31st, Our commissary went on a few miles before
us, and purchased three beeves, we followed between
seven and eight, in the morning; it was then so smoky,
that we proceeded with difficulty. Encamped about
four miles above Wheeling. Several of our men were
indisposed with sore throats, owing probably to colds
contracted from their frequent wettings.—Thermometer rose from 36° to 47°.

November 1st, About one o'clock in the morning
we had a furious gale of wind; it appeared, as if
nature was making an exertion to free the atmosphere
from the astonishing quantity of smoke, with which
it had been filled for many days. Stopped at Wheeling and took the latitude, and then proceeded to the
mouth of Grave Creek and encamped. Went to view
the amazing monuments of earth, thrown up many
ages ago by the aborigines of the country, for some
purpose unknown to us. One of those monuments
is more than 70 feet high: it has a cavity or depres-
sion on the top, in which a large oak tree was growing. The atmosphere again became smoky in the
evening. The thermometer rose from 30° to 52°.

2d, Found that one of our soldiers had deserted
after being detected in stealing liquor: made search
for him but to no purpose. Got under way at ten
o'clock, but our progress was much impeded by
dragging our boats over the shoals. Encamped at
five in the evening. Cloudy with an appearance of
rain most of the day, but cleared off in the evening.
—Thermometer rose from 29° to 50°.

3d, Got under way about 7 o'clock in the morning,
and continued down the river till sun down. The
large boat was impeded by a strong head wind,
and did not overtake us till eight o'clock in the evening.

C

ing. Cloudy in the morning but no fog, clear at night.—Thermometer rose from 36° to 55°.

4th, Set out early in the morning, but our progress was impeded by head winds. Encamped at sunset. The large boat did not overtake us. Cloudy with thick smoke all day.—Thermometer rose from 35° to 56°.

5th, Left the shore before sunrise, and proceeded down the long reach: at the lower end of it the water was so shoal, that we were two hours employed in dragging our boats over the gravel, and then encamped. The large boat still behind. The fog was so thick in the morning, that for four hours, when in the middle of the river, we could see neither shore; some appearance of rain in the evening.—Thermometer rose from 33° to 49°.

6th, Left the shore at seven o'clock in the morning.—Thermometer rose from 37° to 51° a strong head wind all day, and but little smoke or fog.

7th, Set off at sunrise, and arrived at Marietta about eleven o'clock in the forenoon. Unloaded the boats to stop the leaks, and make some repairs. Smoke as in the morning.—Thermometer rose from 25° to 56°.

8th, The men were employed in repairing the boats. Viewed the amazing works thrown up many ages ago by the Indians. They are the most regular of any I have seen. Some smoke and fog in the morning.—Thermometer rose from 31° to 52°.

9th, Our men still employed in repairing the boats. Our large store boat arrived in the evening. The smoke was so thick all day that we could not see over the river.—Thermometer rose from 34° to 53°.

10th, The boats were repaired, and loaded by one o'clock in the afternoon, we then proceeded down the river.

Marietta

Marietta is a handsome town, standing on a high bank, on the west side of the Ohio river, just above the mouth of the Muskingum. The annual rise of the water has sometimes inundated the lower part of the town. The latitude by a mean of four good observations appeared to be 39° 24' 21″.

During our stay, we were treated with great politeness by Col. Sproat, and a sensible young gentleman, by the name of Tupper, a son to the General of that name. I paid a visit to Gen. Putnam, who had lately been appointed Surveyor General of the United States, and presented him with one of my pamphlets upon the variation of the magnetic needle. He did not return the visit, neither did I hear from him afterwards. The fog and smoke was so thick till ten o'clock in the forenoon, that we could not distinguish one person from another the length of one of our boats. Encamped at sun down.—Thermometer rose from 34° to 56°.

11th, Left the shore at seven o'clock in the morning. Passed the little Kanhawa, and afterwards a miserable village by the name of Belle Prae, next a floating mill, and lastly, the mouth of little Hockhocking.

The ordinary streams of water in that part of the western country, so universally fail in the summer, and beginning of autumn, that the inhabitants are under the necessity of having recourse to floating mills, or to others driven by the wind, or worked by horses to grind their corn. Those floating mills are erected upon two, or more, large canoes or boats, and anchored out in a strong current. The float-boards of the water wheels, dip their whole breadth into the stream; by which they are propelled forward, and give motion to the whole machinery. When the waters rise, and set the other mills to work, the floating ones

C 2

are

are towed into a safe harbour, where they remain till the next season. Although floating mills are far inferior to permanent ones driven by water, they are nevertheless more to be depended upon than wind mills, and may be considered as preferable to those worked by horses. The lessening of manual labour and that of domestic animals, is a subject at all times, and in all countries, which merits the attention of the moralist, the philosopher and legislator. The effect produced by either the wind, or water, is not attended with any expense, and while those elements are directed to the execution of some valuable purpose, manual labour, and that of domestic animals, may be employed in a manner equally beneficial to the community, and more to their ease, safety, and convenience.

Encamped opposite to a miserable village called Belle Ville: made 24 miles this day. Fog in the morning, and smoky all day.—Thermometer rose from 37° to 66°—Water in the river 45°.

12th, Left the shore at daylight. Dragged our boats over several shoals, and encamped at sun down. Very smoky all day.—Thermometer rose from 37° to 55°.

13th, Got under way very early; had to drag our boats a considerable distance over the shoals, with which one of them was much injured. Encamped about sun down, and caught a number of fine cat fish, one of them weighed more than 48 pounds. Very smoky all day.—Thermometer rose from 27° to 52°.

14th, Were under way at daylight, and arrived in the evening at Point Pleasant, a small and indifferent village on the east side of the river, just above the mouth of the great Kanhawa. We were politely treated by Mr. Allen Proyer of that place. Near to where

where the village now stands, was fought the memorable battle between a detachment of Virginia militia, (commanded by Col. Lewis,) and the Shawnee and Delaware Indians. The engagement continued several hours, and the victory was a long time doubtful, and alternately appeared to favour each party; courage, address and dexterity equally characterized both; but the Virginians remained masters of the field.

We had a light shower of rain in the morning, and two in the evening. The atmosphere yet filled with smoke.—Thermometer rose from 41° to 62°.

15th, Arrived at Gallipolis about eleven o'clock in the forenoon. This village is situated on a fine high bank, on the west side of the river, and inhabited by a number of miserable French families. Many of the inhabitants that season fell victims to the yellow fever, which certainly originated in that place, and was produced by the filthiness of the inhabitants, and an unusual quantity of animal, and vegetable putrefaction in a number of small ponds, and marshes, within the village. Of all the places I have yet beheld, this was the most miserable.

There are several Indian mounds of earth, or barrows, within the vicinity of the village. Detained the remainder of the day in procuring meat. The smoke yet continues.—Thermometer rose from 40° to 62°.

16th, Left Gallipolis at eight o'clock in the morning. About two in the afternoon, one of our boats went to pieces in a body of strong rough water, and it was with difficulty conveyed to the shore without sinking. Encamped at sunset. A strong north wind all day, which carried off the smoke.—Thermometer rose from 37° to 52°.

17th, Left the shore at daylight: got fast on a shoal, which extends across the river when it is low,

by

by which we were detained two hours in drawing our boats over it : detained again from one till two o'clock in the afternoon in passing another shoal. Shortly afterwards, two black men belonging to a boat we fell in with in the morning, were drowned in attempting to go to the shore in a canoe. We sent some of our people to aid in finding them, one was taken up but could not be revived. Light showers of rain in the evening. —Thermometer rose from 27° to 63°.

18th, Left the shore before sunrise, got fast, and were detained for more than one hour. Passed the mouth of Sandy Creek, which is one of the boundaries between the states of Virginia and Kentucky. Encamped just before dark. A heavy fog in the morning, the afternoon remarkably clear.—Thermometer rose from 43° to 64°. Water in the river 46°.

19th, Set off before day, got fast on a log where we remained till near sunrise. The fog was so thick, that we could neither discover sand-bars nor logs, till it was too late to avoid them. The fog disappeared about ten o'clock in the forenoon : reached the mouth of the Big Scioto a short time before noon, and took the sun's meridional altitude, by which the latitude appeared to be 38° 43′ 28″ N. The waters of the Scioto have a strong petrifying quality. We collected several fine specimens. Proceeded down the river, and encamped after sunset.

Cloudy, with thunder and lightning in the evening, accompanied by a shower of rain. The atmosphere again filled with smoke.—Thermometer rose from 43° to 65°.

20th, Left the shore at daylight, had a sharp thunder gust between six and seven o'clock, in the morning. At ten o'clock, I left the boats, and went on shore with my skiff to view the salt works, which are about one

mile

mile from the river, in the state of Kentucky, and collected the following information, *viz.* that 300 gallons of water, produce one bushel of salt: that they had 170 iron kettles, and made about 30 bushels of salt per day, which sold for 2 dollars cash per bushel, or 3 dollars in trade, *as they term it.* The salt lick, or spring, is situated in the bed of a small creek, which when high overflows it. The back water from the river also inundates the lick, or spring, when high, together with all the works. From these causes, they were not able to carry on the business more than eight months in the year. But the greatest difficulty they found, was with the *bitter water*, which I supposed was what the manufacturers of salt in England, call bittern, and drains from the salt after it is granulated, and stowed away in the drales to dry. However I asked the manager for an explanation, who replied, " Bitter water is mixed with the salt water, and separated from it in this manner. After boiling the water, till the salt will just begin to crystallize, it is laded out into troughs, or vats, and let stand for some time, and the bitter water which assumes a dark brown colour, floats on the top of the salt water, and is skimmed off, and thrown away, and if this separation was not made, the salt would not properly granulate, but become tough, and form a hard mass of a bitter taste, and quite useless: and if the bitter water was evaporated, it would leave a hard mass of matter, of a disagreeable, and nauseous taste, but as it was useless, they had none of it by them." He likewise informed me, that the bitter water was very injurious to cattle, by inflaming the skins of such as frequently drank it, that the same effect was often experienced by their workmen, and that in a few hours it would destroy the quality of leather. The lick, or spring, does not appear to have been much
frequented

frequented either by buffaloes, or deer, and the cattle in the neighbourhood are not remarkably fond of it. The temperature of the water in the spring was 60°.

Returned to the river, and followed the boats, passed two villages, one in Kentucky by the name of Preston, the name of the other I did not learn. Overtook my company about sunset, and encamped. Cloudy in the evening.—Thermometer rose from 45° to 70°. Water in the river 50°.

21st, Set off before day, and arrived at Limestone about ten o'clock in the forenoon. It is a miserable village ; left it in about an hour. Encamped at dark. Cloudy, with mist, and light showers all day.—Thermometer rose from 39° to 42°.

22d, Rain, and hail from four till ten o'clock in the forenoon, when a heavy fall of snow began, and continued till night. The weather was so extremely bad, that we could not proceed.—The thermometer was 42° in the morning, 33° at noon, and 25° at eight o'clock in the evening.

23d, Clear morning, and hard frost, cleared our boats of ice and snow by ten o'clock in the forenoon, and proceeded down the river. Encamped at sunset. —Thermometer rose from 19° to 27°.

24th, Got under way at eight o'clock in the morning. About eleven o'clock in the forenoon my boat struck the root of a lodged tree in the river, and was so much injured by it, that we had to put to shore and stop the leak, which detained us till noon. The river was much lower than it had ever been known, since the first settlements commenced in that country, and it was with the greatest difficulty we made any progress on that day, being obliged to drag our boats over several shoals, of considerable extent, the weather at the same time being so cold, that the men's
clothes

clothes froze stiff almost as soon as they came out of the water. Encamped after sun set on the east side of the river, opposite to a village called Columbia.— Thermometer rose from 14° to 25°. Water in the river 40°.

25th, Proceeded to Cincinnati, where we arrived about ten o'clock in the forenoon, and found ourselves under the necessity of procuring another boat, in place of one which was rendered useless by dragging it over rocks, stones, and shoals, and repairing the one I had from General Wilkinson. The waters were so low that no boats but ours had reached that place from Pittsburgh since the preceding August, and the season was then so far advanced that no others could be reasonably expected. Our success was owing to the number of people we had with us, and whose quiet submission to unusual hardships does them great credit. A clear day.—Thermometer rose from 20° to 25° and fell to 14° at nine o'clock in the evening.

26th, A clear day.—Thermometer 3° below 0 at sun rise, rose to 21° but fell to 9° at ten o'clock in the evening. Water in the river $33\frac{1}{2}$".

27th, A clear day.—Thermometer 7° at sunrise, rose to 25°. The water rose this day about 2 inches.

28th, A little fine snow last night.—Thermometer rose from 15° to 37°. In the evening the water appeared to have risen about one foot.

29th, A fine pleasant day, and the snow began to melt. The boat being repaired, and another procured, we left Cincinnati in the evening. The water had risen about three feet.—Thermometer rose from 35° to 46°.

Cincinnati was at that time, the capital of the North Western Territory: it is situated on a fine high bank, and for the time it has been building, is a very respecta-

D   ble

ble place. The latitude by a mean of three good observations is 39° 5′ 54″ N. During our stay, we were
politely treated by Mr. Winthrop Sargent, secretary
of the government, and Captain Harrison who commanded at Fort Washington.

30th, Floated all night, and passed the mouth of the
Great Miami early in the morning. The river in
much better order for boating. Rain and snow all day.
Encamped in the evening.—Thermometer rose from
26° to 37°. Water in the river 35°.

December 1st, Left the shore at daylight. Snow
and rain the whole day. Encamped about dark.—
Thermometer 37° all day.

2d, Set off at daylight. Stopped and took breakfast at a small village just above the mouth of Kentucky river. Made but little way on account of a
strong head wind. Encamped just before dark. Cloudy
all day.—Thermometer continued at 29°.

3d, Got under way at daylight; but made little way
on account of head winds. Encamped at dark.—
Thermometer rose from 23° to 30°. Water in the
river 33°.

4th, Set off at daylight, and proceeded down to the
rapids, and encamped. The water was so low that the
pilots would not be answerable for the safety of the
boats in passing the falls.—Thermometer rose from
28° to 35°.

5th, Concluded to risk the boats, rather than be detained till the rise of the waters, and sent all the people, who were either afraid of the consequences, or
could not swim, round by land, and a little after noon,
all the boats were over, but not without being considerably damaged: the one that I was in, had nine of
her timbers broken. Squalls of rain and snow, all the
afternoon.—Thermometer rose from 24° to 29°.

6th,

6th, Spent at work upon our boats. Squalls of snow all day.—Thermometer rose from 21ᶜ to 28°.

7th, Finished repairing our boats. Cloudy great part of the day.—Thermometer rose from 18° to 26°.

8th, Detained till evening by our commissary, who was employed in procuring provision. Set off about sun down.

The town of Louis Ville stands a short distance above the rapids on the east side of the river. The situation is handsome, but said to be unhealthy. The town has improved but little for some years past. The rapids are occasioned by the water falling from one horizontal stratum of lime-stone, to another; in some places the fall is perpendicular, but the main body of the water when the river is low, runs along a channel of a tolerably regular slope, which has been through length of time worn in the rock. In the spring when the river is full, the rapids are scarcely perceptible, and boats descend without difficulty or danger.— Thermometer rose from 22° to 29°.

9th, Floated all night. Stopped in the morning to cook some victuals, and then proceeded on till sunset and encamped.—Thermometer rose from 27° to 35°. Water in the river 33°.

10th, Left the shore at sunrise. About nine o'clock in the morning discovered a Kentucky boat fast upon a log, and upon examination found that it was deserted, and suspected that the crew were on shore in distress, which we soon found to be the case. The crew consisted of several men, women, and children, who left the boat two days before in a small canoe when they found their strength insufficient to get her off. They were without any shelter, to defend them from the inclemency of the weather, and it was then snowing very fast. We spent two hours in getting the

D 2   boat

boat off, and taking it to the shore, where we received the thanks of the unfortunate crew, and left them
to pursue their journey.

Having a desire to determine the geographical position of the confluence of the Ohio and Mississippi rivers, and the large store boat not being calculated for
expedition, I left her with directions to follow with all
possible despatch, and pushed on myself for the mouth
of the river. Stopped at sun down, to give our men
time to cook some victuals : set off at eight o'clock in
the evening, and proceeded down the river against a
strong head wind till almost midnight, when it became
so violent that we had to put to shore. Snow great
part of the day.—Thermometer rose from 21° to 28°.
Water in the river 33°.

11th, Left the shore at daylight, and worked against
a strong head wind till sunset, then went on shore to
dress some victuals. Cloudy great part of the day.—
Thermometer rose from 23° to 29°. Left the shore at
eight o'clock in the evening, and worked all night
against a strong head wind.

12th, This morning the country appeared much
lower, the hills or mountains smaller, and more py-
ramidical. No snow to be seen. The day fine and
clear.—Thermometer rose from 32° to 45°. Put to
the shore at sunset to cook. Got under way before
seven o'clock and proceeded all night.

13th, Went to the shore at eight o'clock in the morning to cook. Set off in two hours. Snow and rain
till evening. Stopped at sun down to cook. Set off
at eight o'clock, and floated all night. The country
flat, and a large portion of the river banks subject to
inundation. Passed Red Bank about nine o'clock in
the evening.—Thermometer rose from 33° to 37°.

14th, The country yet continues flat. Put to the
shore

shore about eight o'clock in the morning to dress some victuals. Set off in two hours. Passed the Wabash about nine o'clock in the evening.—Thermometer rose from 28° to 37°. Water in the river just above the freezing point.

15th, Much ice in the river. Stopped at an Indian camp, and procured some meat. Dined at the great cave. This cave may be considered as one of the greatest natural curiosities on the river, and I have constantly lamented that I could not spare time to make a drawing of it, and take its dimensions. It is situated on the west side of the river. The entrance is large and spacious, and remarkably uniform, the dome is elliptical, and the uniformity continues to its termination in the hill.

Stopped about sunset to take in some wood. Set off in half an hour and floated all night. Cloudy part of the day.—Thermometer rose from 21° to 41°.

16th, At eight o'clock in the morning, one of our boats unfortunately ran on the roots of a tree, which were under water, and bilged. We spent till near one o'clock in the afternoon in repairing her, and then proceeded down the river till about sunset and encamped. The weather that day was very pleasant.—Thermometer rose from 35° to 51°. Passed Cumberland river at 3 o'clock in the afternoon.

17th, Set off at day light, and about nine o'clock in the morning passed the mouth of the Tennessee, and in two hours afterwards arrived at Fort Massac, and was politely received by the commandant Captain Pike, who with the surgeon Doctor Hammel dined with me. The fort stands on a high bank, on the west side of the river. The stones appear to be composed of ferruginous matter and gravel. A considerable quantity of land

land both above, and below the fort, is annually inundated.

Left the fort about two o'clock in the afternoon, and proceeded down the river till dark, and then came to. Thunder and lightning in the evening.—Thermometer rose from 48° to 64°. Water in the river 36°.

18th, Left the shore at daylight, and arrived at the mouth of the Ohio about two o'clock in the afternoon. —Thermometer 46° at sunrise; but fell to 24° in the evening. Water in the river 34°.

19th, Set up the clock, and prepared to make some astronomical observations for the purpose of determining the latitude and longitude of the confluence of those great, and important rivers: for those, and the thermometrical observations made at this place, see the Appendix.

The map of the Ohio river which accompanies this work, is laid down from the best materials I could procure, a number of the latitudes between Pittsburgh and the rapids, were taken by myself: from thence down to the Mississippi, the latest charts have been used, except in a few places which have been corrected by my friend Don Jon Joaquin de Ferrer, an ingenious Spanish astronomer. The map is divided into two parts, that it may not be too large to fold in a quarto volume, and at the same time of such a size, as to shew distinctly the errors that may hereafter be discovered, and serve as a basis for future corrections.

The Ohio river, is formed by the junction of the Allegany and Monongahela rivers, at Pittsburgh, which name it retains till it falls into the Mississippi. It may not be improper here to observe, that all the Indians residing on the Allegany, ever since my acquaintance with the western country, have called that

branch,

branch, as well as the main river, the *Ohio*, and appeared to know it by no other name.

The Ohio is certainly one of the finest rivers within the United States, whether considered as to magnitude, the great extent of its course, or the outlet it affords to an immense and fertile country rapidly filling with inhabitants.

The bottom and sides of the river are stony, from Pittsburgh down to the low country, which is generally supposed to be about eight hundred miles. The strata of stone are horizontally disposed, and principally consist of either freestone, or limestone. This horizontal disposition of the strata of stone, is observable through a very large extent of the United States. I have traced it from Oswego, up Lakes Ontario and Erie, with all the waters falling into them, and through all the western parts of Pennsylvania, and down the Ohio, wherever hills or mountains are to be seen.

The flat, or bottom lands on the Ohio, are not surpassed by any in the United States for fertility; but in many places they are small, and inconsiderable; being limited by hills or mountains, on one side, and the river on the other. A large proportion of the hills, and mountains, are unfit for agricultural purposes, being either too steep, or faced with rocks. The hills and mountains on the east side of the river, generally increase in magnitude, till they unite with the great ridge, commonly called the Allegany: but on the west side they decrease, till the country becomes almost a dead level.

The country produces all the immediate necessaries of life in abundance, and far beyond the present consumption of the inhabitants; the residue, with many other articles, such as hemp, cordage, hard-ware, some glass, whisky, apples, cider, and salted provisions, are
annually

annually carried down the river to New Orleans, where they find a ready market. Mines of pit coal (lithanthrax), are not only abundant, but inexhaustible from Pittsburgh many miles down the river.

The inhabitants of no part of the United States are so much interested in establishing manufactories, as of this. They possess the raw materials, and can export their produce with ease, but their imports are attended with difficulty, great risk, and expense. And so long as they receive neither bounties, nor uncommon prices for their articles of exportation, and depend upon the Atlantic states for their supplies of European manufactures, the balance of trade will constantly be against them, and draw off that money, which should be applied to the improvement of the country, and the payment of their taxes. To this source, may in some degree be traced, the character the inhabitants have too generally had bestowed upon them of insurgents, and disorganizers; to a few individuals these epithets may be applied, but not to the body of the people. In order to judge fairly on this question, it will be necessary to take into view the local situation of the inhabitants. In the Atlantic states every article however minute, if a necessary of life, will not only find a ready market, but command cash. On the Ohio, and its waters, almost the only article, which has heretofore found a ready market at home, and would command cash, was their own distilled spirits. The taxing of this article would therefore be but little different from taxing every article in the Atlantic states, which commanded cash. Such a tax as the latter, I am inclined to believe, would be collected with difficulty, and probably with the same propriety, give the same turbulent character to a great majority of the nation.

I am

I am far from justifying any opposition by force, to the execution of laws constitutionally enacted, they must either expire, or be constitutionally repealed; a contrary proceeding must terminate in the destruction of all order, and regular government, and leave the nation in a state of nature : but at the same time, it is a duty incumbent on the legislature, to attend to the local situations of the several constituent, or component parts of the union, and not pass laws, which are feebly felt in one part, and be oppressive in another. That some turbulent persons are to be met with on our frontiers, every person possessed of understanding and reflection, must be sensible, will be the case so long as we have a frontier, and men are able to fly from justice, or their creditors; but there are few settlements so unfortunate as to merit a general bad character from this class of inhabitants.

The people who reside on the Ohio and its waters, are brave, enterprising, and warlike, which will generally be found the strongest characteristical marks of the inhabitants of all our new settlements. It arises from their situation; being constantly in danger from the Indians, they are habituated to alarms, and acts of bravery become a duty they owe to themselves, and to their friends. But this bravery, too frequently when not checked by education, and a correct mode of thinking, degenerates into ferocity.

Vessels proper for the West India trade, may be advantageously built on the Ohio, and taken with a cargo every annual rise of the waters down to New Orleans, or out to the islands. The experiment has already been made, and attended with success.

The climate on the Ohio, does not appear to be inferior to that of any part of the union. The inhabitants enjoy as much health, as they do on any of the

E   large

large rivers in the Atlantic states. At Pittsburgh, and for a considerable distance down the river, bilious complaints are scarcely known; but they are frequent at Cincinnati, and still more so at Louisville near the rapids.

The timber growing on the river bottoms, is with a few exceptions, such as grows on the east side of the mountains in the middle states, *viz.* Black walnut, (juglans nigra,) butter nut, (juglans cinerea of Wengemheim,) juglans hickory of several species. Sugar maple, (acer saccharinum,) button wood, or sycamore, (platanus occidentalis,) tulip tree, (liriodendron tulipifera,) wild cherry, (prunus Virginiana,) papaw, (anona triloba,) spice wood, (laurus benzoin,) black willow, (salix nigra,) ash, (fraxinus Americana,) elm, (ulmus Americana,) mulberry, (morus rubra,) locust, (robinia pseud-acacia,) honey locust, (gleditsia triacanthus,) buck eye, (aesculus flava,) beech, (fagus ferruginea). To which might be added many more of less note and value. The uplands likewise produce many of the foregoing, with a variety of others, such as black oak, (quercus nigra,) white oak, (quercus alba,) red oak, (quercus rubra,) chesnut, (fagus Americana,) dog wood, (cornus Florida,) cucumber tree, (magnolia acuminata,) and sassafras, (laurus sassafras.)

CHAP. II.

Occurrences at the mouth of the Ohio, and down the Mississippi to the town of Natchez.

THE day after we arrived at the confluence of the Ohio and Mississippi rivers, they were both so full of ice, that it would have been impossible to navigate either of them with any degree of safety; and
the

the day following, each appeared like a vast mass of ice and snow in motion.

On the 22d, both rivers closed, and made a romantick appearance, from the piles of ice which were thrown up in a variety of positions.

We now became alarmed for the fate of our store boat, which we left behind on the 11th, and otherwise found our situation very disagreeable; not expecting to be overtaken by such extreme cold weather, we were not prepared to meet it. Great part of our blankets and stores, flour excepted, were behind. Our instruments, baggage, and other articles, were all taken to the top of the bank, on the east side of the river, where we encamped: and for a number of days the cold was so intense, that we had to keep up large fires both day and night, to prevent our being frozen.

In consequence of the severity of the frost, the water in the river had fallen during the first four days after our arrival about four feet, which left our boats frozen so fast in the mud, and loaded with such a quantity of ice, that it would have been impossible to save them, if a sudden rise of the water had taken place; and the loss of our boats, we were sensible, would involve us in very serious difficulties, as a considerable tract of country where we were encamped, was inundated every annual rise of the waters, and this rise of the waters might be expected with the breaking up of the ice.

On the 23d, we sent three men up the river, to obtain if possible, some intelligence respecting our store boat.

On the 25th, about eight o'clock in the evening, the ice gave way, and continued to move about fifteen minutes. We had laboured hard on that and the preceding days to free the boats from ice, and loosen their bottoms

E 2

from

from the frozen mud and sand; and every person was now engaged to save them. Just as the ice gave way the water rose about four feet, and one of the boats which had not sunk very deep into the mud, rose with it, and was immediately hauled out on the beach; but the other continued fast until loosened by the ice, and was carried away about 80 yards; but the ice stopped so quick, that she received no material injury. A passage was immediately opened through the ice to the boat, which was then drawn out of the water, and safely landed with the other.

The next morning about sunrise the ice gave way again, and notwithstanding the extreme degree of cold, it continued to move the whole day in so great a mass, that the water was not to be seen: Both rivers made the same appearance, and as our boats were now safe, we were enabled to contemplate the prospect which was grand and awful, with some degree of pleasure and composure. The concussion of the ice at the junction of the two rivers produced a constant, rumbling noise, for many hours, similar to that of an earthquake.

After this time, neither of the rivers was completely closed at their confluence: but a few miles above our camp, the Ohio continued shut till about the 20th of January following.

On the 2d of January 1797, the party which had been sent up the river returned, after going as high as fort Massac; but could obtain no intelligence respecting our store boat. But on the 6th our anxiety was in some degree removed by the arrival of Messrs. Ellicott, junr. Rankin, and one of the labourers, who had left the boat, notwithstanding the uncommon severity of the weather, and proceeded down the river, sometimes on the ice, and sometimes on the land, till
they

they fell in with us. By them we were informed, that they continued floating in the boat among the ice so long as it was practicable, and after running several risks, they made the land near the mouth of the Wabash, where they landed the stores, and the whole party (being about twenty in number,) oncamped. They likewise assured us, that every precaution they could devise, had been taken to prevent the loss of the boat, when the ice should give way.

This journey, undertaken and performed by such young men, at such an inclement season, does them great credit, and shews a spirit of enterprize, and a voluntary surrender of every comfort seldom to be met with, in committing themselves, (with what they could carry on their backs,) to the wilderness, to perform what they supposed to be a duty.

During the winter season, until the inundation commences, a number of Indians hunt and reside in the swamp; and it happened fortunately for us, that several companies of them were encamped in our neighbourhood, and by whom we were supplied with meat in exchange for flour: but exclusive of what we obtained from them, our men were not unsuccesful, and besides other game, took a great number of raccoons, and opossums, which after being skinned, and hung out in the frost a few days, afforded a pleasant kind of aliment. They appeared to abound particularly in the swamp.

A few days after we had encamped at the confluence of the rivers, Mr. Philip Nolan,* so well known for his athletic exertions, and dexterity in taking wild horses stopped at our camp on his way from New Madrid to fort Massac, having two boats at the latter place shut up by the ice. From him I obtained much useful

* He was killed by the Spaniards in the spring of 1801.

useful information relative to the situations, and characters, of the principal inhabitants of Natchez; which at that time was a matter of mere curiosity, but which eventually I found extremely useful. Being pleased with his conversation, and finding that he had a very extensive knowledge of that country, particularly Louisiana, I requested the pleasure of his company down the river, as we were unacquainted with the navigation of it, to which he agreed. After staying with us one night he proceeded up to Massac, and remained there till our store boat reached that place, and accompanied her, with his two boats down to us. While in our camp he observed a number of Indians, who were from the west side of the Mississippi, and spoke to them in the several languages with which he was acquainted, but they could not understand him; he then addressed them by signs, to which they immediately replied, and conversed for some time with apparent ease, and satisfaction. This was the first time I had either seen, or heard of this curious language, and being led by curiosity to speak to Mr. Nolan upon the subject, he informed me that it was used by many nations on the west side of the Mississippi, who could only be understood by each other in that way, and that it was commonly made use of in transacting their national concerns. A vocabulary of part of this curious language, has been sent on to the American Philosophical Society by William Dunbar, Esq. of the Mississippi Territory, and contains a much more particular account of it than I could give.

About the 16th of January the weather began to moderate, and both rivers rose gradually, and carried off the ice almost imperceptibly.

On the 29th, in the evening the store boat, with Mr. Nolan's two boats arrived.

The

The 30th was spent in loading our boats, and preparing to leave our encampment.

On the top of the stump of a large tree, to which the zenith sector was fixed, a plate of lead was laid, containing the latitude, and longtitude of that place. The stump was then covered by a mound of earth of considerable magnitude ; but which will probably be demolished in a few years by the annual inundations.

31st, About 11 o'clock in the morning got under way, but the weather being bad, attended with a remarkably heavy rain, we had to encamp before sunset.

February 1st, Left the shore at day light, and proceeded down the river to the station of one of the Spanish gallies ; the master behaved very politely, but informed us that it would be proper to remain at his station till the next morning.

2d, Aftert aking coffee with the Commandant of the galley, we proceeded down to New Madrid, where we arrived about eleven o'clock in the forenoon, and were saluted on our landing by a discharge of the artillery from the fort, and otherwise treated with the greatest respect and attention by the Commandant and officers of the garrison.

In the evening, the Commandant told me, that he had a communication to make, and for some reasons, which he did not detail, requested me to continue there two or three days. He was told, that we had been so long detained, for the want of a sufficiency of water in the Ohio river to enable us to descend it with expedition, and by being so long shut up by the ice, that I could not permit myself to think of it. He then desired me to breakfast and dine with him the next day, to which I consented.

3d, After taking breakfast with the Commandant, I
walked

walked about two miles out to the plains, and high lands: the soil did not appear to be of the first quality. Between the town, and plains is a swamp through which a body of water passes when the river is full. Returned about half an hour before noon, and took the sun's meridional altitude.

Immediately after dinner, the Commandant desired me to walk into a private room with him: after being seated a few minutes, he called in a clergyman of the church of Rome, a native of Ireland, of the name of Maxwell, a well informed liberal gentleman, who acted as interpreter on that occasion. The Commandant addressed himself to me nearly as follows. "Sir, I find myself somewhat delicately situated in consequence of your arrival, which you will readily perceive by this letter, which I received last November, from the Governor General the Baron de Corondelet." He then handed the letter to Mr. Maxwell, who read, and interpreted it. It contained an order to the commandant, not to permit us to descend the river till the posts were evacuated, which could not be effected until the waters should rise.

The order appeared extraordinary to me, and I believe not less so to the Commandant, as the state of the water in the Mississippi below the mouth of the Ohio, is at all times such, that no difficulty could arise in the evacuation of any of the posts claimed by the United States. In our conversation upon the subject I endeavoured to convince the Commandant, that our descending the river could not be construed into a violation of his orders. *First*, because if the want of water was an objection, when the Governor General issued the order, it was now done away by the commencement of the inundation. *Secondly*, that the Governor's intention could have been no more, than to

put

put a stop to the descent of such troops as were intended by the United States, to garrison the posts till they were evacuated: and, as I had no orders respecting the posts, nor men sufficient to garrison them, the order could neither affect me, nor my military escort: and *Thirdly*, that it was impossible that the Governor could have intended that myself and party, should be detained, because it would be in direct violation of the treaty we were preparing to carry into effect. To which the commandant observed, "that as the waters had risen, one half of the objection at least was done away, and we should meet with no impediment from him." We then returned to the company.

At four o'clock in the afternoon we took leave of the Commandant, and his officers, whose hospitality and politeness, I shall ever acknowledge with sensibility. As we left the shore, we were again saluted by the artillery of the fort.

Proceeded about two miles down the river and encamped. My mind was occupied the whole evening, in reflecting upon the order of the Governor General, which had been communicated to me by the Commandant at New Madrid. It occurred to me, that if similar orders were given to the other Commandants below, and they should be less liberal and friendly towards the United States, we might be detained several months during a discussion with the Governor General, which from the great distance, would unavoidably be attended with delay, inconvenience and additional expense.

4th, Left the shore about eight o'clock in the morning, and proceeded down the river till sunset.

5th, Got under way before sunrise, but had to put to the shore about ten o'clock in the forenoon in consequence of a violent head wind, which continued till night, accompanied by a heavy fall of rain.

F

6th,

6th, Left the shore early in the morning, but on account of a strong gale of wind, had to make a harbour where we lay till one o'clock in the afternoon, and then continued down the river till after sunset.

7th, Set out at sunrise, put to at the lower end of an island between the first and second bluffs, a few minutes before noon, and took the sun's meridional altitude, then proceeded down the river, and encamped opposite to the third bluff.

8th, Left the shore at sunrise, and continued our journey till a few minutes before twelve o'clock, when we put to, and took the sun's meridional altitude, got under way immediately, and arrived at the Chickasaw bluffs, about four o'clock in the afternoon. The Commandant received us politely, but at the same time in a manner, which convinced me that he did not expect us. He appeared somewhat embarrassed, and directed the military escort to encamp on the upper or north side of Wolf river, the fort being below. Mr. Nolan, and myself at his request, accompanied him to his quarters: after being seated, he enquired about an express which had lately gone up the river, with dispatches from the Governor General, to the Commandant at New Madrid. We told him the express had not arrived at that place when we left it, neither had the Commandant received any communication from the Governor General since the preceding November.

The enquiries about the express were very natural, and possibly had no more in view, than to find whether the person had done his duty, or to relieve his mind from some anxiety about him, as he had a considerable distance to travel through the wilderness: but the orders from the Governor General, to the Commandant at New Madrid, had produced suspicions

picions in my mind, of which I could not divest myself. I thought it probable that the Governor General
had sent on other orders more pointed, and less equivocal, to stop us at that post.

9th, Remained at the fort, and though treated in
the most polite and hospitable manner, my suspicions
were increased from two circumstances. *First*, the
Commandant and officers appeared, (or affected,) to
be almost wholly unacquainted with the late treaty
between the United States and his Catholic Majesty :
And *Secondly*, no preparations either had been, or were
making to evacuate that post. Exclusive of these,
there appeared an unnecessary suspicion and caution
on the part of his Catholic Majesty's officers : two
armed gallies were brought into the mouth of Wolf
river, between our troops and the fort.

In the course of the day, I informed Mr. Nolan that
I strongly suspected something was in agitation respecting the treaty, with which we were unacquainted.
He replied, " keep your suspicions to yourself, by no
means let them appear, you may depend upon me,
whatever I can discover, you shall know, but the utmost caution will be necessary, both for your success
and my own safety."

10th, Left the Bluffs about eight o'clock in the
morning, and put to the shore a few minutes before
noon to take the sun's meridional altitude, and then
continued our journey till four o'clock in the afternoon,
when we encamped at a remarkable place, where the
Chickasaws and Chocktaws formerly held their con-
sultations.

11th, Left the shore at sunrise, and proceeded down
the river till a few minutes before noon, when we
stopped to take the sun's meridional altitude, and then
proceeded down the river till about three o'clock in the

F 2   afternoon,

afternoon, when we had to stop on account of a violent gale of wind, which continued till after night.—The thermometer rose that day to 66°. Thunder gust after night, and the musquitoes began to be troublesome.

12th, Set out about nine o'clock in the morning. Cloudy in the forenoon, and rain in the afternoon, attended with thunder and lightning. Stopped at sun down.

13th, Got under way very early, and made no halt till we came to after sun down. Cloudy all day with some rain.

14th, Set off very early, but had to come to at three o'clock in the afternoon, in consequence of a violent head wind.

15th, Left the shore about sunrise. A smart frost last night. Stopped a few minutes before noon and took the sun's meridional altitude, and then got under way, but were brought to about two o'clock in the afternoon by Col. Howard, an Irish gentleman in the service of his Catholic Majesty, who had two armed gallies with him; after detaining us about one hour, we proceeded down the river till sunset and encamped.

16th, Left the shore at sunrise, took the sun's meridional altitude, encamped in the evening. A fine pleasant day.—Thermometer rose to 64°.

17th, Left the shore at sunrise. A cloudy warm morning, and a light shower between seven and eight o'clock, attended with a thick fog which continued about three hours, and separated our boats so completely that they did not all join me till the next day. Took the sun's meridional altitude. At one o'clock in the afternoon put to the shore on account of the violence of the wind. On the shore we found a large alligator, and endeavoured to kill him with our oars and

and setting poles, but in vain ; got under way in about
an hour, had a thunder gust in the afternoon.   Encamped in the evening.   A heavy rain at night attended with hail, sharp lightning and uncommon loud
thunder.—Thermometer rose to 65°.   Several of our
people indisposed.

18th, Left the shore just after sunrise, a fine pleasant day.   Took the sun's meridional altitude.   The
maple (acer negundo) and some other trees begin to
look green.   Encamped in the evening.

19th, Set out early in the morning.   Took the sun's
meridional altitude on a small island.   Near the place
of observation, our men killed a large alligator.   It
appeared to be a very strong, though dull and stupid
animal ; but the latter might be owing to its just
emerging from its torpid state.   Arrived at the Walnut Hills, where the Spaniards have erected some considerable works.   The post is a very important one,
and capable of being made very strong.   This day was
very warm for the season, the thermometer rose to 79°.

At this post my suspicions relative to delays being
in contemplation by the officers of his Catholic Majesty, to prevent the treaty going immediately into effect, were nearly confirmed.   The Commandant, though
he treated us very civilly when on shore, had us
brought to by the discharge of a piece of artillery,
which was wholly unnessary as we were near the landing, and making to it as fast as we could.

After we landed, Mr. Nolan and myself accompanied the Commandant to his quarters, and after taking
some refreshment, he enquired my business, with
which he appeared to be almost wholly unacquainted,
and was only satisfied by my sending to the boat for
my papers, and producing an authenticated copy of the
treaty in his own language ! That the Commandant
could

could be unacquainted with a transaction so notorious, and stationed at a post in the vicinity of a settlement, in which Governor Gayoso resided, appeared very extraordinary, and could only be considered as the effect of affectation.

20th, The Commandant very politely conducted us to their different works. At noon I took the sun's meridional altitude at the curtain of the lower battery; after which we dined with the Commandant and his officers, and then proceeded down the river, and encamped about sun down.

The Walnut Hills, are so called from the tree of that name, (juglans nigra,) with which they formerly abounded. The situation is handsome and commanding, but said to be unhealthy: a small, beautiful stream of water, falls from the hills into the Mississippi, which the Commandant informed us was, notwithstanding its favourable appearance, of a very bad quality. A number of peach trees which had been planted on the hills were now in full bloom.

21st, Set out at five o'clock in the morning, but were driven on shore about nine o'clock in the forenoon by a violent gale of wind, which continued till some time in the night. Took the sun's meridional altitude.— Thermometer 74°, almost the whole day, and the musquitoes from that degree of heat had become very troublesome.

22d, Got under way about four o'clock in the morning. A few minutes after we had left the shore, I received the following letter from Governor Gayoso.

" Sir,
" Some gentlemen that left you at the mouth of the Ohio, have informed me of your approaching arrival here,

here, and that to attend you on your commission you bring a military guard and some woodsmen.

" It is with pleasure that I propose myself the satisfaction of seeing you here and to make your acquaintance.

" Though I do not conceive that the least difficulty will arise respecting the execution of the part of the treaty in which you are an acting person, yet as we are not prepared to evacuate the posts immediately for want of the vessels that I expect will arrive soon, I find it indispensable to request you to leave the troops about the mouth of Bayou Piere, where they may be provided with all their necessaries, which you can regulate on your arrival here. By this means every unforeseen misunderstanding will be prevented between his Majesty's troops and those of the United States, besides it is necessary to make some arrangements previously to the arrival of the troops, on which subject I shall have the honour of entertaining you when we meet.

" I embrace this opportunity to assure you of the satisfaction I feel in being appointed to act in concert with you, though your first interview is to be with the General in Chief of this Province.

I have the honour to be with the highest consideration,

Sir, your most humble servant,

(Signed) MANUEL GAYOSO DE LEMOS."

Honourable A. Ellicott.

The foregoing letter was sent by an express to the Walnut Hills by land, but we having left that place before he arrived, the Commandant manned a light canoe, and sent him after us.

The request contained in the letter, respecting the escort, was not only a very improper, but an unnecessary one, and was so considered at that time ; but it

was

was thought best, (as it was now certain that difficulties would be thrown in the way to prevent the immediate execution of the treaty,) to give no direct offence to the officers of his Catholic Majesty, but to depend upon discussion and fair argument, rather than irritation, (which might terminate in force) to ensure success. The escort was therefore left at the mouth of Bayou Piere, where we arrived about two o'clock in the afternoon. Immediately after landing, Mr. Nolan and myself, walked to my friend Col. Bruin's, who had resided some years at that place. From him, I expected to obtain much valuable information respecting the principal characters in that country, and the line of conduct it would be proper to pursue, in the present unfavourable appearance of the important business, submitted to me by my country. In my expectations I was not disappointed.

We were received by the Colonel with that politeness and hospitality, for which he has been so long and justly esteemed. In order to render us all the service in his power, it was agreed that he should go on to Natchez; but to avoid that suspicion, which generally characterises arbitrary governments, to take his passage in one of Mr. Nolan's boats, and not be seen with me till after my interview with the Governor; who had the satisfaction of giving us a formal introduction to each other the day after my arrival.

23d, Took the sun's meridional altitude at the mouth of Bayou Piere, where we were detained by a strong head wind till four o'clock in the afternoon, when we left the escort, and proceeded down the river.

24th, Cool in the morning with some rain. The 22d and 23d had been disagreeably warm, but this day as much too cold. Arrived at Natches about two o'clock in the afternoon.

CHAP.

CHAPTER III.

Containing official correspondence with the officers of his Catholic Majesty, connected by a detail of the circumstances which produced it—interview with a mysterious character from Philadelphia—continuation of the official correspondence and detail, with the incidents which produced the general commotion among the inhabitants—the election of a committee, and termination of the commotion by a compromise between the Governor and inhabitants.

THE correspondence with the officers of his Catholic Majesty and other persons, and the incidents relative to the political state of the country contained in the ensuing part of this work, are substantially the same, as detailed to the Secretary of State, and partly copied from my original communications: some things are added which it was not thought advisable to trust to a hazardous conveyance; but no opinion is altered, and no new colouring is given to meet either the changes of sentiment, of men, or of measures.

Immediately after we arrived at the town of Natchez, the following note was sent to Governor Gayoso by Mr. Nolan.

Landing at the Town of Natchez, Feb. 24th, 1797.

Sir,

It is with pleasure that I announce to you, my arrival as commissioner on behalf of the United States, for carrying into effect the third article of the treaty lately concluded between the said United States, and his Catholic Majesty.

G   I wish

I wish to be informed, when it will be convenient for your Excellency to receive my credentials.

I am, sir, with due respect,
Your humble servant,
ANDREW ELLICOTT.

His Excellency Manuel
Gayoso de Lemos. }

In the evening the following answer was received by the hands of his secretary Mr. Vedal.

Natchez, 24th Feb. 1797.

SIR,

By your favour of this day, delivered to me by Mr. Nolan, I learn with pleasure your arrival at this post, in the character of commissionary in behalf of the United States, to ascertain the boundaries between the Territory of his most Catholic Majesty, and that of the said United States.

I have the honour to be, with the highest respect,
Sir, your most humble servant,
MANUEL GAYOSO DE LEMOS.

Honourable Andrew Ellicott.

The Governor in his reply, having made no answer to that part of my note respecting the reception of my credentials, the time when they could be presented of consequence remained uncertain: several verbal messages passed between us, before this point was adjusted. The Governor urged that we had come upon him by surprise, that it would have been proper to have remained at some distance above the town, till he was officially informed of our approach: but it being now too late to go through this ceremony, the Governor at length consented that we should meet at the

government

government house in the afternoon of the 25th. The meeting took place accordingly, and immediately after my credentials were produced, the Governor was pressed to name a day on which our operations should commence. On this subject some discussion took place, which ended with the Governor's naming the 19th of March following.

On the 27th of February, the following letter was written to the Governor General the Baron de Corondelet, at New Orleans, who was named by his Catholic Majesty as principal commissioner.

Natchez, Feb. 27th, 1797.

Sir,

It is with pleasure, that I embrace this opportunity of informing you of my arrival at this place, as commissioner on behalf of the United States, for ascertaining the boundaries between the territories of his Catholic Majesty, and those of the said United States.

The polite manner in which I have been received at the posts on the Mississippi, now in the possession of his Catholic Majesty, demands my thanks and gratitude, and I am in hopes that a similar conduct will be observed on our part.

I have the honour to be, with great esteem,
Your Excellency's humble servant,
Andrew Ellicott.

His Excellency the Governor General ⎱
  the Baron de Corondelet. ⎰

On the same day that the letter was written to the Baron de Corondelet, we encamped on the top of a hill, at the upper end of the town about one quarter of a mile from the fort, and on the 29th hoisted the flag of the United States. In about two hours after

G 2   the

the flag was hoisted, a message was received from the Governor directing it to be taken down! This request met with a positive refusal, and the flag wore out upon the staff. We were several times notified that parties were forming to cut it down, but the attempt was never made; it would have been resisted by force. On the day the flag was hoisted, a course of astronomical observations was begun, the observations will be found in the Appendix.

Before we encamped, the following intelligence was communicated to me through confidential channels. *First,* that in September previous to my arrival in that country, the Baron de Corondelet in a private conversation, declared the treaty would not be carried into effect, that he as principal commissioner should evade, or delay, from one pretence or other, the commencement of the operations. *Secondly,* that a letter had been written bearing date June 16th, 1796, by Governor Gayoso, to a confidential friend, stating that the treaty was not intended to be carried into effect, and that delay on their part would reduce it to a dead letter.* And *thirdly,* that the country either was, or would be ceded to the republic of France. This intelligence was kept a profound secret for two reasons: *first,* because its being known might have produced suspicions injurious to individuals, and *secondly,* that we might be able gradually to effect our object, and secure to the United States a country very important both from its situation and value of its commerce, before any direct explanations should take place. The dispositions of the inhabitants were sounded, and a large majority appeared in favour of becoming citizens of the United States.

The

* The original letter has been in my hands.

The dispute between the United States and the republic of France, presented serious difficulties, owing to the alliance between the latter power, and his Catholic Majesty. It did not appear improbable, that a common cause would be made between those nations against the United States, and Great Britain, who had lately entered into a treaty, which was offensive to the republic of France, and to say the best of it, was very unpopular in the United States. Whatever my prejudices might be in favour of the principles of the French revolution, and of that nation, for the part it took in our arduous struggle with Great Britain for the liberty we now enjoy, I considered it my duty, as a citizen of the United States, not only to retain the post we then occupied, but to extend our limits if hostilities should commence. This is not meant as an apology for my conduct, but a declaration of my sentiments. My commissary Mr. Anderson was directed to procure all the ammunition he could find among our friends, but to do it in as private a manner as possible. My party then consisted of about 30 persons, (exclusive of the escort which yet remained at the Bayou Piere,) well acquainted with the woods, and generally armed with rifles.

Notwithstanding these arrangements, peace was considered the true interest of the United States, and positive orders were several times given to treat the Governor, and other officers of his Catholic Majesty, with all the respect due to their stations, and to which they were particularly entitled from us, for the attention and hospitality we had experienced from them: and that if hostilities should be commenced, we might not be the aggressors.

We had been but a few days at Natchez, before the Indians became very insolent, insulted a number of our men, walked about the camp with drawn knives, and

and one night we were informed that they intended attacking us, and they actually came part of the way from their camp towards ours, but whether for the purpose suggested I am not certain. In consequence of these repeated insults, and to be able to make some stand if attacked, the following letter was written to Governor Gayoso.

Natchez, March 11*th,* 1797.

DEAR SIR,

The conduct of the Indians yesterday, and last night, owing principally to their constant state of intoxication, renders it absolutely necessary in my opinion, to have recourse to my military escort for protection.

The discipline of our army is such, that you may rest assured none of the inconveniencies mentioned in your first communication to me, are to be apprehended from the escort being stationed at this place: And as the attendance of the guard, forms a part of the treaty now carrying into effect between the United States and his Catholic Majesty, and which I am authorised to declare will be observed by the nation I have the honor to serve, with good faith and punctuality. From these considerations I must request the favour of you, to withdraw your objections against my escort's joining me at this place as soon as possible.

I am, Sir, with great esteem and respect,
Your Excellency's friend,
And humble servant,

ANDREW ELLICOTT.

His Excellency Manuel }
Gayoso de Lemos. }

Immediately

Immediately after sending the foregoing letter to Governor Gayoso, the following was received from the Governor General the Baron de Corondelet.

TRANSLATION.

New Orleans, 4th March, 1797.

Sir,

I received with much satisfaction your favour of the 27th of February last, in which you are pleased to communicate to me your arrival at Natchez, in the character of commissioner on the part of the United States of America, for settling the boundary line between the territory of his Catholic Majesty, and the said United States. I am equally well pleased, with the testimony you have given of the civilities and attentions which were shewn to you from the commanders of the different posts; which has been conformable to the intentions of the Sovereign, to my orders, and to the general principles of the nation, and I doubt not but that on every occasion Spaniards would receive a like attention from the citizens of the United States.

May God preserve you, &c.

BARON DE CORONDELET.

Mr. Andrew Ellicott.

It may be observed, that the Baron de Corondelet wholly omitted saying any thing about commencing our operations, this omission was not expected, though I was well aware that delay would be attempted.

Very soon after the letter was received from the Baron, Governor Gayoso called at my tent, and informed me, that the Baron in consequence of some pressing concerns below, had declined to attend, and that the whole business had devolved on him, with which I expressed my entire satisfaction, and particularly as we

were

were both on the ground, we might immediately proceed to make our arrangements. He assured me,
that no time should be lost, although it would be impossible for him to be ready by the 19th. He added
further, that though the Baron could not attend on account of other pressing business, he was nevertheless
very desirous of having an interview with me at New
Orleans, and for that purpose had given orders to have
a galley fitted up for my accommodation to New Orleans, and from thence, wherever my curiosity might direct. In reply, the Governor was informed, that the
proposal would be taken into consideration, and an
answer given the next day. The day following, a
number of gentlemen (in the Spanish interest,) waited
upon me with assurances, that the Baron was anxious to
see me at New Orleans, that he had written to them upon the subject, and that I might depend on every attention in his power. By this time my mind was made up.
The invitation appeared calculated to produce delay,
divide my small party, and leave no rallying point for
such of the inhabitants of the district, as were in our
favour, if the commotions and intrigues in Europe
should produce hostilities between the United States,
and his Catholic Majesty. From these considerations
the invitation was not accepted. Having an opportunity the same day of writing to New Orleans, the following letter was written to the Baron de Corondelet.

Natchez, March 12*th* 1797.

Sir,
Your favour of the 2d of this month has been duly
received, but contrary to my expectation, does not contain any information respecting the time you will be
ready to proceed to the ascertaining of the boundaries
between the United States and his Catholic Majesty.
This

This appears to me the more extraordinary, as his Excellency Governor Gayoso informed me in his first communication, that your Excellency was the person with whom I must have the first interview relative to the arrangements, and manner of carrying into effect that part of the late treaty, so far as it respects the boundaries between the nations which we represent.

Although my detention here at a great expense to the United States, gives me much uneasiness, my concern would be greatly increased, could I for a moment suppose, that any impediment would be thrown in the way, to prevent a speedy and full execution of a treaty, in which both nations from their local situations are so deeply, and mutually interested: that these interests, and a reciprocity of good offices, may produce a perpetual friendship between the nations we have the honour to serve, is the sincere wish of

Your Excellency's friend, and
Humble servant,*

ANDREW ELLICOTT.

His Excellency the Baron }
  de Corondelet.   }

In the afternoon of the same day, the following letter was received from Governor Gayoso.

Natchez, 12th March, 1797.

MY DEAR SIR,

This morning I had the pleasure to receive your amicable communication dated of yesterday. I give you my sincere thanks for having established this form of intercourse, as it will make our business more easy, and indeed it is more conformable to the sincere friendship that we have contracted.

H   In

* This letter was never anfwered.

In answer to your said letter, I will remark, that such conduct of the Indians is not customary here, I foresaw that it would happen, from the moment you shewed a desire of having your colours flying, before all the transactions were terminated ; knowing the Indians as well as I do, this was the reason of the objection I offered the moment I saw it hoisted, for otherwise I know very well, that it is frequently used by the representatives of any nation in a foreign country, it is even done in Spain by foreign consuls. I am sorry that you should have experienced any inconvenience from this particular circumstance, and that urged by such effects, to wish to have by you your escort. I have not the least objection that it should be called from its actual station, but as it is my duty, and that I am answerable for the tranquillity of the country that is entrusted to my charge, I must propose to you a method that will answer every good and satisfactory purpose. Had you not been unluckily stopped on your voyage to this country, you would have had immediately the General of the province here to begin the operation, of demarking the divisory line between the territories of his Catholic Majesty, and those of the United States of America, he had every necessary to attend to the business, but since the time that he had a right to expect the commissionary of the United States, the war with England has taken place, and his cares thereby encreased, yet he expected to have it in his power, to come to meet you at Daniel Clark's, Esquire, which place is near the point of the 31°, but he has found it impossible, as it would oblige him to make too long an absence from New Orleans, therefore it is myself that will have the honour to accompany you on that important commission on behalf of his Catholic Majesty. This is the moment that I am in want of

every

every individual thing, both for my person, and for the
attendants of the commission, though the geometer,
and other officers that are to be employed, are already
on their way from New Orleans, and will stop at
Clarksville, where I shall go myself as soon as my equi-
page arrives from the capital, but this will inevitably
take some time, therefore the plan that I wish to arrange
with you, will be to make Lofftus's Cliffs our point of
re-union, this place is at a short distance from Clarksville, and it is a very healthy situation, there I will
send every thing concerning the Spanish commission,
and that will be the most convenient place to establish
for a while your head quarters under your military
escort. By adopting this measure, you will have all
your people together, and the most distant disagreeable occurrence avoided; as I am positively confident
that some would happen by the conjunction here as
you propose. It is true that by the treaty an escort
is supposed, and even recommended to each commission, but it is to be on the line, and not at a distance
from it, where it would interfere with other business,
therefore I feel sensibly hurt that it is out of my power to consent in the landing of the troops at this place,
though I have not the least objection on their going
directly to Lofftus's Cliffs.

I have given the most positive orders to prevent the
Indians getting liquor, and to their interpreter I have
given the strictest charge to be always in sight, and
to-morrow I expect that they will remove to some distance from hence.

I have the honour to be, with the highest
Respect and esteem,
Your most affectionate
Friend and humble servant,
Manuel Gayoso de Lemos.

The Honourable
Andrew Ellicott.

By

By this letter, it will be seen that my request relative to the military escort had not the desired effect: but in the mean time, an express had been privately sent to the commanding officer of the escort, with directions to proceed down to the town of Natchez.

Shortly after the Governor's letter was received, we had an interview. He immediately undertook to prove the propriety and necessity of our going down the river to Clarksville, where myself and party, might be altogether; and closed his reasoning by declaring, that if the escort did land at the town of Natchez, he should consider it an insult offered to the king his master. He was told, that few observations would be made at present, as his letter should be replied to immediately, but that there was one circumstance which appeared to require some explanation; that was, the desire constantly manifested to draw us from the town of Natchez, to some other place, less convenient, and more out of the way of information: but as the town of Natchez was designated by the treaty as the place of meeting for the commissioners, any propositions to draw us from thence would be rejected without ceremony. To which the Governor replied, " you have either mistaken my meaning, or I have expressed myself very badly, I do not want you to leave this place, on the contrary, I am desirous you would take up your residence at my house, where you would be much more comfortable than in a tent." He was told in reply, that the tent was more agreeable than a palace, and in which that independence, so characteristic of the country I had the honour to serve, could be indulged and gratified.

On this subject the Governor and myself no doubt perfectly understood each other: he wanted us from the town, and in some place of small importance, and distant

distant from the principal settlement, the fidelity of whose inhabitants he suspected; or at his own house, where our intercourse with them would be under his own eye, and where our plans could not easily be carried on, and digested without a discovery: and for the express purpose of making use of the inhabitants to carry the treaty into effect, or secure the country by force, if such a measure should become necessary, was our real motive for continuing at that place

On the 13th at noon, the following was sent to Governor Gayoso, as a reply to his letter of the preceding day.

Natchez, March 13th, 1797.

Dear Sir,

Your favour of yesterday would have been answered sooner, had not the storm last night prevented me from writing in my tent.

Your letter, as well as other circumstances that have come to my knowledge, contain fresh proofs of your desire to promote good order and harmony in this part of the country. But sir, I cannot suppose that any inconvenience could possibly arise, or the peace of the settlement be disturbed, by the arrival and landing of the escort which I left at Bayou Piere. If I did suppose the contrary, I trust that I should be one of the last persons to propose the measure. In my opinion the escort which accompanied me to Bayou Piere, is as much bound to observe good order in this country, as the troops of his Catholic Majesty. This is not an opinion of the day, it has uniformly been mine ever since I left the seat of our government, in consequence of which immediately upon my entering the Mississippi, I issued standing orders, that when any of our party, the military included, should be in any place where the jurisdiction was exercised by his Catholic Majesty, the
laws

laws and usages of that government should be observed, and submitted to, in the most pointed manner.

As I hope that mere punctilios will never interrupt our friendship, and as the conduct of the Indians has become less exceptionable, since the night before last; I am not so anxious for the escort to be stationed at my present encampment. I would therefore, to prevent any misunderstanding or disturbance, propose that the officer who commands the escort, be directed to proceed down the river to Bacon's landing, from whence he may come to this place, and procure such necessaries as he may be in need of for the season.

As this is the place designated by the treaty for our meeting and making the arrangements for carrying on the business, I conceive there would be an impropriety in my leaving it, until your Excellency is ready to join in fixing the first point of latitude.

I have the honour to be,
With great esteem,
Your humble servant,

ANDREW ELLICOTT.

His Excellency Manuel
   Gayoso de Lemos.

I now found myself involved in a dilemma, the troops were by that time (by my order) on their way to Natchez, and that contrary to the orders of the Governor: being unacquainted with intrigue and address, it was determined to support openly the descent, and landing of the escort, and which might have been done upon good ground, and fair argument, if no other considerations had been involved in the Governor's objections; but the discussion was rendered unnecessary by the following letter from the Governor.

Natchez,

Natchez, 14th March, 1797.

My Dear Sir,

I do myself the pleasure, to acknowledge the reception of your favour of yesterday, and am very happy to find that our sentiments uniformly agree in every thing that can combine the mutual interests of our nations, and I pledge to you my honour and friendship, that every step of my conduct shall be guided by this principle, impressed in me by my duty, and by the very particular attachment that I have for you.

I have the honour to be, with the greatest esteem and affection,

Dear Sir,

Your most humble and obedient servant,

Manuel Gayoso de Lemos.

Honourable Andrew Ellicott.

The Governor's letter was handed to me by his aid Captain Stephen Minor, who was asked, whether the Governor meant by his polite communication that the escort might be stationed at Bacon's landing, or to remain at the Bayou Piere, the latter now being impossible, as I hourly expected its arrival. The captain answered, that " the Governor acquiesced in its being stationed at Bacon's landing."

On the 15th, in the evening, the escort arrived, and on the afternoon of the 16th it proceeded down to its station.

A few days after the landing of the escort, the following verbal message was received from the Governor, by his aid Captain Minor. " Sir, his Excellency has been informed, that the officer commanding your escort, has taken up a number of men as deserters from your army, some of whom are detained contrary to their inclinations, he therefore requests that they may

all

all be immediately discharged." Captain Minor was desired in return, to inform the Governor, that a compliance with his request would require some previous consideration, that it was a subject which might be of importance to both nations, in the prosecution of our business, and therefore the line of conduct we intended to pursue, ought to be well designated to prevent disagreeable interferences : that the next day, the Governor should have my answer. And accordingly in the presence of William Dunbar, Esq. (a gentleman whose talents, extensive information and scientific acquirements, would give him a distinguished rank in any place or in any country,) Captain Minor was desired to inform Governor Gayoso, that his request relative to the deserters had been taken into consideration, and that my conduct should be regulated by the following view of the subject, viz. *First*, That all deserters from the army of the United States, who came into that country since the period appointed by the late treaty, for the evacuation of the posts held by his Catholic Majesty within the limits of the United States, should be considered as wholly without the protection of his Catholic Majesty, and liable to be taken, and detained whenever they fell in our way. *Secondly*, such deserters, as came into that country before the time stipulated for the evacuation of the posts, and had taken the protection of the Spanish government, should, as their case was somewhat doubtful, remain for the present unmolested. *Thirdly*, that all persons against whom there were standing proclamations by the executive of the United States, if found north of a line to be drawn east from the Mississippi, and thirty-nine miles south of the town of Natchez, should be apprehended if they fell in our way. Here this subject appeared to rest.

About

About the time my escort arrived, the principal part of the artillery was taken out of the fort, and carried to the landing, and there was every appearance of a speedy evacuation ; but on the 22d, great industry was used in taking it back, and the cannon were immediately remounted. This gave great alarm to the inhabitants of the district, who generally manifested a desire of being declared citizens of the United States, and at once to renounce the jurisdiction of Spain. In order to quiet the minds of the inhabitants, and be able to give them some reason for the Governor's conduct, which they now began to consider as hostile towards the United States, the following letter was written to him on that subject.

Natchez, March 23d, 1797.

Dear Sir,

The remounting of the cannon at this place, at the very time when our troops are daily expected down to take possession of it, the insolent treatment which the citizens of the United States have lately received at the Walnut Hills, and the delay of the business, (on your part) which brought me into this country, concur in giving me reason to suppose, that the treaty will not be observed with the same good faith and punctuality, by the subjects of his Catholic Majesty, as it will by the citizens of the United States. I hope your Excellency will give such an explanation of the above, as to remove my doubts and apprehensions, which I am afraid have been too justly excited.

I have the honour to be, with great

Esteem and respect, your friend and

Humble servant,

ANDREW ELLICOTT.

His Excellency Manuel
 Gayoso de Lemos.

I

The

The foregoing letter was followed by the following *Note.*

Mr. Ellicott presents his compliments to his friend Governor Gayoso, and wishes to be informed, whether it is true or not, that all the works at the Chickasaw bluffs have been either demolished, or carried to the opposite side of the river, and that every exertion is now making at the Walnut Hills to put that post in a complete state of defence. This representation has this moment been made to Mr. Ellicott.

March 23d, 1797.

The letter and note of the 23d, produced the following reply.

Natchez, *23d March*, 1797.

My Dear Sir,

I have just received your communication of this day, by which I am sorry to find the construction you put on the storing of the ammunition that came from the Walnut Hills in this fort, I have no other place to put them in, for it would be imprudent to leave them exposed in an insecure place, in a time that the Indians might take advantage of us, if they found that in the present circumstances we acted without the necessary precautions. At the same time, that you see me conducting ammunition to the fort, you will likewise see as many go out of it for the Arkansas, to reinforce that post, which now will be exposed to the incursions of the Osage Indians, who in the last season pillaged the white hunters of that country.

I am entirely unacquainted of any ill treatment, that the citizens of the United States should have received at the Walnut Hills; if you mean the execution of the orders of the General in Chief of this province, to demolish that post, it was in consequence of our treaty with

with the Indians, that they might have no just reason
to complain of our conduct, but since I have been informed of their unsettled disposition, I have sent
counter orders to suspend every thing that might injure the actual estate of those fortifications, and in such
circumstances shall not move any thing else until
the arrival of the American troops that are daily expected.

The unavoidable detention that has been experienced in beginning the line, you know the reasons, but
they shall soon be removed, as Lieutenant Colonel
Guillemard is far on his way up, and at his arrival this
important business shall be begun.

I do assure you, that there is nothing that can prevent the religious compliance of the treaty, though I
might observe, that the conduct of some persons that
seem to affect an immediate interest for the United
States is such, as to occupy my attention. I request
that you will be so kind as to take such measures, as
to suppress untimely expressions, that can only tend to
disturb the tranquillity of the public, of which I am
solely answerable for the present. As I was finishing
this, your secretary, Mr. Gillespie, brought me your
note, enquiring if the works at the bluffs had been destroyed or removed to the other side of the river.

What I have already said concerning our treaty with
the Indians, I suppose, has guided the Governor General of this province to take that step. I really do not
know whether they are destroyed or not. I give you
my word, that I did not know what was to be done there,
and it is only by Baron Bostrop that I learn, that post
would soon be evacuated; but as this is a thing that only
regards the General of the province, I cannot account
for it, nor can I say a word more on the subject, as all
the

the orders proceed from him, that post being entirely out of my jurisdiction.

I am with the highest esteem and respect,
Dear sir,
Your most humble obedient servant,
MANUEL GAYOSO DE LEMOS.

Honourable Andrew
Ellicott.

Governor Gayoso in this letter showed less caution, address and judgment, than in any other one he wrote during the whole discussion. He begins by stating, that the carrying back and remounting the cannon, was no more than storing ammunition which had been brought down from the Walnut Hills: when the reverse was manifest to every person in the country, and the whole transaction within view of my tent. No military stores whatever had been brought down from the Walnut Hills, on the contrary, they were making that post more tenable, and the ammunition which he pretended to be sending to the Arkansas, was actually intended for, and sent to the Walnut Hills: and again, the absurdity of sending military stores down the river from the Walnut Hills to Natchez, and from thence back to the Arkansas, was too glaring to merit any serious animadversion. Their fears respecting the Indians were merely affectation, the Indians at that time were decidedly in their favour, and no measures had been taken by our administration to secure the friendship of the Chocktaws, (a brave and numerous nation,) and through whose country we had to pass.

Notwithstanding the inconsistency of this letter of the Governor's, I felt inclined to take it up in a serious point of view, but gave way to the opinion of my particular friends, or little council, which consisted of

a

a few of the best informed, intelligent and independent gentlemen of the district, by whom it was thought best for the present to make a short reply, and affect to have no doubt of the truth of the Governor's statement : in consequence of which the following was sent to him the next day.

Natchez, March 24th, 1797.

Dear Sir,

It is with pleasure I acknowledge the receipt of your Excellency's very satisfactory letter of yesterday. You may rest satisfied, that I have, and shall continue uniformly to discountenance every measure, and the propagation of any opinion, which may have a tendency to disturb the good order and harmony of this settlement.

I shall close this with requesting, that the Commandant at the Walnut Hills, be directed to treat the citizens of the United States with politeness when they stop at that post, as a contrary conduct may be attended with disagreeable consequences on a river, which both nations have an equal right to navigate.

I am, sir, with great respect and
Esteem, your friend and
Humble servant,
Andrew Ellicott.

His Excellency Manuel
Gayoso de Lemos.

From this reply, the Governor supposed that he had allayed my suspicions, and that he might now venture one step further, and make use of me as an instrument in stopping some of our troops that were said to be on their way down the river under the command of Lieutenant Pope. For this purpose, he sent to me

by

by his aid Captain Minor, an open letter to Lieutenant Pope, informing him, that for sundry reasons it would be proper, and conduce to the harmony of the two nations, for himself and the detachment under his command to remain at or near the place where that letter should meet him, until the posts were evacuated, and as every preparation was making for that purpose, the delay would be but for a few days, when he would be happy to see him at Natchez. This proposal to Lieutenant Pope he wished me to second, as may be seen by the following letter.

Natchez, 25th March, 1797.

My Dear Sir,

By every report, you are acquainted with the confirmation of every thing I have told you concerning our business, you know that Lieutenant Colonel Guillimard will be here soon, and that immediately we shall proceed to the running of the line. But as nothing than friendly arrangements are to guide our conduct, it is necessary to avoid every shadow of compulsion. By the contents of my letter to Mr. Pope, you will see my reasons, therefore request that you will join a couple of lines to avoid any more writing.

I am hurried by many people that have business, this being court day, though I have tried to disembarrass myself, but cannot wait upon you.

I am with the highest esteem and
Respect, my dear sir,
Your most humble servant,

Manuel Gayoso de Lemos.

Honourable Andrew ⎫
Ellicott. ⎬

After

After reading the Governor's letter, Captain Minor was informed, that it was impossible for me to join with the Governor in his request to Mr. Pope, as it was well known to me, that instead of evacuating the posts, they were making them more defensible; however I would write to Mr. Pope, and requested him the captain, as he was to be the bearer of the Governor's letter, to take charge of mine also, to which he consented: it was in the following words.

Natchez, March 25th, 1797.

Sir,

This will be handed to you by Captain Minor, a friend of mine, and an officer in the service of his Catholic Majesty, your polite attention to him will be considered as a favour conferred on me.

By order of Governor Gayoso, his letter to you of this date has been shewn to me; his request for you, and the troops under your command, to remain an indefinite length of time above this place, appears to me a very extraordinary one: as sufficient time has already been given by the United States, for the evacuation of all the posts on the east side of the Mississippi above the 31st degree of north latitude, and from the circumstance of the cannon belonging to this place, after being taken to the landing apparently for transportation, being taken back and remounted, I cannot pretend to say that an evacuation is really intended in any reasonable length of time. From this, and some other considerations, I should conclude that the sooner you are here the better. However, as I have no control over the destination of the troops of the United States, except my own escort, I shall take it for granted that your instructions are sufficiently pointed to direct your conduct.

Please

Please to accept of my sincere wishes for the safe and speedy arrival of yourself and troops at this place.

I am, Sir,

Your friend and humble servant,

ANDREW ELLICOTT.

Lieutenant Pope.

The letters were taken up to the Walnut Hills, and safely delivered by the Commandant to Lieutenant Pope on his arrival, which was eight or nine days after Captain Minor had returned from that place.

A few days before Captain Minor went up to the Walnut Hills, a gentleman arrived at Natchez, who informed me that he had a communication to make which was for myself only. It was immediately arranged, that the communication should be made in my tent the next day at nine o'clock in the forenoon. At the time appointed he attended, and after the common ceremonies were over, he began a panegyric upon the late Mr. William Blunt of the state of Tennessee, observing that for his knowledge of men, and dexterity at intrigue, he was perhaps unrivalled in the United States, and that the secretary of war had consulted him (the stranger) upon the propriety of sending Mr. Blunt to France, as minister plenipotentiary to adjust our differences with that nation. Our opinions respecting Mr. Blunt not coinciding, no communication was made, unless his informing me that the secretary of war was aware of the difficulties we should meet with in carrying the treaty into effect before he left the city of Philadelphia, (which was near the latter end of the preceding December) can be called a communication.

If those difficulties were known to the administration at that early period, it was certainly very improper

per to leave us in the dark to combat them, without having any line of conduct marked out for us to pursue. It left it in the power of the administration to avow or disavow our proceedings, as they were more or less successful. This gentleman, after remaining a few weeks at Natchez, and in its vicinity, and spending some time with Mr. Anthony Hutchins, who was then a Major on the British military establishment, and with a Mr. Rapleja a refugee from the state of New York, and likewise on the British establishment, he went to Mobile, and Pensacola, where he resided at the house of Panton, Laslie, & Comp. and their connexions until the explosion of Mr. Blunt's plans. Panton, Laslie, & Comp. are equally known to both Spanish and British governments, as British subjects. For a considerable annuity which they pay to the King of Spain, they have the exclusive privilege of trading with the southern Indians east of the Mississippi, from which circumstance they have acquired a great influence over them. Of this distinguished house, I shall have some occasion to speak hereafter. The gentleman on whose account this digression has been made, and whose mysterious conduct embarrassed me exceedingly, was paid for his services, whatever they were, by the public.

On the 29th of March the Governor issued the following Proclamation.

Don Manuel Gayoso de Lemos, *Brigadier of the Royal Armies, Governor Military and Political of the Natchez, and its dependencies, &c. &c. &c.*

Whereas the political situation of this country, offers a large field to busy, and malignant minds, to agitate and disturb the tranquillity of its inhabitants, it is therefore my duty, and in the continuation of that

K   vigilance

vigilance which I have constantly exerted, not only to promote the happiness of every individual of this government; but likewise to support their interest, and secure their tranquillity, that I now step forth to warn the public against being led by their innocent credulity, into any measure that may be productive of ill consequences, and frustrate all the advantages that they have a right to expect, and that by the present I assure to them, if they continue as they have always done with strict attachment to the welfare of his Majesty, from which will depend the following favourable events, viz.

His Majesty has offered to support the rights of the inhabitants to their real property, and until this is ascertained I am bound to keep possession of this country, as likewise until we are sure that the Indians will be pacific.

Contrary to the general expectation, the same indulgence that has until now protected the inhabitants from distress, will be continued during his Majesty's sovereignty in this country, and this being the season in which the planters are employed in preparing for an ensuing crop, none shall be disturbed from that important object on account of their depending debts.

The misconstruction of what is meant by the enjoyment of the liberty of conscience is hereby removed, by explaining it positively to be, that no individual of this government, shall be molested on account of religious principles, and that they shall not be hindered in their private meetings; but no other public worship shall be allowed, but that generally established in all his Majesty's dominions, which is the Catholic religion.

These important objects that until now have not been published, though resolved, I make known to
the

the public, apprehensive of the dangerous insinuations of several persons, who have made it a business to dazzle the public with false notions, to serve their own purposes in their speculations upon the lands that are lawfully held by all the inhabitants of this government.

I therefore firmly rely, that no person will deviate from the principles of adhesion to our government, until the negociations that are now on foot between his Majesty, and the United States of America, are concluded, and thereby the real property of the inhabitants secured.

Given under my hand, and the seal of my arms, and countersigned by his Majesty's secretary for this government, at government house this 29th day of March 1797.

(Signed)   MANUEL GAYOSO DE LEMOS.

(SEAL) (Counter-signed) JOH. VIDAL, Sec.

This proclamation the Governor pretended was issued to quiet the minds of the people, but it had a contrary effect: it was nevertheless well calculated to answer to the purpose really intended; which was that of attaching two powerful classes of the community for the present, (at least) to the Spanish government: these were *first*, the holders of real property, whose cases were not recognized, and provided for by the Treaty, and *secondly*, those in debt. But the people had been so often deceived, under the arbitrary government which had been exercised there, that they had lost all confidence, and the proclamation served more to irritate than conciliate. As soon as this was discovered by the Governor, he requested William Dunbar, Esq. and Mr. Philip Nolan, to inform me

K 2   that

that he had just received directions from the Governor General the Baron de Corondelet, to have the artillery, and military stores, immediately removed from the forts which were to be given up to the troops of the United States, immediately on their arrival.

The truth of this information was generally doubted, although great pains was taken by the Governor to circulate the report. In order therefore to draw him into a direct explanation, the following letter was sent to him.

Natchez, March 31*st,* 1797.

Dear Sir,

I was last evening addressed by a number of respectable inhabitants of this district. They are very much alarmed for their situations, in consequence of having expressed their satisfaction since my arrival at this place, of very soon becoming citizens of the United States: but your proclamation of the 29th inst. they conceive renders that event very doubtful. They have therefore from considerations of personal safety, and to avoid the insults which many of them have experienced from one or more officers of a small grade in this district, called upon me to use my influence with your Excellency, to grant to them, and all others who are inclined to leave this country, the privilege of disposing of their property, and passports to enable them to reach the frontiers of such states as they may be inclined to remove to.

I have now stated the substance of their application, and assure your Excellency, that from the respectability of the applicants, it is a subject in which I feel myself interested, and to which I request your Excellency's attention.

Ever since I arrived in this district, I have uniformly recommended to the inhabitants a quiet submission

to

to the government now in force; but at the same time, they have in the most explicit manner, been informed that the period could not be far distant, when the jurisdiction of the United States would be extended to them: but they are not satisfied, they have their suspicions, and it is your Excellency alone who can quiet them. Let the cannon, and military stores be again taken out of the fort, withdraw your objections to the descent of the American troops, and their apprehensions will subside. I do not pretend to say that their apprehensions are well founded, it is possible they are not, but your objections to my escort being stationed with me, your hauling back, and remounting the cannon at this place, your despatching Capt. Minor to delay the arrival of the American troops at this place, added to your proclamation however well meant, have had a contrary effect.

I have enclosed two paragraphs from the address, which was handed to me last evening.*

I am, Sir, with esteem,
Your friend and humble servant,
ANDREW ELLICOTT.

His Excellency Manuel }
  Gayoso de Lemos. }

To

---

* The address was drawn up by the late Mr. Narsworthy Hunter who was at that time a military officer under his Catholic Majesty, and had been an active person against such citizens of the United States who were preparing to attack the Spanish colonies by the advice of Mr. Genet. He was since member of Congress from the Mississippi Territory —The paragraphs are verbatim as follows, viz. " Many whose ideas of allegiance had been preponderant from the treaty until the time of your arrival at this place, thought themselves now at full liberty to announce their sentiments in any way that might not affect the operations of peace and good order in society. But the result is a melancholy contrast to the construction.—Some have already been torn away from the bosom of agricultural life and conveyed to prison with every indignant epithet that malevolence could invent. Scouts are crossing the country in various directions, breathing threats of

To this letter the Governor returned the following answer:

Natchez, March 31*st*, 1797.

My Dear Sir,

I have just now received your favour of this day, in which you inform me of the application made by several respectable inhabitants of this government to you, requesting your interposition to facilitate to them a privilege that they never ceased to enjoy, and in which consists the greatest liberty of a Spaniard. There is not one single example in our government, of having made opposition to any person selling his property, and leaving the country whenever they called for a passport, and as our system is not altered, I shall not refuse the same privilege to any person that may apply to me for it.

I am very sorry that the persons that addressed you, have imposed on your credulity, and goodness, making use of remonstrances proper to make sensations on the feelings of a good citizen of the United States; but there is not a word of truth in what they have advanced. I have not taken any notice of the satisfaction that some persons have expressed on the prospect of becoming citizens of the United States, nor has any body been apprehended for it, nor have I issued any order for such a purpose, but against Mr.

vengeance against those who had unguardedly thrown aside the mask of duplicity.—Numbers are waiting with solicitude the moment of their fate.

There are many in this country to whose exertions America is much indebted for her political existence.—We call upon you in the name of every friend to that emblem of peace and science which has recently been displayed to us, to stand forth with a confidence suitable to the dignity of your commission and demand of the Governor passports, with leave for all such as would dispose of their property and avail themselves of a change of situations by withdrawing to the United States."

Mr. Green, senr. who made his escape conscious of the criminality of his conduct, which is notorious; indeed in all the extent of this government there is but one single individual confined, and that is for a criminal proceeding. There is not a single patrol out in pursuit of any body, nor just in this moment do I find occasion for it; but if I should, I would employ every possible means in my power to suppress disorders, and to keep the peace of the country as I have already done.

I doubt not of the assurances you pretend to give me, of the good advice you have uniformly given to the inhabitants, it being conformable to a gentleman of your character, and whose object is another than that of interfering in the affairs of government.

My proclamation I found absolutely necessary to calm the minds of the people, stating to them, the true situation of the political arrangements between His Majesty, and the United States of America; which does not dissolve the treaty, but requires an essential explanation, not only with regard to the points alluded to in my proclamation, but likewise as I am authorized to declare to you, that the General in chief of the province finds himself under the necessity to consult His Majesty concerning the manner in which the posts are to be evacuated, as it appears from General Wayne's communication to him, that he expects the posts will be delivered with the buildings standing as they are, and by the treaty we conceive that the posts are to be demolished before we quit them, and as such explanations of the true meaning of the treaty either one way, or the other, it might produce unnecessary ministerial contests. My General has given me positive orders, to suspend the evacuation of the posts until the matter shall be amicably
settled

settled between the Courts. In the mean while, if the troops of the United States that are daily expected arrive, they shall be received at the Walnut Hills in the most friendly, and hospitable manner, as is due to a nation with whom we are at perfect peace, and with whom we wish to keep the most perfect harmony.

I flatter myself, that you will do me the justice to acknowledge the propriety of my conduct, in obeying the superior orders of my General, who is actuated by the principles of the strictest honour in supporting the interests of his Majesty entrusted to him.

The uniform good harmony that we have promised reciprocally to one another, will subsist, and it will not only be our duty but likewise our glory, to banish every shadow of misunderstanding which is wrong-fully interpreted by the public, without any more foundation than asserted by those that tried to per-suade you of wrongs that they never suffered.

I am with the most sincere sentiments
of esteem and true friendship,
My dear Sir,
Your most humble servant,
MANUEL GAYOSO DE LEMOS.

Honourable Andrew }
   Ellicott. }

This letter of the Governor's convinced me of the truth of the confidential communications which I have already mentioned to have received on my arrival, and to bring him to an official, unequivocal explana-tion for his conduct, was the principal design of the preceding correspondence.

The true cause of the delay being now avowed, the correspondence with the principal part of the foregoing detail, was forwarded with all possible expedition by
a young

a young lawyer by the name of Knox, to the Secretary of State, that government might not be ignorant of our situation, and be enabled to take such prompt measures as the nature of the case appeared to require.

The securing the country to the United States, and the safety of such of the inhabitants as had appeared openly in our favour, were objects of no small importance. Some of the inhabitants had been imprudently warm, among whom was Mr. Green, senr. the same person mentioned in Governor Gayoso's last letter. A very short time after my arrival, he offered me his assistance with that of an hundred volunteers, who he assured me would join in an enterprize, to take the Spanish fort: But he was not the only one who offered his services, they were more general than could be reasonably expected. It was Mr. Green's misfortune that he could not keep his own secrets, and his conduct became known to the Governor, who ordered him to be apprehended; but he made his escape, and retired to the state of Tennesee a few days after I received the Governor's letter of the 31st of March. But of all the propositions that were made to me, that of Anthony Hutchins was the most extraordinary; it was no less than to take the Governor by surprize, and convey him a prisoner into the Chickasaw nation. This proposition was rejected, but not with contempt. Mr. Hutchins was popular with one class of the inhabitants, and it would have been improper to offend him, as his popularity might possibly be made use of to our advantage. This proposition he aftewards made to Lieutenant Pope, but it met with the same fate. The attempt would have been wholly unjustifiable unless in case of open hostility, and being of so singular a nature, it rendered the design very suspicious, and he

L   being

being at that time a British officer, it did not appear improbable but he had the interest of that nation in view. These propositions were made by Mr. Hutchins a few days after his interview with a confidential friend of Mr. Blunt's! the mysterious gentleman already mentioned.

The alarm was now so great, notwithstanding the professons of the Governor, that it was with difficulty the people could be prevented from acting offensively, and that a general commotion in favour of the United States would take place in the course of a few weeks was evident; the difficulty was, how to direct its effects to the advantage of our country, without committing our government. The attempt was made, and the public is left to judge of its success.

Any further correspondence with the Governor upon the subject of my mission now becoming unnecessary, our views were directed to the increasing of our strength. For this purpose the officer commanding my escort, (which was stationed less than two miles from my encampment), inlisted a number of recruits; but none of them could be considered subjects of his Catholic Majesty. On this subject the Governor sent me the following letter.

Natchez, 13th April, 1797.

My Dear Sir,

I am informed that the officer commanding your escort, has inlisted several persons residents of this government, which being against the laws of nations, it cannot pass unnoticed, it being an infringement on the sovereignty of the King, my master, and a disregard of the authority residing in me.

I cannot persuade myself that it was done intentionally, nor thinking that it could give the most remote offence;

fence; but as the matter is of the most delicate nature, I request you, to give the necessary orders, that the men so inlisted may be discharged, and delivered to Captain Minor whom I commssion for this purpose.

The object of the escort not being to raise men in this country while under his Catholic Majesty's dominions; I request of you likewise, to give the most precise, and positive orders to the officer of the troops, or to whom it may appertain, to discontinue such proceedings, or any thing that may injure the immunity of the King's dominions, or any of his rights.

The most perfect harmony, and friendship subsisting between his Catholic Majesty, and the United States of America, and the same being recommended in a very particular manner to the individuals of both nations, it would be unaccountable if we, that have the honour to be distinguished by our appointments, did not promote this friendly reciprocity, which not only consists in a hospitable, and polite intercourse, but in guarding, and keeping to one another the prerogatives, and privileges, that are due.

Enclosed I have the honour of transmitting to you a list of the men that to my knowledge, have been recruited in this government by the officer commanding your escort.

> I have the honour to be,
> With the sincerest friendship,
> My dear sir,
> Your most humble servant,
> MANUEL GAYOSO DE LEMOS.

Honourable Andrew Ellicott.

To which the following answer was returned.

Natchez,

Natchez, April 13th, 1797.

DEAR SIR,

Your Excellency's favour of this date has been handed to me by Captain Minor, but the request it contains,
is of so general, and important a nature, and affecting
so deeply the privileges of the citizens of the United
States, that I must take a short time to investigate its
ultimate tendency; as part, if not all the persons named
in your Excellency's list, cannot by any construction
of the late treaty, or the laws of nations, be considered
as subjects of his Catholic Majesty. You may rest assured, that having in view the sacred, and honourable
principles, which are the basis of that government
which I have the honour to serve, and by which treaties are considered the most sacred of all obligations, I
shall be careful neither to infringe the rights of the
subjects of his Catholic Majesty, nor willingly suffer
an infringement of those of the citizens of the United
States.

I have the honour to be,
With great esteem and respect,
Your sincere friend,
ANDREW ELLICOTT.

His Excellency Manuel }
  Gayoso de Lemos. }

Here the discussion on this subject ended. The
men were neither given up, or dismissed.

Several of our soldiers at Bacon's landing became
unwell about the beginning of April, owing to their
disagreeable situation on the bank of the river, being
almost surrounded by the annual inundation. They
were removed to high ground, about one mile and an
half from the river, and the same distance from my
own camp.

Having

Having heard nothing from the troops said to be descending the river under the command of Lieutenant Pope but from the Kentucky boats, which occasionally stopped at Natchez on their way to New Orleans, I became very anxious to know their real situation; but my anxiety was released on the 17th of April by a letter from the Lieutenant, by which I found that he had halted at the Walnut Hills in consequence of Governor Gayoso's letter to him.

Immediately upon receiving Lieut. Pope's letter, the following was written, and sent off in the night by a confidential, active person, but the distance being considerable, and the person having no passport, there was more than a probability of his being taken up, searched, and the letter found and opened; it was therefore necessary to be somewhat guarded; but the person was directed to inform Lieutenant Pope, that it would be proper to leave the Walnut Hills, provided it could be done without blood-shed, and to ascertain this fact, he must make the attempt.

Natchez, April 14th, 1797.

Sir,

Your favour of the 13th has just been received. It is my opinion, that the proper place for yourself, and detachment to be stationed, is at this post—here you can be of more service to the United States than at any other place on the river. Nine tenths of the inhabitants, whom I found numerous beyond my expectation, are firmly attached to the United States; but until your arrival, have no rallying point, in case of a rupture between the United States and his Catholic Majesty, which from the conduct of Governor Gayoso I am under the necessity of concluding cannot be very distant.

For

For particular information I must refer you to the bearer,

And am with respect,
Your friend and humble servant,
ANDREW ELLICOTT.

Lieutenant Pope.

After sending off the above letter, doubts began to arise as to the propriety of bringing the troops into the settlement without the approbation of the Governor, at least it appeared best to have it done by his consent: In consequence of which I waited upon Capt. Minor early the next morning, and requested him to be so good as to inform the Governor that I wished to see him at my tent at nine o'clock of that morning. The Governor attended at the time, when Lieutenant Pope's situation was represented to him—that being a military man, with a separate command, ordered by his superior to perform a certain duty, he had no choice left, he must perform, attempt, or resign: that Lieut. Pope had shewn on the present occasion, a spirit of accommodation which was not expected, and perhaps not strictly justifiable: But come, or attempt it, he must,* and that being the case, it was certainly better that it should be done in peace, than provoke hostilities by meeting with opposition. The Governor after a little hesitation agreed that the Lieutenant, and his detachment should proceed down the river without opposition.

An express was immediately despatched at our joint expense to the Commandant at the Walnut Hills, with directions to permit the troops to leave that place without opposition.

I had

---

* I afterwards discoverd that his orders were provisional.

I had some expectation that the second express would arrive as soon, if not sooner, than the one sent off the preceding night ; which might be the means of preventing disagreeable consequences, if the opposition to the troops leaving that place should extend to force ; and to increase the expedition of the second express, I made an addition to his pay on my own account: And though he left the town twelve hours after the first, (who was on foot,) the first arrived but about one hour before him—and delivered the letter to the Lieutenant, who immediately began to prepare for his departure. The Commandant after protesting against his proceeding, retired into the fort: at this critical moment the second express arrived, and delivered the Governor's orders to the Commandant, who immediately hastened to the landing, and with great satisfaction informed the Lieutenant that he had that moment received orders from the Governor, to permit him to proceed down the river.

On the 24th of April in the forenoon, the detachment arrived at the landing at the town of Natchez, where they remained till the next morning ; in the mean time arrangements were made for my escort to leave its encampment at a certain hour the next morning, and join the detachment under the command of Lieut. Pope at the north end of the town. The two companies met in most excellent order, with the colours flying, and attended with their music, and after the usual salutations, marched a short distance into the rear of my tent, and encamped on a commanding eminence, having both the fort, and government house in full view.

This junction of the two detachments was neither expected, nor intended by the Governor, who saw with extreme chagrin the whole parade ; but it was now too
late

late to provide against it. This measure, with the good appearance of the men, produced such a confidence in our friends, that they entertained but little doubt of our being able to keep possession of the country.

Lieutenant Pope's descending the river was certainly a fortunate circumstance for the United States, though in doing it, he did not strictly comply with his orders from General Wayne, by whom he was instructed to remain at fort Massac, till he obtained some information respecting the evacuation of the posts. And if a judgment was to be formed from the provision made for the detachment, it could not be supposed that it was really intended to descend the river. It was in want of artillery, tents, money, medicines, and a physician. In conseqence of this omission, or bad management, I had to furnish the men with such articles as they were in need of, out of the stores appropriated for carrying the treaty into effect: and after all that I was able to do, we had, (to our great mortification) to borrow some tents from the Governor.

From the arrival of the detachment under the command of Lieutenant Pope, till the first of May, there was a perfect silence respecting our business, but on that day the following letter was received.

Sir,

I have the honour to acquaint you, that the Commander General of this province, desires me to inform you that his Majesty's Envoy in the United States, has given him the intelligence of an attack proposed against our part of the Illenois by the British from Canada, and as such an expedition cannot take place without passing through the territory of the United States, said Envoy did officially communicate what was necessary

to

to the Secretary of State of the United States, requiring that convenient orders should be issued, to have their territory respected, and provide for their own safety, which we doubt not but the United States will acquiesce to, in consequence of the treaty, and good harmony that subsists between the United States, and his Catholic Majesty.

The said Commander General of this Province in consequence of the foregoing information, finds himself under the necessity of putting in a state of defence several points of this river, and particularly Nogales, (the Walnut Hills) to cover Lower Louisiana, in case the British should succeed in their project against Illinois, for which purpose a convenient force shall be sent to Nogales to repair, and defend that post, which far from being against the interest of the United States of America, will in case of being agreed to, leave the military post in that state which it may be found.

As this is a powerful reason, in addition to those that I have offered to suspend the evacuation of the posts, and of running the line, as our attention is entirely drawn towards the defence of the Province. The said Commander General orders me, to pass to you this official communication, and in consequence of the unavoidable delay, to repeat to you in his name, the proposal of remaining here, to go down to Lower Louisiana, or as he thinks might be preferable to remove to Villa Gayoso, where there are sufficient buildings to accommodate you. This insinuation, being an effect of the desire we have to shew every degree of consideration, as a proof of our disposition to improve the friendship between our nations, assuring you that in any part that you should determine to remove to, or stay, the Commander General will faci-

M   litate

litate every conveniency in his power for your satisfaction.

I have the honour to be,
with the highest consideration,
Your most humble servant,

MANUEL GAYOSO DE LEMOS.

Honourable Andrew }
   Ellicott.   }

Natchez, 1*st May,* 1797.

A reply of considerable length was immediately
drawn up to this letter and communicated to Lieut.
Pope, who had likewise received a similar one from
the Governor. The Lieutenant objected to my reply,
as he thought it would with more propriety come from
him, some paragraphs of which he made use of.
Upon hearing his objections, which appeared to have
some weight, I acquiesced, and only sent the following short reply.

Natchez, May 2*d,* 1797.

DEAR SIR,

Your Excellency's favour of yesterday is now before me, but as it principally concerns the commanding officer of the troops of the United States in this
quarter, who I presume will give a satisfactory answer, it will be unnecessary for me to make any
remarks upon it.

In a former communication, you were apprized of
my determination to remain at this place until we proceed to the tracing of the boundary, or recalled by
the executive of the United States.

I am, Sir, with great respect and esteem,
Your friend,
and humble servant,

ANDREW ELLICOTT.

His Excellency Manuel }
   Gayoso de Leṁos. }

On

On the 2d of May Lieut. Col. Guillimard, the surveyor appointed on behalf of his Catholic Majesty under the late treaty arrived; I was then informed, that
the Governor would be ready to co-operate with me in
a few days, but in this report I had no confidence.

On the 3d of May a number of labourers, and arti-
ficers, were engaged in repairing the fort, and several
more pieces of artillery were mounted. On the 7th
a reinforcement of about 40 men arrived. On the
9th Lieut. Col. Guillimard, and a number of officers,
with a boat load of intrenching tools, left the town
for the Walnut Hills. Of the truth of Mr. Guillimard's
departure I was not certain until the morning of the
11th, when the following letter was immediately sent
to the Governor.

Natchez, May 11th, 1797.

Dear Sir,

I am informed, that Mr. Guillimard, the surveyor
on behalf of his Catholic Majesty, has left this place
for the Walnut Hills. From this circumstance, and
the delay on your part, in carrying the late treaty
between the United States, and his Catholic Majesty
into effect, I feel myself impelled, by the duty which
I owe to my country, to request a definitive answer
from you, as to the time you will be ready to proceed
to the determination of the boundaries between the
two nations, agreeably to the stipulations contained
in the treaty above mentioned. The harmony, and
friendly intercourse between the nations we have the
honour to serve, can only be maintained, while they
promptly fulfil their contracts with each other.

I have the honour to be,
With great esteem,
Your friend and humble servant,
Andrew Ellicott.

His Excellency Manuel }
Gayoso de Lemos. }

To

To which the Governor returned the following answer.

Natchez, 11*th May,* 1797.

Sir,

I have received your communication of this day, in which you express to me, that Lieut. Col. Guillimard's absence to Nogales impelled you, to demand of me, a definitive answer as to the time that I should be ready to proceed to the determination of the boundaries between our nations, in compliance with the late treaty.

Mr. Guillimard's absence is not to be long, and it was in consequence of the suspension that I announced to you the 1st instant, as his presence was not essential here for the present.

By my said communication of the 1st instant, you will find that it is out of my power to give you the definitive answer that you require, as it depends on the ministers of both nations to whom this business is intrusted, and through which channel both you, and the commander General of this Province, will be informed of the time that the boundaries are to be determined.

I have the honour to be,
with the highest esteem,
Your most humble servant,
MANUEL GAYOSO DE LEMOS.

Honourable Andrew
   Ellicott.

On the 16th of May, a company of grenadiers arrived at Natchez, from New Orleans, and after staying about 36 hours, proceeded up the river to the Walnut Hills.

By

By this time we had received satisfactory information from the Chickasaw, and Chocktaw nations of Indians, that they had for 8 months past been tampered with by people said to be Spanish agents, to oppose the demarcation of the boundary; they were told that immediately upon the establishment of the line, the United States would take possession of all the lands on the north side of it, and drive them off by force, if they made any opposition. To counteract the effects of these improper suggestions, negotiations were immediately set on foot with the Chocktaws, from whom we had the most to dread, being equally as brave as the Chickasaws, much more numerous, and residing as it were in one neighbourhood. On this subject I shall be more particular in another place.

Mr. Philip Nolan whom I have already mentioned, had now been some weeks in New Orleans; he had at different times been much favoured by the Spanish government, particularly in being permitted to take, and dispose of wild horses, which are to be found in vast numbers west of the Mississippi: and from his singular address, and management had much of the Governor General the Baron de Corondelet's confidence, who informed him, (Mr. Nolan) that the troubles were becoming serious up the river, (meaning Natchez) but that he was determined to quiet them, by giving the Americans lead, and the inhabitants hemp; and asked Mr. Nolan, if he would take an active part in the expedition, to which he replied, " a very active one."

The Baron had carried his plan so far, as to direct a camp to be marked out at Batton Rouge for a considerable body of men, and a contractor was engaged to supply the provision. This intelligence was conveyed to me through a confidential channel, but a knowledge
of

of it was kept from the inhabitants of the district, *first*, because its being known would injure, if not ruin Mr. Nolan, and a few others, and *secondly*, had it been made public, it would have been impossible to restrain some of the inhabitants from committing hostilities. It was thought best, to counteract secretly the plans of the Baron in the city of New Orleans, and turn his weapons upon himself should he persevere in executing his design.

Having heard nothing respecting the intended British expedition from Canada, but from the officers of his Catholic Majesty, it appeared to us, that it was probably no more than a pretext for putting the country in such a state of defence, as to render our getting possession of it difficult, and expensive, and enable his Catholic Majesty to retain a part of it by the negotiation which Governor Gayoso informed us officially was then carrying on.

From every circumstance which came to our knowledge, it appeared certain that there was no design on the part of the officers of his Catholic Majesty to co-operate with us, in carrying the treaty into effect, and the discussion being already carried to a great length, in which we constantly found evasion and finesse, substituted for argument, the correspondence was for the present closed on our part by the following letter to Governor Gayoso.

Natchez, May 16*th*, 1797.

Dear Sir,

Any observations on your favour of the 11th instant, in reply to mine of the same date, appear to be wholly unnecessary as it contains a specific declaration, that the business which brought me into this country is suspended, and the execution of it, to depend upon
future

future negotiation. I shall now take leave of the subject, by laying before your Excellency a retrospective view of some part of our correspondence, and state some facts which occurred antecedent to your Excellency's letter of the 1st instant.

In your Excellency's letter to me of the 17th of February we find these words, " I do not conceive, that the least difficulty can arise respecting the execution of that part of the treaty in which you are the acting person." The day after my arrival at this place, we agreed to proceed down the river on the 19th of March last to meet the Baron de Corondelet, and commence our operations: But previous to that day, I was given to understand by yourself, that the Baron could not attend, and that the business devolved upon you. In my communication of the 23d of March, you will find after mentioning your remounting the cannon at this place, these words, " and the delay in the business upon which I came, concur in giving me reason to suppose, that the treaty will not be observed with the same good faith, and punctuality by the subjects of his Catholic Majesty, as it will by the citizens of the United States." In your reply of the same date, we find the following expression. " The unavoidable detention that has been experienced in beginning the line, you know the reasons; but they shall soon be removed, as Lieut. Guillimard is far on his way up, and at his arrival this important business shall be begun: I do assure you, that there is nothing can prevent a religious compliance of the treaty." Although your Excellency here declares, " that Lieut. Guillimard was far on his way up," he was certainly at home, in New Orleans, sixteen days after the date of your Excellency's letter. In your letter to me of the 25th of the same month you say, " by every report

report, you are acquainted with the confirmation of every thing I have told you concerning the business, you know that Lieut. Col. Guillimard will be here very soon, and that we shall proceed immediately to the running of the line." On the same day you wrote a letter to Lieut. Pope, which was shewn to me by your direction, in which you informed him that the evacuation of the posts was going on, and would be completed in one month. At this very time, you were remounting the artillery in the fort at this place, and rendering it more defensible ; of this circumstance you could not suppose me ignorant, as I had written to you upon that subject only two days before. On the 29th of the same month you issued a proclamation, which contained certain evidences that you did not intend strictly to carry the late treaty into effect. This proclamation created considerable discontent, its design was too obvious, to be hidden by the specious pretence, of delaying the execution of the treaty for the purpose of securing to the inhabitants of the district of Natchez their real property. This finesse not succeeding, I was waited upon by William Dunbar, Esq. and Mr. Nolan, who informed me, that you had declared to them, you had just received directions from the Baron de Corondelet, to evacuate the posts within the United States, then occupied by the Spanish troops, and deliver them to the troops of the United States immediately on their arrival ; and that boats were then on their way from New Orleans to transport the artillery and military stores, into the territory of his Catholic Majesty. Mr. Dunbar waited upon you the same evening, and gave you to understand that he had communicated the intelligence to me. However respectable the characters who gave me this intelligence, and the source from whence they had it, I entertained strong

strong doubts of its authenticity; and therefore to draw from you its certainty, sent my communication of the 31st of March. In your reply of the same date is the following expression: " My General has given me possitive orders, to suspend the evacuation of the posts, until the matter shall be amicably settled between the two courts." This confirmed my suspicions. I am wholly unacquainted with any " matter" to be " settled," or any negotiation carrying on " between the two courts." And I think I may with confidence say, that the Executive of the United States had no idea on the 27th of last March, that his Catholic Majesty would decline carrying into effect a treaty which he had so lately, and with a deliberation of near six months finally ratified: especially when we recollect, that the Court of Madrid, has been remarked beyond any other Court in Europe, for the good faith it has observed, in complying with its national contracts.

From the contents of your last letter, and having no definitive evidence that any Commissioner is authorized to co-operate with me in ascertaining the boundary between the territory of the United States, and that of his Catholic Majesty, any more correspondence between us upon that subject, will for the present be unnecessary.

I have the honour to be,
with great esteem and regard,
Your friend and humble servant,
ANDREW ELLICOTT.

His Excellency Manuel
Gayoso de Lemos.

To this letter the Governor returned the following answer.

Natchez,

Natchez, 17*th of May*, 1797.

Sir,

I have received your communication of yesterday, by which you are pleased to signify to me, that you find unnecessary the continuance of our correspondence, as you are not persuaded that any commissioner is authorized to co-operate with you, in ascertaining the boundaries between the territory of his Majesty, and that of the United States. I have informed you, that I am the Commissioner in behalf of his Catholic Majesty, and I have likewise communicated to you the reasons, that have caused the suspension of our business. I still subsist under the said character, but I am not authorized to proceed, until I receive further orders, which I doubt not will reach you, and me, at the same time: therefore as matters are situated, I shall not trouble you with justifying the motives that have caused some disagreement in my communications; they are far from being insincere, but they have originated from the various, momentous occurrences, influenced by the distance from New Orleans, to this place, and time will evince that our conduct is irreproachable.

> I have the honour to be,
> with the greatest friendship,
> and attachment, and respect,
> Your devoted, humble servant,
> MANUEL GAYOSO DE LEMOS.

Honourable Andrew }
Ellicott. }

On the 19th of May, more troops passed Natchez on their way to the Walnut Hills. The reinforcing of that post, and the fort at Natchez, kept the inhabitants in constant fear; they considered the whole as designed

designed against them, and in order to avert, what they conceived would shortly become a serious calamity, a number of plans were now devised, and communicated to me for attacking the Spaniards; but they were objected to as being premature, and having a tendency to involve the United States in a war. The inhabitants were constantly told, that self defence ought to be their object, and to make that effective, they ought at all times to be ready to repel an attack, and if ready, there could be not a doubt of their success.

One of those plans for attacking the Spaniards was of a very general nature, and covered many sheets of paper; it was drawn up by a Mr. Dayton,* a native of the state of Connecticut, but being a suspicious character, his plan was detained and put into the hands of George Cochran, Esq. to be used against himself, if he should be found playing a double game, or joining the Spanish interest.

About this time a serious difference took place between the Governors, the Baron de Corondelet, and Gayoso, which no doubt must have embarrassed their proceedings, and weakened, if not entirely disconcerted their plans. A number of conjectures were made to account for this difference; but none of them hit upon the true cause. Upon this subject I received the following letter from Governor Gayoso.

N 2

DEAR

---

* He was generally called diving Dayton, from the following finesse, which it is said he used, to get clear of his creditors in New England. After procuring a new suit of clothes, he went to the bank of Connecticut river, where he left his old ones, and put on the new, and wrote on the sole of one of his old shoes, these words "*the last of poor Dayton,*" and then left the country, and proceeded to Natchez. From the circumstance of his clothes being found on the bank of the river, and himself missing, it was generally supposed that he had at once put a period to his life and troubles, but some years ago a person went from the same part of Connecticut to Natchez, and finding Mr. Dayton at that place, concluded that he certainly must have dived from Connecticut river to the Mississippi: hence the cant name.

Concord, May 28*th*, 1797.

DEAR SIR,

I have the honour to address you on a subject, that though it does not concern our public business, it is connected with my conduct towards you. I find the Commander General of this Province, is informed that there has passed several occurrences between you and me, of which I have not given him any notice. I cannot recollect any of our transactions that is not either expressed, or alluded to in our correspondence. With regard to my intercourse with you merely as a gentleman, I hoped it only belonged to us to judge of, but yet it might be such, through inadvertency, as may have drawn the attention of the public, who sometimes misplace the man from his private, to his public character; but even in this case it is not in my principles to act any otherwise than as a gentleman.

I request you therefore, to remind me of any particular circumstance that is not comprehended in the heads that I have expressed, and to be very particular to remark if my conduct towards you, either in a public or private character, has given you the least cause of displeasure.

I have the honour to be,
With the highest esteem and regard,
Your most humble and obedient servant,
MANUEL GAYOSO DE LEMOS.

Honourable Andrew Ellicott.

This letter of Governor Gayoso's appeared in some measure calculated to make me a party in the dispute, the appearance of which I was determined to avoid, and therefore endeavoured to be as guarded as possible, and made no reply till the 31st, when the following was sent to the Governor.

Natchez,

Natchez, May 31*st*, 1797.

Dear Sir,

I have the honour to acknowledge the receipt of your Excellency's favour of the 28th. I cannot recollect any transactions between us, which can be considered as official, "that are not either expressed, or alluded to in our correspondence," in which I presume you have acted agreeably to your instructions, and therefore, (though I lament the delay on your part, in carrying the late treaty between the United States and his Catholic Majesty into effect, as it will have a tendency to disturb the harmony, now subsisting between the nations we have the honour to serve,) I do not impeach your motives.

" With regard to" your " intercourse with" me, " merely as a gentleman," it has constantly been such, as became a person in your station, and consequently entirely satisfactory.

I have the honour to be, with great esteem, And regard, your humble servant,

Andrew Ellicott.

His Excellency Manuel }
  Gayoso de Lemos. }

On the first day of June, I received the following proclamation of the Baron de Corondelet's, by a private conveyance from New Orleans, and not having heard of it from Governor Gayoso, I had some doubts of its authenticity, and called upon Captain Minor to know the truth of it; but it appeared that neither he, nor Governor Gayoso were acquainted with it at that time: it was announced officially two days after, and had an effect very different from what the Baron expected.

Province

PROVINCE OF LOUISIANA.

By his Excellency FRANCIS LEWIS HECTOR, BARON DE CORONDELET, *Knight of the order of Malta, Major General of his Armies, Commandant General of Louisiana, West Florida, Inspector of the Troops, Militia, &c. &c. &c.*

PROCLAMATION.

Whereas it has come to our knowledge, that some evil disposed persons, who have nothing to lose, have been endeavouring to draw the inhabitants of Natchez into improper measures, whose disagreeable consequences, would only fall on those possessed of property, whilst the perturbators would screen themselves by flight. We have thought convenient, in order to dissipate the reports, which without the least foundation, are intentionally propagated to alarm the inhabitants, to declare authentically, as we do by these presents, that the suspension of the demarcation of the limits, and the evacuation of the forts, which will be comprehended on the other side of the line, is at present only occasioned by the imperious necessity of securing Lower Louisiana, from the hostilities of the English, who without regard to the inviolability of the territory of the United States, have set on foot an expedition against Upper Louisiana, which they cannot however attack, without traversing the aforesaid territory, an act as violent, as unjust towards the United States, leaving no room to doubt, that if they make themselves masters of the Illinois country, they would avail themselves of the articles of the last treaty, concluded between the United States and Great Britain, in appearance contradictory to that concluded between the former and Spain, by which they guarantee the navigation

tion of all rivers, on which the said United States hold posts, to attack or molest Lower Louisiana. We have thought proper to put the posts of Walnut Hills in a respectable, but provisional state of defence, until the United States are informed of these motives, by the Minister Plenipotentiary of his Majesty, to whom we have communicated them, to provide against these inconveniencies, and by taking the proper steps to cause the territory to be respected, shall put it in our power to fulfil without danger the articles of the treaty concerning limits.

In consequence we indulge the well grounded hope, that the inhabitants of Natchez will behave with the same tranquillity, and entertain the same affection, of which they have (given) the proofs, on occasions towards the Spanish government, which could not, without feeling in the most sensible manner, see itself forced to compel the unsubordinate minds, to hear the dictates of national gratitude in a settlement, which it has been at so much pains and expense, to form and protect.

And, that the present proclamation may get to all, and every one in particular, we order that it may be published, and posted up in all the districts of the government of Natchez in the usual places.

Given under my hand and seal, at the house of government, in New Orleans, the 24th of May, 1797.
(Signed)   BARON DE CORONDELET.
(Counter-signed)   ANDRES LEPOZ. ARMETRO.

It has already been remarked, that the foregoing proclamation was not attended with any beneficial effects to the Spanish government: on the contrary, it served to convince the inhabitants, that his Catholic Majesty intended if possible, to retain the country under one pretence or other, till the treaty should become a dead letter.

ter. The most common observer, could not fail to contrast the reasons given by the two Governors, in their
proclamations for retaining the posts. Governor
Gayoso by his proclamation of the 29th of March, informed the inhabitants, that it was for the purpose of
having their real property secured to them: and the
Baron de Corondelet, that it was for the purpose of
opposing the British, who were meditating an attack
upon that country. The Baron was much more unfortunate in the motive he assigned for keeping the posts,
than Governor Gayoso, and much less acquainted with
the political sentiments and prejudices of a large class
of the inhabitants, who had formerly been British subjects, and to which government many of them were still
attached; both from principle and habit, and no intelligence could have been so pleasing to them, as that of the
British preparing to repossess that country: in this business the Baron was guilty of committing a very glaring oversight for a person of his extreme caution, and
sound judgment. He appears extremely anxious, that
the United States should cause their neutrality to be respected, if the British should attempt to pass through
any part of their territory, to attack the possessions of his
Catholic Majesty; but at the same time, insists upon
holding posts within the United States, to oppose the
same power upon the same principle, the British would
have an equal right to complain of our submitting to it.

After the appearance of the Baron's proclamation,
the public mind might be compared to inflammable gaz;
it wanted but a spark to produce an explosion! A country in this situation, presents to the reflecting and inqui-
sitive mind, one of the most interesting and awful spec-
tacles, which concerns the human race.

About the beginning of June, an itinerant Baptist
minister of the name of Hannah, called upon me, and
asked

asked permission to preach a sermon in my camp the following sabbath, which was the 4th of the month. As no public worship was allowed in any of the Spanish colonies, but that of the Roman Catholics, there appeared to be a difficulty in complying with his request; but to get clear of this obstacle, and to give no just cause of offence to the officers of his Catholic Majesty, I spoke to the Governor upon the subject; who gave his consent without hesitation. On the morning of the 4th, it was stipulated with the preacher, that he should not touch upon political subjects in his discourse, that the public mind was already extremely agitated, and that a few observations however just, and well intentioned, might be productive of great mischief.

A public protestant sermon, being a new thing in that country, drew together a very large, and tolerably respectable audience: and though the preacher meddled not with politics, the effect was nearly the same; the hearers who were generally protestants, wanted liberty of conscience in its fullest extent, and very naturally preferred a sermon which they understood, to a mass, which few of them knew any thing about. The preacher being a weak man, was extremely puffed up with the attention he received on that occasion, which arose more from the novelty of the case, than his own merit and talents, and paved the way for the commotion which took place a few days after.

In case of a rupture with the United States, the officers of his Catholic Majesty calculated largely upon the effects of their intrigues, and the money they had expended in the states of Kentucky, Tennessee, and other districts, west of the Allegany mountain, for the purpose of detaching the inhabitants from the Union. These intrigues so far as I was able to discover, appeared to have originated with Mr. Gardauqui, at the

O   time

time he was his Catholic Majesty's minister to the United States. But the advantages to be derived from these intrigues, were certainly very much overrated.

From a conviction founded on the undeniable evidence contained in several authentic documents, of the reality of those intrigues, suspicion naturally attached itself to every equivocal character who was observed to be passing and repassing between those states, and New Orleans. These suspicions in one instance fell upon a gentleman, who had been very active in these intrigues, and who I was informed on the 5th of June, was immediately setting out by order of the Baron de Corondelet, for the states above mentioned. The critical situation of the country at that time, warranted a conclusion, that his business was to serve the Spanish government, at the expense of the United States. From this impression, measures were immediately taken to embarrass him in his progress, by writing to certain characters in those states, of whose fidelity to their country, there could be no doubt, to have him detained and examined, as often as possible ; the success was as great as could be expected. The secretary of state of the United States was likewise written to on the same subject, on the day before mentioned.

My first written communication to the Indians was likewise sent on the 5th of June : till that time, our correspondence with them had been merely verbal. It required some time to discover the inclinations and wishes of the traders and interpreters, and after being fully satisfied on this head, a circular letter was addressed to such of them as appeared to merit confidence, to be communicated to the chiefs. As this subject would probably be very uninteresting at this time, but little will be said upon it ; it was however attended with considerable

siderable difficulty, and if circumstantially detailed, would of itself require a volume. It was a subject that required great caution in the management, so as to give no offence to the officers of his Catholic Majesty. Our whole view, was to render the Indians harmless, in case of a rupture between the United States and Spain, and to convince them that it was their true interest, to take no part in the quarrels between white nations. War of itself, with all the alleviating circumstances introduced by the present refined state of civilization, should be considered as one of the greatest scourges of the human race; why then add to its calamities by employing savages in it?

The success of those negotiations with the Indians was so complete, that in less than three months they were almost wholly detached from the Spanish interest, and although the United States had no treaty with the Chocktaws, through a large extent of whose country we had to pass, they gave us no molestation, in the execution of our business. A copy of every paper and message relative to this subject, was with my other communications forwarded to the secretary of state, where I presume they remain filed.

The afternoon of Friday the 9th of June, I spent at the Spanish commissaries, and after taking tea in the evening, rode to my camp, which I found to be in great confusion, and upon inquiring the cause, was informed that the Baptist minister was taken and sent to prison; but on what account I could obtain no information. From the state of the country at that time, the worst of consequences were to be expected from this measure. After staying about ten minutes in the camp, and recommending in the strongest terms the necessity of keeping good order, I rode to Captain Minor's, and desired him to wait upon the Governor as quick as possi-

ble,

ble, and request in my name, the liberation of the minister; not as a matter of right, but for the purpose of preserving peace in the country. The Captain lost no time in repairing to the Governor at Concord;* where he found him in a state of considerable agitation, and deaf to the request. I remained at the Captain's till his return, and after receiving the Governor's answer, inquired the cause of the minister's confinement, and received the following statement, which upon further inquiry, I found to be correct. The minister being elated with the attention he had received on account of his sermon, and imboldened by having the permission to speak publicly, he had with enthusiastic zeal, which was a little heightened by liquor, entered into a religious controversy in a disorderly part of the town, generally inhabited at that time by Irish Roman Catholics, who took offence at the manner in which he treated the tenets of their church, and in revenge gave him a beating. He immediately called upon the Governor, and in a peremptory manner demanded justice; threatening at the same time to do it for himself, if his request was not complied with. The Governor with more patience and temper than ordinary, desired him to reflect a few minutes, and then repeat his request, which he did in the same words, accompanied with the same threat. Upon which the Governor immediately ordered him to be committed to the prison, which was within the fort, and his legs to be placed in the stocks.

Between ten and eleven o'clock in the evening, I returned to my camp, and went to bed; but spent great part of the night in devising plans, to direct the commotion which was now inevitable, to the advantage of the United States, without committing either the government or its officers.

On

* The name of his seat about two miles from the town.

On the morning of the tenth, agreeably to my constant custom, I rose about daylight, and walked into the town; when to my surprise I found many of the inhabitants up, and the place in considerable confusion; upon inquiring the cause, I was informed that the Governor, with the officers of government and several Spanish families, had taken refuge in the fort, to avoid the fury of the country inhabitants! Thus in less than ten hours, by an unnecessary, (and at that time an impolitic) exertion of power, the authority of the Governor was confined to the small compass of the fort.

This proceeding of the Governor, was considered by the inhabitants an attack upon the privileges of the citizens of the United States, (Mr. Hannah being one,) and a determination at all events to enforce the laws of Spain, both civil and religious with rigour.

The tumult appeared to have no direct object in view, it was without system, or a rallying point. Some were for immediately attacking the fort, and others for taking the gallies, and making themselves masters of the river; but much the greater part were for taking the fort. By the evening of the tenth, the opposition to the Spanish government had become very general over great part of the district.

On Sunday the 11th, a number of the enterprising opposers of the Spanish government, called upon Lieutenant Pope, and myself, and declared their determination of commencing hostilities in consequence of the imprisonment of Mr. Hannah, and the following address of the Baron de Corondelet's, which they considered as a declaration of war against the United States. The address was in those words, *viz.*

" The government being informed by his Majesty's ambassador to the United States of America, that an expedition assembled on the lakes, was intended to attack

tack the Illinois, has judged necessary for the surety
and tranquillity of Lower Louisiana, to suspend the
evacuation of the post at Natchez and the Walnut
Hills, being the only posts that cover it : the possession
of which will put the English in a situation to disturb
and ravage the country, in case they rendered themselves masters of Upper Louisiana with so much more
facility, as by an article of the treaty concluded poste-
riorly with Great Britain, the United States acknowledge
that the English may freely navigate and frequent the
posts belonging to the United States, situated on the
rivers in general, lakes, &c. being a manifest contradic-
tion to the treaty concluded with Spain, which it appears to annul, because by this the United States acknowledge that no other nation can navigate upon the
Mississippi without the consent of Spain.

Notwithstanding the legitimacy of these motives,
the suspension has been represented to the congress of
the United States, with all the necessary veracity, and
intimated by our orders to the commissary of limits, as
well as to the Commandant of the detachment of American troops now at Natchez. We are now informed,
that a detachment of the army of the United States can-
toned on the Ohio, are on their way by Holstein towards
Natchez, while the militia of Cumberland are intimated
to hold themselves ready, to march at the first notice.

These hostile dispositions can naturally only concern
these provinces, because the United States are in peace
with all the savages. The anterior menaces of the
commissary of limits, and the Commandant of the detachment of Americans now at Natchez, the immediate
rupture, (and if the American gazettes are to be believ-
ed,) already between France, our intimate ally, and the
United States, engage us to be on our guard, to defend
our property with that valor and energy, which the inhabitants

habitants of these provinces have manifested on all occasions, with the advantage and superiority which a
knowledge of our local situation will procure, and with
that confidence which right and justice inspire. If the
congress of the United States have no hostile intention against these provinces, they will either leave the
post of Natchez, or the Walnut Hills, the only bulwarks
of Lower Louisiana, to stop the course of the British,
or give us security against the article of the treaty with
Great Britain, which exposes Lower Louisiana to be
pillaged and destroyed down to the capital, we will then
deliver up the said posts, and lay down our arms,
which they have forced us to take up, by arming their
militia in time of peace, and sending a considerable body
of troops by round about ways to surprise us."

New Orleans, 31*st May*, 1797.

(Signed)   BARON DE CORONDELET.

I shall make a few remarks on this address of the
Baron's, and then pass on to the subject of the commotion.

The Baron in this address, pursues the same inconsistency as he did in his proclamation; he appears not
to be aware of the impropriety of fortifying within the
territory of a neutral power, (without previous consent,)
to oppose the enemies of his sovereign. He likewise
seems to be wholly ignorant of the geography of the
United States, or he could never suppose, that a body
of troops were preparing to march from the Ohio by the
way of Holstein to attack them, which would be an undertaking little short of Ferdenand de Soto's, when he
traversed the Floridas. But why march many hundred
miles through the wilderness, and consume the best
part of a year to attack them, when the same effect might
be produced in a few days, by descending the river?

The

The conduct of the United States, in admitting the British to participate in the navigation of the Mississippi, I never attempted to justify.

The assertion of the Baron, that I had menaced their government, was without foundation, but it is not improbable that he had received such information: the close of the last paragraph admits that they had " taken up arms," which many of the inhabitants of the district of Natchez were of opinion amounted to a virtual commencement of hostilities, if not to a declaration of war: but it is certain this was rather a forced, than a just and liberal construction. But to return to the subject of the commotion.

To have opposed the inhabitants directly in their opposition to the Spanish government, would have put an end both to our influence and power of being useful; and to encourage them, would in my opinion have been improper, as the United States had not extended their jurisdiction to that territory. I therefore on my part, resolved to do neither, but to direct if possible the attention of the people from immediate acts of hostility, by address and management, to other objects, till their proceedings were reduced to system, under which they might be more easily checked if necessary, or their force rendered more efficient, if the officers of his Catholic Majesty should commence hostilities against them.

In pursuance of this plan, the spirit of the people was highly complimented on account of their present exertions, but in the conclusion they were informed, that before they could call with propriety upon the United States for aid or support, in case they were unfortunate, or likely to be overpowered, it would be necessary that the United States should have some evidence of their having made an election in their favour. It was

was therefore proposed, that they should subscribe a specific declaration for this purpose as generally as possible, before hostilities were attempted; but in the mean time, not to lose sight of their personal safety, and to be ready at a moment's warning to act in concert and repel an attack if made upon them. This measure was generally approved, and the subscription papers put into immediate circulation.

On the evening of the 12th, Lieutenant Pope and myself, received a verbal message from the Governor, by his aid Captain Minor, to the following purport, " gentlemen, Governor Gayoso requests the favour of an interview with you to-morrow, as private gentlemen; the interview to be without the fort, to see if some plan cannot be devised to quiet the present disturbance in the country." To this message, I replied that I had no objection to the proposed interview, that I approved of peace, and would join in any measures for that purpose, consistent with the honour and safety of the inhabitants, who generally considered themselves citizens of the United States. Lieutenant Pope's answer was the reverse, he refused to have any thing to do with the Governor, or his messages, unless delivered in writing. As the message was jointly to Lieutenant Pope and myself, and as the Lieutenant would not agree to the interview, I informed Captain Minor that I should not attend alone, upon which he returned to the fort.

On the 13th I received the following letter from Governor Gayoso.

Sir,

By repeated informations, and by every appearance, it seems past a doubt that a number of the inhabitants of this government, subjects of his Majesty, are at present in a state of rebellion, with the hostile design of attacking this fort.

P   I am

I am informed that yesterday, several of the said insurgents were riding through the country, soliciting subscribers to a list that already contained the names of several persons, who declared themselves citizens of the United States of America,* though they are actually under oath of allegiance to his Majesty, and under whose dominion and protection they have lived, and enjoyed the benefit thereof, and the bearers of this list declare themselves commissioned by you for that purpose.

I cannot prevail upon myself, to believe that you have either authorised or encouraged such proceedings, as a conduct of that nature would unavoidably produce the most disagreeable and fatal misunderstanding between our nations, and the total destruction of this district.

Therefore I request you, to give me such a positive answer as will enable me, to inform the Commander General of this province for the intelligence of his Majesty, of the part you take in these transactions, and should you take such an active part in them, as it is represented you do, from this moment I protest in the name of the said Commander General, against such conduct, and make you answerable for the fatal consequences that may ensue. I repeat the request of a positive answer on this subject.

I have the honour to be, with the greatest regard,
Sir, your most humble servant,
(Signed) Manuel Gayoso de Lemos,
Brigadier of the Royal Armies, Governor of Natchez and its dependencies, &c. &c. &c.

Honourable Andrew }
   Ellicott.

Fort at Natchez, June 13th, 1797.
         To

* The Governor alludes to the paper already mentioned, which was put into circulation to prevent the commission of hostilities, and which had been previously explained to his aid Captain Minor.

To this letter the following answer was immediately returned:

Natchez, June 13th, 1797.

DEAR SIR,

In order to answer your letter of this day, which from the spirit of it, denies the existence of that principle which has been the object of a long train of discussion between us, I must refer to your letter, dated the 12th of March last. In that letter, you admit not only that at Daniel Clark's will be about the point of demarkation, but that the Commissioner of his Catholic Majesty, would in all probability meet me at that place.

As the treaty itself was a fact notorious, so likewise ought to be all the transactions attending it, either in direct performance, or open violation. The people therefore became acquainted with those circumstances, that were the result of my observations, or of the acquiescence of the Spanish government. They were matters which involved their felicity, and could not from decency or duty be withheld.

If on the present occasion, the people have thought proper to act in conformity to the intelligence received, which intelligence had the combined sanction of the agents of both governments for its support; is my agency or my conduct, to be called to account with regard to the effects?

A little inquiry into the human mind, would have enabled you, sir, to have discovered a more powerful cause, than any operation of mine concerned in producing the present commotion. The people conceived themselves citizens of the United States, they had a right to conceive themselves so, and they have lately individually come forward to express their wishes and intentions.

P 2

After

After this short detail, of what is the real cause of the present disturbance, I might flatter myself with a complete acquittal on your part, did not the first paragraph of your last letter compel me to form a different conclusion.

On what principle do you still retain the idea, that the citizens of this country are subjects of his Catholic Majesty? Is there not a compact deliberately entered into by the two nations, to the contrary of your opinion? Have not you acknowledged me to be the agent of the United States to carry that compact into effect? And have you not repeatedly pledged your word to co-operate with me in that desirable object? Here I might with propriety ask, what human assurances could have gone farther than those that have been made on your part? Do all solemn obligations between nations depend upon chance or caprice, or is there such a principle universally acknowledged among different powers as the law of nations? If your Excellency admits that there is such a principle as national law, I assert that the inhabitants of this district, cannot be considered in any wise subject to the Spanish monarchy. If you deny the existence of the principle, I have only to observe, that the people cannot with propriety be censured for recurring to that conduct, which will ultimately secure their felicity.

I have proceeded thus far by way of argument, in answer to your communication, from the whole of which you will readily infer a very natural conclusion, that the delay on your part, in carrying the treaty into effect, added to the invariable nature of the human heart, have produced the evils of which you complain. But since you demand a positive reply to the general question, whether I am concerned in measures destructive of

his

his Catholic Majesty's interest, or in an attempt to attack the fort, I give you my honour, that I am not.

As you have assisted me in confirming the sentiment that this territory belongs to the United States, I do now on the part of the said United States, (as their commissioner,) solemnly protest against the officers of his Catholic Majesty, landing any troops, or repairing any fortifications in the territory before mentioned, as I shall consider such conduct a violation of the treaty, and an immediate attack upon the interest, honour, and dignity of my country.

I shall now finally observe, that from your verbal message by your aid Capt. Minor, I expected that your Excellency would have proposed some plan of accommodation consistent with the justice and sentiment of the countries we have the honour to serve: and should you have any such proposals to make, I assure you that I feel every wish to enter into a discussion for that purpose.

I have the honour to be,
  With great esteem and regard,
   Your friend and humble servant,
(Signed)   ANDREW ELLICOTT.
His Excellency Manuel ⎫
 Gayoso de Lemos. ⎭

The foregoing reply to the Governor's letter, was sent to him by a flag about four o'clock in the afternoon. About eleven o'clock the ensuing evening, I received a verbal message by George Cochran, Esq. from the Governor, requesting a private interview with me at the house* of the said Cochran, at nine o'clock the next morning. To this I had no objection, as I supposed the object of the interview was to fall upon some

           plan

* In the neighbourhood of the fort.

plan of accommodation. The next day being the 14th, I met the Governor agreeably to his request. He at first appeared much agitated, and intemperate, and endeavoured to intimidate by threatening to bring the Indians on the settlement, upon which I put on my hat, as I was going to leave him; but he insisted upon my staying a few minutes longer. He was then given to understand, that the interview was in consequence of his own request, that if he had any proposal to make for quieting the disturbances in the country, it would be attended to, and calmly discussed, provided it was neither accompanied by threats, or attempts at intimidation. To which he assented; we then entered on the subject, and mutually agreed upon certain principles, which appeared well calculated to produce the desired effect: but the difficulty was how to bring Lieut. Pope into the measure, without which the whole would be abortive; this was however fortunately effected by the address of Mr. Cochran, and a few other well disposed gentlemen. On the 15th, the Governor published a proclamation, embracing in part the terms we had agreed upon, and containing some expressions very offensive to the people. The proclamation was communicated to me for my approbation previous to its publication; but as it did not completely embrace the objects we had previously settled, my assent was withheld, though an assurance given, that it should meet with no opposition from me. Its fate was such as might reasonably be expected from the state of the country. In some places it was torn to pieces, and in all, treated with contempt. As soon as I discovered that the proclamation, instead of quieting, only served to irritate, and render the inhabitants more violent, I gave the information to the Governor's aid Capt. Minor, but it was now too late to remedy it.

The

The commotion now assumed a very serious aspect, and hostilities appeared inevitable; but even at this period, it was my opinion that an honourable and amicable compromise would take place.

By this time the opposition to the Spanish government had acquired some form, and more strength: a number of militia companies had elected their officers, and were ready to take the field.

On Friday the 16th it was agreed, that on Tuesday the 20th following, a meeting of the principal inhabitants of the district, should be held at Mr. Belts, about eight miles from the town. The design of calling this meeting, was for the purpose of taking the business out of the hands of the people at large, and commit it to a committee of their own electing. In the mean time both sides continued their preparations, companies of militia were forming and organizing in the country; and the Governor exerting himself in reinforcing and strengthening the fort: he called to his aid, every person who would join him either through fear or affection, but was nevertheless too weak to attempt offensive operations.

On Saturday the 17th, about ten o'clock in the evening, a Spanish patrol fell in with a patrol from my camp, and without hailing or other previous ceremony, fired upon it; the fire was immediately returned, but I believe little or no damage was done. Immediately on the commencement of the firing, all the lights in my camp were extinguished, they might have served as a good direction for the Spanish artillery, one piece having been brought to bear upon my tent for a number of weeks. Two or three days after I had first observed it, the impropriety of such conduct was mentioned to Governor Gayoso, who ordered the direction of the

piece

piece to be changed, but it was brought back again in a few days.

On the evening of Sunday the 18th, I received a verbal message from the Governor, by his aid Capt. Minor, requesting a private interview with me the next morning, at the house of his aid, to which I immediately consented.

The next morning the Governor left the fort, and by a circuitous route, through thickets and cane brakes, made his way to the north side of his aid's plantation, and thence through a corn field to the back of the house, and entered the parlour undiscovered, where I joined him. Our conversation immediately turned upon the state of the country. He assured me that he was sincerely desirous of coming upon some terms of accommodation with the inhabitants, and as he understood I was going to attend the meeting at Mr. Belts, requested that I would be so good, as to use my influence in bringing about a compromise. He was told that was my object, and that a plan was already arranged, which would check, and finally put an end to the present disturbance: but that no terms could now be expected, that were not safe and honourable to the people, they had felt and knew their strength, and would only agree to disband and return home, by being admitted to enjoy a qualified state of neutrality till the treaty between the United States and his Catholic Majesty, should be carried into effect: to this privilege I thought them entitled, but to go further, would, in my opinion be impolitic, and probably attended with ruin to individuals, if not to the district. As the Governor neither commented on, nor appeared dissatisfied with these observations, it was taken for granted that he would agree to the qualified neutrality proposed. Before we parted, the Governor was informed of my determination, to abide by

that

that declaration contained in my *last letter*, to protest against the landing any more troops on the east side of the river, above the 31st degree of north latitude, except for the purpose of refreshment; which he ever afterwards observed in the most honourable and punctilious manner.

My feelings were scarcely ever more affected, than in this interview with Governor Gayoso. The humiliating state to which he was reduced, by a people whose affections he had courted, and whose gratitude he expected, had made a strong and visible impression upon his mind and countenance. His having been born and educated with high ideas of command and prerogative, served but to render his present situation the more poignant and distressing.

A circumstance took place on the morning of the 20th, which had a considerable effect in attaching the Chocktaws to the interest of the United States. A short time after our arrival at Natchez, a body of those Indians crossed the Mississippi, to make war upon the Cadoes. In this expedition they were very successful, and returned with a number of poles filled with scalps; but in place of finding the Governor at his usual residence, they had to pay their respects to him in the fort. From this time their respect for him and his people as warriors, was diminished, and their attention to the Americans increased.

After spending a short time with the Indians above mentioned, I went on with a number of gentlemen to the meeting at Mr. Belt's, which was large and respectable. In consequence of the previous arrangements, that had been agreed upon by the gentlemen of property and influence in the country, but little difficulty was found in prevailing upon the people, to submit the future management of their affairs to a committee, to be

Q   chosen

chosen by themselves. In this stage of the business, Mr. Hutchins took an active, useful and decided part, which to me appeared not only extraordinary, but inexplicable, when I reflected on his proposition to take the Governor by surprise, and his wishes frequently manifested, to remove the Spaniards by force.

About three o'clock in the afternoon, the people proceeded to the election of the committee, when the following gentlemen were almost unanimously chosen.

Anthony Hutchins,	Cato West,
Bernard Lintot,	Joseph Bernard,
Isaac Gaillard,	Gabriel Benoist.
William Ratliff,	

To the above committee Lieut. Pope and myself were added, by a unanimous vote of the meeting.

The same evening the committee assembled in the town of Natchez, and informed the Governor by a note of their election, to which he immediately returned a polite answer.

On the 21st, the committee proceeded to business. The Governor offered them the use of government house, which was then unoccupied, but they declined accepting of it, and made use of one which I was preparing to go into. It was a good new building, nearly finished, the property of Mr. Dunbar, who offered me the use of it, free of expense to the public: upon these terms only did I consent at any time during my absence, to reside in a house.

On the 22d the following letter and propositions, were presented to the Governor for his concurrence.

Natchez, June 22d, 1797.

Sir,

The following propositions being unanimously agreed to by us, the underwritten, being a committee appointed

appointed by a very respectable, and numerous meeting of the inhabitants of this district, and Andrew Ellicott, commissioner and citizen of the United States, and P. S. Pope, commanding the United States troops on the Mississippi, are submitted to your Excellency, with a request that you may accede to, and transmit a copy of the same to the Baron de Corondelet, and obtain his concurrence, in order to restore tranquillity to this government.

1st. The inhabitants of the district of Natchez, who under the belief and persuasion that they were citizens of the United States, agreeably to the late treaty, have assembled and embodied themselves, are not to be prosecuted or injured for their conduct on that account; but to stand exonerated and acquitted.

2dly. The inhabitants of the government aforesaid, above the 31st degree of north latitude, are not to be embodied as militia, or called upon to aid in any military operation, except in case of an Indian invasion, or for the suppression of riots during the present state of uncertainty, owing to the late treaty between his Catholic Majesty and the United States not being fully carried into effect.

3dly. The laws of Spain in the above district shall be continued, and on all occasions be executed with mildness and moderation; nor shall any inhabitant be transported as a prisoner out of this government on any pretext whatever: and notwithstanding the operation of the law aforesaid is hereby admitted, yet the inhabitants shall be considered to be in an actual state of neutrality, during the continuance of their uncertainty, as mentioned in the second proposition.

4thly. We the committee aforesaid, do engage to recommend it to our constituents, and to the utmost of

Q 2

our

our power endeavour to preserve the peace, and promote the due execution of justice.

We are your Excellency's most obedient humble
servants,

(Signed)

ANTHONY HUTCHINS,
BERNARD LINTOT,
ISAAC GAILLARD,
WILLIAM RATLIFF,
CATO WEST,
JOSEPH BERNARD,
GABRIEL BENOIST.

*Don Manuel Gayoso de Lemos, Brigadier
in the Royal Armies, Governor Military, and Political, of the Natchez,
and its dependencies, &c.*

Being always desirous of promoting the public
good, we do join in the same sentiment with the committee, by acceding to their propositions in the manner following.

By the present, I do hereby accede to the four foregoing propositions, established and agreed upon for
the purpose of establishing the peace and tranquillity
of the country, and that it may be constant and notorious, I sign the present under the seal of my arms, and
countersigned by the secretary of this government at
Natchez, the 22d day of June, 1797.

(Signed)   MANUEL GAYOSO DE LEMOS.
(Signed)   JOSEPH VIDAL, Secretary.

On the 23d the Governor and his officers left the fort,
and returned to their houses. Thus ended this formidable tumult, without a single act of violence having
been committed by the inhabitants of the country, during a suspension of the government and laws, for the
space of two weeks !

The propositions were immediately transmitted to
the Baron de Corondelet for his approbation and signature, who agreed to them without hesitation, except
to a part of the third; which relates to the transportation
of

of any inhabitant out of the district as a prisoner. By a royal edict, trials for capital crimes must be held in New Orleans, and to capital crimes only the Baron's exception extended. It was out of his power to set aside a royal edict. This was well understood by the committee, when the propositions were under consideration; but it was thought best to require more than was expected, to obtain as much as was necessary for the safety of the people.

As the Governor retired from the fort on the 23d, he called at my quarters where we had a conversation of considerable length upon the state of the country.

During this interview the necessity of electing another committee, to aid in preserving good order and the peace of the country, was strongly impressed upon the mind of the Governor, who appeared fully aware of the propriety of the measure, and the day following issued his proclamation for that purpose.

The election took place about the beginning of July, when the following gentlemen were chosen. Joseph Bernard, Peter B. Bruin, Daniel Clark, Gabriel Benoist, Philander Smith, Isaac Gaillard, Roger Dixon, William Ratliff and Frederick Kimball.

The election of this committee, as was really intended on my part, put the finishing stroke to the Spanish authority, and jurisdiction in the district. The members, with the single exception of Frederick Kimball whose sentiments were doubtful, and who fell below the line, were decidedly republican, and firmly attached to the government and interest of the United States. This committee held their first meeting about the 15th of July, at the house I occupied: all their subsequent meetings were held at the same place, although they were offered the use of government house, they declined to accept of it.

Having

Having been very minute, and I fear tedious, in detailing the difficulties which occurred in carrying the treaty into effect, and in the account of the commotion, I shall in the next chapter take up a subject more interesting.

CHAP. IV.

Containing some account of the Mississippi river—of the settlements, and part of the adjacent country, &c.

TO say any thing new respecting this river, whose magnitude and importance has for more than a century past, employed the pens of some of the ablest historians, philosophers and geographers of most nations in Europe, as well as in our own country, is not to be expected from me. In following such characters I shall proceed with diffidence, and confine my remarks to that part of this celebrated river, which I had an opportunity of examining myself, and which lies between the mouth of the Ohio and the Gulf of Mexico.

The confluence of the Ohio and Mississippi rivers, is in 37° 0' 23" N. latitude, and about 5^h 55' 22".8 W. from Greenwich, agreeably to the observations in the Appendix to this work: but since those observations were printed off, my friend Don Jon Joaquin de Ferrer, whom I have already had occasion to mention, has determined at my request, by one of Arnold's best chronometers in descending the river from Pittsburgh, to New Orleans, the difference of meridians between the mouth of the Ohio, Natchez, and the two places first mentioned; and by a careful comparison of the difference of those meridians, the longitude of the mouth of the Ohio appears to be 5^h 56' 24", which exceeds the
                                                    determination

determination in the Appendix by 1′ 1″.2: and by combining this determination with the observations in the Appendix, the longitude of the mouth of the Ohio will be 5ⁿ 55′ 38″.1 west from the royal observatory at Greenwich, and which is the position I have given it in the map. I am well aware, that this position differs nearly two degrees in longitude, and 14 minutes in latitude, from our best maps or charts. I have not adopted this alteration without some hesitation, and should still have been more cautious, if I could have found any other authority in favour of the former position, than charts unaccompanied by any observations.

Those who are descending the Ohio and Mississippi, and have been pleased with the prospect of large rivers rushing together among hills and mountains, will anticipate the pleasure of viewing the conflux of those stupendous waters. But their expectations will not be realized, the prospect is neither grand nor romantic: here are no hills to variegate the scene, nor mountains from whose summits the meandering of the waters may be traced, nor chasms through which they have forced their way. The prospect is no more than the meeting of waters of the same width, along the sounds, on our low southern coast.

These great rivers after draining a vast extent of mountainous and hilly country, join their waters in the swamp through which the Mississippi passes into the Gulf of Mexico. This swamp extends from the high lands in the United States, to the high lands in Louisiana; through various parts of which the river has at different periods made its way. From the best information I could obtain, the swamp is from thirty-six to forty-five miles wide, from the boundary many miles up, (the whole of which is several feet under water every annual inundation) and much the greater part of it lies

on

on the west side of the present bed of the river. From the mouth of the Ohio, to the southern boundary of the United States, the Mississippi touches but two or three places on the west side that are not annually inundated, and even these are for a time insulated; but on the east side it washes the high land in eleven places.

The swamp appears to be composed of the mud and sand, carried by Mad river into the Missouri, and by the Missouri into the Mississippi, to which may be added, the washing of the country drained by the Mississippi and Ohio rivers, with their numerous branches, which furnish a fresh stratum every inundation. This stratum is deposited upon a stratum of leaves and other dead vegetables; which had fallen the preceding autumn. These strata may be readily examined in many parts of the swamp, and banks of the river. The thickness of the deposited strata differs considerably, and principally depends upon the duration of the different inundations. In 1797, the inundation was complete by the last of February, and the river was not entirely within its banks till the beginning of September following. But in the year 1798, the inundation was not complete till after the middle of May, and the river was generally within its banks by the first of August. The mean perpendicular height to which the river rises, (at the time of the inundation,) above the low water mark at the town of Natchez, is about 55 feet.

In descending the river, you meet with but little variety; a few of the sand bars and islands, will give a sample of the whole. When the water is low, you have high muddy banks, quick-sands, and sand bars; and when full, you might almost as well be at sea: for days together you will float without meeting with any thing like soil in the river, and at the same time be environed by an uninhabitable, and almost impenetrable wilderness.

This

This river, like all others passing through flat countries, and not checked or confined by hills or mountains, is very crooked as may be seen by the chart. This arises from a very natural cause, and may be explained in the following manner. Suppose in the figure below, the lines *a b*, and *c d*, to be the banks or margins of a portion of a river, and the water moving in the direction *ef*, but meeting with an obstruction

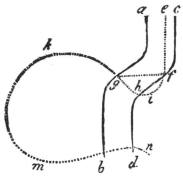

at *f*, it will be reflected in the direction *fg*, and at *g*, as well as at *f*, the bank will be worn away. About *h*, an eddy will be formed, where sand, earth, and rubbish will be deposited, and continually increase the convex parts, while the concave parts will be worn away, and in time a loop will be formed something like the dotted curve line *i*, *h*, *m*, and *n* in the figure, which will increase in magnitude till the river, aided by an inundation, breaks through a shorter way, and the convex part will become an island. If the loop should be very large, and the water cease to have much current along it, the two ends in a short time will be filled up by the great quantity of mud and sand, which are constantly mixed with the water of the Mississippi, and a lake will be formed. These lakes are to be met with in various parts of the swamp, and bear evident marks of having

R   been

been at some former period, a portion of the main bed of the river.

In consequence of the great body of water in the Mississippi, and the light and loose nature of the soil, the concave banks of the river are falling in, more or less during every general fall or rise of the water ; and I believe but few people have ever descended it, in either of those states, who have not heard or seen large portions of the banks give way, which are instantly carried off by the current, and the earth, sand, and some of the rubbish again deposited in the eddies formed by the convex points below.

From what has been said, one general caution must necessarily present itself to those concerned in navigating the Mississippi, which is *to avoid the concave banks or shores.* Many fatal accidents have happened on this river, either through ignorance of the danger, or inattention in coming to at improper places on the shore to cook, procure fewel, or for other purposes. We have a late instance of a Mr. M‘Farling, and part of his crew, being lost by the falling of a bank. When the banks are inundated they are less dangerous, being in some measure supported by the water, and not so liable to give way ; but the concave shores are still to be avoided, because the water near the bank and elevated above it, not being confined to the course of the river by the lower current, rushes straight forward among the cane and timber, and if Kentucky boats (as they are called,) fall within the draught of this upper current, it will be extremely difficult to relieve them, or prevent their being lost in the woods ; many losses have been sustained from this cause.

A boat may at all times come to with safety at a sand bar, the upper or lower end of an island where young bushes are growing, or just at the beginning of eddy,

below

below any of the points that are covered with young cotton wood, (the populus deltoida of Marshal,) or willows (salix nigra.) From the mouth of the Ohio, down to the Walnut Hills, it is not safe to descend the river in the night, unless the boat be uncommonly strong, on account of the sawyers and planters. The former are trees slightly confined to the bottom by some of their roots or limbs, and the loose or floating ends continue a vibratory motion, generally up and down, some of them rise five or six feet above the water, every vibration. The latter are more dangerous, being firmly fixed or planted in the bottom. They are all easily avoided in daylight. With these precautions, the Mississippi may be navigated with as much, if not more safety, than any other river upon this continent.

It may generally be observed, that the banks of all our rivers subject to inundation, are higher on the margins of the rivers than some distance from them, and commonly terminate by a gentle declivity in a swamp: this is the case the whole length of the Mississippi from the mouth of the Ohio, to the gulf of Mexico: hence some superficial observers, have been led to believe, that the river passes along the top of a hill with a valley on each side of it. After the water, at the time of the inundation rises above the banks, it runs from the river into the swamps with great rapidity till they are filled to a level with the main current. Those swamps which communicate immediately with the gulf of Mexico, or the salt water lakes, never fill during the inundation; consequently the current continues over the banks into them, till the waters fall. Advantage hath been taken of this circumstance, in a number of places about New Orleans, for the erection of saw mills, which are found to answer a valuable pur-

R 2   pose,

pose, and are kept constantly going during the whole term of the inundation.

The first large body of water which leaves the Mississippi, and falls by a regular, and separate channel into the gulf of Mexico, is the Chafalia. It leaves the Mississippi in the westernmost part of that remarkable bend just below the boundary, and has every appearance of having been formerly a continuation of the Red river, when the Mississippi washed the high land from Clarksville, to the Bayou Tunica, (or Willing's creek,) the traces of which are yet visible by the lakes, through which a large current yet passes when the river is high. The distance on a straight line from Clarksville to the Bayou Tunica is not more than eight miles, but by the present course of the river, it is supposed not to be less than fifty miles. Should the Mississippi break its way through by a shorter course, (which is more than a mere probability,) the Chafalia will again become a part of the Red river.

When the Mississippi is high, the draught into the Chafalia is very strong, and has frequently carried rafts, and likewise some few flats, or Kentucky boats down it, which are generally lost. This branch notwithstanding its magnitude is not navigable to the gulf of Mexico, owing to an immense floating bridge, or raft across it, of many leagues in length, and so firm and compact in some places, that cattle and horses are driven over on it. This surprising floating bridge or raft, is constantly augmented by the trees and rubbish, which the Chafalia draws out of the Mississippi.

During the annual inundation, a considerable stream of water called the Bayou Manshack, or Iberville, leaves the Mississippi at Manshack, and after joining the Amit, falls into lake Maurepas, thence into lake Pontchartrain, and communicates with the gulf of Mexico,

near

near the mouth of Pearl or Half-Way river. During the passage of the water along this channel, New Orleans stands upon an island, which may be considered the Delta of the Mississippi. This channel might be rendered navigable for boats during the inundation by removing the timber and rubbish, with which it is at present choked up: and no doubt, when the population of the country will justify the measure, it will be made sufficiently deep to communicate with the lakes Maurepas and Pontchartrain, and the coast of West Florida at all times, which will be found a much easier and cheaper conveyance than by the way of New Orleans.

Below Manshack a few miles, but on the west side of the river, another branch called the Plaquemin, makes out of the Mississippi, and communicates by several mouths with the gulf of Mexico : from this branch there is a water communication with the Opelousas.

Between Evan Jones's place and the church, another branch makes out on the west side of the river, called La Fourche, (or the Fork,) from its dividing and falling into the gulf of Mexico by two branches. From the Mississippi along this branch to the sea coast, the settlement is compact.

Between New Orleans and the Balise, the Mississippi has several communications with the gulf of Mexico ; but they are generally too shoal to be of much importance.

After this short account of the river, I shall proceed to take some notice of the settlements on it below the mouth of the Ohio.

Ferdinand de Soto, after traversing the Floridas, discovered the Mississippi in the year 1541. The place where he first struck it is uncertain, but generally supposed to have been about the latitude 34° 10′ north.

Notwithstanding

Notwithstanding this early discovery the river re,
mained unexplored till 1682, when the enterprising La
Salle, in an excursion from Canada fell upon it, and
followed its courses to its mouth; and is said to be the
first person, who discovered that it discharged its waters into the gulf of Mexico. He was afterwards trea-
cherously murdered on the coast, about one hundred
leagues west of the Mississippi by his own men, where
he was endeavouring to establish a colony.

No permanent settlement was attempted on the Mississippi till about the year 1712, when Crozet obtained
a patent for the exclusive trade of Louisiana: but previously to the obtaining this patent, a few miserable families had settled at, or near the place where New Orleans now stands. These settlers were the remains of
two small colonies, that had been settled on the coast,
east of the Mississippi in the years 1699, and 1701.
One of these colonies was settled at the bay of St.
Louis, and the other near the bay of Mobile. But the
country being low, sandy, and miserably poor, and
producing little beside pitch pine, added to the coast
being too shoal for any other than the coasting trade,
(of which at that time there was none,) those colonies
after enduring innumerable hardships, and a number
of the adventurers dying for want of the necessaries of
life, the remainder quitted their habitations, and followed the coast to lake Pontchartrain, which they likewise coasted to the Bayou St. John's, and after ascending it a few miles they crossed to the banks of the
Mississippi, the distance across being less than a league.
Here those miserable people found a soil, not exceeded by any thing in the world for fertility; but the
banks of the river being subject to the annual inundation, their situation was still deplorable. Immediately

ately after Crozet obtained his patent, a number of adventurers, (some of whom were very respectable,) arrived, who began with spirit to bank out the river, but the labour being great, the progress was small, until Crozet's patent was relinquished to the Mississippi company in the year 1717. The plan of this company was projected by John Law, a Scotsman, during the regency of the Duke of Orleans, and shared the fate of all speculations which have paper only for their foundation. The failure of this celebrated company checked the progress of the settlement; but it had taken too firm a hold to be abandoned; the banking out of the river had been carried on with great spirit, and the plantations thus protected, were not exceeded by any thing in America for beauty and fertility. Notwithstanding the misfortunes which had attended the first adventurers, the settlement extended as early as 1727, up to the present town of Natchez, where a fort was erected, but owing it is said to the improper conduct and tyranny of the French, the Indians to get rid of their troublesome guests, in a treacherous and barbarous manner, about the year 1731 massacred almost every French inhabitant in the upper settlement: but the year following, the French retaliated in a manner equally treacherous, and nearly extirpated the whole nation of the Natchees; the few that escaped, took refuge among the Chocktaws, and other neighbouring nations, where some of their descendants yet remain. From this time the French had possession of the country until the peace of 1763, when all the French and Spanish possessions east of the Mississippi, except the island of Orleans, which has already been designated as the Delta of the Mississippi, were ceded to the crown of Great Britain. A few years afterwards, by an arrangement between the crowns of France and

Spain,

Spain, the latter became possessed of Louisiana and the island of Orleans, to which they yet belong.*

The

* The following is a translation of the French king's orders for delivering to the Spaniards, all his possessions in North America, which had not been ceded by the definitive treaty to Great Britain, from the original, printed by Dennis Braud, printer to the King at New Orleans.

"*Extract of the king's letter to M. D'Abbadie, Director General and Commandant for his Majesty in Louisiana.*

" Mons. D'Abbadie, by a special act, done at Fontainbleau, Nov. 3d, 1762, of my own will and meer motion, having ceded to my dear and best beloved cousin the king of Spain, and to his heirs and successors, in full property, purely and simply, and without any exceptions, the whole country known by the name of Louisiana, together with New Orleans, and the island in which the said city is situated ; and by another act done at the Escurial, November 13th, in the same year, his Catholic Majesty having accepted the cession of the said country of Louisiana, and the city and island of New Orleans, agreeable to the copies of the said acts, which you will find hereunto annexed : I write you this letter to inform you, that my intention is, That on receipt of these presents, whether they come to your hands by the officers of his Catholic Majesty, or directly by such French vessels as may be charged with the same, you are to deliver up to the Governor, or officer appointed for that purpose by the King of Spain, the said country and colony of Louisiana, and the posts thereon depending ; likewise the city and island of New Orleans, in such state and condition as they shall be found to be in on the day of the said cession, willing that in all time to come they shall belong to his Catholic Majesty, to be governed and administered by his governors and officers, and as possessed by him in full property without any exceptions. At the same time, I hope for the prosperity and peace of the inhabitants of the colony of Louisiana, and promise myself, from the friendship and affection of his Catholic Majesty, that he will be pleased to give orders to his governor and all other officers employed in his service in the said colony, and in the city of New Orleans, that the ecclesiasticks and religious houses who have the care of the parishes, and of the missions, may continue to exercise their functions, and enjoy the rights, privileges and immunities granted by their several charters of establishments. That the ordinary judges do continue, together with the superior council, to administer justice according to the laws, forms, and usages of the colony : that the inhabitants be preserved and maintained in their possessions : that they be confirmed in the property of their estates, according to the grants which have been made by the governors and directors of the colony, and that all the said grants be holden and taken as confirmed by his Catholic Majesty, even though not as yet confirmed by me.

" Hoping, above all, that his Catholic Majesty will be pleased to bestow on his new subjects of Louisiana, the same marks of protection and good will, which they enjoyed while under my dominion, and of which the misfortunes of war alone have prevented their experiencing greater effects ; I command you to cause my present letter to be recorded in the superior coun-

The country on the east side of the Mississippi, and north of the island of Orleans, was peaceably possessed from the peace of 1763, till after the commencement of our revolutionary war in the year 1775, by Great Britain. In the mean time, the country increased rapidly in population, by the number of adventurers that went into it from England, Ireland, Scotland, and the colonies, now the United States. Among those adventurers was the late Mr. James Willing, of Philadelphia, who resided on the Mississippi several years, during which time he became acquainted with the inhabitants generally, and their particular sentiments, as they related to the contest between Great Britain and her colonies. After the commencement of hostilities, he returned to Philadelphia, and was entrusted with a command down the Mississippi. On his arrival at Natchez, he entered into an agreement with the inhabitants, by which they were permitted to enjoy a state of neutrality during the controversy. As Mr. Willing conceived Mr. Anthony Hutchins to be the most dangerous and determined royalist in the settlement, he took him a prisoner to New Orleans; from whence he made his escape, returned to Natchez, and put an end to the neutrality. The particulars of this important transaction, which kept the United States out of the possession of that country at least fourteen years, will be found in the following deposition, which is only one, out of several others to the same import, sent to the department of state in the year 1797.

S *Government*

cil of New Orleans, to the end that the several estates of the colony may be informed of its contents, and may have recourse thereto when necessary. And the present being for no other purposes, I pray God, Mons. D'Abadie, to have you in his holy keeping. Given at Versailles, April 21st, 1764. Signed LOUIS, and underneath Le DUC De CHOISEUL."

Government of Natchez,
   Villa Gayoso District. } *ss.*

Personally appeared before me William Ferguson, one of the justices assigned to keep the peace for the said district, James Truly of the same place, aged about forty-three years, who being duly sworn on the Evangelists of Almighty God, deposeth and sayeth, that he has been an inhabitant of this country since the year 1773. That Capt. James Willing, in the service of the United States, with an armed force, did arrive at Natchez landing about the middle of February 1778. That the very night he arrived, or soon after, he detached a party of soldiers, piloted by the deponent, to the house of Alexander M'Intosh, where they seized and carried to the Natchez landing aforesaid, about half a dozen of the said M'Intosh's negroes, also a number of hogs; but on the said M'Intosh's conforming with the arrangements, which the inhabitants of Natchez had made with said Willing, he, the said Willing, did return to the said M'Intosh his slaves and hogs. That on the night of the said Willing's arrival, he also detached Lieut. Thomas M'Intire, with another party of soldiers to the plantation of Col. Anthony Hutchins, where they seized the said Col. Hutchins, together with three or four of his slaves, and carried them to Elles's Cliffs, (commonly called the White Cliffs) where his boat lay: the said slaves were put on board Capt. Barber's flat laden with corn, the Colonel himself being taken as a prisoner aboard said M'Intire's boat.

On the arrival of the Colonel and slaves at New Orleans, Governor Galvez prevailed on Oliver Pollock, agent for the United States, to allow the Colonel the liberty of the town, on his parole of honour, not to depart thence without permission: regardless of which, he the said Colonel broke his parole of honour, and made the best of his way home to Natchez. Before the said

said Col. Hutchins left New Orleans, Mr. Oliver Pollock, the agent of Congress, fitted out a boat under the command of Mr. Reuben Harrison, Lieutenant in the armies of the United States, who proceeded up the river Mississippi to the White Cliffs above mentioned. In the mean time Col. Hutchins had, (as he arrived before the said boat,) excited the inhabitants of Natchez to take up arms, by declaring on OATH to the people, that this detachment was coming up with a determination of robbing the inhabitants of their property without exception. This declaration alarmed the people when they associated in arms to attack the boat aforesaid. John Tally, who lived about a league below the said cliffs, informed Lieut. Harrison on his arrival there, that the people armed as aforesaid were to attack him, and his party at the Cliffs aforesaid. Mr. Harrison then proposed to Tally, to go to the Cliffs where the people were assembled, and inform them, that he was going to the Natchez in peace, and that on his arrival opposite to the landing at said Cliffs, he would fire a gun; and if the people under arms at said Cliffs were disposed for peace, he desired that they would give him a gun as a signal of such. Accordingly Lieut. Harrison fired a gun, and the Natcheans returned one, upon which Mr. Harrison turned to cross the river: but prior to this, it was urged strongly by the Col. upon Tally's information as above, to make the signal required, in order to intice them over; but to fire upon them as soon as they came within gun shot, without speaking to them! This the inhabitants objected to, saying it was time enough to fire when they found there was a necessity, and appointed Captains Bingaman and Hooper, to remain open at the water side, (the rest being concealed,) to know their intentions; but when the said Harrison came near enough to speak, discovered that he had been basely decoyed over, spoke aloud, desiring all

those

those that were friends to the United States, to separate themselves from those that were not. In answer to which, Captain Hooper desired all those on board said boat, that were friends to the Natchez (meaning as the deponent presumes those attached to the English,) to fall below the gunwales of the boat, or jump ashore, as the boat had gotten into an eddy near the shore. In this confusion, one Cephas Kenard who was previously engaged by the said Col. Hutchins, (as was then conjectured,) to begin the attack, fired a gun in, or towards the said boat, then the firing commenced on all sides, five of the Americans were killed, and the rest jumped ashore, and called for quarters. Further a man named Gardner, whom Col. Hutchins sent down the river a few days before as a spy, and who was taken prisoner by said Harrison near Point Coupie, still continued aboard the boat. The said Col. Hutchins, after the surrender of the Americans, came from his place of concealment and safety, ran down a small hill to the place of action, and seeing Gardner still about the boat, fired a ball through his shoulder! so eager was the Col. for shedding of blood, that he did not know the man he had employed as a spy, though he was within 30 or 40 yards of him!

The deponent has frequently heard that Lieut. Harrison was sent by Oliver Pollock, agent of the United States at Orleans, to remain at Natchez, with a view to preserve the peace of the country, and the convention agreed on between the inhabitants and Capt. Willing, and also to watch that the neutrality secured to them by the said convention was not violated. The deponent has frequently heard the Colonel express himself in such a manner, as proved him to be an enemy to the United States.

Sworn before me this 6th day of November, 1797.

(Signed) WILLIAM FERGUSON.

(Subscribed) JAMES TRULY.

Thus

Thus ended the neutrality after a continuance of a few weeks. The settlement now became again subject to his Britannic Majesty, under the auspices of Col. Hutchins, in which state it continued till the 21st of September 1779, when it was surrendered by Col. Dickson, who commanded the British forces at Baton Rouge, to General Bernard de Galvez, who commanded the troops of his Catholic Majesty. From this time until after my arrival in that country, it continued subject to Spain, except for a few weeks during an insurrection in the year 1781, in which Col. Hutchins was a principal actor.

From Natchez up to the mouth of the Ohio, there are no settlements of much account. Those at the Walnut Hills and Chickasaw Bluffs, consist of but few inhabitants, and they are of that class, who support themselves by supplying the soldiers with vegetables and other articles they may be in want of, and may be more properly denominated suttlers than settlers. The Spaniards have a small settlement at New Madrid, which was planned by Mr. Gardauqui his Catholic Majesty's minister to the United States. Col. Morgan of New Jersey was some time Governor of that colony which was evidently on the decline when I descended the river.

The soil in the district of Natchez is at present uncommonly fertile: but the country being high, hilly and broken, the fine rich mould will be washed away after a series of cultivation, and the country become less productive. This tract of good upland is not very extensive, being about 130 miles in length along the Mississippi, and not more than 23 in breadth.

The staple commodity of the settlement of Natchez is cotton, which the country produces in great abundance, and of a good quality. The making of indigo,
and

and raising tobacco, were carried on with spirit some years ago; but they have both given way to the cultivation of cotton. The country produces maize, or Indian corn, equal, if not superior to any part of the United States: the time of planting it is from the beginning of March, until the beginning of July. The cotton is generally planted in the latter end of February, and the beginning of March. Rye has been attempted in some places, and raised with success; but wheat has not yet succeeded. Apples and cherries are scarce, but peaches, plumbs and figs are very abundant. The vegetables of the middle states generally succeed there. The sugar cane has been attempted in the southern part of the district, near the boundary; I have not yet heard with what success: but from Point Coupie, down to the gulf of Mexico, it answers at present better than any other article; and sugar has within a few years past become the staple commodity of that part of the Mississippi. A variety of oranges, both sweet and sour, with lemons, are in great plenty on that part of the river.

From the great number of artificial mounds of earth to be seen through the whole settlement of Natchez, it must at some former period have been well populated. Those mounds or tumuli, are generally square and flat on the top: add to this circumstance in favour of the former population of that district, the following fact, which is very conclusive. In all parts where new plantations are opened, broken Indian earthen-ware is to be met with, some of the pieces are in tolerable preservation, and retain distinctly the original ornaments; but none of it appears to have ever been glazed.

The climate is very changeable during the winter, as may be seen in the Appendix; but the summer is regularly hot. During my residence at Natchez the

greatest

greatest degree of cold was about 17° and of heat 96° by Farenheit's scale.

The permanent degree of heat may be stated at about 14° beyond that of Pennsylvania. The conclusion is drawn from the following facts. In Pennsylvania the mean temperature of the best spring and well water, is about 51° and from the Mississippi, east to the Atlantic, in the parallel of 31° I found it about 65°, the difference is 14°.

The natives of the southern part of the Mississippi are generally a sprightly people, and appear to have a natural turn for mechanics, painting, music, and the polite accomplishments, but their system of education is so extremely defective, that little real science is to be met with among them. Many of the planters are industrious, and enjoy life not only in plenty but affluence, and generally possess the virtue of hospitality, which never fails to impress the stranger and traveller with a favourable opinion of the country, and its inhabitants.

A large proportion of the inhabitants below the boundary, are descended from the original French settlers and adventurers, and still retain in a great degree, the language, manners and customs of their ancestors.

The horses are tolerably good, but not equal to those of Pennsylvania. Many of them have been taken wild on the west side of the Mississippi, and are used both for the saddle and draught. Few animals are reduced to obedience, and taught subordination more readily.

Contrary to my expectation, I found the cattle in the settlement of Natchez but little inferior in size to those of the middle states. They are extremely numerous, and it is not uncommon for the wealthy planters to possess from one to two hundred head, and sometimes
more.

more. The cows yield much less, and poorer milk than those of the northern states.

The domestic animals of that country, are not so gentle as those of the northern states. This probably arises from the little dependence they have upon man for their support. In the middle and northern states, they have to look up to their owner for their daily support; but in that country they can pass through the winter without his aid. If this idea be correct, may not the domestic situation of animals be considered a forced state, and will not the degree of their domestication be in proportion to their dependence?

The mutton of that country is well tasted; but the wool of the sheep is more hairy, and less valuable than in the middle and northern states.

The hogs are but little, if any thing inferior to those of any part of the United States, provided they receive the same attention.

The wild animals of the middle states will generally be found as far south as the boundary, except the red fox, (canis vulpes,) ground hog, (arctomys monax,) and musk rat, (mus zibethicus,) but they are evidently somewhat smaller.

I shall now proceed to give some account of the construction of the map of the Mississippi. A continued, and correct survey of this river will scarcely ever be obtained on account of the swamps, lagoons, thickets, and cane brakes on its banks: and below the banks, the impediments will be equally great. In some places impassable quick-sands will be met with; in others the water will be found washing the high, and almost perpendicular banks, and no place left for foothold. Some other mode, different from the common method of surveying must therefore be resorted to. The following was used in constructing the map to which

which this refers. The mouth of the Ohio and town of
Natchez, were taken as given points, both as to latitude
and longitude. An excellent surveying compass, corrected for the variation of the needle, was used in taking the courses, which were entered in time, instead of
space. Every day in descending the river when the
sun shone at noon, his meridional altitude was taken,
from the artificial, or reflected horizon, with an excellent sextant made by Ramsden, which graduated by the
vernier to twenty seconds, and was generally found by
a very great number of observations to determine the
latitude true, within less than a minute. The latitudes
determined by those observations, are entered on the
chart of the river at the places where the observations
were made : all the courses between each two of those
points were protracted in time, instead of space, that is,
by calling the time space. Each set of courses were
then expanded, or contracted, so as to agree with the
points of latitude to which they belonged. From the
number of latitudes taken, I expect that no part of the
river will be found very erroneous in that respect: so
much cannot be said in favour of the longitude, except
at the mouth of the Ohio, and the town of Natchez,
which are considered as given points: the latitude and
longitude of the latter being determined with as much
precision as any point within the United States.

Since my first chart of the river was made for the use
of our government, I have been enabled to correct some
points of longitude between the mouth of the Ohio and
Natchez, from the observations of Mr. Ferrer.

In consequence of the banks of the river constantly
giving way, no map or chart of it can be expected to be
tolerably correct for more than a century to come.
The chart of the Mississippi is divided into two parts,
for the same reason already given for the division of the
Ohio : the division takes place at latitude 33° north.

T   CHAP.

CHAP. V.

Containing an account of some of the occurrences which took place in the settlement of Natchez after the election of the second, (commonly called the permanent,) committee, until the author left the Town to commence the demarcation of the boundary.

THE occurrences which took place in the settlement of Natchez after the termination of the commotion, and the election of the permanent committee, until my beginning the demarcation of the boundary, must daily become less interesting; they will therefore generally be but slightly mentioned, and some of them wholly omitted. The difficulties were however as great, if not greater, than any we met with from the Spanish government, but as some of them arose from the conduct of certain citizens of the United States, a few of whom did at that time, and still continue to enjoy the patronage of our government, it is not impossible but they acted in conformity to directions they had received, or agreeably to a plan previously devised. It would therefore be improper to bring their conduct before the public, which possibly had its origin from a higher source, and which was fully competent to decide on its propriety.

I have ever been an enemy to the abuse of the officers of government, unless after conviction by a competent tribunal; it is lessening them in the esteem of the public, and not unfrequently renders both a useful office and officer contemptible: added to which, it is either insulting the judgment, or arraigning the motives of the executive, who made the appointments.

The

The press cannot be too free, when directed to a manly, and candid discussion of principles; but its usefulness ceases, when it waves the principle, and attacks the individual. From a full persuasion of the correctness of this opinion, in opposing plans brought forward, or seconded by the officers of the United States, which appeared injurious to the interest of my country, the plans, and not the individuals, (when they could possibly be seperated,) have felt my opposition.

After Governor Gayoso had issued his proclamation for the election of the permanent committee, a number of gentlemen were anxious to have Mr. Hutchins elected a member of that body; not from any influence he had with the well informed part of the settlement, but from his being popular with that class of the populace, who regard men more than principles. Contrary to expectation, he declined serving, on account (as he said) of his age and infirmities.

The committee was no sooner organized, than it was evident its measures would be directed to the attainment of two objects: *first*, the securing the country to the United States, and, *secondly*, the preservation of peace and good order in the settlement. The *first* was contrary to the wishes of the officers of his Catholic Majesty, and the *second* to those attached to the British interest, to which may be added another class, who had nothing to lose, but hoped to gain by the tumult and disorder.

Mr. Hutchins attended the first meeting of the committee as a spectator, but finding the views of that body, so different from his own, he became discontented with its proceedings, which circumstance was immediately taken advantage of by Governor Gayoso, who expected by dividing the inhabitants, to regain the power he had so lately lost.

On

On the 26th of July, Governor Gayoso received his appointment from the court of Madrid as Governor General in place of the Baron de Corondelet, who was promoted to the government of Quito. On the 27th, Governor Gayoso informed me by a polite note of his promotion, and that he should leave the settlement on the 30th, and proceed to New Orleans; that for the present Captain Minor would represent him in the government of Natchez. But previous to his departure, he directed Captain Minor not to oppose Mr. Hutchins in the election of another committee, if he should attempt it.

A few days after the Governor's departure for New Orleans, Mr. Hutchins came to the house I occupied, and requested my aid in dissolving the permanent committee, which was then in session, and to let the principal power be lodged in his hands and that of another committee, which he would have elected. This proposition met with my decided disapprobation, not only from its being unnecessary, but from the impropriety of being instrumental in placing a British officer, in a situation, by which he might be enabled materially to injure the United States. Notwithstanding my opposition and remonstrances, Mr. Hutchins went into the hall where the committee was on business, and after a few preliminary observations, accompanied with abusive language, he told the members they were "no committee, that they were dissolved, and he would direct the election of another, that it was a hard pill, and rough bur, for them to swallow, but he would force it down their throats." To which the honourable Judge Bruin, (who was a distinguished officer in our revolutionary army,) coolly replied "Col. Hutchins you appear to be acting the dictator, and at the same time

time affect to be waving the American cap of liberty; but they are incompatible, the cap of liberty but ill becomes you, who opposed in arms the independence of the United States." Mr. Hutchins then left the hall exclaiming, "you are no committee, you are dissolved"!

In this extraordinary proceeding Mr. Hutchins was seconded by some citizens of the United States, several of whom held commissions under our government. It is possible they were deceived.

Immediately after this singular transaction, Mr. Hutchins applied to Captain Minor, and obtained permission to have another committee elected: but this election met with great opposition, and was generally considered by the well disposed inhabitants, as an artful measure, calculated to divide the people between the two committees, which if effected would, in all probability, end in a breach of the neutrality by one, or the other of the parties, and thereby produce the reestablishment of the Spanish government with all its terrors. Under this impression, six out of the ten subdivisions of which the district was composed, protested against the election, of course there were but four elections holden agreeably to the permission obtained from Captain Minor. These four returns were sent to Mr. Hutchins sealed up, who presented them to the judges, but they refused to act, he then presented them to Captain Minor who declined having any thing further to do with the business.

On the day appointed for the meeting of this new committee, the four members elected by the four subdivisions, with Mr. Hutchins assembled at Mr. Belts to proceed to business: but the difficulty which first attended opening the returns still existed, however men void of principle, and determined to carry a

favourite

favourite object, are seldom arrested in their progress by considerations of propriety. Mr. Hutchins therefore resolved to stop the first three persons who might be passing along the road, and constitute them judges of the returns of the election. A short time after he had taken this resolution, Mr. Justice King, (an equivocal character,) and his two sons Richard, (a Captain in the Spanish militia,) and Prosper, who were on their way to the town of Natchez, were called in by Mr. Hutchins, who constituted them judges, after which they opened the returns, and declared Thomas Green, James Stuart, a Mr. Ashly, and a Mr. Hocket, to be duly elected.

Mr. Green, (although a Captain in the Spanish militia,) I always found to be both a republican and friend to the United States; but being an easy, quiet man, and not calculated to fathom political intrigue, it was supposed that he would on all occasions be influenced by Mr. Hutchins, with whom there was a family connexion. Mr. James Stuart was only entitled to notice from the active part taken by himself, and some of his relations in favour of the British during our revolutionary war.

Mr. Ashly was a Baptist minister, he went to Natchez from the state of Georgia, and it was affirmed by most respectable authority, that he was followed for taking property not his own.

Mr. Hocket's honesty I never heard called in question, but his other qualifications were below mediocrity.

From this statement which is certainly correct, it appears that but four, out of ten members were duly elected. The elections were holden on Saturday the 2d of September 1797, and three days after, the four members already mentioned, with Mr. Hutchins at their head, proceeded to business: on the 9th following

ing, an itinerant attorney, of some education and abilities, by the name of Shaw, held an election, (without any other authority than from Mr. Hutchins,) in the subdivision of Homochitto; when a Mr. Davis was elected by ten voices, no return was ever made of this election, but Mr. Davis nevertheless took his seat. He was justly esteemed a steady friend to the United States, and being independent in his sentiments, he disapproved of great part of the proceedings of Mr. Hutchins's committee. The week following, Mr. Dayton who I have already had occasion to mention, procured the election of Mr. Justice King and Mr. Abner Green, son-in-law to Mr. Hutchins, by subscription: the number of signers did not exceed thirty. This method was resorted to, because the inhabitants of the two districts for which these two men were returned, had protested against the election of Mr. Hutchins's committee: this private mode by subscription was therefore resorted to, as a general election could not be had. The two last members appointed, served to increase the number of the committe, which yet consisted of but seven instead of ten members.

This imperfect representation of the settlement un-the direction of Col. Hutchins, after a session of three weeks, produced a petition and memorial to congress; which was equally remarkable for its misrepresentation, composition, and absurdity of its requests or prayers, for it contained many; but its great length would not justify the insertion of it in a work of this kind.

One of the most prominent features of the petition, was a paragraph calculated to injure Lieut. Pope and myself with our country, and at the same time to furnish the minister of his Catholic Majesty with materials to enable him to make good his charges against us. This petition and memorial, after being finished by Mr.
Hutchins,

Hutchins, and agreed to by the committee, was circulated with great secrecy, and only submitted to the perusal of Mr. Hutchins's confidential friends, and when read at small, partial meetings, for the purpose of obtaining signatures, the paragraph reflecting upon " the persons sent there by the United States," (meaning Lieut. Pope and myself,) *was generally*, *if not always omitted*. It was by accident that a true copy of it was obtained. Mr. Hutchins had sent one on, with a number of papers, by the way of New Orleans, for the Spanish Minister, which were intercepted, opened, and handed to me. The petition and memorial was immediately copied by the late Mr. Benoist, chairman of the permanent committee, and my secretary Mr. Gillespie, after which the packet was made up and forwarded. From this circumstance I was enabled to furnish the department of state with a copy of the petition and memorial, accompanied with remarks, some time before the original forwarded by Mr. Hutchins and his committee, was received.

Upon shewing a copy of the petition and memorial, to some of the signers, they were astonished at the deception which had been practised upon them by Mr. Hutchins and his committee, and declared in the most solemn manner that part of it had never been read to them, in consequence of which, a number of protests were drawn up and signed, by many of the respectable inhabitants, against the paragraph above alluded to, and presented to me for the purpose of being forwarded to the department of state, to counteract any impression that might otherwise have been made by the deception. These protests were all of the same import, the following is an exact copy of one of them.

" Whereas there has been a memorial drawn up by Col. Hutchins, (and a committee stiling themselves a
committee

committee of safety and correspondence,) to the congress of the United States, intended as we conceived to represent only the grievances of the people of this government; but among other representations, we find since signing it, a paragraph reflecting very severely upon the conduct of the honourable Andrew Ellicott, Esq. and Lieutenant Pope, commanding the troops of the United States here, for exciting the inhabitants of this place to an insurrection against the government.

Therefore we the subscribers, as conceiving ourselves over-reached in this particular, not comprehending the meaning of such paragraph, or as we are more inclined to believe, not hearing it read by the person, or agent employed for that purpose, and being now willing to do justice to the characters of the said honourable Andrew Ellicott, Esq. and Lieut. Pope, do most solemnly protest against such paragraph, and make this our recantation, at Natchez, October 24th, 1797."

(Signed by) BALEY CHANCY, JOHN ERWIN, and many others.

Mr. Hannah the Baptist minister, whose name has already been frequently mentioned, with a number of his friends who had entered their names on the petition and memorial, (as it was called,) finding that it contained a paragraph which was not read to them when they signed it, waited upon Mr. Hutchins and requested their names to be stricken out, unless the obnoxious paragraph was expunged. To which he replied " I am much less anxious about retaining any other part of the memorial, but I now have your names, and shall make what use of them I see proper."

U   After

After this transaction, Mr. Hannah immediately called upon me, much alarmed on account of Lieutenant Pope and myself, as it was now evident our injury, more than the good of the settlement, was Mr. Hutchins's real object, and proposed several plans to obtain and destroy the petition and memorial: these plans were not only objected to as improper; but Mr. Hannah was requested to oppose every attempt to get possession of it for any such purpose. He was told that no injury could arise from it, because the government of the United States was not a government of mere opinion, in which an individual could be affected by the caprice of any man, whatever might be his talents, and standing in the community; but a government of laws which served equally for the direction of the first magistrate and the private citizen. That the executive would be cautious in censuring or dismissing a person, (who had devoted more than twenty years of his life in various employments to the service of his country,) without either a hearing, or an investigation to gratify any man, or party of men, much less a stranger almost unknown, but for the part he had taken in opposition to the independence of the United States, and in favour of monarchy.

The declaration of Mr. Hutchins relative to that particular paragraph of the memorial being made public by Mr. Hannah and his friends, turned the popular torrent against him so effectually, that his influence was but trifling during my subsequent continuance in that settlement, though he frequently endeavoured to regain it by artifice and slander.

Notwithstanding the opposition I had uniformly given to taking the memorial, or arresting it on its way to the seat of our government, the irritation was so great that the packet which contained it, together with many other

other papers, was intercepted and brought to me un-opened, in which condition it was returned to Mr. Hutchins, and his committee, who to the best of my recollection never met afterwards.

Having now given an account of the election of Mr. Hutchins's committee, and the sanction it gave to his labours, every part of which can be substantiated by documents furnished to the department of state where they no doubt remain filed, I shall return to the history of the proceedings of the permanent committee, and of my own conduct, which were too intimately conected to be wholly separated. Notwithstanding the rude, and almost unprecedented manner in which Mr. Hutchins treated the permanent committee, and which was seconded by menaces from various parts of the country, that body continued firm in the discharge of its duty.

In the beginning of September 1797, I received from the department of state a communication, containing an account of the detection of Mr. Blunt's plans for conquering Louisiana and the Floridas, for his Britannic Majesty ; which was the second despatch I had received since I left the seat of our government, the other was received on the 25th of July preceding. The communication relative to Mr. Blunt was immediately laid before the permanent committee, and measures taken to prevent any part of the plan being carried into effect, if attempted. The traders and interpreters among the Indians were written to upon that subject, and requested to be vigilant in preventing the circulation and suppression of any improper talks that might be sent among them.

From the part which Mr. Hutchins took in quieting the commotion, it was my opinion for some time after I had received the communication, that he was unacquainted with Mr. Blunt's designs, notwithstanding

U 2

his

his interviews with one of his friends who had left Philadelphia the preceding December, as stated in the third chapter; but his subsequent conduct compelled me to change this opinion, and to conclude that his opposition to the commotion arose from its being either premature, or not in unison with Mr. Blunt's plans. For it is to be observed, that the country had scarcely become tranquil, before Mr. Hutchins began to form a party against the permanent committee, and was desirous of having the principal power placed in his own hands; to accomplish which no art was left unpractised, and no falsehood but was propagated to secure this favourite object. Could this be done to serve the United States? Certainly not; he was well known to have been at all times an enemy to them, and to republican forms of government; and was moreover at that very time an officer on the British military establishment. It is likewise a fact, that three days previous to my arrival at Natchez, when it was known that I was on the river, he went and renewed his oath of allegiance to his Catholic Majesty. In consequence of his inflammatory libels, which he industriously circulated through the settlement, he brought many well meaning inhabitants into the belief that they were in a state of slavery, (though at that time the most free people upon the continent,) and that nothing could prevent their chains being rivited, but a spirited opposition to the permanent committee, and " some of the persons sent there by the United States." Those misrepresentations had nearly proved fatal to the district by arming one part of the inhabitants against the other. The inhabitants of the Bayou Piere being the most distant from the seat of information, were the most easily imposed upon, and some of them were at one time actually imbodied, in consequence of which I received the following letter from the permanent committee.

Committee

Committee room, 12*th September,* 1797.

S<small>IR</small>,

Information has been received by a member present, that forty armed men were on their way from the Bayou Piere, and that the inhabitants of Coles-Creek were in an ill humour, and threatening to arm also. The designs of those preparations seem either to be to interrupt the permanent committee in its proceedings, or otherwise to act hostilely against it. The committee conceive it their duty to make this communication to you in consequence of your having made yourself guarantee for the preservation of peace and good order in this country, by the instrument of writing you was pleased to sign the 22d of June last.

I have the honour to be, with great esteem,
Your most obedient humble servant,
(Signed)   J<small>OSEPH</small> B<small>ERNARD</small>,
Chairman of the permanent committee.

Honourable Andrew }
 Ellicott.   }

To the foregoing letter, the following answer was immediately returned.

Natchez, September 12*th,* 1797.

S<small>IR</small>,

I am sorry to find from your communication of this date, that some of the inhabitants of Coles-Creek and Bayou Piere, continue their opposition to good order. You may depend upon my influence and exertions, both in supporting your authority, and preserving inviolate the present neutrality of this district.

I have the honour to be, with great esteem,
Your friend and humble servant,
A<small>NDREW</small> E<small>LLICOTT</small>.

Joseph Bernard, Esq. chairman }
 of the permanent committee. }   The

The good sense of the people alluded to in the communication from the permanent committee, aided by proper advice, prevailed over their prejudices and passions, and they returned home without committing any act of violence.

On the 14th of September, I received the following letter from the permanent committee.

Sir,

The many proofs that the committee has had of your desire to contribute to the welfare of this country, encourage it to request of you the service mentioned in our first resolve of yesterday, of which this encloses a copy.

I am, sir, your most obedient servant,

Committee room, Sept. 14th, 1797. (Signed) Joseph Bernard,
Chairman.

Honourable Andrew ⎱
    Ellicott.   ⎰

The resolution was in these words.

Sept. 13th. *Resolved*, That the 5th resolve of the 29th ultimo be rescinded, and that Mr. Ellicott, whose inclination for the interest and happiness of this country, we have a convincing proof of in his former communications to the general government published since, and now in our hands, and who from his residence for several months among us, is well acquainted with the circumstances of this country, be requested to represent our present situation to his Excellency the President of the United States, and likewise all the measures which he shall deem conducive to the future welfare of this country, in the event of the late treaty between his Catholic Majesty and the United States being carried fully into effect.

(True copy.)
(Signed)   G. Benoist, *Secretary*.
                                                     The

The fifth resolve of the 29th ultimo, mentioned in the above resolution, was rescinded, as not being sufficiently comprehensive, and the object included in that of the 13th.

By the resolution of the 13th, the committee imposed a very difficult task upon me; but with which I nevertheless endeavoured to comply, and after my ideas were thrown together, they were submitted to that body, and approved of before they were transmitted to the department of state. As that communication contained my sentiments, (which have been extremely misrepresented,) relative to the local and political situation of the country, I shall give the substance of it from my original notes.

The *first*, and principal object with the committee was a constitution, or form of government, and though not expressly mentioned in the resolve, (on account of the neutrality, and the Spanish government having yet a nominal existence,) was nevertheless well understood.

On the subject of government, there have ever been such a variety of opinions, that there is no plan which human wisdom could devise that would not find opponents, and none so bad, that would not have advocates. This diversity of opinion arises in part from habits early acquired, and which vary gradually with the different stages of civilization, and the unequal distribution of wealth in a country.

In framing a government for a district or settlement, it will be proper to inquire into the population, habits, state of civil society, and circumstances of the inhabitants: because these for a time, may be such that a government purely representative, would be very improper, by being placed completely in the power of the vicious, indigent, and uninformed, would oppress the wealthy

thy and industrious, on whom the burden of supporting government generally falls ; and which would probably be the case at present in Natchez,* for this like other new countries, is peopled by the following descriptions of persons, viz. people of ambition and enterprize, who have calculated upon an increase of fame and fortune, others who have fled from their creditors, and some, (not a few,) from justice ; to which may with propriety be added, those who fled from the United States during the revolutionary war, for their monarchical principles, or treasonable practices.

When settlements as they grow up from the causes above mentioned, become constantly incorporated with old and stable governments, they generally produce but a small inconvenience by having a proportionable share in the general representation; but the effect would be very different, if such a settlement without any qualification of the electors, as to property and allegiance, should be invested with the sovereign power of legislating for themselves. In case of such an event, creditors might expect to be injured, if not ruined, gentlemen of probity, worth, and information neglected, if not persecuted, and public confidence annihilated.

It appears to me, that a territorial government simi lar to that of the North Western Territory, is less expensive, and better calculated than a representative one, for doing justice in a district populated from the causes above mentioned, and where the habits of the people have in part been formed under a despotism, and by whom the principles of representative government must be but imperfectly understood, and the free white population supposed not to exceed five or six thousand souls. The Governor, in conjunction with the judges, being

* This representation was made to the department of state, September 24th, 1797.

being competent to the selection and adoption of laws for the district, from the codes of the different states, (comprized in the Union,) and those laws thus adopted, being again subject to the approbation of congress is as great a change from despotism, towards represen tative governmont, as ought suddenly to be made in the situation of any people, (however enlightened,) until their habits, circumstances and morals become more congenial to the true principles of liberty ; otherwise there will be great danger of falling into licentiousness which is the natural extreme. This may be considered political heresy, but it will be found orthodox in practice.

Although domestic slavery is extremely disagreeable to the inhabitants of the eastern states, it will nevertheless be expedient to tolerate it in the district of Natchez, where that species of property is very common, and let it remain on the same footing as in the southern states, otherwise emigrants possessed of that kind of property, would be induced to settle in the Spanish territory.*

The manner of disposing of the vacant land, is a subject in which the inhabitants are materially interested. The mode heretofore pursued by the United States, would neither give satisfaction to the present inhabitants, nor in my opinion be good policy, setting aside the advantage it gives the wealthy, in a monopoly the most dangerous of any other to the liberties of the people.† By disposing of the vacant land in small tracts, and at a moderate price, the preference being given to actual settlers, a firm, compact settlement

X

would

---

* Mr. Hutchins to aid his plans, asserted in the most solemn manner, that I had not only recommended to our government, the abolition of slavery in that territory, but represented it to be the wish of the inhabitants !

† It was likewise represented by Mr. Hutchins and his party, that I had recommended, and advocated the disposing of the vacant land in large tracts only.

would speedily be formed, which from its local situation, would be very advantageous to the United States in case of a war with Spain : another reason for this practice is, the danger of losing a number of our citizens, who would be induced to settle in the Spanish territory, where lands are obtained in any quantity, (great or small,) upon very easy and advantageous terms.

There is yet one other source of uneasiness among the inhabitants, and which relates to their titles. It appears that much the greater part of the lands now occupied, are covered by old British grants. The occupiers of those lands may be divided into two classes. *First*, those who continued in the country after its conquest by the Spaniards, and renewed their titles under his Catholic Majesty, and *secondly*, those who are seated on old British grants, which became forfeited to the crown of Spain by their owners or attornies, not appearing, and occupying them agreeably to the tenor of two proclamations or edicts, issued by his Catholic Majesty ; the one dated in 1786, but whether this was the first or last, I am unable to say, as I have not yet been able to procure either of them. The lands thus forfeited, have been granted by the officers of his Catholic Majesty, in the same manner, as practised in granting vacant lands. This class of settlers may be considered as composing the body of the settlement. With respect to the *first* class, there cannot possibly be any doubt as to the validity of their titles: and the *second*, upon the principles of justice and equity, are perhaps equally safe ; but they have their fears, and are therefore desirous that an act of congress may be passed confirming all their titles, that were good under the crown of Spain, at the time of the final ratification of the late treaty. So far the representation was made

to

to the department of state, agreeably to the request of the permanent committee.

About the 20th of September, the committee met with a great loss in the death of its chairman, Mr. Bernard. He was a gentleman of good understanding, sound judgment, and of the most inflexible integrity. From his youth he was strongly attached to republican principles, and it may truly be said, that he expired serving the United States. His easy manners, benevolence and hospitality, were of that cast, that he only needed be known, to be esteemed.

Upon the death of Mr. Bernard, Mr. Benoist was unanimously elected chairman of the permanent committee, the duties of which he performed with singular assiduity, judgment and integrity. He was a French gentleman, of very respectable connexions; but from an ardent passion for liberty, he left his own country, and espoused the cause of the United States, in their arduous struggle for independence; and afterwards retired into the settlement of Natchez, under the full persuasion, that it would be shortly annexed to the United States, where he married an amiable lady, the daughter of an honest, worthy planter, by the name of Dunbar.

Mr. Benoist was no sooner elected, than he was attacked with all the abuse, obloquy, detraction and misrepresentation, that could be devised by Mr. Hutchins and his party: his being both a Frenchman and republican, were sufficient causes to merit the hatred of Mr. Hutchins, by whom he was loaded with the epithets, French jacobin and democrat, together with the whole catalogue of kindred terms, invented for party purposes, and intended by an association of ideas, to lessen the characters of those whose conduct would not be injured by an exhibition of facts.

X 2

Mr.

Mr. Benoist being a gentleman of great sensibility, could not but feel the injustice done to his character, and though his natural vivacity veiled from the public eye, the injury done to his feelings, it laid the foundation of a disorder, under which he sunk the following summer.

The permanent committee took little or no notice of Mr. Hutchins's committee ; but depended on its own integrity, and a conscientious conviction in its own mind, that its endeavours and exertions, were directed to the true interests of the United States for support.

My communications to the department of state, and which I did not think myself justifiable in making public, (particularly that one drawn up at the request of the permanent committee,) were so wantonly misrepresented, that it produced such a degree of irritation among some of the inhabitants, that I found it necessary for a short time to augment the number of my guard. To allay those prejudices, and if possible prevent the deluded from committing acts of violence, the following address was circulated through the district, and read by my secretary at a public meeting, about seven miles from the town.

To the inhabitants of the district of Natchez.

I have received certain information, that the following reports evidently calculated to injure me in the estimation of the good people of this district are in circulation. *First*, that I have in my official communications to the government of the United States, recommended that the vacant lands in this country, be laid off, and sold in squares of six miles to a tract. *Secondly*, that slavery ought to be prohibited here, as in the North Western Territory, and *thirdly*, that I am, or have been extensively

extensively concerned in large landed speculations, particularly in the purchase of old British grants.

I now in the most unequivocal manner, declare the above reports to be without the least foundation. The *first two*, you will find contradicted by my official communications, when they are published. In those communications, I have recommended, that the vacant land be disposed of in such a manner, as to accommodate actual settlers of all descriptions, and that the system of slavery be continued upon the same footing, that it is in the southern states. The *third charge*, of being concerned in landed speculations, will in time be found equally false with the others.

These reports have originated with the enemies of the United States, and are calculated to answer the worst of purposes. They have been brought forward with so much art, and propagated with so much address, that many well disposed, honest, upright characters have given them credit. They are of the same stamp with Mr. Blunt's letter to Carey, and intended to weaken the confidence of the inhabitants of this district, in the agents of the United States, that in case of danger, they may have no rallying point, and thereby become an easy prey, to some one of the European powers now at war.

My duty and inclination, have both impelled me to use all my interest with the executive of the United States in favour of this district, to which I feel a strong partiality, a partiality not of the moment, but the result of several months experience. These exertions in your favour will be continued with zeal and assiduity.

I am with sentiments of high respect,
Your humble servant,

Natchez, October 13th, 1797.   ANDREW ELLICOTT.

Notwithstanding

Notwithstanding the industry of the designing and turbulent, in the propagation of reports injurious to the characters of the members of the permanent committee, as individuals, and to their conduct as a body, they in both capacities met with the most decided support, from the honest, intelligent, independent, and well informed; who will at all times have great weight, in all well regulated governments; and when they cease to be regarded by an executive, and lose their influence with the populace, either anarchy or tyranny is the certain consequence.

From the able support given to the committee, it was enabled to surmount all the difficulties, by which it was at various times surrounded, and triumph over the friends to disorder and confusion, who could not at that time on account of the neutrality, be publicly supported even by the Spanish government, whatever might have been its strength in political mercenaries, who are easily, in all countries converted into military ones.

Although the members of the committee felt themselves thus secure, they feared the effect of the misrepresentations of Mr. Hutchins, and his followers, upon the executive of the United States, so far as they related to Lieut. Pope, and myself. To counteract the effect of those misrepresentations, the committee drew up, and presented to me the following address, which though evidently intended to be made public, was only transmitted to the department of state.

To the honourable ANDREW ELLICOTT, *commissioner of the United States of America, for running the line of demarcation between the United States and Spain.*
SIR,
Permit the members of the permanent committee of the district of Natchez, to accost you with all the attach-
ment

ment and respect, which a just sense of your talents, patriotism, and truly amiable manners is calculated to inspire. To the judicious arrangements entered into with the Spanish government, and which you had the happiness to concert with the commanding officer of the United States troops, and with certain well disposed, and influential characters in this district, we feel ourselves indebted for the neutral position which we at present hold, and which it is our particular duty, interest, and inclination to preserve inviolate, by all the means in our power: And we consider it sir, as one of the most agreeable consequences of our neutrality, that it affords us the pleasure and advantage of a safe, and unreserved communication with you: it surely is but justice to add, that when difficulties and doubts, have arisen in the discharge of our duty, from the novelty of our situation, your friendly advice has contributed greatly to remove them, and that aided by your experience we have been enabled to act a consistent, if not a popular part, though placed in circumstances embarrassing in the extreme, and altogether without precedent or example.

These sir, are the sentiments of the committee, and it is with pain they observe, that through the restless and intriguing disposition of a designing individual, attempts have been made to injure you in the public mind, and to prejudice you, not only in this district, which you have so essentially served, but also with the executive of the United States, whose dignity and interest you have so well supported. This sir we consider a censure so ungenerous and unmerited, and the whole procedure so base and ungrateful, that so far from concurring therein, we should hold ourselves criminal if we remained silent on the occasion. With a view sir to do justice to your character, so far as it

has

has been connected with the proceedings of this committee, and at the same time, to remove any improper impressions which the executive of the United States may have received, with regard to ourselves, from the misrepresentations of Col. Hutchins, we have thought proper sir, to offer you free access to our files with the privilege to make such extracts therefrom, as you will think necessary for your justification.

Although the committee have already made honourable mention of Lieutenant Pope, in one of their resolves, they cannot with justice close this address to you sir, without expressing in the most unequivocal manner their approbation of his conduct in this business, and giving it as their opinion, he has deserved well of his country.

That your well meant endeavours to serve this district, may be productive of consequences salutary to the inhabitants, and honourable to yourself, is the sincere wish of

Sir, your very humble servants,

Gabriel Benoist Chairman,

Philander Smith	Roger Dixon
Peter B. Bruin	William Ratliff
Daniel Clark	Frederick Kimball.
Isaac Gaillard	

Natchez, October 21*st* 1797.

The permission given in the foregoing address, to have access to the files of the committee, was never made use of; because it was impossible for me to suppose, that any measures injurious to the character, or reputation of a citizen, in a public capacity, would be attempted by the first magistrate of a great, free,

free, and powerful nation, who held his office by the voice of a watchful people, (ready at all times to scrutinize his conduct, and make the cause of an injured citizen their own,) without a regular investigation, to which every freeman ought to be entitled, and from which none but the guilty would shrink.

In November 1797, the appointment of Col. Grandprie by the court of Madrid to the government of Natchez, and its dependencies was publicly announced. Immediately upon receiving this information, the permanent committee took the subject into consideration, and in a firm, and manly manner, resolved that Col. Grandprie (who was then at New Orleans) could not be received in the district of Natchez, in the quality of Governor. The proceedings of the committee were immediately transmitted to Governor General Gayoso, with a request to put a stop to Col. Grandprie's going into the district, if he should attempt it, as it would be considered a breach of the neutrality, and resented accordingly. This conduct alone, ought to be sufficient to convince every unprejudiced person, of the attachment of the permanent committee to the government, and interests, of the United States.

Very soon after the part, which the permanent committee had taken relative to the admission of Col. Grandprie was publicly known, Mr. Hutchins entered into a correspondence with him, and it was currently reported in New Orleans that he had offered to aid him with two hundred men, in taking possession of the government. But the firmness of the committee, added to the general disposition of the inhabitants, rendered it improper, and perhaps unsafe for Col. Grandprie to make the attempt: in consequence of which he remained quietly at New Orleans, until
Y   he

he could be otherwise provided for. One of the letters from Col. Grandprie, to Mr. Hutchins, *passed through my hands.*

In the beginning of December, a considerable detachment of troops from the army of the United States arrived at Natchez: they had been long expected, and as long desired by the friends of the United States, as it was presumed their presence would have a happy effect, in keeping good order, by awing the turbulent, and rendering the possession of the country more certain. But it unfortunately happened, that the Commandant who superceded Mr. Pope, was much indisposed by an inflammatory complaint on one side of his head, and face, at the time of his arrival, that evidently had an effect upon his understanding, which was naturally very far above mediocrity: in this state, he was immediately surrounded by a number of unworthy characters, who took advantage of his situation, to prejudice his mind against the permanent committee, and other friends of the United States; who were treated by him in the most opprobrious manner. One evening he came to the house which I occupied, and in which the committee held its meetings, and after insulting his Catholic Majesty's consul Mr. Vidal, who was there on a visit; he inquired whether or no the committee was in session? and being answered in the negative, asked if none of the members were present? Upon which Mr. Gaillard answered "I am one of the members." The Commandant then inquired "by what authority they met."? That he was determined not to be made a cypher of, and would rule the district with a rod of iron. That the meetings of the committee were improper, and seditious, and must henceforth, consider itself dissolved, or he should treat it worse than Mr. Hutchins had done. Mr. Gaillard

Gaillard being a gentleman of considerable wealth, independence of sentiment, and firmness of mind, added to true republican principles, for which he had suffered severely under the Spanish government, could not brook the idea of again becoming subject to a military despotism. He therefore replied with great warmth to the observations of the Commandant, who after having exhausted his vocabulary of abusive epithets, took leave with expressions too indelicate to have a place in language.

Notwithstanding this outrageous conduct of the Commandant, the committee met the next morning without opposition; but the circumstance of his abuse of that respectable body, was taken advantage of by the discontented, who proposed that the district should immediately be put under military government. This, as might reasonably be expected, met with great opposition; and I considered it my duty, as a citizen of the United States, to prevent if possible, so dangerous and unnecessary a measure being carried into effect.

Among those who laboured with the most assiduity in favour of the military government, was the late Mr. Hunter, who was afterwards appointed by the influence of Mr. Hutchins, a member of congress from the Mississippi territory. Mr. Hunter was employed by me in May 1797, to carry my despatches to the seat of our government, and returned a strenious advocate for the omnipotence of presidential power, and pretended that he had received a commission from the United States, which enabled him to borrow a little money : the commission was probably a forgery. General Mathews likewise exerted his talents on the same side of the question with Mr. Hunter, but the behaviour of the Commandant, (already exemplified) on several occasions, had convinced every person in the district, who had

Y 2   the

the least regard to justice and liberty, that the measure
would be attended with serious evils to individuals,
and dishonour the United States. It therefore had
an abortive issue.

In revenge for the failure of the above plan, my arrest was frequently spoken of, and as a foundation to
ground it upon, an officer, with two other persons were
despatched into the Chocktaw nation, to procure my
letters; but as a cover to this expedition, a message or
talk of Gen. Wilkinson, was sent along. The day previous to the departure of those messengers, I met with
the officer, and told him the expedition was unnecessary,
as copies of all my letters were transmitted to the department of state, and if any of them should be found
improper, or reprehensible, there could be no doubt
but I should hear of it from the secretary of state, whom
I would request to furnish them with copies, but if that
would be attended with too much delay, they should
willingly have the perusal of copies of them, in my possession. The offer was not accepted, and the party
went, and returned, without procuring any materials
for an arrest; but succeeded in persuading one of our
deputy agents of Indian affairs by the name of Mitchell,
that I had prevailed upon the Indians to drive him out
of the nation. A more bare-faced falsehood was never
propagated!

For several months, the public mind was frequently
agitated by anonymous papers that were circulated
through the district; some of which were evidently
written by Mr. Hutchins; but those that were entitled
to the most attention, in point of composition, were
penned by a Mr. Payne, and a Mr. * * * * * ; the latter
for particular reasons, found it most convenient to
go by an assumed name. Mr. Payne had followed
trading and swindling on the Ohio, till his safety rendered

dered it necessary to descend the river, and he arrived at Natches a few weeks after I did: but it will only be doing justice to his character, to state that he voluntarily came in, and acknowledged his fault, and was afterwards useful in exposing to public view the insidious conduct of Mr. Hutchins. Mr. * * * * *, had been a soldier in General Wayne's army, but after being twice publicly whipped for forgery, (at which he was very dexterous,) and other misbehaviour he was ignominously discharged. He was a person of excellent understanding, and good education, but to all appearance totally lost to every sentiment of honour and honesty. Nature appeared to have intended him for an ornament to his country; but from a defect in the moral principle, he became the cause of sorrow to his connexions. After being compelled to leave the army, he took up his residence in the district of Natchez.

These two young men, almost strangers, without property, standing connexions, or character in the country, became the champions of liberty, and the rights of the people. When men of this class become patronized for party, or political purposes, the public mind may be truly said to be taking in a slow poison, which though like the forbidden fruit, does not produce immediate death, the effect is nevertheless certain, as well (to use the expression of the late Gen. Lee,) might the community be inoculated for the leprosy, as be governed or influenced by such characters. This sentiment I am well aware is not popular, neither was it in the republics of Greece and Rome. Those republics were constantly convulsed, and their political existence terminated by the violence of party, which was kept alive by artful demagogues, whose want of industry and character, prevented their obtaining a live-
lihood

lihood by honest, regular pursuits. When this class of men come forward as reformers, these questions ought to be asked. What interest have they in the community? "Are they honest, are they capable;" what have they done to merit the confidence of the public? But it is said, that as liberty is as dear to one person as another, they are equally entitled to the use of their exertions, either in the obtaining or preservation of it. This is certainly true, so far as it goes merely to the preservation, or obtaining of liberty; but there may be an essential difference in their views: A person of character, and respectable standing in the community, and possessed of property, has infinitely more at stake, than one possessed of neither; and consequently much more interested in keeping good order, and securing to individuals the unmolested enjoyment of their property. Many of those itinerant reformers, who have been falsely called politicians and philosophers, have under the specious garb of liberty, nothing but disorder and anarchy in view: they delight in confusion, for they are nourished and supported by it, like vermin by putrefaction.

Bad men, and fugitives from justice, think all governments however lenient, oppressive, they hate law, and are at all times ready to oppose it. It is therefore necessary to inquire dispassionately into the situation and probable views of every officious patriot, before we submit to become scaling ladders to his ambition, or instruments to impede justice, or prostrate government.

The very name of liberty, like that of religion, has in all ages entitled the true patriot, as well as the divine, to singular attention, respect and confidence; hence those characters, like valuable coin, hold out strong inducements to the artful and designing, to counterfeit them,

them, from whence arises the necessity for honest men to be on their guard against them.

The permanent committee, by neither submitting to be guided or influenced in any of its measures, by the approbation of noisy or pretended friends, nor regarding the abuse of its opponents, gave such a stability to the public mind, that though the shadow of the Spanish jurisdiction, which had remained in the district since the termination of the commotion, was withdrawn in January 1798, and the inhabitants left without law or government, till September following, I never heard of a single outrage being committed in the territory, except by the Commandant, and one or two other officers.

On the 18th of January 1798, the disagreeable state of suspense we had been in for almost one year, relative to the fate of the treaty, was partly terminated by the following letter from Governor Gayoso.

New Orleans, January 10th, 1798.

Sir,

By a packet just arrived, I have received orders from court, by which I am authorised and ordered, to evacuate the forts of Natchez and Nogales, (Walnut Hills,) in consequence thereof by this express, I send the necessary orders to withdraw the artillery, and other military effects. As the gallies will not be sufficient, other vessels shall be sent from this to complete the operation with all possible speed.

Please to furnish Major* Minor with the information I request, that I may be enabled to provide every thing concerning the execution of the boundary line between his Majesty's dominion, and the territory of the United States.

It

* He received this title from his office of fort major, which he held whilst a subaltern.

It is with the greatest satisfaction that I have the pleasure to announce to you this agreeable event, as it justifies our disposition in complying with our engagements as soon as political circumstances would justify it.

I have the honour to be,

with the highest consideration,

Sir, your most obedient humble servant,

MANUEL GAYOSO DE LEMOS.

Honourable Andrew }
Ellicott. }

Immediately upon receiving the above letter, I had it made as public as possible, for the satisfaction of our friends, and the same evening waited upon Capt. Minor, and gave him what information I could relative to the arrangements and preparations necessary to be made on their part, agreeably to the request of Governor Gayoso,* and the next day forwarded to him the following reply.

Natchez, January 19th, 1798.

DEAR SIR,

Your favour of the 10th, came to hand yesterday in the evening. The intelligence which it contains is agreeable and interesting. Nations like individuals, can only be respectable in proportion to the good faith they observe in complying with their contracts : in this particular, the court of Madrid has generally been more exact than any other in Europe.

I have handed to Captain Minor, the arrangements made by the United States, for the demarcation of the boundary ; but as this relates principally to the number

of

---

* Governor Gayoso in his letter to me of the 12th of April 1797, stated that all the necessary preparation on their part was made before my arrival.

of persons to be employed, we shall find it necessary on our meeting near the point of beginning, to settle many particulars which could not possibly be taken into view by the legislature and executive of the United States, owing to a want of the necessary information relative to the face of the country, and many obstacles which could not reasonably be expected by persons only acquainted with the Atlantic states.

I am with great esteem and regard,
Your friend and humble servant,
ANDREW ELLICOTT.

His Excellency Manuel ⎱
  Gayoso de Lemos. ⎰

Although our business now began to assume a more favourable aspect, and had I not been taught by experience, to suspect every thing that came from the officers of his Catholic Majesty, I should have concluded our difficulties at an end; but I still had my suspicions, which were in some measure realized on the 31st of January; when Capt. Guion handed me a letter which he had just received from Governor Gayoso, in which he informed the Captain, "that he would come up to Natchez, and make the arrangements with him for furnishing the military escort, and supplying it with provision, likewise a plan for running the boundary." Upon reading this curious letter, it was observed to the Captain, " that delay and embarrassment, still continued to be an object with Governor Gayoso; but that the present finesse would, and must fail." The Captain replied, that he " was certainly the proper person to make the arrangements, but did not intend to interfere with the astronomical operations." Finding from this reply, that the Governor's finesse had taken with the Captain, the following letter was

Z   sent

sent off to New Orleans, for the Governor the next day.

Natchez, February 1st, 1798.

DEAR SIR,

That our proceedings in carrying into effect, that part of the late treaty between the United States and his Catholic Majesty, which has been submitted to us, may be commenced with system, it will be necessary that we should understand each other as to the place, and precise time of our meeting: by the third article of the treaty, my present situation appears to be the place contemplated by the contracting parties for the meeting of the commissioners; however as that cannot be very material, I shall have no objection to meet you at Clarksville, which will be near the beginning of the line of demarcation. With respect to the time I wish it to be at as early a period as possible; and as I am at times ready to proceed to business, I wish you to name the day of meeting.

Captain Guion has communicated to me the contents of a letter, which he has lately received from you relative to the arrangements for furnishing the military escort, supplying the provisions, and a plan for carrying on the line. With respect to the *first* of those objects, I beg leave to observe, that the escort has already been furnished by Colonel Butler, agreeably to instructions which he received from the secretary of war: of this circumstance you could not possibly be unknowing, as the escort descended the river with me, and was for some time a subject of discussion between us. As to the *second point,* the supplying of provisions, it is equally well known to your Excellency, that a commissary has been appointed by the secretary of state of the United States, for the purpose of procuring the

necessary

necessary supplies, and attending to the transportation of provisions, instruments, &c. So far, I thought the arrangements would be considered without the reach of criticisms or objections, and I confess that I am unable to account for your letter to Captain Guion upon any other principle, than the contemplation of further delay. The plan, which you have proposed to the same gentleman, for carrying on the line, however proper and judicious in itself, is wholly unnecessary, as he is not the person appointed to carry that part of the treaty into effect. My instructions, and those to the surveyor, I am fully persuaded will be a sufficient guide to us in the execution of the business, without any foreign or domestic advice.

I now give you my candid opinion, that I think the arrangements on behalf of the United States, fully sufficient to give validity to the work when executed, and if yours should not be much more exceptionable, there will be no objection from the government I have the honour to serve, which would spurn at the idea of criticism on extraneous minutia, which could neither affect the accuracy, nor due execution of the work.

I have the honour to be,
With great esteem and respect,
Your sincere friend and humble servant,
ANDREW ELLICOTT.

His Excellency Manuel
Gayoso de Lemos.

To the foregoing letter Governor Gayoso returned the following answer.

New Orleans, February 13*th,* 1798.

SIR,

I have received your favour of the 1st instant, by which you propose our meeting at Clarksville, as soon

as

as possible, finding yourself in readiness to proceed to the demarcation of the boundary line prescribed by the treaty.

In consequence of the measures that I have taken for evacuating the posts, I am persuaded that some time next month that the operation will be completed, at the same time I shall be at Clarksville, disposed to begin the demarcation of the boundary line ; but previous to my arrival, I shall give you timely notice, that we may meet about the same time.

My communication to Captain Guion on the same subject, ought not to appear strange to you. General Wilkinson speaking of Captain Guion to me says, " this officer's experience and good sense, the powers with which he is elevated by the President of the United States, conspire to promise a happy result to his command, in which I flatter myself, I shall not be disappointed." Under such circumstances Captain Guion is not an indifferent person to me, and the double application I have made to you and to him, does not imply the disposition that you are pleased to interpret: the executive of the United States can give his powers either to you, or to Captain Guion, or to both, and where I find that the authority resides, I have no manner of objection to act with it, for in this important business, the depending interests are those of the United States, and the king my master executed by their representatives.

I am, with great esteem and
  Friendship, sir,
    Your humble servant,
     MANUEL GAYOSO DE LEMOS.

Honourable Andrew }
 Ellicott.

The

The latter part of the above letter from Governor Gayoso is certainly very confused, he must have been sensible, that his finessing with Captain Guion was highly improper, and could not be justified by any character given of him by Gen. Wilkinson: he therefore found it difficult to reconcile his conduct with that candour he had constantly professed.

Not being by any means certain of the extent of Mr. Blunt's plans and intrigues, (a friend of his being then in the settlement, and in the pay of the United States,) or in what manner they might operate in embarrassing our business, or how far those delays were in unison with another plan, of much greater magnitude, the outlines of which I obtained in October 1797, and communicated confidentially in cypher to the department of state, by a communication dated the 14th of November following, it was therefore resolved, to bring the business to issue at all events, and risk the consequences, by beginning the demarcation of the boundary, the instant the posts were evacuated by the Spaniards; although the officers of his Catholic Majesty should not co-operate, and Captain Guion should detain my escort. This resolution was not made known to an individual in that country; but communicated to the department of state by two despatches, the one dated February 1798, and the other the 25th of the same month.

The French privateers had now began to be very troublesome to the trade of the United States in the West Indies, and about the Gulf of Mexico. A number of our captured vessels were taken into the port of New Orleans, condemned, and disposed of with their cargoes for a trifling price, our seamen treated in a most shameful manner, and our trade otherwise brought into great jeopardy.

This

This subject became a matter of serious considera-tion, and the United States having neither a con-sul nor vice consul at that port, I interested myself in procuring the privilege for Daniel Clark junior, a dis-tinguished merchant of that place, to act as consul for the United States, till the executive should make a re-gular appointment.   Immediately upon the application being made to Governor Gayoso, he directed that Mr. Clark should be received as consul from the United States, and regarded as such by the merchants and officers of his Catholic Majesty.

The firm, manly, and decided conduct of Mr. Clark, in a short time put a new face upon our commerce in that quarter, and obtained some privileges we had not before enjoyed.   The correspondence between Gover-nor Gayoso, Mr. Clark and myself, on the various sub-jects which invited discussion, would of itself make a volume; but as it more particularly concerned Mr. Clark, it is hoped he will some time make it public. The conduct of Mr. Clark was so acceptable to the ex-ecutive of the United States, that he was thanked through my hands, and requested to continue his good offices in favour of our citizens : the appointment of con-sul was nevertheless given to a Mr. Jones, and that of vice consul, to a worthy native of the United States, by the name of Hulings.   Upon the late change of admi-nistration taking place, the merit of Mr. Clark was so conspicuous, that he was appointed consul in the place of Mr. Jones.

During the years 1797 and 1798, the character of the United States stood very high in the Floridas and Louisiana, and even those who were directly in favour of the republic of France, admired the firm manner in which Mr. Adams began his administration ; and could not withhold their approbation of the threatening aspect assumed

assumed by one of the youngest nations in the world, that dared boldly to come forward, and oppose a power under which all Europe was bending. This conduct produced such a confidence in the friends of the United States in that quarter, that a plan was early formed, to add to the Union, the two Floridas, with the island of Orleans, provided the Spaniards either committed hostilities against the citizens of the United States at Natchez, or joined France in the contest against us. From the secrecy, talents and enterprise of those concerned, added to a temporary system of finance, and a deposit of arms, there could not possibly be any doubt of the complete, and almost instantaneous success of the plan had it been attempted. But the threatening aspect which was assumed by our government, like a meteor, flashed but for the moment, left the nation paralyzed and damped, or extinguished the spirit of enterprise, without obtaining a single permanent advantage.

If Mr. Adams was right in the manner he commenced his administration, he was wrong in abandoning the ground he had taken: but if he began wrong, his subsequent conduct was by no means calculated to do credit to the country, or give the shadow of consistency to the measures of government, which were so capricious, that they left neither the French nor British satisfied with us, who may hereafter combine their intrigues and forces, to prostrate the only free national government upon earth.

The existence of the plan above mentioned, for annexing the Floridas and the island of Orleans to the United States, is mentioned in a long communication to the department of state, dated January 10th, 1799. A further public developement would for very obvious reasons, be yet improper.

Being

Being fully satisfied, that delay was yet a favourite object with the officers of his Catholic Majesty, and having taken the resolution already mentioned, to commence the business without them so soon as the posts were evacuated; I waited in daily expectation of that event. The time when the evacuation was to take place, was kept a most profound secret by the Spaniards, and managed with all the caution of a retreat. On the 29th of March late in the evening, I was informed through a confidential channel, that the evacuation would take place the next morning, before day; in consequence of which, I rose the next morning at four o'clock, and walked to the fort, and found the last party, or rear guard just leaving it, and as the gate was left open, I went in, and enjoyed from the parapet, the pleasing prospect of the gallies and boats leaving the shore, and getting under way: they were out of sight of the town before daylight. The same day our troops took possession of the works.

CHAP.

CHAP. VI.

The author leaves the town of Natchez—difficulties which attended the beginning of the boundary—joined by Governor Gayoso and other officers of his Catholic Majesty—Governor Gayoso returns to New Orleans and sends back a communication concerning the hostile disposition of the Indians—Opinion of it—moves on by several stations to the Pearl or Half Way River —on the way gets possession of a curious letter— difficulties at the Pearl river—finishes the course of observations, and sets out for New Orleans—arrives there on the 4th of January 1799—some account of the Pearl, or Half way river, and lake Pontchartrain.

I now began to make my arrangements for commencing the important business of my mission, and left the town of Natchez the 9th of April following.

I confess my feelings were much alive on leaving that town; the attention, politeness, and hospitality which I had experienced from the inhabitants on all occasions, for more than a year, had made strong impressions upon my mind, which can only be obliterated by the loss of recollection. And though it was frequently the scene of difficulties, the constant support I found from the friends of the United States, and the ultimate success of the important business with which I was intrusted, served to render the place more interesting. Our boats were under way by sunrise; but I could not direct my face from the town, until the last house disappeared.

On the 10th early in the morning, we arrived at Clarksville and encamped, and on the 11th I set up the

A a   clock

clock, and small zenith sector, and proceeded to take the zenith distance of pollux, for five evenings successively, the first three, with the plane of the sector to the east, and the others with the plane west. From the result of those observations, it appeared that we were three miles, and two hundred and ninety perches too far north. This distance my assistants Messrs. Gillespie, Ellicott, junior, and Walker, traversed with a common surveying compass and chain, to the south, in order to discover, (nearly,) a proper place to encamp, and set up the large sector, to determine the first point in the line with accuracy. When this traverse was completed, it was found to be impracticable to convey our instruments, baggage and stores directly from Clarksville, to the most eligible place, owing to the extreme unevenness of the country on the one hand, and the banks of the Mississippi not being sufficiently inundated on the other, to give us a passage by water through the swamps and small lakes: it was therefore determined to descend the Mississippi to the Bayou Tunica, (or Willing's Bayou;) from whence I understood we could convey our instruments, stores and baggage, either by land or water, almost to the place of beginning; though not without some difficulty. The distance from Clarksville to the Bayou Tunica by land, is but about eight and an half miles, but by the Mississippi more than fifty.

On the 24th we left Clarksville, and arrived at the Bayou Tunica on the 26th, being detained one day by head winds.

On the 27th my assistants were sent to carry a line east from the termination of the traverse already made, into the high land, and on the 28th, I went and examined the country over which the guide line passed, and fixed upon a very elevated situation, about one thousand

four

four hundred feet south of it, for our first position :
but the difficulty of getting our instruments, baggage
and stores to it, appeared much greater than I first expected. A party of our men were directed to open a
road from the height already pitched upon, to Alston's
Lake ; the distance was about one mile. The road was
completed on the 30th, and on the first of day May we
moved and encamped on the top of the hill. Our instruments, baggage, &c. were first carted from the
Bayou Tunica, to Alston's Lake, into which I had previously taken through the swamp two light skiffs : the
articles were then taken by water, up the lake to the
point where our road from the hill struck it, and
from thence packed on horses to our encampment.
The country was so broken, and covered from the tops
to the bottoms of the hills, with such high, strong cane,
(arundo gigantea,) and a variety of lofty timber, that a
road from the Bayou Tunica, to our camp, could not
be made by our number of hands, in less than a month
passable for pack-horses.

The situation of our encampment on the top of the
hill, was both pleasant and beautiful, the prospect very
fine, particularly to the south-west, which opened to
the Mississippi swamp, and gave us an uninterupted
view, which was only terminated by the curvature of
the earth. The hill appeared to have been under cultivation some years ago, and the cane entirely destroyed ; but a number of splendid trees were left standing,
among which we encamped.

Our observatory tent being worn out by the military,
who had no tents when they arrived at Natchez, I was
now under the necessity of erecting a wooden building for that purpose ; which I began on the 2d of May,
and with the aid of four men finished on the 4th, and
set up the clock, and large zenith sector ; but the wea-

ther

ther being unfavourable, the course of observations was not began till the 6th, and was completed on the 16th, which with the results, and manner of commencing the demarcation of the boundary, may be seen in the Appendix. On the 21st we were joined by Capt. Minor, and a party of labourers on behalf of his Catholic Majesty, and on the 26th by Mr. Dunbar, the astronomer in the same employ.

On the 31st of May Governor Gayoso, with his secretary and several other officers arrived at our camp. The Governor had written me a number of letters to delay any proceedings till he joined me; but being well convinced, if it had been left to that issue, he would have found reasons for continuing at New Orleans the whole season.

On the 1st of June, the Governor accompanied me to the line, and approved of the work. On our return to camp, I requested him to join me in a report confirming the work already done, particularly as he was yet the principal commissioner, and had not under the powers with which he was invested by the court of Madrid, authorised any other person to execute the commission; but this under various pretences, he declined doing. And the day following set out for New Orleans, after impowering Capt. Minor and Mr. Dunbar, to execute the commission on behalf of his Catholic Majesty.

On the 7th of June, we moved our camp to Little Bayou Sara. The weather had now become extremely hot, and the season being uncommonly wet, and our men badly provided for with tents and other covering, they were generally indisposed and unfit for duty. We were therefore reduced to the necessity of either abandoning the business for some time, or employing slaves; the latter was adopted.

The

The first twenty miles of country over which the line passed, is perhaps as fertile as any in the United States; and at the same time the most impenetrable, and could only be explored by using the cane knife and hatchet. The whole face of the country being covered with strong canes, which stood almost as close together as hemp stalks, and generally from twenty to thirty-five feet high, and matted together by various species of vines, that connected them with the boughs of the lofty timber, which was very abundant. The hills are numerous, short and steep: from those untoward circumstances, we were scarcely ever able to open one-fourth of a mile per day, and frequently much less.

On the 10th of June, an official communication was received from Governor Gayoso informing us of the hostile disposition of the Indians, and their determination to put a stop to the demarcation of the boundary; and that their enmity was directed against the people of the United States: this intelligence was considered as a part of the system of delay, which had already been so injurious and expensive to the United States, it was therefore disregarded; but from an impression of duty, the communication with some observations upon it, was forwarded immediately to the department of state.

On the 17th of July, we moved our camp to Big Bayou Sara; but a few days previous to our removal, we received information that a constitution had been framed for the Mississippi territory, and that Winthrop Sargent, Esq. was appointed Governor. This intelligence was not only agreeable to us, but highly acceptable to every friend to order and good government in the territory. We were further informed, that General Wilkinson was expected down to take the command of the troops.

Before

Before the line was extended to the Bayou Sara, Mr. Hutchins, and several others made application for lands south of the line, and requested permission to remove to them, but Governor Gayoso denied the request to Mr. Hutchins, and some other turbulent characters ; but permitted one of Mr. Hutchins's sons to remove within his government, where I am informed he continues to reside : those turbulent characters finding now no alternative left, they then, and not till then, became violent republicans, and may now be said to direct generally the public affairs of that territory.*

On the 6th of August Governor Sargent arrived at Natchez, but in so bad a state of health, that he did not begin to organize the government till in September following. On the 26th of the same month General Wilkinson arrived.

Thus it will appear, that all the difficulties we had to encounter were surmounted, and the demarcation of the boundary commenced several months before the arrival of either the Governor or General Wilkinson.

In the beginning of September Mr. Dunbar left us, and returned to his seat, a few miles from the town of Natchez. This circumstance I considered a real loss to the public. To myself it was irreparable. The day after the departure of Mr. Dunbar, we moved to Thompson's Creek, where we continued till the 27th of October, when we broke up that camp, and proceeded to the Pearl, or Half-Way River : on the way I halted a few days at Darling's Creek, for the purpose of refreshing our pack horses, and making up a communication to the department of state. While at that place, by a very extraordinary accident, a letter from the Governor

vernor

* Since this paragraph was written, I have been told a change has taken place in the legislature of that territory.

vernor General, on its way to a confidential officer in the Spanish service, fell into my hands for a few hours.

This letter contained the most unequivocal proof, of the late existence of a plan, calculated to injure the United States; but which appeared then to be abandoned, and in which a number of our citizens had been actually engaged. From this letter it was rendered evident, that the suspicions of the late General Wayne, respecting an improper correspondence being carried on between the officers of his Catholic Majesty, and some gentlemen residing in the western part of the United States, were well founded; but it was equally certain, that he was mistaken in several cases, as to the individual objects of his suspicion. It is likewise a fact, that the despatches, and nearly twenty thousand dollars in silver, to be paid to certain characters were on board of the boat from New Orleans, which was taken by his order, and examined by Licut. Steel; but the articles were overlooked!

The interesting parts of the above mentioned letter, were reduced to cypher, and accompanied my despatches of November 8th 1798, to the department of state.

On Saturday the 17th of November, we arrived at the Cane Brake on the west side of Pearl river, and the 18th were employed in opening a road to the river, making rafts, and ferrying our baggage over, and on the 19th encamped and set up the clock.

In our journey from Thompson's Creek, we had many difficulties to encounter. The swamps were numerous, and many of them so deep, that we had to go considerably out of our way either to cross, or go round them, and others we had to causeway: add to those difficulties, a total want of information respecting the face of the country, which in our direction, did not

appear

appear to have ever been explored by white people; some of the streams were so deep, that we had to cross on rafts, in the constructions of which my assistants already mentioned, were singularly useful.

From Thompson's Creek, east along the boundary, the soil is of an inferior quality, except on the margins of creeks and rivulets, which is very fertile, and covered either with the large cane, (arundo gigantea,) or the small cane or reed, (arundo tecta.) The face of the country is gently waving with hills, which in some places have a most beautiful appearance. The prevailing timber on the upland is pine, (pinus,) of several species. The grass is high, coarse and hard, and when full grown is only eaten by horses and cattle, through necessity. The soil of the upland is composed of a large portion of sand, with a small mixture of yellowish clay or loam. On one of the pine ridges I saw a few stones, which were evidently ferruginous; but this appearance was not promising.

The small streams of water that rise among the sandy hills are remarkably pure, clear and light.

The day on which we encamped, a number of our men were set about making a canoe, to descend the river, and meet our provisions that were expected from New Orleans; the small supply we had brought on from Thompson's Creek being nearly exhausted.

On the 21st the canoe being finished, Mr. Robins the superintendant of our labourers, with three hands, were despatched down the river; but returned on the 23d, in company with a small, light skiff, which had been sent up from the mouth of the river to examine the state of the navigation. The hands who had the care of the skiff, informed us that our stores and the large sector, were at the Bluffs above the mouth of the river; but could not possibly be brought up, till a large

large quantity of timber was removed, and channels cut through two rafts or floating bridges, which extended from one side to the other; and those rafts or bridges, being in the swamp, the articles could not be carried round them.

On the 24th, my assistant Mr. Gillespie, with a number of our labourers were despatched down the river to remove the obstructions; from thence he was to proceed to New Orleans, and make arrangements for an immediate supply of some articles we were in want of. Our provisions, (beef excepted,) were exhausted on the 27th.

Having two more canoes finished on the 28th, the superintendants of both parties, were sent down the river with some of our most active men, to bring us a supply of flour with all possible expedition.

On the 30th a small supply of provisions arrived on pack-horses, from Thompson's Creek. The pack-horse-men likewise brought on my small zenith sector. This instrument was not intended to be made use of in the determination of any points in the boundary, and merely brought along for common geographical purposes; but owing to the uncertainty of the time when the large one would arrive, which was too weighty to be conveyed by land, and therefore sent round by water, added to the fickleness of the weather at that season, and being in want of some of the necessaries of life, it was thought proper and expedient to use the small one. The 1st of December, I polished the mirrors of the eye piece, which were tarnished by the great moisture of that country, and set the instrument up.

The weather was cloudy until the 3d, when a course of observations was begun, which was closed on the 13th, much more to my satisfaction, than could reasonably

B b   be

be expected from so small an instrument.* From the time these observations commenced, until they were completed, I had but few hours sleep; for the space of three successive days and two nights, I slept but three hours.

The day on which the observations were closed, Mr. Gillespie arrived from New Orleans, and brought with him a few barrels of flour. His expedition on this occasion, and the manner in which he executed his trust, do him the greatest credit.

On the 15th and 16th, we were employed in laying off the correction, and making the necessary arrangements for carrying on a guide line to the Mobile, and correcting back to Thompson's Creek. The former was submitted to Mr. Daniel Burnet, and the latter to Mr. Gillespie.

The difficulty of passing through the country from Thompson's Creek to the Pearl river, was so great, owing to the swamps and morasses which lay in the way, and were daily filling with water, that the principal part of our baggage and clothes, which we had left behind, had not yet overtaken us. I nevertheless found it necessary to set out immediately for New Orleans, with no other clothing than what was immediately calculated for the woods. This measure had become necessary for the following reasons. It has already been mentioned that our tents were worn out before we commenced our business, and myself and people without the requisite covering. The escort was without either pay or clothing. On these subjects I had early written to the department of state, and received assurances that the articles should be immediately forwarded; but from some cause or other, it was never done. We had therefore to procure them at an advanced

* These observations with the results, may be seen in the Appendix.

advanced price in New Orleans, or suspend our operations. It has likewise been observed, that Governor Gayoso left us without officially confirming the work that was executed before he joined us, his signature to the report was yet wanting, and it did not appear probable that it would be had without waiting upon him. Experience had already taught us, that it would be impossible to convey our apparatus, baggage and provision wholly by land ; a vessel to carry the heavy articles was therefore wanting, calculated to follow the coast, and ascend the navigable rivers, to or near the points where the line of demarcation crossed them. With this, another object which appeared of considerable importance was combined, which was to obtain as accurate a knowledge as possible of the sea coast, and of the navigation of the rivers that rise in the United States, and fall into the Gulf of Mexico.

On the 17th in the afternoon, I left the encampment, accompanied by a part of the military escort. Our passage down the Pearl river was extremely disagreeable, the rain was cold and almost incessant, and our canoes small and uncovered, which added to other obstacles, prevented our reaching the Bluffs on the tide water, till the 25th. From the Bluffs a person was immediately despatched to New Orleans, to procure a vessel to convey myself and party across Lake Pontchartrain, which by the exertions of Governor Gayoso, was immediately obtained, and arrived at the Bluffs in the forenoon of the 1st of January, 1799. On the same day about three o'clock in the afternoon we got under way, but the tide being against us, we came to an anchor about six o'clock in the evening. Early the next morning we were under way, but the tide failing, and the wind being ahead, we came to an anchor in the Rigolets, where we lay until the morning of the 3d ; when we got under way, and entered Lake Pontchartrain about ten o'clock

B b 2

in

in the forenoon, and having a light, fair breeze, we arrived at the fort, at the mouth of the Bayou St. John's in the
evening. Early the next morning, being the 4th, the
Governor's barge was sent to carry me to New Orleans,
(the distance was about six miles,) where I arrived at
ten o'clock in the forenoon, and was received by the
Governor and officers of government, in the most polite and friendly manner. I shall now close this chapter with some account of Pearl river.

The Pearl or Half-Way River, is navigable for small
craft many miles north of the boundary. It is remarkably crooked, and full of logs and lodged trees ;
which are at present very injurious to its navigation.
Its banks for some distance above the boundary, and
almost the whole of them below, are annually inundated. The banks, with a considerable extent of country
become very low, below the Indian house, (marked on
the map,) over the whole of which the water passes,
when the river is high; and here it begins to divide
into a number of branches, some of them maintain an
open channel until they unite again with the main
branch; and others are lost in the swamp. Those
branches appear so nearly of the same size, that a person not acquainted with the river, will be as likely to
take a wrong, as a right one. This happened to several of our parties and to myself, although I had two
persons with me, who had been up and down twice before : we were a part of two days and one night, before
we got back to the place where we made the mistake.
The officer of my escort, with several of his men, were
still more unfortunate ; they took another branch, and
were a greater length of time before they discovered
their error, and on half allowance of provision.

In consequence of the water extending over such a
considerable space, it never acquires a sufficient head
to force away the lodged timber, which in two places
extend

extend across the river. The upper raft is of considerable magnitude, and covered with grass and other herbage, with some bushes. Through those rafts our men had to make channels, by removing and cutting away the logs, until they had a sufficient depth of water to float loaded periaguas and canoes. This was an arduous undertaking, and executed at the most unfavourable season of the year.

Nearly the whole of the provision, made use of at our station up the river by both parties, including the military escorts, and for extending the guide line east to the Mobile, was taken from New Orleans through the east end of Lake Pontchartrain, thence up the river to the boundary.

The tide ebbs and flows, a few miles above latitude 30° 21′ 30″, where there was formerly a trading house, and to where any vessel that can cross the bar into the Lake, may ascend with ease. The banks of the river above the old trading house, so far as the tide is perceptible, are too low and marshy for a settlement. The river has several communications with the Gulf of Mexico and Lake Pontchartrain, but they are all too shoal for vessels drawing more than six or seven feet water, and therefore only fit for the coasting trade.

The coasting vessels which visit New Orleans from the eastward, pass by the mouth of the Pearl river into Lake Pontchartrain, thence through the west end of the Lake, and up the Bayou St. John's to the canal, executed by the Baron de Corondelet, thence to the end of the canal, which terminates at the walls of the city, immediately behind the hospital. This canal requires cleaning every year, which is done by slaves and criminals, condemned to hard labour; but might be done more effectually, by conveying a stream of water into it from the Mississippi, at the time of the annual inundation,

tion, which might be effected with but little trouble and expense.

Lake Pontchartrain which connects the mouths of Pearl river, with the Bayou St. John's and thence with New Orleans, is a beautiful sheet of water, but unfortunately surrounded with marshes, and the landing in many places is attended with difficulty on account of the mud. There are some places towards the east end, where the beach has a fine appearance, being composed of large bodies of cockle shells, from which all the lime used at New Orleans, and about the Lake is made. The water in the Lake is not deep, being generally not more than twelve or fifteen feet.

CHAP. VII.

The author makes a course of astronomical observations—obtains a vessel—some account of the city of New Orleans—ceremony at signing the reports—proof of Mr. Hutchins being at that time a British officer, with some remarks on that subject—leaves New Orleans, and arrives at the guide line on the Mobile river—an observation relative to the Pascagola river.

BEING anxious to examine the geographical position of the city of New Orleans, the large sector, telescope and clock were unpacked, and set up on the 10th and 15th of January, and a number of observations made during my stay, which with the results will be found in the Appendix.

Immediately on my arrival in New Orleans, arrangements were made for procuring the articles we were in want of; but it was found difficult to obtain a vessel properly constructed, to answer our purpose both on the

the coast, and for ascending the rivers. A hull, without a deck was at length procured, built of live oak and red cedar ; it was very light, but well put together. On the 24th of January several hands began to work upon her, whom I superintended myself from daylight until dark, until she was ready for sea, (Sundays not excepted,) for which permission was had from the bishop.

New Orleans has now become a place of very considerable importance, both on account of its population and commerce, and some gentlemen of respectable talents are looking forward with pleasure to a period, which they conceive not distant, when it will be annexed to the United States. For my own part, I do not see any advantage we could derive from the possession of it at present. The United States are already in a great degree possessed of its commerce, and draw from it annually a very large sum in specie, and that probably, with much more ease than if it was in our possession. When I give this opinion, I would only be understood to mean while it is in the possession of his Catholic Majesty. Rather than a transfer should be made of it to any power in Europe, or than it should become a part of a new empire, I should think it our interest to possess it.

It has been doubted whether the local situation, or scite of the city of New Orleans, is the best that could be chosen to combine generally the greatest number of advantages, with the fewest disadvantages. Lower down the river would be more convenient as a sea port; but the ground is lower, softer, and the country less healthy : further up the river, the country is higher, firmer, and more healthy; but the difficulty of ascending with shipping, would increase almost in geometrical ratio. For it must be observed, that although there is a small swell in the river, which is sometimes
perceived

perceived as high as New Orleans, the current is nevertheless always strong into the Gulf of Mexico ; and therefore, no advantages are ever to be expected from the tides. And when the winds have been unfavourable, vessels have been known to be upwards of six weeks in going up to New Orleans from the Balize ; which is a serious drawback upon the profits of a voyage ; add to this the danger of sickness among the hands, if they should be unfortunately delayed in that low, marshy country in summer, or the beginning of autumn, and it will probably appear, that the city is already sufficiently distant from the mouth of the river. There is one argument in favour of the present situation which has not been answered by the advocates for a position higher up, and that is, the facility with which all the coasting trade east of the Mississippi, is connected with the city of New Orleans, by means of the canal already mentioned, the Bayou St. John's and the Lakes, and which could not be carried on with the same ease at any other point. However if the situation is not the best, it is now too late to remedy it as the wealth, population and capital in trade is so considerable, that the certainty of a market will prevent any competition for many years, and consequently impede the growth of any other place within a reasonable distance.

No place upon this continent, and perhaps in the world, can command the trade of an equal extent of fertile country as that of New Orleans; and as that vast country increases in population, so must that city in magnitude, wealth and commerce.

The weather during the summer season at New Orleans is warm, sultry, and disagreeable; but during the cool months there are few places more desirable : it then abounds with health, and a variety of well conducted amusements; which are encouraged and protected

tected by the government; but this, though pleasing, it may be observed, is characteristic of despotism, and naturally grows out of an arbitrary government. The mind of man being active, must be employed, and if not occupied by amusements, may in its pursuit of objects to rest upon, be directed to the investigation of the principles of liberty, and inquiries into the conduct of public officers, which are of all things the most to be dreaded, and are the most exceptionable to the feelings of an arbitrary magistrate.

The plan of the city of New Orleans is regular; the streets cross each other at right angles; and are accommodated by their narrowness, to the heat of the climate. It is fortified on the sides exposed to the land by a work, which though not strong, is far from being contemptible.

The city has suffered several times severely by fires, but has entirely recovered from the effects of them; by the last, the greater part of it was laid in ashes. It now affords many good houses, built in a handsome style.

On the 23d of February, Governor Gayoso and my self signed four reports, two in English, and two in the Spanish language, confirming all the work done before the 7th of June, 1798; after that day, the execution of the work on behalf of his Catholic Majesty, was submitted to William Dunbar, Esq. and Capt. Minor; but Mr. Dunbar continued but a few months in the employ, after which the whole duty devolved upon Capt. Minor. One report in each language was intended for the executive of the United States, and the other two in the same manner for his Catholic Majesty.

Great ceremony was used at signing the instruments. The Governor had a large table covered with fine green cloth placed in the hall of the government house,

C c
on

on which the reports were laid. A lighted wax taper for melting the sealing wax was placed by the side of a new silver standish, which appeared to have been made for the occasion: the workmanship was well done, but the construction and form of the different parts was very whimsical. The sand-box was in the form of a drum, braced with fine silver wire, and ornamented with engravings, representing various implements of war. The vessel that contained the ink represented a bedded mortar, which could be elevated and depressed at pleasure, as occasion might require, and was likewise decorated with engravings; this device the Governor observed was in character, as the matter drawn from the mouth of the vessel frequently proved very destructive. The pounce-box was in the form of a globe or sphere, on which was engraven the equator, ecliptic, colures, tropicks, &c. After a short dissertation upon this standish, the manufacturing of which I presume delayed for several days the execution of the instruments, the Governor and myself, seated ourselves at the table and signed the reports; they were then handed to our secretaries and attested.

During my residence at New Orleans, a number of curious documents fell into my hands, particularly a packet from Mr. Hutchins, containing a number of letters to his friends in London. One of the letters had enclosed two certificates for drawing his pay as a British officer, one of them bears date subsequent to the arrival of Governor Sargent in the Mississippi territory. They are in the following words.

"Major Anthony Hutchins maketh oath, that he had not between the 24th day of December, 1797, and the 25th day of June following, any other place or employment of profit, civil or military, under his Majesty, besides

besides his military allowance as a provincial officer.

Sworn before me, the 2d day of January, in the year of our Lord, 1799.

(Signed) ANTHONY HUTCHINS.

(Signed) ISAAC JOHNSON.

Major Anthony Hutchins maketh oath, that he had
not between the 25th day of June, 1798, and the 24th
day of December following, any other place or employment of profit, civil or military, under his Majesty, besides his military allowance as a provincial officer.

Sworn before me, the 2d day of January, in the year of our Lord, 1799.

(Signed) ANTHONY HUTCHINS.

(Signed) ISAAC JOHNSON.

The first paragraph of the letter which covered the
foregoing certificates, directed the manner in which the
money was to be disposed of, and is in the following
words.

" *Natchez, 25th of January,* 1799.

JOHN MILLER, Esq.

DEAR SIR,

I send this only to enclose my certificate in hopes
it may arrive safe, and as you will receive the amount,
I will thank you to purchase two London state lottery
tickets. One for my wife Ann Hutchins, and the other
for my eight children, Samuel, John, Mary, Elizabeth,
Nancy, Magdaline, Charlotte, and Celeste Hutchins,
and have them recorded in their names, in the lottery
office as formerly."

It is presumed those documents are sufficiently
conclusive to prove, that it would have been improper for me to have countenanced Mr. Hutchins's
plan of placing himself at the head of the inhabitants

C c 2

of

of the district of Natchez, particularly during the existence of Mr. Blunt's intrigues in favour of the British government. On the contrary, I considered it my duty, to oppose all foreign influence within the limits of the United States, and therefore, if possible by the aid of the friends to our government, in that territory, to destroy the influence, and destroy the power of Mr. Hutchins and his party in that country. The success after a contest of some months, may be said to have been complete : but a change of the administration of the United States, and an affected change of political opinions in Mr. Hutchins, and some of his party, has again brought them into consequence : thus circumstanced they can only be viewed in the light of political mercenaries, and ought as such to be guarded against.

Here I wish to be indulged in an observation or two relative to the conduct of Winthrop Sargent, Esq. late Governor of the Mississippi territory. It appears that Mr. Sargent, either knowing or suspecting, that Mr. Hutchins was a military officer on the British establishment, refused to gratify him with any appointment whatever within his gift in that territory, and for which he openly and candidly gave his reasons ; which were so offensive to Mr. Hutchins, that he became his decided enemy, as he had before become mine, and in like manner declared his determination to effect his removal.

From the conduct of Mr. Sargent on this occasion, it is evident, that let his political sentiments be what they might, his regard for the honour and reputation of his country was such, that he spurned the idea of giving an appointment to a person whose attachment to the government of the United States was suspected, though he well knew at the time, that a large share of his popularity would depend upon his acquiescence.

Although

Although those documents concerning Mr. Hutchins, must be conclusive with every person who reads them, they are not more so, than those I saw relative to the plan already mentioned, for the effecting of which a number of our citizens received considerable sums of money from the Spanish government; the difference is, I am not yet at liberty to make the same use of them.

On the 1st of March, our vessel being completed, we proceeded down the canal to Bayou St. John's, and the next day gave the Governor and officers of government, an entertainment at the drawbridge. The day following we passed the fort at the mouth of the Bayou, or Creek, which was saluted by my escort, and returned by a discharge of artillery from the fort. The winds were very unfavourable, which delayed our arrival at the end of the guide line on the Mobile, until the 17th in the evening.

At New Orleans, I was able to engage but two sailors, and they were both deserters from a British privateer, which lay some days off the mouth of the Mississippi. With those two sailors, who were completely illiterate, I undertook to navigate the vessel. Several masters of vessels offered their service, but the price they demanded was so high, that it was thought more economical to do it myself.

Here it appears proper to make an observation respecting the Pascagola, which is a large river, between Pearl river and the Mobile. It is navigable for small craft a considerable distance above the boundary, and from the report of some of my people who descended it, it is very deep, and falls with a number of smaller waters into a bay opposite to Horn Island: but the bay and mouth of the river, being full of shoals and oyster banks, it appears only adapted to the coasting trade.

CHAP.

CHAP. VIII.

The author begins and completes a course of observations—opposition expected from the Creeks—writes to Col. Hawkins upon that subject—leaves the encampment and sails to Mobile point—some account of Mobile river and the town—arrives at Pensacola—joined by Col. Hawkins—interview with Governor Folch—treaty with the Indians at Miller's place—observes the transit of Mercury—makes a course of observations on the Coenecuh—returns to Pensacola—difficulty with the Indians—account of the Coenecuh and city of Pensacola—leaves Pensacola and arrives at the end of the guide line on the Chattahocha—makes a course of observations—treaty with the Indians—descends the river, to the mouth of Flint river—makes a course of observations—menaced by the Indians—retreats—interview with Mr. Bowles and a British officer—letter to Col. Hawkins on that subject—arrives at St. Mark's—account of the Chattahocha river, West Florida, and its importance to the United States.

THE observatory being erected before we arrived at the end of the guide line on the Mobile, the instruments were up on the 18th of March, when a course of observations was begun, and completed on the 9th of April following : for the results and difficulties we met with in carrying the line over the Mobile swamp, see the Appendix.

We had now passed through the Chocktaw nation without interruption, but from the conduct of some Creeks or Muscogees, who had visited our camp, it was evident we should meet with difficulties from that nation. I therefore sent off on the 23d of March, a special
cial

cial messenger to Col. Hawkins, our principal agent of
Indian affairs for the southern department, requesting
an interview with him, and some of the principal chiefs,
at Pensacola about the 20th of April following, that we
might fall upon some plan to ensure safety to our party,
and success to the execution of our business.

While at Natchez, I wrote several letters to Mr.
Mitchell, one of the deputy agents for Indian affairs,
enclosing others for Col. Hawkins, and though delivered
to Mr. Mitchell, they were either suppressed by him,
or intercepted afterwards, as they were never received by the Colonel.   The former I am inclined to believe
was the case, as Mr. Mitchell was evidently deceived,
and impressed with unfavourable sentiments of me, either by the Commandant at Natchez, or some of the
persons already mentioned, who visited him when in
search of my letters.   But in this there appears to
have been a systematic plan, for although Col. Hawkins wrote a number of letters to me, not one ever
came to hand, (until the return of the special messenger,) which effectually prevented our communication of
sentiments during a very important and critical period.

A few days after our arrival at the end of the guide
line on the Mobile, Mr. Gillespie was despatched up
to Fort St. Stephens, with an Hadly's sextant, to take
the latitude of that place, and a sketch of the river,
which he executed with his usual promptitude; the latitude is probably sufficiently accurate for geographical
purposes.

The face of the country, and soil between the Pearl
and Mobile rivers, are similar to those already described between the former and Thompson's Creek.

The 10th of April the instruments were taken down
and packed up, and on the 11th I descended the river
to the city of Mobile ; on the same day a party was sent
through

through the Mobile swamp, to extend a guide line to the Coenecuh, (commonly called the Escambia.)

The 13th I set sail for Mobile point, where I arrived in the evening, and came to an anchor; that night the wind shifted, which prevented the vessel from crossing the bar for several days; but the delay gave me an opportunity of determining the latitude with considerable precision.

The Mobile is a fine large river, and navigable some distance above the boundary for any vessel that can cross the bar into the bay. One square rigged vessel has been as high as Fort St. Stephens, in latitude 31° 33' 44".

When the river is low, the tide ebbs and flows several miles above the line, and is sometimes observed as high as Fort St. Stephens; but when full there is but little, if any tide above the city of Mobile. It was in the latter state when I ascended it, and notwithstanding the current being constantly against us, and but little fair wind, we reached the place of our encampment north of the boundary in four days, my vessel was 38 or 40 tons burthen.

About six miles north of the boundary, the Tombeckby and Alabama rivers unite, and after accompanying each other more than three miles, separate: the western branch from thence down to the bay, is called Mobile. The Alabama retains its name, until it joins some of its own waters, which had been separated from it for several miles, and then takes the name of Tensaw, which it retains until it falls into the bay.

The easiest way from the Gulf of Mexico by water into the United States, is up those rivers, the navigation of each being equally good.

The upland on those rivers is of an inferior quality from their mouths up to the latitude of Fort St. Stephens,

phens, and produces little beside pitch-pine and wire-grass; but is said to become better as you ascend the rivers. The lands on those rivers have notwithstanding had a good character for fertility; but this has arisen from not discriminating between the upland which is generally unfit for cultivation, and the banks of the rivers, which are fertile in the extreme, and to which agriculture is almost wholly confined for a number of miles above the boundary. But those lands are subject to a great inconvenience from the inundations of the rivers.

Planting is not attempted in the spring, until the waters have subsided; and it sometimes happens, that inundations follow the first fall of the waters in the spring, and wholly destroy the previous labours of the planters. This was the case in May 1799, after the corn was two feet high: But this inconvenience is by no means so great as it would be in a more northerly latitude, there still remains summer sufficient to bring a crop of corn to full maturity.

The large swamp through which the rivers meander after their separation above the boundary is intersected in almost all directions by smaller water courses, which maintain a constant connection between the main branches; such of them as were used by our people in passing, and repassing from one side to the other are laid down on the map.

At the mouth of the Mobile river, and on the west side, stands the town, or city of Mobile. The situation is handsome, and some of the houses are tolerably good, and for so small a place, the trade is considerable; but it is said to be unhealthy during the months of July, August, September and October.

The fort is of brick, and stands a short distance below the city; it is a well built regular work, and

was taken from the British during our revolutionary war, by Don Galvez, who commanded the troops of his Catholic Majesty. Since that time, it has been rebuilt, and put in a good state of defence.

From the traverse of the river between the boundary, and city, the latitude of the latter appears to be about 30° 36' 30" north, and the longitude, 5^h 52' 17" west, from the royal observatory at Greenwich.

The bay is extensive, and supposed to be about 9 leagues in length; but too shoal for large shipping. The latitude of the bar, at the entrance into the bay from the Gulf of Mexico, I found by a mean of two good observations to be 30° 12' 30" north, and as the course of the bay is nearly north and south, the longitude must be nearly the same as that of the city.

On the 19th, in the morning, the wind serving we crossed the bar, and sailed for Pensacola, but the wind dying away, we did not reach the battery at the Cliffs, until after nine o'clock in the evening; where we were detained until ten o'clock the next day for examination. The wind serving in the afternoon, we sailed up to the city of Pensacola; but on the way, were obliged to come to a few minutes under the stern of a forty four gun frigate, and produce our passport. On my arrival at Pensacola, I found elegant, and convenient lodgings provided for me, which I had reason to believe, were at the expense of the house of Panton, Laslie, Forbes & Co. but on this subject I made no inquiry.

The 25th of April, late in the evening, Col. Hawkins arrived, and the next morning about ten o'clock, we waited upon Governor Folch, who in a short time informed us that he had that morning to give audience to two Seminole Chiefs; upon this we withdrew to Capt. Minor's quarters, which were within the Go-

vernor's

vernor's inclosure, and a few minutes afterwards, saw two Indians go into the Governor's house : Capt. Minor followed them, and heard their conversation with the Governor: in less than an hour he joined us, and observed, that the Chiefs gave a strong talk against running the line, and that they were Seminoles; the subject then passed over.

Col. Hawkins and myself, after some consultation, were of the opinion that the proper place to meet the Indians, who were then on their way, would be as nearly as we could judge on the Coenecuh, where the guide line would cross it: but the officers of his Catholic Majesty were of a different opinion, and proposed the city of Pensacola, which would have given them considerable advantages over us in point of intrigue, at which they were habitually dexterous; and what was equally to be dreaded, the delay that might reasonably be expected from intoxication, in which the Indians always indulge themselves at treaties where liquor is to be had: after some conversation on this subject, the officers of his Catholic Majesty gave way, and on the 28th, in the afternoon, Col. Hawkins, Capt. Minor, and myself sailed to the head of the Bay. As soon as we came to anchor, Col. Hawkins went on shore to meet the Mad Dog Chief, who was the speaker of the nation, and who we were informed had just arrived. This Chief immediately informed Col. Hawkins on his landing, that two Indians* had just gone to the Tallesee's with bad talks from the Governor. The Col. assured him it was impossible, that the Indians he alluded to were Seminoles, and had gone on to their nation. An Indian standing by, observed that the Mad Dog was

D d 2   right,

---

* These were the same Indians to whom the Governor gave an audience, as already mentioned.

right, that he himself saw the two Indians at Pensacola, and conversed with them, that he knew them to be Tallesees and that they had bad talks.

The Mad Dog wanted to come immediately on board, and give Capt. Minor, and myself the information; but Col. Hawkins prevailed upon him to defer it until the next morning, when he came on board each of our vessels, and gave the information separately; and proposed sending a runner after the two Indians immediately, but Capt. Minor conceived it to be wholly unnecessary, as he was confident the Indians in question were Seminoles, and not Tallesees, in consequence of which no more notice was taken of it at that time.

On the 29th we rode up the river to Miller's farm, which was the place agreed upon to meet the Indians. The day following they began to assemble, but from their slow movements in treaty business, it was not expected that we should finish our conferences with them in less than ten or twelve days. I therefore made the necessary preparation for observing the transit of Mercury, which was by calculation to happen on the 7th of May in the forenoon. The observation will be seen in the Appendix.

Two or three days before our public conferences took place with the Indians, the Mad Dog asked Col. Hawkins, and myself, if we supposed that Governor Folch would attend at the treaty: to which we answered in the affirmative. " No replied the Mad Dog, he will not attend, he knows what I shall say to him about his crooked talks. His tongue is forked, and as you are here, he will be ashamed to show it. If he stands to what he has told us, you will be offended, and if he tells us that the line ought to be marked, he will contradict himself; but he will do neither, he will not come."

On

On the 4th of May, we were joined by Col. Maxant, and several other Spanish officers. Col. Maxant represented Governor Folch, who was taken so unwell on his way to the treaty, that he thought proper to return back to Pensacola! So soon as the Mad Dog discovered that Governor Folch had returned to Pensacola, and was not going to attend the treaty, he called upon Col. Hawkins and myself, and with some degree of pleasantry said: "well the Governor has not come, I told you so, a man with two tongues can only speak to one at a time."

The 5th of May Col. Hawkins and myself, had several conversations with the officers of his Catholic Majesty, in which the Colonel stated, that many crooked talks had some time since been sent out among the Indians, that they had been taught to believe, that his Catholic Majesty had no desire to have the line determined or marked. Whether those talks had the sanction of the officers of his Catholic Majesty, or made by interested traders, he should not attempt to determine: but they had had their effect, and he saw but one way to remedy it, which was that Col. Maxant, (who represented Governor Folch,) and Capt. Minor the Commissioner, should in the most explicit manner, declare to the Indians, that it was not only the wish, but determination of his Catholic Majesty to have the boundary determined.

On the evening of the same day, the Mad Dog as speaker of the nation, informed us that the principal Chiefs had arrived, and would meet in council the next morning, and that it was expected by them the white people would open the conference.

The 6th about ten o'clock in the forenoon we met, and the business was opened by Col. Maxant, who went into an explanation of the late treaty between the United

United States and his Catholic Majesty, and ended by an unequivocal declaration, that it was the wish of his master the king of Spain, to have the treaty carried into effect, and the boundary determined and marked. Col. Maxant was followed by Capt. Minor, who explained in a forcible manner, the nature of our business: that the line we were tracing, was not a line of property, but of jurisdiction, a line between white people, and not intended in any way to affect the Indians in either their property, manners, customs or religion. These gentlemen went so fully and explicitly into the nature of the business, that Col. Hawkins, and myself, had little more to say, than to assent to what the others had advanced.

Col. Hawkins reminded the Chiefs of their treaty with him at Colerain, in the year 1796, and called upon them for a fulfilment of their stipulations, which closed the business on our part. The Chiefs after a short consultation among themselves, gave us to understand, that they intended to reply the next day.

On the 7th, the Chiefs by their speaker the Mad Dog, delivered their answer, which was short and satisfactory. They observed that many crooked talks had been sent into their country; but now they had seen and heard the representatives of both nations, and found that their talks were the same and straight. That being the case, they were perfectly satisfied, and with pleasure concurred in the determination, of marking off the boundary, and would agreeably to their stipulation with Col. Hawkins at Colerain, send on their Chiefs and warriors, as an escort to the surveying parties

The 8th we rode up to the Coenecuh, and fixed upon a proper place for encamping, and erecting an observatory

tory, which was immediately begun and completed the next day, and the instruments set up. Our instruments, baggage and provision, had been taken up by water in boats and periaguas, to the place of our encampment. The observations* were completed on the 20th, and the instruments taken down and packed up on the 21st.

On the 22d of May, Mr. Gillespie, the surveyor on behalf of the United States, began the guide line from the Coenecuh to the Chattahocha, being escorted by the military of the United States, and of his Catholic Majesty, together with two Chiefs and twenty warriors of the Creek nation, agreeably to the stipulation already mentioned, made at Colerain.

In the afternoon of the 23d, Col. Hawkins and myself, set off down the river in a canoe for Pensacola, where we arrived on the 26th in the morning, when I took possession of the lodgings prepared for me before my first arrival. As it appeared probable, that if any intrigues should be set on foot with the Indians, to induce them to oppose the completion of the line, they would originate at Pensacola, we therefore concluded to stay a few days, to watch equally the conduct of the Governor and the Indians, till the surveyor should have proceeded so far on his way to the Chattahocha, that there would be no doubt of his reaching that river.

We had been but a few days at Pensacola, when Col. Hawkins was informed by a confidential Indian, that a large body of the Upper Creeks were on their way to that place in consequence of an invitation from Governor Folch, that the talks were crooked, and the line would be stopped. This information the Colonel immediately communicated to me, and after a little consideration we thought it would be most prudent to be wholly silent on the subject, and affect the most perfect confidence

* For the observations and results see the Appendix.

confidence in the candour of the Governor.   This intelligence was followed by information from the surveying party, that they had been menaced by a body of Indians. By this time it was generally known, that a large number of Creeks were on their way, and might be daily expected.   The Governor affected to be entirely ignorant, either of the reason of their coming, or of their business. They at length arrived, and encamped about three miles from the city, when the Governor immediately left the place.   The Indians were nevertheless determined to have an interview with him, as they had come in consequence of his invitation.   Col. Hawkins and myself being desirous to bring this curious business to a close, which now began to wear a disagreeable aspect, requested Capt. Minor to write immediately to the Governor, and hasten his return.   On his return, he requested Col. Hawkins and myself to be present the next day, at ten o'clock in the forenoon at his house, when he was to receive a visit of ceremony from the Chiefs ; but the cause of their coming being unknown to us, we declined attending.

The Governor at this time certainly found himself much embarrassed between us and the Indians.   To deliver talks, and issue presents to those who resided a great distance north of the boundary, and within the United States, would have a strange appearance to us, and to send them away without any, after an invitation, would give them great offence. The Governor at length informed them, that as they fell north of the boundary, and that being now marked, they must look to the United States for presents, and deliver their talks to Col. Hawkins. In consequence of the direction which the business now unexpectedly took, we were in our turn called upon for presents.   It was in vain to tell them that they came without our invitation, and therefore

fore not entitled to any, some must be given, and a compliance was a matter of course. After receiving from us to the amount of two or three hundred dollars, they left the place apparently well satisfied. During those transactions, which were not closed until after the 20th of June, a number of letters passed between Col. Hawkins and Governor Folch on the subject of Indian affairs : in this correspondence the Colonel manifested that firmness, caution and candour, for which he has been so justly esteemed. Copies of all those letters were handed to me and transmitted to the secretary of state ; but as they properly belong to Col. Hawkins's department, I shall forbear to publish them.

Before Col. Hawkins and myself left Pensacola, we called upon Governor Folch, and requested him to send an agent immediately among the Lower Creeks and Seminoles, to quiet their minds, and explain to them the nature of our business. To which the Governor assented without hesitation, and assured us in the most unequivocal manner, that it should be done immediately ; but notwithstanding this solemn declaration, it was not done.

Immediately after dismissing the Indians, Colonel Hawkins set out for his station among the Upper Creeks, by the way of Mobile, and on the 24th I proceeded down the bay to the bar; but the wind failing, we were detained until the 2d of July. These calms are very common in that season along the coast. While laying at anchor I drew up the following short account of the Coenecuh river, and the bay and city of Pensacola.

The Coenecuh has generally, though erroneously been called the Scambia and Escambia, which is the name of a much smaller stream that falls into it from the west, a short distance above Miller's place, where

E e we

we had our conference with the Indians, and observed the transit of Mercury.

The banks of the Coenecuh during a large portion of the spring, are inundated for many miles above the line, down to Pensacola bay, with very few exceptions. The upland is poor as far up the river as we saw it, but it was said to be tolerably good about the head branches.

The river is navigable for small crafts a considerable distance above the boundary. All our tents, stores, instruments, &c. were taken up to our camp by water. The tide ebbs and flows but a few miles up the river.

The Coenecuh falls into the head of Pensacola bay, which is a beautiful body of water, well stored with a variety of fine fish, crabs and oysters, and is justly considered one of the best harbours on the whole coast. Vessels not drawing more than twenty-one feet water, may cross the bar at all times with safety.

Pensacola stands on the west side of the bay, the situation is delightful, and the place remarkably healthy; but the water is shoal in the front of the city. It was the capital of West Florida, while that province was in the possession of his Britannic Majesty, when it made a very respectable appearance; but since the conquest of that colony by the Spaniards under Don Galvez, it has been on the decline.

The old fortifications stood on some sand hills back of the city, and too distant to yield it any substantial protection; notwithstanding this circumstance, the Spaniards never once attempted to molest the inhabitants, or injure the buildings, during the siege of the forts, which lasted two months. The garrison made a gallant defence, and the surrender was hastened by one of the magazines accidentally blowing up. During the whole siege, as well as after the surrender, Don Galvez

conducted

conducted himself both as a man of courage and humanity. Mr. Bowles, (commonly called General Bowles,) Mr. Philip Key of the state of Maryland, and several other Americans of distinction, were at that time officers under Gen. Campbell who commanded the troops of his Britannic Majesty.

The trade of Pensacola, is at this time principally carried on by the house of Panton, Laslie, Forbes and Company. Mr. Panton resides at Pensacola, and Mr. Forbes at Mobile, where they live in an elegant stile, highly esteemed for their great hospitality and politeness by all classes of people.

From a number of good observations, the latitude of Pensacola appears to be about 30° 23′ 43″ north, and the longitude by our measurement from the Mississippi and traverse of the Coenecuh river is about 87° 14′ 15″ west from Greenwich: but from the observations of Sir John Lindsay and Dr. Lorimer 87° 40′: it may lie between the two, but I suspect much nearer to the former. The latitude of the bar at the entrance into the bay, is about 30° 18′ north, and the longitude from our measurement and traverse 87° 17′ west from Greenwich. This harbour as well as all the others on the coast of East and West Floridas, is rendered much less valuable on account of the worms. They are so numerous in this bay, that a vessel's bottom has been known to be ruined in two months: and it is absolutely necessary for all vessels not copper bottomed laying in the harbour to be hove down, cleaned and payed, every five or six weeks.

The entrance into the bay is defended by a small fort on the west end of St. Rose's island, and a battery on the main land nearly opposite to it.

July 2d, a very light breeze serving, we crossed the bar about eleven o'clock in the forenoon and steered

E e 2   for

for cape Blass, which we made early in the morning of the 4th, when the breeze which had continued to be very light died away, and we come to an anchor. From the time we weighed anchor on the 2d, until we reached cape Blass, the breeze was so regular that we never once found occasion to shift a single sail, and the sea almost as smooth as a mill pond. On this passage we were a few hours out of sight of land, a phenomenon which I observed for the first time.

Shortly after we came to anchor at cape Blass, we were enveloped by a thick fog, or mist, which was followed by a gale of wind. We immediately got under way, and stood for the entrance into St. George's Sound. The gale continued to increase until near noon, but we received no other damage than springing our bowsprit. At one o'clock we entered the sound, and come to an anchor. The day following we began to search along the north side of the sound for the mouth of the Chattahocha river; but found the coast so intersected, and cut up by numerous water courses, nearly of the same magnitude, that the true channel was not ascertained until the 13th, when a fair wind serving, we ascended about thirty miles; and afterwards warped for two days more; but the labour being very hard, the weather extremely hot, and our progress slow, I left the vessel and proceeded up the river in an open canoe, having our apparatus with me.

My journey up the river was disagreeable and painful, being blistered by the rhus radicans, (poison vine,) from head to feet. This aptitude to be disordered by this poisonous vegitable I have been subject to from my infancy, and have generally been confined in consequence of it, at least one week every summer since. The evaporation from the dew from this plant

plant in the morning, falling upon me, is sufficient to produce the effect. The irritation and heat of this complaint was frequently so excessive, that I had to plunge into the river many times in the day, and lay whole hours in it during the night, which was the only relief I could find; medical aid had at all times proved ineffectual to relieve me.

On the 21st, I arrived at an Indian village, where I remained until the 23d, when the horses arrived, and after they had rested a few hours, I set off for the camp, which I reached on the 25th in the evening in the midst of a heavy shower of rain. The canoe in which I ascended the river to the Indian village, arrived at our camp with the instruments, tents, &c. on the 26th. The observatory was finished on the 27th, and the instruments unpacked and set up; but the rain continued until the 30th, and prevented any observations being made until that day: the course was completed on the 19th of August. See the Appendix.

From an apprehension that difficulties might possibly arise with the Indians at that position, Col. Hawkins had written to Mr. Timothy Barnard, one of our deputy agents, to meet us on that river, and explain the nature of our business to the Indians, if they should appear discontented with our proceedings.

Mr. Barnard arrived five days before me, and as it was evident we could proceed no further without an explanation, Mr. Barnard had taken measures for assembling the chiefs. But previous to our arrival, the Indians on the east side of the river, had assembled in considerable numbers to stop, and plunder the Surveyor; but his movements were so rapid, that he had arrived at the river, and was well posted before their main body had crossed, and their spies had fortunately been looking out too low.

On

On the 15th of August the Indians were assembled, and we proeeded to the conference: a number of speeches were delivered on both sides, and the business appeared to terminate as favourably as could be expected, and the Indians declared themselves perfectly satisfied: but I nevertheless had my doubts of their sincerity, from the depredations they were constantly committing upon our horses, which began upon the Coenecuh, and had continued ever since; and added to their insolence, from their stealing every article in our camp they could lay their hands on. Those doubts I frequently communicated to our agent Mr. Barnard, but who on his part had none.

It will be but justice to observe, that this disposition to plunder and impede our business, was by no means general: great part of the upper Creeks, the tame king, and his people excepted, behaved uniformly well, and upon a report reaching some of their towns, that the Seminoles, and Euphales intended abusing us, and plundering our camp, a large body of them flew to our assistance, and offered to protect us through the country to the source of the St. Mary's; but their services were objected to by his Catholic Majesty's commissioner on account of the expense, who proposed as a substitute, to send to Fort Wilkinson for a troop of American horse which we were informed was stationed at that post: but this measure would probably have been attended with bad consequences, because it would have given the Indians reason to believe, that it was not his Catholic Majesty, as they had been frequently though improperly informed, but the United States alone, that wanted the boundary ascertained, and were determined to carry it through by force. Resistance would certainly have followed. But it would have been im-
                                                proper

proper on another account; because it would be imposing an additional burden upon the United States, beyond that borne by his Catholic Majesty, which ought not to be expected, especially when it is recollected that the impediments which were thrown in the way by the officers of his Catholic Majesty, delayed the commencement of the business for more than a year; during which time the expenses of the United States were nearly the same as if the work had been progressing. And again, a troop of Spanish horse were stationed at Pensacola, which might much more readily have come to our assistance; but this, for some reason could not be agreed to by the Spanish commissioner.

The friendly Indians, who had come to our protection, and offered their assistance through the country to the source of the St. Mary's, were thanked for their conduct, and good intentions, and dismissed.

About this time, we received an account of the death of the late Governor General Gayoso, which I then, and yet consider a great loss to our western citizens concerned in the Mississippi trade, to whom he paid particular attention, and who frequently partook of that hospitality, for which he was so highly esteemed. As the Governor of an arbitrary monarch, he was certainly entitled to great merit, and it appeared in an eminent degree to be his pride, to render the situation of those over whom he was appointed to preside, as easy, and comfortable as possible, and in a particular manner directed his attention to the improvement of the country, by opening roads which he considered the arteries of commerce. He was educated in Great Britain, and retained in a considerable degree the manners, and customs, of that nation until his death, especially in his style of living. In his
conversation

conversation he was easy and affable, and his politeness was of that superior cast, which showed it to be the effect of early habit, rather than an accomplishment merely intended to render him agreeable. His passions were naturally so strong, and his temper so remarkably quick, that they sometimes hurried him into difficulties, from which he was not easily extricated. It was frequently remarked of him as a singularity, that he was neither concerned in traffick, nor in the habit of taking doceurs, as was too frequently the case with other officers of his Catholic Majesty in that country. He was fond of show and parade, which he indulged to the great injury of his fortune, and not a little to his reputation as a paymaster. This fondness for parade showed itself in all his transactions, but in nothing more than the ordinary business of his government, to which, method and system, were too generally sacrificed. In his domestic character he merited imitation : he was a tender husband, an affectionate parent, and a good master. In his correspondence with me relative to the late treaty, it is presumed he was governed by his instructions, and therefore no conclusion ought to be drawn from that discussion to his disadvantage as a man, and gentleman.

One or two days before we left our position on the Chattahocha for the mouth of Flint river, Mr. Burgess, who had lately been one of our deputy agents, and interpreters, and who had agreeably to the Creek custom intermarried with several of their females, who then lived with him, informed me confidentially, that a plan was laid to plunder us on our way to the St. Mary's, and requested me to write to Col. Hawkins, to join us at the mouth of Flint river immediately, as his influence would effect our safety,

if

if it was in the power of any man to do it. Upon taking leave of me he observed, that for certain reasons it would not then be proper to mention the information he had communicated; but to be careful to take such measures as would secure the safety of the party.

The night of the 22d was wholly spent in writing and copying my despatches to the Department of State, and to Col. Hawkins, which were forwarded with all possible expedition by a runner to the Colonel.

On the 23d Capt. Minor and myself, proceeded by water down to the mouth of Flint river, and on the 25th began a course of observations, which will be seen in the Appendix.

In the beginning of September, Capt. Minor dismissed his military escort agreeably to instructions which he had received from the late Governor General Gayoso, as early as the 14th of May preceding; he also discharged great part of his labourers, and sent away a large portion of the baggage of his department, and the only valuable part of their apparatus. As soon as this was done, he became very importunate to set out for the St. Mary's. In one of our conversations upon that subject in the Contractors tent, he was told that the work must be finished at that place before we left it, and which could not possibly be completed before the 14th, admitting the weather to be favourable. And moreover, that I was desirous of seeing Col. Hawkins before I ventured upon a journey, the success of which was, in my opinion, at best, very doubtful; and further, that my commissary Mr. Anderson had just reported, that our remaining number of horses were scarcely sufficient to transport the requisite stores, baggage and apparatus to the St. Mary's: it therefore became necessary for our agent,

F f   if

if possible to obtain some security from the Indians, for
the remainder. But that his (Capt. Minor's,) situation was very different, his military escort was dismissed, almost the whole of his labourers discharged,
and great part of the baggage, and apparatus sent
away; he would therefore have horses sufficient for
his purpose, if some should happen to be stolen on
the way. To which he answered, " I suppose you
will be angry, but I must now tell you that those men
of yours are no longer necessary." This expression
was certainly a hasty one, and made without reference to
the subsequent part of the work; for there yet remained
more than 150 miles of line for the surveyors to trace,
correct, and mark, by erecting a large mound of earth
at the end of each mile, (stones not being to be had,)
which would have required our whole joint force, if he
had not discharged one of his labourers, to accomplish
in any reasonable time. It is true, that there remained
but one point more for the commissioners to determine, which was the source of the St. Mary's. The
Surveyor on behalf of the United States, (Mr. Gillespie,) was gone back to the Coenecuh for the purpose
of correcting the guide line; if we went on before his
return, he and his party might be plundered and abus-
ed by the Indians, and would have no place to retreat
to nearer than Pensacola, or St. Mary's. Capt. Minor
was told, that my situation was similar to that of a
passed pawn in the game of chess, and that it did not
appear prudent to make another move, until supported
by a piece, and if Col. Hawkins upon his arrival should
be of opinion that appearances were favourable, I
would immediately proceed, but not otherwise.

On the 9th Mr. Burgess paid us a visit. After
dinner he took me into the observatory, and asked
this question, " Did you write to Col. Hawkins while

at

at the Upper Camp agreeably to my recommendation"?
To which he was answered in the affirmative. " You
have not", says he, "written as pointedly as was necessary, or he would have been here before this: you
must write to him immediately, and procure support
from the Upper Creeks, which may be had, or you will
positively be plundered on your way to St. Mary's;
you may think me a fool, but mark the end." He was
told that the letter to Col. Hawkins was sufficiently
pointed, and if he was well, there could be no doubt
of his joining us in a few days.

The 14th of September Col. Hawkins joined us,
and being of opinion that every thing relative to the
Indians was in a good train, and that we might go on
with safety, my objections were then immediately withdrawn, and I began the arrangement of the astronomical journal, that it might be understood, if any accident
should happen to me, and it be preserved. The commissaries of both parties, were directed to have every
thing ready for our moving on the 20th.

Early in the morning of the 17th, we received a
message from Indian Willy, (a person of property,)
who resides on the Chattahocha, a few miles above
the mouth of Flint river, to the following effect:
" Gentlemen, I have sent my Negro, to inform you
that about twenty Indians lay near my place last night,
they intend mischief; many more are behind: they
say they are Chocktaws: but this is not true. Be on
your guard, and remember I have nothing to do with
it: my Negro goes at midnight." Although this information was not slighted, it was not pointedly attended to. About two o'clock in the afternoon, some
Indians belonging to our escort, were sent over the river to make discoveries; but returned in two or three
hours, without making any; but at sun down, our

doubts

doubts were at an end: we then received positive intelligence, that a number of strange Indians had just
crossed the river; upon which my escort was immediately called to arms, and my son and labourers, who
were armed with rifles joined it. The Big Lieutenant,
(a Creek Chief,) who commanded our Indian escort,
was directed to go, halt the strangers, demand their
business, and give us immediate information. They
halted but for a short time, and declared " their object
was to plunder the camp, scatter the people, and let
them go home what way they pleased." They then
proceeded to within about two hundred yards of our
camp, when they were again halted by our Indian escort, and interpreter; but still persisting in their determination to take and plunder our camp, we had only
to choose between submission and resistance; the
latter was immediately resolved upon, and Col. Hawkins requested Capt. Bowyer, (who commanded my
escort,) to arrange his men in the best manner he
could: the labourers, with their rifles, being stationed
on the flanks. This was done with great expedition,
and the party marched within about twenty yards of
the hostile Indians, and was then halted by Col. Hawkins, who stepped forward, and addressed the strangers, who still persisted in their determination to
plunder the camp, and told us, that if they met with
no opposition no blood should be shed; but vengeance
would follow resistance. The Colonel with great firmness replied, " that we were willing to put it to issue,
and if any one of their party, should attempt to remove
any one article in the camp, he should instantly be
put to death, and if the party presumed to march one
step nearer, it should instantly be fired on." This
parleying continued until about ten o'clock in the evening, when the Indians became more cool, and agreed
to

to remain quiet until the next morning, when they would hold a talk; but at the same time, gave us to understand, that they were determined to carry their design of plunder into effect, which they should be able to accomplish with ease, as their strength was hourly increasing. Upon the assurance of their remaining quiet until the next day, our armed party marched back, and guarded the camp until morning.

About three o'clock in the afternoon of the arrival of the Indians, Capt. Minor's riding horse, with another very valuable one, were stolen from within two hundred yards of the camp: upon receiving this intelligence, orders were immediately given to bring all those belonging to our party into the camp, and secure them, when we found that eight or ten were already missing. The Spanish horses were also collected, and put into a pen made for that purpose.

The hostile Indians kept moving about in small parties the whole night, and sometimes came within gun-shot of our tents. They threw down the contractor's bullock pen, and let his cattle out, and opened the pen which contained the Spanish horses, and haltered four of them; but were driven off with but two. Three of the horses belonging to my party broke loose, and ran without the camp, and though every exertion was made to bring them back, they were mounted by some Indians, who rode off on them. In this manner the night was spent.

From a suspicion that we should meet with some difficulties at that place, I had detained a small Spanish schooner, which was in the employ of our commissary Mr. Anderson; the United States schooner which I had fitted up at New Orleans, was too large to ascend the river with ease, I had ordered her to Apalachy (St. Marks,) a few days before, and to wait

further

further orders. The principal part of the loading of the small schooner, I had very fortunately taken to our camp a short time previous to the alarm. The fate of this vessel we did not learn until early in the morning of the 18th, when we were informed that she had been plundered about midnight; that the sails were cut to pieces, and the running rigging carried away. Upon receiving this information, my son with two of the labourers, armed with rifles, went to repossess her; on their way they saw a small party of armed Indians, who fled on their approach: as they drew near the vessel, they discovered three Indians on board of her; seeing that their numbers were equal, they gave a whoop, and sprang forward, on which the Indians jumped on shore, and fled with precipitation into the woods. The master and other persons on board, had been robbed of all their cloathing, even their handkerchiefs from their necks, and heads, together with their bedding. The public property was of no great value: twelve or fifteen guns which wanted repairing, a case of claret, a small quantity of brandy, a chest of axes with other tools, and a few blankets were the principal articles taken.

We waited impatiently until nine o'clock in the morning, but heard nothing of any Indians coming to the conference they had proposed the preceding evening. We called upon the Big Lieutenant, and asked his opinion of our situation; he answered " that it was far from being good: the Indians on the river about us had taken the bad talks of the strangers: that he had no dependance, but on his own, and our people; with them he thought he could take us safely to St. Mark's, (Apalachy)." Upon receiving this information, Capt. Minor and myself thought it best to retreat. It was agreed that he should proceed by land

to

to Colerain, if not followed the two first days by the Indians; but in case he were, to proceed to St. Mark's, and wait for a vessel to carry him, and his party, round Cape Florida to St. Mary's: the vessel he had heretofore used was discharged, (I believe,) by an order from the late Governor Gayoso. To render his journey as safe as possible, I sent Capt. Bowyer and all my escort, a corporal, and three privates excepted, with him.

I went on board the small schooner myself, in which was put the apparatus, with all our provision, and baggage, except what would be wanted by the party who went by land, determined to force my way down the river if opposed: my armed party consisted of sixteen persons, twelve of whom were expert rifle men.

Before I left the camp, I wrote a letter to our surveyor Mr. Gillespie, to be forwarded to him by Col. Hawkins, who proposed remaining on Flint river a few days, to endeavour to give a more favourable turn to the disposition of the Indians. A message was likewise sent to the two sailors on board the United States schooner at St. Mark's, to meet me with all possible expedition in St. George's sound. The party who went by land, with the remaining pack horses set off at four o'clock in the afternoon, and the schooner was under weigh at five: we manned eight oars and relieved the hands every hour.

Immediately after we left the shore, it began to rain, but we soon made such a covering with our tents, the cut sails, and some oil cloths, that our people and their arms were kept dry. We continued down the river until after dark, when we stopped for fear of injuring the vessel against logs. The next morning, although it was raining, the moon gave us so much light, as to enable us to proceed, and about eleven
o'clock

o'clock in the forenoon of the 19th, we passed the lowest Indian village on the river. The rain continued without intermission, and so heavy that it would have been impossible for the Indians to attack us with success in open canoes, and they have no other.

On the 21st of September, we came near to St. George's sound, where we halted to repair the rigging of the vessel. Thus ended this disagreeable business. It was alarming, because we had savages to deal with. To the American party, (who a few days before had been declared useless,) both camps were indebted for their safety, and by them public and private property, to a considerable amount, together with all the papers, observations, and other documents, relative to the boundary were preserved. The Spanish party was too small to make even the shew of resistance, those few however behaved• with great firmness. Here it will be justice to add, that it is my opinion, the Spanish commissioner, (Capt. Minor,) was as much in the dark respecting the conduct of the Indians as we were, and was wholly regulated in his conduct by his instructions, and that if any thing improper has been done by other officers of his Catholic Majesty, it was wholly without his knowledge.

The following statement of facts, may perhaps satisfy the reader on this subject.

First. In the month of May preceding, Capt. Minor received instructions from Governor Gayoso, to dismiss his escort on his arrival at the Chattahocha, and return himself to Pensacola, and wait there until he could be furnished with a passport from the Bahama Islands, that he might be enabled to go with safety round Cape Florida to St. Mary's. That their surveyor should go by land from the mouth of Flint river,

ver, and carry on a line east until it intersected the Apalachy, after which he should proceed to the source of
the St. Mary's, and when the geographical position of
that point was determined, the work might be considered as complete. These instructions were shown
separately to Col. Hawkins and myself; what were
the Colonel's comments on them I know not; but my
own opinion of them was given very freely. They
were considered, as calculated for the purpose of delay. The directions to the surveyor, to carry on a
line east from the mouth of Flint river, until it intersected the Apalachy, was not only unconnected with
our business, but embraced an absurdity; because a
line drawn east from the mouth of Flint river would
pass many miles north of the source of the Apalachy.
The orders respecting the military escort were certainly improper: it was a subject submitted to the
commissioners of the treaty.

Captain Minor was not pleased with the instructions,
and immediately by letter to Governor Gayoso proposed some alterations, who dispensed with his returning to Pensacola, and waiting for a Bahama passport, and with the east line to be carried on to the
Apalachy.

Secondly. The two Indians, whom Governor Folch
assured Col. Hawkins and myself were Seminoles,
were Upper Creeks from the Tallisee town, and bro-
thers-in-law to his interpreter Antonio.

Thirdly. That instead of going to the Seminoles,
they returned home to their town, of which the Tame
King was Chief.

Fourthly. A few days after their return home, the
Tallisee, or Tame King, with about two hundred of
his people including the two already mentioned, proceeded to Pensacola, and menaced our surveyor and

G g   his

his party on their way. An account of their proceedings at Pensacola has already been detailed.

Fifthly. The party who came down to plunder us, were a part of those who came to Pensacola with the Tame King.

Sixthly. Governor Folch promised Col. Hawkins and myself, when in Pensacola, that he would immediately send agents among the Indians, particularly the Seminoles, to quiet their minds, which was never done!

Seventhly. Had the officers of his Catholic Majesty been careful to have agents among the Indians, to cooperate with ours, in keeping up a good understanding, and allaying their fears and suspicions, our business would have been completed in all its parts.

On the 23d in the forenoon, my two sailors arrived in an open boat. The United States schooner, could not be got out of the harbour, on account of a head wind. On their landing, they handed me two letters, over the superscription of one was written these words, " On his Britainic Majesty's Service." The following is a true copy of it.

Fox Point, September 22d, 1799.

Sir,

I beg leave to make known to you, that I am at present on a small island on this coast, which is well known to the bearers, with the crew of his Britainic Majesty's schooner Fox, late under my command, but which was unfortunately wrecked five days since, on this coast. As there is no possibility of saving the schooner, I trust sir, your humanity will induce you to stop here, and devise with me, some means of removing those unfortunate men, who have nothing

more

more than some provisions saved from the wreck to exist on; the island producing nothing; on the contrary, for two days, during the late gale, the sea made a breach over it, so that for those two days, we were with nearly two feet water on the ground.

Understanding that you have been driven by the Indians from the country where you were employed, I beg leave to inform you, that General Bowles, the Chief of the Creek nation is with me, he expresses his wishes to see you much, as he thinks your unfortunate differences may be settled: he has no force here, therefore you may be assured no treachery can be intended, as I shall consider you under my protection, and use the force under my command to the utmost for your security, which is not inconsiderable, as I have been enabled to save my arms, ammunition, &c. With the most anxious wishes of seeing you soon,

I am your most humble servant,

(Signed)　　　　JAMES WOOLDRIDGE,
Lieutenant in the Royal Navy.

Andrew Ellicott, Esq.

The other letter was in the following words.

Fox Point, September 22d, 1799.

SIR,

I am now at the mouth of this river on my return from Spain by the way of London, and the West Indies, in order once more to rejoin my nation the Creeks. The vessel that brought me here, was four days since unfortunately run on shore at the entrance of the bay, but having saved all my effects, with my boat, should have proceeded into the country, until hearing of your being near, I determined to stay, and wish much to see you. Although we may differ in politics, yet as gentle-

G g 2　　　　　　　　men

men we may associate, and be friends, at least we may be civil to each other; I pledge my honour to be so to you and rely on yours.

> I have the honour to be,
>> Your obedient servant,
> (Signed)   WM. A. BOWLES.

Andrew Ellicott, Esq.

It had been for some weeks previous to this time, rumoured among the Indians, that Mr. Bowles was on his way to join them; but whether they had this information from himself while in the West Indies, or whether it had been communicated to them in consequence of some injudicious publications which appeared in several of our news papers is uncertain; but it evidently had a bad effect.

The line of conduct which was thought proper to pursue on this sudden and unexpected incident, will be found minutely detailed, in the following letter to our principal agent Col. Hawkins.

> *Apalachy, October 9th,* 1799.

DEAR SIR,

On the 23d of last month, at the mouth of the Chattahocha, where my people were repairing the rigging of the vessel, which had been cut to pieces by the Indians on the morning of the 18th preceding, the enclosed letters* Nos. 1 and 2, were put into my hands by my sailors, who had come on from Apalachy in an open boat to meet me; the United States schooner could not be got out of that harbour on account of a head wind. On their passage, they were brought to at the east end of St. George's island, by some people in distress. Upon going ashore, they were

---

* The letters from Lieutenant Wooldridge and Mr. Bowles.

were critically examined by one of the gentlemen respecting the employ they were in, and where they
were bound; to which they gave satisfactory answers.
They were then informed that the people they saw
there, were the officers and crew of his Britannic Majesty's armed schooner the Fox, which had been
wrecked at that place five days before, and that Gen.
Bowles, and his suit were among them, and requested
the sailors to be the bearers of some letters to me, to
which they consented. On receiving those letters
which was in the forenoon, I did not decide in what
manner I should act until some time in the afternoon,
when I concluded to go on immediately in the open boat
to those unfortunate people, and leave the schooner,
(which was in the employ of our commissary Mr.
Anderson,) to have her rigging repaired. At five
o'clock in the afternoon I set out, and proceeded along
the sound until one o'clock in the morning of the 24th,
when I wrapped myself up in my cloak, and slept on
one of the benches; the men being much fatigued
with rowing, likewise went to sleep. At day break
they took in the anchor, and a light breeze serving,
we arrived at the east end of the island about ten
o'clock, A. M. where I met with the unfortunate crew,
and after receiving an account of their misfortunes
from the commanding officer, he was informed that
their situation had been taken into consideration, and
my mind was made up upon it. That the country
which I had the honour to serve, and of which I was
a native, had early resolved to observe a strict neutrality between the present belligerent powers in Europe. This resolution I thought a wise one, and could
not therefore on any occasion, consent to any one act
which might be construed into a deviation from that
principle. That the officers and crew were certainly
in

in their enemies country, and came into it with hostile views; an attempt therefore on my part to extricate them, might be viewed by the Spanish government, as a deviation from that line of conduct we had determined to observe. From that view of the subject, which I thought a correct one, they were not to expect any other aid from me, than what was immediately connected with humanity; that when my commissary arrived, which would probably be the next day, I should direct him to furnish them as liberally as our circumstances would justify, and if I could be of any service to them in a negotiation with the officers of his Catholic Majesty, they might rely upon my interest and exertions in their favour. The officer, (Lieut. Wooldridge,) who appears to be a man of liberality, and good understanding, made no objection; it was therefore concluded that he admitted the justness of the principle. The next day the commissary arrived, and delivered to the Lieutenant 15cwt. of flour, and three bags of rice; the crew were then on half allowance, great part of their provision being lost when they were wrecked.

I shall now proceed to take some notice of Mr. Bowles, (commonly called Gen. Bowles,) who, with his suit, came in the vessel under the command of Lieut. Wooldridge. I had many conversations with Mr. Bowles, both of us being detained together eight days on the east end of St. George's island, by a violent gale of wind. He is certainly a man of enterprize, and address, added to considerable talents. He declared to me, that he was not taken by the Spaniards some years ago at Apalachy in the manner reported; but for political reasons it was necessary to give it that appearance. That in 1794, it was proposed to him by the Minister of his Catholic Majesty, to receive

a

a commission in that service, and return to his nation, and attack the United States ; which he declined in a pointed manner, and was shortly after, and not until then confined. Soon after Mr. Pinckney arrived in Spain, he was informed by the Prince of Peace, that the American Minister was his enemy, and was again offered a commission which he declined to accept, though in confinement. That in the year 1797, if my recollection serves me, he was informed by the same Minister, that the Floridas were ceded to the Republic of France, and to be taken possession of as soon as convenient to the Republic, and was offered a commission in that service, which he also declined: And that immediately upon the late treaty between the United States, and his Catholic Majesty, being made public, he protested against it to the Ministers of the court of Madrid, as interfering with the dignity of his people and nation, the Creeks, who were as free, and independent as any other nation in the universe. That the article by which the United States, and his Catholic Majesty, are bound to restrain the hostile attempts of the Indians within their respective territories, was an atrocious violation of the law of nations, and should never be submitted to whilst his people had a drop of blood to spill. He declared that he had arrested that part of the treaty at Madrid, and that it must be done away by the executive of the United States. And further, that he had warned the court of Madrid against running the boundary, and expected from assurances given, that it had been suspended some months ago, and had also demanded in the name of his nation an immediate evacuation of the post of St. Mark's, which if not done immediately, he should fall upon measures to compel a compliance, and had he arrived in time, he should have arrested the Spanish commissioner,

commissioner, and his party. He likewise intends to seize Mr. Panton's property at Apalachy.

This is the substance of all the conversation I had with him interesting to our country. What credit may be due to his information, and what we have to fear from his threats, you are better able to judge of than myself: some Indians will probably be led away by him, and some temporary inconvenience experienced by the United States; but I cannot think that the nation generally, will risk its existence to gratify either his ambition or resentment. He speaks in the style of a King; " my nation," and " my people," are his common expressions.

Whether he is supported, or countenanced by any foreign nation is a question that scarcely needs a conjecture. Certain it is, that on his arrival last spring at Barbadoes, he was treated with the utmost respect, and at Jamaica with singular attention, both by the Governor and British admiral on that station. This attention induced two young gentlemen to become his followers, the one a Scotchman by the name of Ferguson, and the other a Mr. Nuvelle, a French gentleman, now or lately a Captain in the Prince of Wales's regiment of colonial light dragoons; which is manifest from his commission. These gentlemen begin to fear a deception, and suggested their doubts to me, and at the same time asked my advice respecting a relinquishment of their plan of proceeding into the nation. They were told, that their present situation was such, that I should forbear saying any thing to them on that subject, but would furnish them with a line to you, and doubted not but in a few weeks they would be able to judge correctly for themselves.

Although the officers of his Catholic Majesty have certainly been very remiss, in obliterating the impressions

sions which were made upon the minds of the Indians two years ago against running the boundary, I am nevertheless of opinion, that Mr. Bowles's plans, which are unquestionably hostile towards Spain, ought to be counteracted by every citizen of the United States. It is not only a duty we owe to the supreme law of the land, but involves a point of national honour: a compliance with the most important of all contracts.

I have now my dear friend, given you as correct an account of my interview with Mr. Bowles, as comes within the power of my recollection, and feel a confidence in your taking such measures, as will preserve the honour of our country, and effectually thwart the views of a bold, daring, adventurer.

I cannot close this letter without observing in justice to Mr. Bowles, that he behaved on all occasions whilst with me in a polite and friendly manner, and generously furnished me with the necessary charts and directions, for sailing round Cape Florida, a matter of great importance to me, as I shall have to navigate our vessel myself.

Mr. Panton and Governor Folch, have been written to on the subject of Mr. Bowles's arrival in the nation, a copy of my letter to the latter, you will find inclosed.

I am my dear Sir,
Your sincere friend
ANDREW ELLICOTT.

Col. BENJAMIN HAWKINS, princi-
pal agent of Indian affairs for }
the southern department.

My passage from the mouth of the Chattahocha, to St. Marks, (Apalachy,) where I arrived in the evening of the 7th of October, was truly disagreea-

H h   ble,

ble, being part of the time at sea, in an open boat, and detained thirteen days by violent easterly winds, on dry islands of sand, which was blown about like snow, filled our blankets, and fell in great quantities in what little victuals we had, which for seven days was bread and coffee, and what few fish we caught. On my arrival at St. Marks, I received a note from my friend Col. Hawkins, informing me that Mr. Gillespie our surveyor, had joined the party which had gone on by land. This intelligence eased my mind of many uncomfortable reflections.

Having now navigated the Chattahocha up to, and down from the boundary, and traversed the whole coast of West Florida, I shall proceed to give some account of that river, and the province.

The Chattahocha, (sometimes called the Apalachicola,) is a fine, large river, and navigable for boats, and gallies, which use oars a considerable distance north of the boundary. A sloop in the service of his Catholic Majesty's commissioner, and a small schooner in our employ, ascended up to the mouth of Flint River, which falls into the Chattahocha about twenty-one miles below the parallel of 31°; but this was attended with some difficulty. The United States schooner ascended more than 30 miles, but for want of oars and hands, had to stop. From the mouth of the river up, for the distance of at least forty miles, the banks are very low, and with the exception of a few places, inundated whenever the water is moderately high. But as you ascend, the banks become more elevated, and some of them which may be called bottom land, are seldom overflown: these are remarkably rich, and extremely fertile, and are almost the only lands under cultivation by the Indians, who reside on the river.

A few

A few miles below the mouth of Flint River, limestone begins to make its appearance, and extends very far up into the country; it is open and porous, and of a dirty bluish colour. On the east side of the mouth of Flint River, and for a considerable distance up it, large quantities of iron ore may be seen.

The up-land on the Chattahocha, and Flint Rivers, from the boundary southward is of an inferior quality, though much better than on some of the waters already mentioned.

The Chattahocha, communicates with St. George's Sound by three mouths, or channels. The most eastern, is at present only navigable for canoes, and small boats, on account of the lodged timber, and rafts. Our vessels ascended the most western one, which is at this time the main channel; but the navigation of this is troublesome for those not acquainted with it, though not on account of logs, and such impediments, but from its connection with lakes and swamps, by branches apparently as large as itself. We took two of them coming in from the westward, the first led us into a lake about three leagues in length, and an half in breadth. The other, a few miles from the main branch, was divided in such a manner, into smaller ones, that we soon discovered our mistake. The latitude of the mouth of the western branch is about 29° 42′ N. and the longitude by a lunar observation 5ʰ 39′ 23″ west from the royal observatory at Greenwich.

St. George's Sound, is principally formed by three islands, between the most westerly one, and the main land, the channel is narrow, and shoal, and only fit for canoes; between this island and St. George's, which gives name to the sound, is a bar on which some bushes are growing. The coasting vessels pass between these islands. St. George's Island is supposed to be about

six

six leagues in length, but in no place more that one
wide. The distance from St. George's Island across
the sound, is from one to two and an half leagues. The
next island is not laid down in any of our charts: it
is about two leagues in length, and two miles east of St.
George's Island. The main channel into the sound,
is near the west end of this third island. From this
third island to a fourth, which at low water sometimes joins the main land, the water is too shoal for any
other than coasting vessels.

The latitude of the east end of St. George's Island
where the schooner Fox, (already mentioned,) was cast
away, is 29° 44′ 38″ N. and the longitude, (by taking
the result of a lunar observation made at the mouth of
the Chattahocha as a correct point,) 5ʰ 38′ 35″ west
from Greenwich. The sound is so full of oyster
banks, and shoals, that it is difficult to navigate it,
without a pilot.

The coast on the north side of the sound, is intersected and cut to pieces by such a variety of water
courses, several of which have evidently at some former period been mouths of the river, that it is extremely difficult to find the true branches: of this we had
sufficient evidence.

The up-land of West Florida, as it is now bounded,
is generally of a very inferior quality, except on the
Mississippi, and is of but little value for either planting or farming. The river bottoms, or flats are all
fertile; but too inconsiderable as to quantity, or too
low and marshy, to give much value to the province.

It may be observed, that no restrictions in this country, have been found so effective, as to prevent settlements being made where the land has been good. A
conclusion may therefore be fairly drawn, that this province, which has been aided by France, Great Britain
and

and Spain, each in her turn, and yet remain in a great degree unsettled, must be materially defective in point of soil.

It is true, that the cities or towns of Mobile, and Pensacola, have been flourishing places, but this was owing to causes not immediately dependent upon the soil. The latter was the seat of government while the province was held by Great Britain, and from the excellence of the harbour was much frequented by the shipping of that nation, and both places well situated for carrying on the Indian trade, which was at that time very considerable; but that trade having greatly decreased, from want of inhabitants, and the necessary articles of exportation, those cities have declined also. Mobile is now beginning to recover, but this is owing to the settlements forming north of the boundary, on the Tombecby, and Alabama Rivers. Notwithstanding the favourable situation of those cities, they can never be of much consequence but from the settlement of the country north of the boundary, which has greatly the advantage in point of soil and climate.

Although West Florida is of but little importance, when considered alone, and unconnected with the country north of it, it is of immense consequence when viewed as possessing all the avenues of commerce to, and from a large productive country. A country extending north from the 31st degree of north latitude, to the sources of the Pearl, Pascagola, Tombecby, Alabama, Coenecuh, Chattahocha, and Flint Rivers, and at least 300 miles from east to west. The coast of this province abounds in live-oak and red cedar, in considerable abundance, fit for ship building, which is not to be met with north of the boundary.

From the safety of the coast of this province, added to the great number of harbours proper for coasting vessels,

vessels; that of Pensacola into which a fleet may sail, and ride with safety, and that of St. Joseph's, into which vessels not drawing more than seventeen feet water may sail at all times ; it must be highly important in a commercial point of view, and if connected with the country north of it, capable of prescribing maratime regulations to the Gulf of Mexico.

In a political point of view, West Florida may be considered as an object of the greatest importance to a large division of the United States; because that power, which holds the avenues to commerce, may give a tone to the measures of another, should it be unfriendly to liberty, and public happiness.

The population of West Florida is very inconsiderable. The principal settlement is on the Mississippi, between the boundary and the Iberville. On the north side of the Iberville, and the lakes, to the Gulf of Mexico there are a few scattering inhabitants. Thence along the coast, to Mobile Bay, there are a few more. There are likewise a few about the Bay. From the city of Mobile, up the Mobile, and Tensaw Rivers, to the boundary, there may possibly be forty families. From Mobile Point to Pensacola Bay, there are no inhabitants, and not more than half a dozen farms on the Bay. From the head of the Bay, up the Coenecuh to the boundary, there are two plantations or farms. The population of the cities of Mobile, and Pensacola, does not exceed fifteen hundred inhabitants. From Pensacola Bay to St. Mark's, there are no inhabitants.

CHAP.

CHAP. IX.

Occurrences at St. Marks—account of the adjoining country—The author sails from St. Marks—arrives at Cayo Anclote—thence at the Florida Keys—examines the Keys, and Reef to the Key Biscana—sails into the Gulf Stream—a violent gale of wind—velocity of the Gulf Stream—another storm—one of the men dies—arrives at the west end of St. Simon's Island in the state of Georgia—theories of the Gulf Stream examined—arrives at the town of St. Mary's.

IMMEDIATELY on my arrival at St. Marks, I communicated Mr. Bowles's design of taking that place to the Commandant, and two or three days after forwarded despatches to Governors White, and Folch, with copies of the foregoing letter to Col. Hawkins, in order that they might be on their guard, and that the officers of the United States might not be accused of improper conduct, or duplicity. But the caution had no effect: Mr. Bowles remained unmolested, until he had in part regained his former influence with the Indians, and then besieged and took the Fort of St. Mark's, which was defended by about one hundred infantry, and more than one dozen pieces of good artillery.

At St. Mark's, I was treated by the Commandant Mr. Portel and his lady, with politeness and hospitality. Madam Portel is an agreeable Spanish lady, and possesses a considerable share of vivacity, and good understanding. She speaks the English language tolerably well, and assisted an interpreter in a verbal communication which I received at that place relative to the money that was put on board a boat at New Madrid, for certain citizens of the United States, as already

ready stated: the names of the persons for whom the money was intended, and for whom the receipts were given by the person who had the distribution of it, were likewise communicated. One of Mr. Panton's clerks was present when the communication was made.

Fort St. Marks, (frequently called Apalachy,) is situated on a point of land at the confluence of the Apalachy, and another stream of nearly the same size; they are too small to be called rivers. The Fort is built of hewn stone, and the work tolerably well executed: on the north side of the Fort, and adjoining the wall, is a deep wet ditch, which extends from one of the streams of water to the other.

The country round the Fort, is almost as level as the water in the Bay, and but little elevated above it: so that when the tides, which rise but between two and three feet, are aided by a brisk S. W. wind, it is overflown. This low tract of country is covered with high grass, and has every appearance of being a deep marsh; but this is not the case; the soil generally, does not appear to be more than two or three feet deep; and in many places much less, and is supported by an horizontal stratum of lime-stone of an indifferent quality. The Fort is built of this stone, and likewise an old tower, which stands about a league S. W. from the Fort. The foundation of the tower, is evidently on this extensive stratum of calcarious matter. The quarry from whence the stones were raised to build the tower is but a short distance from it.

When, or for what purpose, this tower was erected appears to be uncertain; but from its mouldering condition, and the total decay of the wood formerly connected with its walls, it is probable that it was built shortly after the Spaniards took possession of that country. On the top there appears to have been a light-house;

light-house ; but from the condition of the bay, being so shoal and full of oyster banks, as to render it useless to ordinary shipping, it appears to have been unnecessary. There is about half an acre of ground round the tower, raised by art so high, as not to be overflown, which was probably used as a garden.

The stratum of lime stone extends northerly a considerable distance, and is possibly connected with those extensive strata on the Chattahocha and Flint rivers, which may be considered the base of a large tract of sandy country. I frequently observed rocks of it, standing several feet above the poor sandy soil, (which appeared only adapted to the production of pitch pine and wire grass,) on the path between the lowest Indian village on the Chattahocha, and the boundary.

The principal source of the Apalachy, is from a single lime stone spring ; many others are to be met with in that sandy country almost as remarkable for their magnitude ; but they all issue from lime stone. The first lime stone observed on the boundary, east from the Mississippi, was between the Coenecuh and Chattahocha rivers.

Some miles north of St. Marks, there is a tract of country, though not extensive, which is tolerably good, and here the Spaniards had a small settlement or colony ; but it was conquered about sixty years ago, by an enterprizing party from Charles Town, South Carolina ; it is now totally abandoned, and scarcely a vestage of the settlement remains, except the ruins of a fort, and one or two pieces of old artillery, almost in a state of complete decompostion.

The latitude of St. Marks, by two good observations appears to be 30° 8′ 29″ N. I had no opportunity owing to bad weather, of making a single observation for the longitude.

I i

I ex-

I expected to have been overtaken at St. Marks, by a vessel laden with a quantity of provision from New Orleans, which had been deposited at that place by our contractor. Supposing this vessel would pass through St. George's Sound, and if so, be liable to be captured by Lieut. Wooldridge, and his men, who had saved their boats. I mentioned the circumstance of this vessel, and provision to the Lieutenant, his officers, and Mr. Bowles, while with them on St. George's Island : and requested them to furnish her with a passport to follow me round Cape Florida, to St. Mary's if I should have left St. Marks before she arrived. They were likewise informed that no objection would be made to their taking such a supply of provision as their immediate necessities required, provided they gave the master a receipt for it. They appeared to be highly satisfied, and returned me many thanks, and in the most positive terms, assured me that the vessel should not be detained if she fell in their hands ; but forwarded immediately agreeably to my request, after supplying themselves with some necessary articles.

The vessel, with the provisions not arriving at St. Marks so soon as I expected, and the stormy season setting in, it was thought best to proceed without waiting longer for her. On the 16th of October, our commissary Mr. Anderson, procured some fresh beef, which he had salted, and barrelled up, and we made ready to set sail the day following.

My undertaking this voyage, was a matter of necessity, and not of choice, and could it have been avoided with advantage to my country, I certainly should not have taken upon myself so important a charge. Having on board the commissary Mr. Anderson with all his accounts, and vouchers, for the money expended since we left the city of Philadelphia in 1796: and all the papers,

drafts,

drafts, and astronomical observations, relative to the boundary, and some other important geographical positions, with the originals of all my correspondence, for more than three years, together with the apparatus, and baggage of the party, including the military escort: to which may be added, about twenty persons, of whom but five had ever been at sea before, and of those five two only were sailors, and totally illiterate.

Thus circumstanced, I left St. Marks on the 18th of October, in a small light built schooner, of not more than 38 or 40 tons burden. The water being low, the vessel stuck some time on the oyster banks. At four o'clock P. M. we took our departure from the last stake in the channel, and at sun down were out of sight of land. About three o'clock in the morning of the 18th, we had a gale of wind from the east, attended with a dark mist, which obliged us to return into Apalachy Bay for shelter. The storm continued until the morning of the 20th, when we got up the yards, and prepared to take advantage of the first fair wind.

On opening one of the barrels of beef, which had been salted up at St. Marks, it was found to be so much damaged, (with the exception of a few pounds,) as to be rendered useless: an examination was then made into the remainder, and it was unfortunately found to be in the same situation.

This discovery appeared to produce some uneasiness among the crew, several of whom were for returning to St. Marks for a fresh supply, but as we had a great sufficiency of bread and flour on board, the propostion met with such a decided negative, accompanied with a reprimand, that it prevented any complaints during the voyage, though we were frequently in disagreeable situations.

About

About eight o'clock in the evening of the 20th, we had a light breeze from the north, and got immediately under way, and put to sea.

21st. After midnight had a violent gale from the east; hove to under the double reefed foresail. About nine o'clock A. M. the wind abated, and shifted to the north. At ten o'clock P. M. from our soundings, it appeared that we were in the great cove, or bay, between the Cedar Keys, and Kayo Anclote, the latter are three small islands off St. Clement's point.

22d. Still in the cove, and though out of sight of land until ten o'clock A. M. our soundings were commonly less than 10 feet, and in some places on an horizontal stratum of stone or rock, of a rough surface; on which was seen large patches of turtle grass, and sand, some of which is remarkably white, and large quantities of sponge. This horizontal stratum of stone, is probably connected with that already described at St. Marks. We arrived at the Keys in the evening, and came to an anchor between the northern one and the main land. In the night had a violent gale of wind, and were under the necessity of putting out our heaviest anchor.

23d. Early in the morning got under way, and sailed to the anchor ground between the main land and southern Key, in an excellent harbour, where we intended laying until the weather became more settled. In the afternoon caught a number of fine fish.

24th. Very squally with dark mists.

25th. Weather the same as yesterday.

26th. Wind very violent from the S. E. until eight o'clock in the evening, when it shifted to the S. and brought on the heaviest fall of rain I had ever known. About midnight the wind changed, and came with such violence from the north that the vessel dragged both anchors a considerable distance.

27th.

27th. Wind moderated about one o'clock P. M. when we immediately got under way and passed Hillsborough Bay, (Spirito Santo or Bay Tampe,) about seven o'clock P. M. This Bay I suspect is laid down in all our charts too far north, by at least fifteen minutes. Kayo Anclote opposite to St. Clement's Point, is laid down seventeen minutes too far north.

28th. The wind fair. The sun was eclipsed whilst I was taking his meridional altitude.

29th. From a meridional altitude of Capella taken after midnight, we appeared to be opposite to Punta Larga, (Cape Roman,) and having a sufficient offing we steered for Cape Sable, the most southern promontory of east Florida, which was seen from the mast head at noon. At three o'clock in the afternoon came to an anchor on the west side of Kayo Ani, or Sandy Key, which is a small island a very short distance south of the Cape. After coming to an anchor, myself and some of the crew, took our boat, and went to the island; where in a very few minutes, we shot about twelve dozen plover. There are some bushes scattered over the island; but what particularly attracted my attention was the amazing piles, or stacks, of the prickley pear, (opuntia a species of the cactus,) the fruit was large and in high perfection: we eat very plentifully of it; but my people were not a little surprised the next morning, on finding their urine appear as if it had been highly tinged with cochineal; no inconvenience resulting from it, the fruit was constantly used by the crew during our continuance among the keys or islands. Though this island is called Sandy Key, and has certainly the appearance of a body of sand; it is little more than a heap of broken and pulverised shells, which were found to effervesce freely with the vitriolic acid, and little or no quartz was perceptible in the solution.

30th.

30th. Weighed anchor and sailed to Key Vaccas, or Cow Island, and moored in a small harbour among a cluster of little islands. Stormy all the afternoon. The soundings from Sandy Key, to Key Vaccas, were regular and generally less than nine feet, and on an horizontal stratum of stone, similar to that described between the Cedar Keys, and Kayo Anclote.

31st. Went on shore on Key Vaccas, where our people in a short time killed four deer, of that small species, common to some of those islands. They are less than our ordinary breed of goats.

November 1st. Examined a number of the small islands, they all appeared to be lime-stone, or calcareous rocks, the tops of them were flat, and elevated but a few feet above the surface of the water, and covered with a thin stratum of earth. These rocks are evidently a congeries of petrefactions, in which may be traced a variety of plants, particularly the roots of the great palmitto, or cabbage tree, (corypha or palmitto of Walter). The mud in the harbour where we lay was of a fine white, and resembled lime, or whiting, and was found to effervesce with the vitriolic acid; from which it is probable, that it is no more than shells, and other calcareous matter, levigated by the friction of the particles, produced by the constant motion of the water.

2d. Took some large turtle, and fine fish. Visited by Captain Burns of New Providence whose vessel lay at the east end of Key Vaccas. He was on a turtling and wrecking voyage. Wind still from the east and squally.

3d. Killed some more small deer and salted them up. Calm the whole day.

4th. A light breeze in the afternoon, got under way, and proceeded about five miles along the north side of Key Vaccas. Soundings generally from seven

to

to eight feet; the bottom horizontal rock with a rough surface.

5th. Got under weigh early in the morning, but the wind being ahead, come to an anchor under a small Key, a short distance from Duck Key. Soundings as before. On the small Island there was some appearance of a clear field, manned the boat and went to examine it; but had proceeded but a short distance among the bushes, when I was compelled to return by the incredible number of musquetoes; on coming to the boat, I found the men had jumped into the water to avoid the attacks of those troublesome little animals.

This island is similar to those already described, but surrounded by a greater number of ragged rocks near the surface of the water.

6th. Got under way at eight o'clock A. M. and beat out into the channel between the Keys and reef, and came to an anchor in a good harbour at the east end of Viper Key.

7th. Made sail early in the morning, and came to an anchor at one o'clock P. M. in the harbour at the north east end of the old Matacombe, where we found it necessary to take in wood and water. This island is noted for affording a greater quantity of good water than any other of the Keys; on which account it is much frequented by the turtlers, and wreckers. The water is found in natural wells about four feet deep, which are no more than cracks or cavities in the rock, and not the effect of art as some have imagined. This island, like those already mentioned, may be considered as a large flat calcareous rock, elevated but a few feet above the water, and covered with a stratum of earth. This is said to have been the last residence of the Coloosa Indians, the original inhabitants of East Florida: From whence they were gradually expelled by the Seminoles,

or

or Wild Creeks. From Matacombe they were taken to the island of Cuba by the Spaniards, and incorporated with their slaves. But this measure does not appear to have been taken without provocation: these Indians were remarkable for their cruelty, which they exercised indiscriminately on all the unfortunate people, who were wrecked within their reach on that dangerous coast. The island of Matanza, (slaughter,) which lies about one mile north east from the watering place, was so called from those Indians massacring about three hundred French, who had collected on it, after being wrecked on the reef.

On the north east side of Matacombe, there is a beautiful beach, which has the appearance of whitish sand, but on examination is found to be broken shells, coral, &c.

8th. Spent in taking in wood and water. In the afternoon the schooner Shark, late the property of Messrs. Panton, Laslie and Company, of Pensacola arrived; being a prize to Lieut. Wooldridge and crew, (of whom mention has already been made,) who captured her near St. George's island on her way to Apalachy. The schooner Shark was loaded with provisions, and as we had no meat, our commissary Mr. Anderson made application to the prize master for a barrel of pork; the prize master Mr. Barnet made no direct answer, but said he would see about it the next day.

9th. Got under way at nine o'clock A. M. The schooner Shark done the same. It was previously agreed, that we should anchor together in the evening at Key Rodriguiz, where the prize master was to furnish us with a supply of meat, in return for what flour they had from us on St. George's island. We sailed rather the fastest, and so soon as we came to an anchor in the harbour, she crouded all her sail, and stood over

the

the reef for New Providence. Thus were we requited for our favours. Soon after we came to an anchor, we were joined by Captain Watkins, who commanded a privateer from New Providence. He behaved with politeness, and furnished me with about five pounds of excellent salt pork.

10th. Wind ahead, were not able to make any way. Our men caught a number of fine fish.

11th. Calm until about eleven o'clock A. M. when we had a light breeze and immediately got under way, proceeded to Key Large, and came to an anchor between the Key and Gulf Stream. At the same time a sloop that we were meeting, came to an anchor about two leagues from us.

12th. About two o'clock in the morning, I was called up to see the shooting of the stars, (as it is vulgarly termed,) the phenomenon was grand and awful, the whole heavens appeared as if illuminated with sky-rockets, flying in an infinity of directions, and I was in constant expectation of some of them falling on the vessel. They continued until put out by the light of the sun after day break. This phenomenon extended over a large portion of the West India islands, and was observed as far north as St. Mary's, where it appeared as brilliant as with us. During this singular appearance, the wind shifted from the south to the north, and the Thermometer which had been at 86° for four days past, fell to 56°.

Many ingenious theories have been devised to account for those luminous and fiery meteors, but none of them are so satisfactory to my mind as the *conjecture* of that celebrated chemist M. Lavoisier, who supposes it probable that the terrestial atmosphere consists of several volumes, or strata of gaz or elastic vapour of different kinds, and that the lightest and most difficult

K k   to

to mix with the lower atmosphere will be elevated above it, and form a separate stratum or volume, which he supposes to be inflammable, and that it is at the point of contact between those strata that the aurora borealis, and other fiery meteors are produced.*

About eight o'clock in the morning, the sloop we saw the preceding evening passed by our stern, and upon being hailed answered, " it is a prize," she was then ordered to come to, to which a person answered " ay," and at about 400 yards from us, hove to, and brought her boat, which was in tow along side ; but contrary to our expectation, it was immediately taken in, and the sloop with all her sails set, bore away. Orders were then given to get under way, and give chase, from an idea that it was an American vessel taken by the French, and if possible to retake her, several of her people not having the appearance of Americans or Englishmen. As soon as we got under sail, a gun was discharged towards the sloop, but to which no attention was paid ; but in about one hour we came within rifle shot, when one was discharged, and with such a direction that convinced the crew their safety depended upon coming to ; which was immediately done, and we passed under her stern. The master was requested to come to anchor, and bring his papers on board of us. We anchored about rifle shot from the sloop, after which the request was repeated, but one of the persons on board the sloop observed, that the sea was rough, and they had but one oar and a paddle for their boat : upon which our commissary Mr. Anderson took the boat belonging
to

* The conjecture of M. Lavoisier is expressed in the following words : " Les phénomènes qui accompagnent les météores ignés me portent à croire qú il exist ainsi dans le haut de l'atmosphère une couche d'un fluide inflammable, & que c'est au point de contact de ces deux couches d'air que s'opèrent les phénomènes de l'aurore boréale & des autres météores ignés." *Traité élémentaire de chimie par M. Lavoisier*, tom. 1. chap. 2.

to our vessel, and brought the master and his papers on board. The papers were satisfactory. The vessel and loading were lately Spanish property, and had been taken about fifteen days before by a New Providence privateer near the Havannah, and sent on for Nassau; but got becalmed in the Gulf Stream, which carried her almost to Cape Carnaveral, when the wind served, the master then kept the Florida coast until we met with him. He and his people had been seven days on allowance of one biscuit, and a pint of water each per day, with what fish they could take, which they had to eat without salt. The master took breakfast with me, and when he was ready to return, I directed our commissary to furnish him with a barrel of biscuit, and some salt, upon which he observed, that he had "never before been so fortunately chased and taken." One half of his crew consisted of the Spaniards taken on board the vessel, and they all equally had done duty. Immediately after this fruitless adventure, we got under way, and the wind began to blow with considerable violence, which gradually increased until we found it necessary to come to anchor, and were very fortunate in making a harbour near the mouth of Black Ceasar's Creek.

13th. The gale continued with violence. Took some fish.

14th. The wind continued very violent until the evening.

15th. The wind violent from the north, until one o'clock P. M. when it shifted in a few minutes, and came from the east; which was the only wind from which we were not protected by shoals, and which would in a short time have rendered our situation extremely uneasy. We got under way as soon as possible, and beat out in order to fall into the northern channel of Black Ceasar's Creek; but having the wind

K k 2

and

and a strong current against us, we did not clear the
shoal between the two channels until a few minutes before sunset, and then took the northern channel, which
is very narrow at the entrance, not exceeding fifteen
yards wide, but gradually widens to more than one
hundred, and has between two and an half, and three
fathoms water, except at the entrance where there is but
seven or eight feet.   We came to an anchor near the
mouth of Black Ceasar's Creek, which is only the entrance into an extensive sound between the Keys and
main land.   The sides of the channel are almost perpendicular, like those at old Matacombe, and composed
of a soft, whitish mud, which appears to be wholly
calcarious.

16th. Capt. Watkins beat up to us ; he was the whole
day making two leagues, in a vessel calculated to sail
on a wind.   He had with him the crew of the prize before mentioned: the vessel was wrecked by the violence
of the wind the day we left her.

17th. The wind still continued very unfavourable.
Took a considerable number of fine fish.

18th. The wind was more moderate, and we got under way early in the morning, and beat along Hawk
Channel.   In the afternoon were brought to by a New
Providence privateer, commanded by Captain William
Ball, who had been but a short time from Ireland, and
who treated us for some time with a degree of insolence far beyond any thing I had ever before experienced.   But after examining my instructions and commission, and viewing the signature of President Washington with all the attention and veneration that would
have been paid to a holy relick, he became more moderate, and made us sufficient compensation for his insolence, by presenting us with a fine turtle, and after
wishing us a pleasant passage, we parted.

About

About sunset there was an appearance of a storm, and we came to an anchor in a small, but excellent harbour, where we were defended by shoals from the violence of the sea on every side : before midnight the storm came on.

19th. The storm continued the whole day.

20th. The storm still continued.

21st. Very strong gale from the N. E. Saw a ship early in the morning, (which had certainly missed her way,) nearly on the reef, and in very great danger, but she fortunately wore off.

22d. Got under way, and beat along the sound to the mouth of Fresh Water river, which is nearly opposite to the southern part of Key Biscanio.

23d. Went on shore at the mouth of the river, filled our water casks, and gathered a large quantity of very fine limes : a party of our people likewise took their rifles, and went into the country, and were uncommonly fortunate in killing deer and turkies.

Fresh Water River is said to be no more than the outlet to a large lake, but a few leagues distance from the coast. At the mouth it is not more than five or six perches wide, and ten or twelve feet deep, and middling rapid. The sides are nearly perpendicular, and composed of calcarious stone or rock, similar to that described at Apalachy. This stratum of stone appeared to be very extensive and horizontal.

Key Biscanio is one of the last islands on the reef, and situated in lat. 25° 37′ N.

The Florida reef, (as it is called,) appears to consist of a number of coral banks on the outer edge of an extensive stratum of calcarious stone, which extends from the main land, to the edge of the Gulf Stream : the general position of this stratum is nearly horizontal, and is possibly a continuation of that observed at Apalachy.

lachy. If this should be the case, it may be considered as the base of East Florida, and conform to the general law observed in the disposition of the strata of
stone on our western waters.

On this stratum of stone, which serves as a helmet
to the southern promontory of East Florida, and de-
fends it from the violence of the Gulf Stream, is situated the whole of that cluster of innumerable islands
and shoals, which have been so troublesome and dangerous to navigators.

These islands and shoals, may be viewed as protuberances, (standing on the surface of this extensive
stratum,) gradually formed during a period of many
centuries, by the constant accretion of calcarious matter. Many of those islands and shoals have evidently
had their origin from coral banks, which not only like
those of oysters, are known to increase, but to surpass
them greatly in magnitude : and it is now reduced to a
certainty, that a number of the islands in the South Sea
are coral rocks covered with a stratum of earth. It is
likewise well ascertained by naturalists, that coral is
not, as was formerly supposed a vegetable substance,
but a vast collection of small animals which build up
those rocky edifices from the bottom of the ocean !

The navigation between the Gulf Stream and Florida Keys, has at all times been considered as very difficult and dangerous, which it certainly is for those not
acquainted with it ; but with a competent knowledge of
the Keys and reef, added to ordinary caution, I know
of none more safe for coasting vessels, and others
drawing not more than nine feet water. Such vessels
as are sailing from the northward into the Gulf of
Mexico, and prefer the passage between the Gulf
Stream and Florida coast, after entering the reef a few
miles north of Key Biscanio, should be careful to give
that

that Key a birth of about one and an half miles, on account of a shoal that makes out from it : it will likewise be necessary to observe, that opposite to the south end of the Key, there are but eleven feet water.

After entering the reef, it will be proper for a careful peroon to be kept aloft, who will be able for a considerable distance, (at least one mile,) if the weather should be fair, to discover the coral banks, rocks and shoals, which in some places are numerous, by which means the danger may easily be avoided. It will likewise be necessary on coming to an anchor, which must be done every night while on the reef, to look out for clear ground, otherwise a cable may be fretted off in a few hours by the coral rocks, or other protuberances, and the vessel go adrift.

As a knowledge of this navigation is of very great importance to the mercantile interest of the United States, it is a subject of regret that we have no charts in common use of the reef and Keys, (or islands,) upon a scale sufficiently large and accurate, to be useful. Mr. Gauld's survey of the Dry Tortugas and the Florida reef and Keys, easterly to Key Largo, made by the direction of the Board of Admiralty of Great Britain, may justly be considered as one of the most valuable works of the kind extant, but unfortunately it is little known. From Key Vaccas to Key Largo, I carefully compared Mr. Gauld's charts with the soundings, and perspective views of the Keys, and found an agreement which excited my surprise, and am induced to believe that not a single rock or shoal, so far as the work extends, has been omitted, and that not an error of three feet will be found in any of the soundings. If this work had been completed, it might be esteemed one of the most perfect and useful of the kind. The copy which I had the good fortune to obtain, (and without
which

which it would have been very difficult for me, being not only a stranger to the coast, but no seaman, to have made my way with safety,) I deposited since my return in the office of the secretary of the navy.

Along the Florida Reef, and among the Keys, a great abundance and variety of fish may be taken : such as hog-fish, grunts, yellow tails, black, red, and gray snappers, mullets, bone-fish, amber-fish, margate-fish, barracoota, cavallos, pompui, groopers, king-fish, siberfish, porgys, turbots, stingrys, black drum, Jew fish, with a prodigious variety of others, which in our situation we found excellent. Turtle are also to be had in plenty ; those we took were of three kinds : the loggerhead, hawk-bill and green; the two last are much the best. We likewise found a remarkable species of prawns, which live in great numbers in holes in the rocks : they frequently weigh two or three pounds a-piece, and are improperly called lobsters ; they want the large claws that lobsters have. Their meat is harder, and less delicate than that of the lobsters of the northern states.

Some of the Keys or Islands, were formerly very well timbered, but the the most valuable kinds, such as lignum vitæ, fustick and iron wood, have generally been cut off by the inhabitants of the Bahama Islands.

Key Biscanio is much frequented by the privateers, wreckers and turtlers from the Bahama Islands. At the south end there is an excellent harbour, and the shore so bold that a vessel not drawing more than ten feet water may be careened with safety. In that harbour we found several of those privateers, wreckers and turtlers, by whom we were politely treated, particularly by a Capt. Johnston, who furnished me with seven or eight pounds of salt pork.

Having

Having filled our water casks, salted up some fish, and the wind serving, on the

25th, about noon, we got under way, and proceeded over the reef into the Gulf Stream. Shortly after we had entered the Stream, we saw a vessel bearing down upon us, but did not discover that she was a privateer until she attempted to bring us to by a shot: being determined to make the best use we could of the first fair, strong breeze we had had since our arrival at the Keys, we crowded all our sail, and the privateer did the same, but in two hours she gave up the chase.

In the evening we had a sudden and violent gale from the west, which laid the vessel almost on her beams before the sails could be handed: continued our course north, under the gib and double reefed mainsail.

26th. At break of day the wind shifted to the north, and continued with such violence that we had to heave too under a ballanced main-sail. By a good observation our latitude 27° 2′ N.

27th. The gale continued until about noon, when the wind shifted to the N. E. and became moderate. By a good observation our latitude 28° 12′. From which it is evident we made our way good 1° 10′ in twenty-four hours against a very strong gale, whilst lying to under the ballanced main-sail, in which situation our drift would have been at least 1½′ south, the current must therefore have set 1° 46′ north during that time, or at the rate of nearly 5.1 English miles per hour! Such is the effect of this surprising Stream. Being convinced from the last observation, that a N. W. course would carry us clear of the northern pitch of Cape Carnaveral shoal, which is laid down in our charts in lat. 28° 18′ N. that course was sailed on with a light

breeze

breeze until four o'clock P. M. when we were becalmed. At eight o'clock P. M. a light breeze from the
east, made sail to the west, in order to get clear of the
Stream, which north of Cape Carnaveral sets north-east-
erly. At ten o'clock P. M. becalmed.

28th. At one o'clock A. M. a light breeze from the
north: made sail to the west. Just after sun rise had
soundings in eighteen fathoms on red shells: at this
circumstance I was not a little surprised, as red shells
are not met with much north of Cape Carnaveral, and
as we had evidently been drifting seven or eight hours
in the Stream, it was taken for granted that we were
north of the Cape, eight or nine leagues. Continued
west; kept the lead going, and gradually shoaled to
ten fathoms, when land was seen from the mast head:
the same course was continued until we had seven fathoms water, and a point of land to the north ; bottom
still red shells. Our latitude at that place by a good
observation was 28° 14'. Our course west, was continued until the observation was worked, when we had
10 fathoms and muddy bottom. It was then certain
that we had passed over the southern part of the Cape
shoal, and that the point of land to the north, was the
Cape itself. From this it appears evident, that after
leaving the Gulf Stream, we must have fallen into a
strong counter current setting southerly, having made
but two minutes northing in twenty-four hours, seven
or eight of which we were driving northerly with the
Stream. A case of the same kind I find related by
Mr. De Brahm. These currents on the coast baffle
all calculation, and doubtless occasion the loss of many vessels, for which the masters are unjustly censured.

Becalmed from one o'clock P. M. until seven, when
we had a brisk breeze from the S. W. made sail to the
east for three hours, in order to clear the dangerous
shoal

shoal off the Cape, and then stood north until midnight.

29th. From midnight until two o'clock A. M. stood N. W. to regain the coast; but the wind then shifted to the N. W. and became so violent that we hove to under the double reefed fore-sail. At day light, to our mortification, we found ourselves in the Gulf Stream. At noon our latitude appeared to be 29° 2′ N. In the afternoon the vessel shipped a sea which parted the lashing of one end of our boat, and nearly carried it off the deck, broke one of the stanchions, and injured the hand rails; handed the fore-sail, and laid to under the balanced main-sail.

30th. The gale still continued with great violence, and the appearance of the sea was truly alarming, and though our vessel laid to with ease, and laboured but very little, the main deck was constantly covered with water, and the seas broke over us with such rapidity for some hours that I was seriously apprehensive of foundering.

By a good observation found our latitude to be 30° 10′ N. from which it appears that we made 1° 8′ northing during the preceding twenty-four hour whilst laying to against a violent N. W. gale, in which, had it not been for the stream, our drift to the S. E. could not have been less than 1 1-2 miles per hour.

About three o'clock in the afternoon the wind shifted to the north, and became less violent. At eight o'clock in the evening John Ransom the vessel's cook died, after about two weeks illness: he was a soldier in the revolutionary army of the United States, and continued in the service of his country, until discharged on account of his age at Loftus's Heights on the Mississippi. From thence he descended the river to New Orleans, to procure if possible by his labour a scanty

pittance

pittance for the remainder of his days under a despotism, after devoting the prime and vigour of his life in assisting to establish the freedom and independence of the United States! At New Orleans I took him into employ through charity, and to gratify his wishes to return and die in the land of liberty for which he had fought.

About nine o'clock P. M. the wind had fallen so much, that we were able to make sail to the west under the gib, and double reefed main-sail. This night we had ice upon the decks.

December 1st. Wind shifted to the N. E. but very light, continued our course west. At ten o'clock A. M. committed the body of John Ransom to the sea.

By a good observation our latitude was found to be 30° 50′ N. Becalmed in the afternoon. Light breezes from various quarters during the evening, but generally from the southward, and we were not able to make good our course to the west.

2d. Soundings at two o'clock A. M. in eighteen fathoms, the bottom black and white sand, with some brown shells. The whole of this day we had a gentle breeze from the S. W. At ten o'clock A. M. soundings in ten fathoms water, when land was seen from the mast head. By a good observation our latitude 31° 13′.

Not having the latitude of St. Mary's in any publication, but from a small mutilated chart it appeared to be about 31° N. it was therefore expected that our course would carry us to the north end of Cumberland Island, the wind not permitting us to lay more south. At four o'clock in the afternoon came to an anchor at the north end of St. Simon's Island in a good harbour. The satisfaction which the crew, and myself experienced on this occasion may be more easily conceived than expressed. We were now able to take a night's repose, free from those cares, and anxieties which must

ever

ever attend the reflecting mind in our past situation; exposed to the turbulence of the sea in a little vessel, having but two young illiterate sailors on board, along a dangerous coast with which we were all unacquainted, and experiencing three violent gales of wind, which we afterwards found had wrecked as many vessels, much better calculated to resist the fury of the winds, and billows than ours. So great was the dependence on observation, and so little on dead reckoning among the currents near the coast, that the log was never hove once during the passage.

My reason for being so minute in noting the results of the observations, and the direction of the winds, with the courses we steered after leaving Key Biscanio, was for the purpose of giving some idea of the velocity of the Gulf Stream, from a retrospect of which, it will appear that while we were in it from Key Biscanio, to about latitude 30° it must have set northerly from 4 to 5 1-2 miles per hour: but it may be necessary to observe, that it is not regular, it has frequently been found less and sometimes more.

The advantages to be gained by vessels taking the stream, which are sailing from the Gulf of Mexico northward, are too obvious to merit a single remark. From Key Biscanio, the course of the stream is a few degrees east of north, until it comes opposite to the shoal of Cape Carnaveral, from thence it forms a curve, still inclining more and more easterly to the shoals of Nantucket, and from thence, it is said, towards the Western Isles until it loses itself in the Atlantic.

In sailing south into the Gulf of Mexico, the stream should be avoided with as much care as it is sought for in the other case. The stream in its progress from the Florida Keys, forms three large eddies on the coast: the first is south of Cape Carnaveral, the second between
Capes

Capes Carnaveral and Hattaras, and the third between Cape Hattaras and Nantucket shoals. Such vessels as are sailing to the southward between the coast and stream, will frequently be benefitted by the eddy currents setting southerly. In taking this passage, it will be proper to give the shoals of both Cape Hattaras, and Cape Carnaveral good births; particularly the latter, which is said to extend eight leagues from the Cape, and so soon as they are cleared haul in a little for the land. In latitude 26° 30′ N. the stream passes near the land, and sometimes touches it. The passage between the stream, and coast was much used by small vessels, whilst the British nation held the Floridas.

The breadth of the Gulf Stream is somewhat uncertain, and has been differently estimated by different writers; but by taking a mean of the several determinations, it will probably be near the truth: Between Key Biscanio and the Bahama Banks, it is about fifteen leagues broad; in latitude 28° 30′ N. about 17. Opposite to Charles Town 20. Off the Capes of Virginia 31 and, in latitude 40° about 38 leagues broad. As the stream proceeds northerly and eastwardly, it is naturally increased in width, and diminished in velocity: But its velocity from various causes is considerably accelerated or retarded, and as those effects are produced by causes operating in a different part of the ocean, the changes in velocity are not subject to any regular calculation.

Various theories have been devised to account for the phenomenon of the Gulf Stream. By one, the Gulf of Mexico is considered as a great whirl-pool, occasioned by the water being thrown into it between the western extremity of the island of Cuba, and Cape Catoch by the trade winds, and tides, and thrown out by

by a rotatory motion between East Florida and the island of Cuba, where it meets with the least resistance.* By others it has been attributed to the water thrown into the Gulf of Mexico between the west end of Cuba and Cape Catoch, by the trade winds alone, and making its way out through the Gulf of Florida, where it is the least obstructed†.

The latter theory scarcely merits a discussion, for it must be evident that though the winds are for the most part easterly within the torrid zone, yet whenever calms happen in the West Indies, and south along the coast which are not uncommon, the water must recede back to restore equilibrium, and not only cease to be pressed into the Gulf of Mexico, but rush out where it had before been pressed in, and an equilibrium take place between the Gulf and the Ocean, which is never the case.

The first theory appears to be correct in part, for it is impossible upon any principle of hydrostaticks, to account for the Gulf Stream without admitting a rotatory motion of the waters; but the centre of this rotatory motion is no more in the Gulf of Mexico, than the earth is in the centre of the solar system, and one is not more absurd than the other. I had an opportunity of examining the coast of the Gulf of Mexico from the out-let of Lake Pontchartrain, to Florida Point, and neither the currents, nor any other appearance would justify a supposition that the Gulf had any more similitude to a whirl-pool, than our lakes which are supplied with water at one place, discharge it at another.

It will be evident upon a moment's reflection, that the vast body of water carried northerly and easterly

by

* Transactions of the American Philosophical Society, vol. 1. page 252, first edition, and the account of M. Gauld's Surveys, page 22.
† See Directions for Sailing through the Gulf Passage, page 25.

by the Stream, must in some manner be returned southerly and westerly : if this be taken for granted, it follows of course, that the Atlantic Ocean, or a part of it, must have a rotatory motion about some centre within itself.

By admitting this circular motion in the water of the Atlantic, and though this motion be but small, it will nevertheless in a great degree be sufficient to account for the phenomenon of the Gulf Stream.

The water in its circular, or rotatory motion, is thrown upon the coast of America a little north of the equator, where from its centrifugal or projectile force, it becomes a little elevated, and still being carried along the coast northerly and easterly, on which the water continues from the same cause to be thrown, and at length meets with another body somewhat elevated, and upon the same principles carried westerly along the southern coast of the island of Cuba, until at length this column of water so united, and thus set in motion, constantly contracted in width, and proportionably elevated above the true level of the sea, is brought as it were to a focus between the western extremity of Cuba and Cape Catoch, where it discharges itself into the Gulf of Mexico, which serves as a great reservoir, and contributes to the uniformity of the Gulf Stream. The water thus thrown into the Gulf of Mexico, issues out between East Florida, and the eastern part of the island of Cuba and the Bahama Banks, where the water of the Ocean is less elevated.

The quantity of water thrown into the Gulf of Mexico, is no doubt considerably increased and diminished by the different courses of the winds and calms ; but never so much diminished as to render the velocity of the Gulf Stream inconsiderable ; which would certain-

ly

ly be the consequence if the cause depended immediately on the winds.

Whether the general rotatory motion of the water in
the Atlantic is effected wholly by the action of the
trade winds, or combined with the tides, and other
causes, is a subject which yet remains to be determined:
but this is certain, the motion must be constant, though
not necessarily uniform to produce the effect.

Several writers have remarked that the water of the
Gulf Stream is five or six degrees, (and sometimes
more), of Farenheit's thermometer warmer than the
adjoining water in the Atlantic, and between the Stream
and our coast. This is certainly true, and thereby
furnishes an easy method for seamen who are accommodated with those useful instruments to determine
when they are in the Stream.

This difference of temperature arises from the water
in the stream remaining a considerable time near the
equator, and then flowing with rapidity into a colder
climate, and though as it proceeds northward, it continues to lose its heat, it is nevertheless passing through
water which still becomes colder, as it advances north :
so that the relative difference continues nearly the same
for a great distance. The difference which I generally found between the water in the Stream, and the eddy
water on the coast, was about seven degrees.

It has been supposed by some ingenious writers, that
because, after leaving the Stream, and having soundings on our coast and a diminution in the heat of the
water about the same time, it followed of course, that
the water on soundings and banks is always colder
than the adjoining. Though this may constantly be
the case on our coast, it is probable the conclusion
ought to be considered a particular, and not a general
one. On our coast the Stream passes nearly along the

M m   great

great bank of soundings, it is therefore very natural to suppose, that soon after leaving the Stream, you will have soundings, and be in one of the large eddies on the coast whose waters being nearly stationary, and therefore colder than that moving with rapidity from the southward. Again, it may be observed that the adjoining water in the Atlantic without the Stream is also colder, as well as that on soundings; but on the contrary fathomless. Hence the difference in this case, does not appear to depend upon the depth of the water, but upon the current setting rapidly from a warmer into a colder climate. From this a conclusion may very fairly be drawn, that the sudden changes found in the temperature of the water in the ocean, are more immediately the effects of currents, than of banks and soundings; but as those currents are generally near coasts, and frequently occasioned by them, the thermometer may be considered a good monitor.

It has been mentioned by Dr. Franklin, that the water of the Gulf Stream does not sparkle in the night*. This, so far as my observations go, is incorrect: I saw little or no difference between that and the other water on the coast; but if there was any, that of the Gulf Stream was the most sparkling and luminous: It may however be observed, that the same water is very different, at different times in this respect.

The same ingenious writer and philosopher, likewise observes, that the Gulf weed is a sign of being in the Stream. This is in part true, but by no means to be considered a general rule, because the water on the borders of the Stream, is constantly mixing with the adjoining water, and leaving some of the weed behind, which consequently falls into the eddy currents, and is carried off many leagues: we met with it on soundings,

* Transactions of the American Philosophical Society, page 316.

soundings, in the eddy current, setting southerly.
These remarks cannot effect the character of Dr.
Franklin, either as a writer or philosopher: his character is formed of materials which will elude the de-
stroying hand of time itself, and will be revered so
long as liberty and science command the affections and
esteem of mankind. I merely think the Doctor was
mistaken, and conceive it my duty to state facts.

December 3d. Sent our boat to the island to procure
some provision, and obtain information relative to the
in-land passage to St. Mary's. By the return of the
boat, we were informed that there was a good, and
safe in-land passage to St. Mary's; but that we should
have to employ a pilot. In the afternoon, the wind
serving, we sailed into a large opening which we supposed led into the Sound.

4th. Before sun rise despatched the commissary
Mr. Anderson to the village on St. Simon's to employ
a pilot. A severe storm, with cold rain all the afternoon, and night.

5th. Clear all the afternoon with a strong gale from
the S. W. In the evening the commissary returned
with a pilot.

6th. The pilot removed the vessel into a harbour
much less secure than where he found it. A heavy
storm all night.

7th. Got under way, but the pilot soon run the vessel aground between two good channels. At low water we had but eight inches at our stern, and exposed
on one side to the sea. Finding the pilot extremely
stupid, and unacquainted with the channels, as soon as
the tide rose, and the vessel was afloat, we moored into deeper water and came to an anchor. My own
people then went, sounded the bar, and staked out the
channel.

8th.

8th. Wind fair, weighed anchor, crossed the bar, and entered a branch of the Alatamaha which is connected with, and forms a part of the in-land communication between Savannah and St. Mary's.

9th. Arrived at the village of St. Simon's, (properly Frederica,) about eight o'clock in the forenoon, and engaged another pilot. After engaging the pilot, I spent a few hours in examining the ruins of that once handsome and flourishing town; which during the whole or part of Gen. Oglethorpe's administration was the seat of the colonial government of Georgia.

The town of Frederica, as nearly as I could judge, appeared to have been regularly laid out, that is, the streets at right angles to each other, and the whole surrounded by a wall of earth, except that part lying immediately on the water,* which was defended by a small battery of tabby work, (as it is called in that country,) which is a composition of broken oyster shells and lime. The walls of the principal houses in the town were also of the same composition. The appearance is similar to rough-cast, and some of the walls seemed as solid as though they had been cut out of a rock.

The town was destroyed during our revolutionary war with Great Britain, and it is probable that it will not be rebuilt for many years to come: at present the population does not exceed twenty families.

The seat of Gen. Oglethorpe, the Governor, and protector of the colony in its infancy, was on St. Simon's Island, and not far from the town of Frederica. Although the character and services of Gen. Oglethorpe, do not appear to be sufficiently appreciated, the monuments of his industry will long continue to do him that justice which his country denied him. While his time

* One of the mouths or branches of the Alatamaha.

time was employed either in defeating the Spaniards, (by whom his little colony was several times invaded,) erecting forts, joining the meandering waters in the low flat country by canals, to render the communication more expeditious, and certain, and otherwise in crossing the value and consequence of his government, he was assailed both at home and abroad, by a host of complainers, and fault-finders, who having no intrinsic worth of their own, felt a pleasure in endeavouring to lessen that of others: And as it is much easier to find fault than to plan and execute, the illiberal, idle, and envious will ever be found attacking distinguished worth, industry, and talents, and too often be attended to, and patronized by those whose stations in government ought to render them inaccessible to the tongue of detraction, slander, and obloquy.

At half an hour after twelve o'clock, the tide serving, we left Frederica and arrived at St. Mary's at half past six the same evening. This passage was one of the quickest ever known. At St. Mary's we had the satisfaction of meeting with our companions, who came through the wilderness from the mouth of Flint River by land: their journey was tedious and disagreeable, on account of the autumnal rains then prevailing.

CHAP.

CHAP. X.

*Encamp at Point Peter and set up the instruments—
Provisions scarce—Observations on East Florida—
Provisions from New Orleans captured—Proceed
higher up the St. Mary's, and encamp near Okefonoke
swamp—Alligators, some particulars respecting them
—Astronomical observations completed—The river
St. Mary's described and the proper positions for mi-
litary works on the Mississippi, &c. pointed out—
Strictures on those already erected and on the state of
military science in the United States—Botanical list—
Conclusion.*

WHEN I arrived at the town of St. Mary's, the
effects of Mr. Bowles's return to the Creek nation was not known, in consequence of which a messenger was immediately despatched to our agent Col.
Hawkins, to obtain some information on that head, before we ventured to proceed into the country to determine the source of the St. Mary's River.

Finding that I could not obtain quarters in the town
for myself and people, free of expense to the public,
I removed on the 12th to Point Peter, and encamped
in a forest of live oak, where a number of people were
engaged in cutting ship timber for the United States:
the offal wood served us for firing. This system I
pursued from the time I left Pittsburg in the year 1796,
until my return to Philadelphia in the year 1800; and
whatever attention, and shelter the men might require,
I occupied no quarters myself at the expense of the
public.

After we had encamped, the instruments were unpacked, and set up, and a course of observations, and
some mathematical operations begun, which will be
found in the Appendix.

We

We found provisions in that part of Georgia very high and scarce, and many of the inhabitants were importing corn, and other necessaries of life for their own consumption : from this circumstance we kept but a small supply by us, being in daily expectation of receiving *that load from New Orleans, about which I had spoken to Lieut. Wooldridge and Mr. Bowles, when at St. George's island, and who had pledged their honour not to detain it, if it fell in their hands.*

I shall now proceed to make a few observations relative to East Florida.

East Florida is but little better than a wilderness, the soil is not superior to that of West Florida, and none of its navigable waters rising in the United States, it does not appear equally interesting. It is nevertheless of immense importance to the United States, being from its pecular situation, well calculated to give security to the commerce between the Atlantic and western states, and may be considered one of the main keys to the trade of the Gulf of Mexico. On the west side, it affords two remarkably fine harbours : one is known by the name of Hillsborough Bay, (Bay Tompa, or Spirito Santo.) The latitude is stated to 27° 36′ N. and the longitude 83° west from Greenwich. It is very capacious, and will admit any vessel over the bar not drawing more than twenty-four feet water.

The first Englishman who explored, and gave an account of this bay was a Capt. Braddock, who commanded a privateer from Virginia, and cruized on the west coast of East Florida, in the years 1744 and 1745 : his survey is yet considered as good as any extant.

The other harbour is called by the Spaniards Boca Grande, and by the English Charlotte Harbour, and stated to lay in latitude 26 43 N. and 82° 30′ west
longitude

longitude from Greenwich. It has fifteen feet water on the bar, and good anchorage within. Exclusive of those harbours, there are several others well calculated for coasting vessels, that draw not more than seven feet water; but their situations are so badly determined, that an enumeration of them would be unnecessary.

The Florida Keys and reef, likewise furnish a great number of harbours proper for coasting vessels, and advantageous stations for cruizers; particularly that of Key Biscanio, situated at the northern entrance of the reef, and capable of commanding the whole coasting trade which should take that passage. This being the entrance of the reef, and the most proper place to depart from in sailing northerly, would be one of the most eligible positions on the whole coast, and perhaps on the continent for a light house.

But instead of any advantage being derived, either to the United States or his Catholic Majesty, from those favourable situations, they serve as dens and hiding places for the privateers and pickaroons of the Bahama islands, by which the trade of both nations has suffered immensely in spoliations: and extraordinary as it may appear, it is no less true, that nearly the whole coast of East Florida, so far as maritime possession gives a right, is under the dominion of the Bahama islands. The coast and islands being uninhabited even by a single solitary settler from Apalachy, almost round to St. Augustine! from which the inhabitants of the Bahama islands cut and carry off, without interruption, as much of the valuable ship timber as they find necessary or convenient.

On the east side of the coast south of St. Augustine, there are a number of small harbours, proper for coasting vessels; but their positions are too badly determined to entitle them to attention.

We

We have not at this time, one chart of the coast of East Florida, except Mr. Gauld's survey of a part of the keys and reef, entitled to any confidence. The making a survey of the eastern side of it, was submitted by the British government, while his Britannic Majesty was in possession of that country, to M. de Brahm, and the west side to Mr. Gauld; but the labours of those gentlemen have never been communicated to the public! An accurate knowledge of the dangerous shoal off Cape Carnaveral, is of great consequence to the commercial interest of the United States. It frequently happens that those places, which from the want of a competent knowledge of them are avoided, when critically examined, will be found to afford places of safety, and good harbours, for such vessels as are driven upon them by bad weather. Such was the case with the Dry Tortugas until examined by Mr. Gauld.

The discovery of East Florida is generally attributed to Juan Ponce de Leon in 1512; but it is probable the eastern coast was discovered about fifteen years before that time by Sebastian Cabot.*

After the coast of East Florida had been discovered by Juan Ponce de Leon, the country was visited by a number of adventurers; but the first patent was obtained by Francis de Geray, who did not live to take possession of the province.† Francis de Geray was succeeded by Luke V. de Allyon, who visited Florida about the year 1524, and was succeeded by Pamphilo de Narvaez in 1528, or 1529, who died on the coast, and was succeeded by that celebrated adventurer Ferdinando de Soto; who traversed both the Floridas, and part of our western country from the year 1539, to

N n   1542,

* Hakluyt's voyages.
† Oglevy's history of America.

1542, and died at the forks of the Red River, or as some writers state on the Mississippi.*

The first permanent settlement in East Florida, was attempted by some French protestants in the year 1562, to secure to themselves a retreat from religious persecution. But as soon as the king of Spain received an account of the commencement of this infant settlement, he despatched Don Pedro Malendez de Aviles, into East Florida, with a considerable force to destroy it, which he effected in a most cruel and barbarous manner, in the year 1565,† and established a colony at St. Augustine.

For this service, it appears that Malendez obtained a grant for all Florida, which grant included the whole coast on the Gulf of Mexico, and as far north and east as Newfoundland; to which was added a number of privileges, for which he was to perform some signal services : one was to make a chart of the coast of Florida for the use of the Spanish navigators who visited those seas, but this service was never performed. Neither does it appear, that any measures were taken for that purpose until about 1718, when Don Gonzales Carrenza, the principal pilot of the Spanish flota undertook it, but his observations remained in manuscript, and were little known, until published in London in the year 1740 : they are however very imperfect.

In 1586 St. Augustine the capital of the province was taken and pillaged by sir Francis Drake, and in 1665 it was again taken and plundered by Capt. Davis, who headed and commanded a body of Buccaneers. In 1702 an expedition was carried on against it by Col. Moore, Governor of Carolina; his force consisted of five hundred English troops, and seven hundred Indians, with whom he besieged the city for three months

* Roberts's account of the first discovery of Florida.
† Charlevoix Historie de Nouvelle France.

months without success, and then retired. Except those incidents, the history of East Florida from the settling the colony in 1565, is little more than a succession of Governors, until Gen. Oglethorpe took possession of Georgia, which circumstance excited considerable jealousy at the court of Madrid, and a large force was sent against him, which he not only defeated, but after various encounters carried his conquests to the gates of St. Augustine, and laid siege to that city in 1740; but being badly supplied with almost every article necessary to give success to such an undertaking, he was obliged to relinquish his design.

By the peace of 1763, the Floridas were ceded to his Britannic Majesty George the third; but who in consequence of the ill advised war he made upon his American colonies, now the United States, and which involved France, Holland and Spain in the contest, was reduced to the necessity in 1783 of acknowledging the colonies independent states, and restoring the Floridas to his Catholic Majesty, who yet retains them.

Notwithstanding the early discovery of East Florida, the interior of it yet remains but little known, and uninhabited, except by the wandering Creeks or Seminoles. It cannot therefore be expected as the Indian trade is now of little importance, that his Catholic Majesty can draw any advantage from the province, to compensate for the expense he is at in supporting the government at St. Augustine.

On the 10th of January 1800, I received a letter from Mr. Panton, informing me, " that when our provision arrived at Pensacola from New Orleans, it was discovered that the vessel was in bad condition, and the master unacqainted with the coast, he thought it prudent to have the loading taking taken out, discharge the vessel and hands, and forward the provision after

us

us in his own vessel the Shark, which was unfortunately captured somewhere on the coast; but by whom he knew not." This was the same vessel loaded with provision, that joined us at Matacombe as already related, and from which we were not able to obtain one single pound of meat, though it is now certain the provision was our own, and captured contrary to an express stipulation between Lieut. Wooldridge, Mr. Bowles and myself.

Upon the receipt of the letter above mentioned, orders were immediately given to the contractor, to lay in a quantity of provision sufficient to serve the whole party, (including the military,) while ascending the St. Mary's river, and employed in ascertaining its source and geographical position.

On the same day that I received the letter from Mr. Panton, I also received one from our agent Col. Hawkins, in answer to mine from St. Mary's, by which it appeared, that he had not then understood how Mr. Bowles was received by the Creeks, and therefore prudently declined giving any opinion respecting the further prosecution of our business.

On the 19th the observations at Point Peter were closed, and the instruments taken down and packed up.

The 23d we left the town of St. Mary's, and proceeded up the river as far as it was navigable for the United States Schooner, and then made use of canoes until an end was put to our navigation on the 6th of February by drift wood, logs and other impediments.

Part of our journey up the river, after leaving the schooner and taking to canoes was extremely disagreeable, owing to bad weather, cold rains, and the wet marshy ground on which we encamped.

February

February 7th, we began our observatory, and sent a party to examine whether there was any communication between the river and Okefonoke Swamp, which after our arrival at St. Mary's to our surprise, we found doubtful. The same day a number of canoes were sent down to the vessel to bring up some of our instruments and other articles, we were under the necessity of leaving behind.

On the 12th the instruments and other articles arrived, and a course of observations was began as soon as the weather permitted. In the evening the party that was sent to explore the source of the river, or its communication with the Okefonoke Swamp returned; but without making any satisfactory discovery, and the day following another party was despatched on the same business.

This being the season that the Alligators, or American Crocodiles were beginning to crawl out of the mud and bask in the sun, it was a favourable time to take them, both on account of their torpid state, and to examine the truth of the report of their swallowing pine knots in the fall of the year to serve them, (on account of their difficult digestion,) during the term of their torpor, which is probably about three months. For this purpose two Alligators of about eight or nine feet in length were taken and opened, and in the stomach of each was found several pine and other knots, pieces of bark, and in one of them some charcoal; but exclusive of such indigestible matter, the stomachs of both were empty. So far the report appears to be founded in fact: but whether these substances were swallowed on account of their tedious digestion, and therefore proper during the time those animals lay in the mud, or to prevent a collapse of the coats of the stomach, or by accident owing to their voracious manner of devouring their food, is difficult to determine.

The

The Alligator has been so often, and so well described, and those descriptions so well known, that other
attempts have become unnecessary. It may nevertheless be proper to remark, that so far as the human species are concerned, the Alligators appear much less
dangerous, than has generally been supposed, particularly by those unacquainted with them. And I do
not recollect meeting with but one well authenticated
fact of any of the human species being injured by them
in that country, (where they are very numerous,) and
that was a negro near New Orleans, who while standing in the water sawing a piece of timber, had one of
his legs dangerously wounded by one of them. My
opinion on this subject is founded on my own experience. I have frequently been a witness to Indians,
including men, women and children, bathing in rivers
and ponds, where those animals are extremely numerous, without any apparent dread or caution: the same
practice was also pursued by myself and people, without caution, and without injury.

Some of the Alligators we killed were very fat, and
would doubtless have yielded a considerable quantity
of oil, which is probably almost the only use that will
ever be made of them; however their tails are frequently eaten by the Indians and negroes, and Mr. Bowles
informed me that he thought them one of the greatest
of delicacies.

The Alligators appear to abound plentifully in musk,
the smell of which is sometimes perceptible to a considerable distance, when they are wounded or killed; but
whether the musk is contained in a receptacle for that
purpose, and secreted by a particular gland or glands,
or generally diffused through the system appears somewhat uncertain: and I confess their appearance was so
disagreeable

disagreeable and offensive to me, that I felt no inclination to undertake the dissection of one of them.

The second party which had been sent to ascertain the connexion, (if any,) between the river St. Mary's and the Okefonoke Swamp returned on the 17th, having discovered the communication, and the day following a traverse was began, to connect the observatory with that part of the Swamp from whence the water issued, in order to determine its true geographical position. For the whole operation, with the observations see the Appendix.

On the 25th the observations were closed, and a large mound of earth thrown up at the observatory.

The 26th Capt. Minor his Catholic Majesty's commissioner and myself, with a party of labourers went to the Swamp, and the day following had a mound of earth thrown up on the west side of the main outlet, and as near to the edge of the Swamp as we could advance on account of the water. The next day we proceeded down to the vessel, and arrived at the town of St. Mary's on the 3d of March.

The astronomical part of the boundary between the United States and his Catholic Majesty, being now completed, it only remained to make out the report, with the maps or charts of the line. As a proper place for doing this business, we agreed to go and encamp on the south end of Cumberland island, where fire-wood could be had without any expense to the public, and where we could be more retired and less interrupted by company. Agreeably to this plan, we left the town of St. Mary's on the 6th day of March and encamped. The instruments were likewise unpacked and set up, that no opportunity should be lost for determining with precision, every important point on the coast, where our residence for a few days became necessary.

necessary. These observations with the results are the last in the Appendix.

I shall now proceed to make some observations relative to the St. Mary's River, and the proper positions for military works within the United States on the Mississippi, and along the boundary from that river to the Atlantic ocean.

The main branch of the river St. Mary's, which is part of the southern boundary of the United States, has its source in the Okefonoke Swamp, from whence the water issues along several small marshes or drains,* which soon unite in one. This Swamp which is also said to be the source of the river St. John's,† which falls into the Gulf of Mexico, is certainly very large, though much less than has generally been supposed: it is watered by a vast number of small streams and drains, which generally rise within its vicinity. Exclusive of two rivers, it has also been the source of a number of ridiculous and fabulous stories.‡

The river St. Mary's is at all times navigable for topsail vessels as high as Trader's Hill, and would be from thence up almost to the Swamp for boats and canoes, when the water is moderately high, were it not for logs, drift wood and rafts, which in many places extend across the stream. A large branch of the river comes in from the west, above the place where we encamped and built our observatory, which is marked in the map. The river is extremely crooked, and a large proportion of its banks are annually inundated. The upland is generally of an inferior quality, producing little besides wire-grass, pitch-pine, (pinus) and broom pine, (pinus palustris). I shall now proceed to note the positions for military works.

There

* These drains are sometimes quite dry.
† Another of the same name falls into the Atlantic between St. Mary's and Augustine.
‡ For one of them see Morse's Geography.

There are several places on the Mississippi between the mouth of the Ohio and southern boundary of the United States, that would answer very well for military establishments; but the best appear to be at the Chickasaw Bluffs, Walnut Hills, and Loftus's Heights. At one of the three Bluffs above the Chickasaw Bluffs, but I cannot recollect which, a fort might be advantageously erected. Fort Prudhome (or Prud'homme,) was built upon the middle one.

It will be difficult to erect works on any part of the Mississippi, below the mouth of the Ohio, that will prevent the descent of troops. The rapidity of the water, and width of the river, will enable a boat with some exertion to pass any of the forts with but little, if any damage, and there is no place where a cross fire could be brought to bear with much advantage: but the ascent of boats and gallies is so slow, that a few pieces of artillery well directed and served, would stop the progress of any vessel employed on the river.

On the Pearl or Half-Way River, a very short distance above the boundary is a commanding eminence, where a fort might be erected that would easily prevent the ascent of such boats and periaguas, as would be proper for that navigation.

My knowledge of the Pascagola is too limited to justify an opinion, but from its distance both from the Pearl and Mobile rivers, and direct communication with the Gulf of Mexico, added to its magnitude, I should suppose it worthy of as much, if not more attention than the Pearl river.

The Mobile, Tombeckby and Alabama Rivers, are at this time of much more importance to the United States than all the other waters between the Mississippi river and the Atlantic ocean: being the only rivers which are navigable for square rigged vessels from the

O o   Gulf

Gulf of Mexico, into that part of the United States, lying on the north boundary of West Florida. But exclusive of this consideration, there is another, which arises from the lands on those rivers being already partially settled, and at this time the most vulnerable part of the Union.

The position of Fort Stoddard, on Ward's Bluff below the confluence of the Tombeckby and Alabama rivers, is a very proper one, but the works are neither sufficiently extensive nor strong, to oppose an enemy possessed of artillery, and so long as his Catholic Majesty holds West Florida, so long will it be necessary for the United States to be formidable in that quarter.

Any works on the Coenecuh river will be unnecessary for some time to come, there being no inhabitants on it to protect, nor a sufficient number of Indians residing on its waters, to make that trade worth attending to. About one mile and an half above the boundary on the east side of the river, there is a place where a trader formerly resided, that would answer tolerably well for a small military establishment.

At the confluence of the Chattahocha and Flint rivers, the ground is swampy, and annually inundated, and therefore unfit for military works: but there are some Bluffs on the east side of the Chattahocha, which begin about one mile and three quarters above the mouth of Flint river, where works might be advantageously erected.

On the St. Mary's river we have two military establishments, one at Colerain, and the other at the mouth of the river on Point Peter. Neither of them ever have, or will be of any advantage, either in protecting our trade, or adding to the security of our citizens: they possess neither advantage in situation, merit in design, nor strength in the execution. If a fort up the river

were

were at any time necessary, the proper situation would have been at Trader's Hill. In fixing upon Colerain, the maxim, that the interest of an individual is to yield to that of the community, has evidently been reversed, and the interest of the nation has yielded to that of an individual; the same may in part be said of the position at Point Peter.

The plan of the fort at Point Peter, and the execution of the work are not only equally defective, but the very end,* or design of a fortification appears to have been overlooked; being even deficient as a demi-lune, to which it bears some faint resemblance, and covered by no other work. The embrasures are so injudiciously opened, that a vessel may come to an anchor opposite to one part of the work, and have sufficient room to ride to her cable, and not a single gun can be brought to bear upon her.

It may be objected, that the fortifications, (if they merit that term,) of the United States were merely intended to answer temporary purposes, and that there was no necessity of attending to that strength and accuracy in their construction, which would be proper in permanent works: this may be true, so far as it respects defence against Indians, for which purpose a block-house, surrounded with palisades is sufficient. But the case is widely different with scientific warlike nations, and the causes which rendered temporary works necessary against them, may so frequently recur, that permanent ones would in a few years be found the least expensive, and accord more nearly with the principles of national economy. On this subject one general, though

O o 2

* Le but de la fortification est de mettre un petit nombre d'hommes en état de résista à un plus grand. Il faut par conséquent dans l'attaque des places supplíer par le nombre de attaquans, aux avantages qui résultent de la fortification.

Traite de l'attaque des places par M. Le Blond.

though disagreeable remark will be sufficient: perhaps no civilized nation in the world, is as deficient in the knowledge of this important part of the art of war, as the United States.

An attempt was made during the administration of President Washington to form a military school, in which the scientific principles of fortification, and projectiles were to be taught; but the professorship, or command was given to a person ignorant of the common properties of a right lined triangle, and the institution naturally fell into contempt. In Europe great care is taken to select the best informed scientific characters, to fill the professorships in their military schools, not merely for the purpose of instructing such as are intended for officers, but to make useful citizens, and subjects; for it is certainly a truth, as well established as any mathematical deduction, that the arts, sciences, and literature are the pillars of civilization, and open the way to ease, plenty, and comfort, and without which man must in a short space of time, occupy his primitive state of barbarism, ignorance, distress, and perpetual want; and it is no argument against this general position to say, that those acquirements are useless, because a portion of mankind in all civilized countries, are rich, and comfortable without having any knowledge of them, for such persons, notwithstanding their deficiency in those branches of knowledge, nevertheless enjoy in common their share of the benefits. Being insensibly led into this digression, I shall now resume the original subject.

The situation selected by the very judicious Gen. Oglethorpe, on the south end of Cumberland Island, where he erected Fort William, appears to me the most eligible, and better calculated for a permanent work to give security to the harbour, and sound, than any other position about St. Mary's.

It

It will probably be expected by some readers, and gratifying to others, to have a list of the indigenous plants, shrubby, and herbaceous, to be met with on the Mississippi, along the boundary, and in the Floridas; but being an indifferent botanist, I am constrained to be very limited on that subject, and shall note but few productions, which did not attract my attention either for their use, quantity, beauty or singularity. To the popular names, those used by the botanists are added, in the manner practised by the ingenious, learned, and truly patriotic author of the Notes on Virginia.* The botanical name constantly follows the popular one, and is included within a parenthesis.

At the mouth of the Ohio, and down the Mississippi swamp, one of the prevailing species of timber is cotton-wood, (populus deltoides of Marshall,) it bears a very striking resemblance to the lombardy poplar, is equally quick in growth, open, soft, and porous. Black-willow, (salix nigra,) black-ash, (fraxinus nigra,) sugar maple, (acer saccharinum,) but not in great abundance, and becomes more scarce as you descend the river. I do not recollect seeing but one tree of it south of the boundary. Water maple, (acer negundo,) pec-can, (juglans illinoinensis,) this is met with as high as the Wabash, where it is not scarce, but becomes more abundant from thence down to the Gulf of Mexico. Papaw, (annona triloba,) I have eat of the fruit in great perfection as early as the 17th of July, in the Mississippi Territory. Button wood, or sycamore, (platanus occidentalis,) hickory, (juglans hickory of three species.) The cypress, (cupressus disticha,) begins to make is appearance about the Arkansas, and becomes

* This learned work alone is a sufficient evidence of the equality of the American genius with that of the old world, but which the writer of the Notes has established from other facts, contrary to the opinion of several celebrated European writers, particularly Mons. de Buffon.

becomes very abundant a little further south, and appears to be inexhaustible before you reach the 31st degree of north latitude. It occupies many parts of the swamp almost to the exclusion of any other timber. The cypress is a very useful wood, and generally used in that country for covering, flooring, and finishing buildings. It grows in swamps, marshes, and ponds, but not on high dry land. The stem, or body of the tree, generally rises from the apex of a large conical base, above which the workmen have frequently to erect scaffolds before they fall the tree. From the roots of the tree a number of conical excrescences grow up, which are called cypress knees, some of them are eight or ten feet high, and being hollow are used for bee-hives, and other purposes. The long moss, (tillandsia usneoides,) makes its appearance on the Mississippi nearly in the same latitude with the cypress, and almost covers some of the trees to which it is appended before you reach the Walnut-hills. This is a very useful article, and answers almost as well for beds, and mattrasses, as craped horse hair : it is nearly as elastic, and almost as incorruptible. Although this moss, is not like the misletoe immediately connected with the trees on which it hangs, it will not live long on a dead tree. Sweet bay, (laurus borbonia,) magnolia grandiflora : this most splendid, and beautiful tree, I do not recollect seeing above the Walnut-hills; but have no doubt of its growing much further north. It is common through all the rich lands of Natchez, and east to the Atlantic. The foregoing appear to be confined either to very wet, or very rich land, and will be met with in all such places along the boundary, and through the Floridas, with the exception of the peccan, sugar maple, and one or two others. The katalpa, (bignonia catalpa,) is not uncommon; but ap-,

peared

peared the most abundant on the banks of the Coenecuh. The nyssa aquatica, is common on the Chattahocha below the boundary. Exclusive of those plants,
which are generally confined to low, or very rich
grounds, the following will be met with in various
parts of the country. Sassafras, (laurus sassafras,)
which grows to a large size about the Natchez. Sweet
gum, (liquid-amber,) common swamp gum, (nyssa integrifolia,) holly, (ilex opaca,) in great abundance in
some parts of the Mississippi Territory, and frequently
becomes a large tree. Parsimon, (dyospyros virginiana,) very common. Locust, (robinia pseud-acacia,)
honey locust, (gleditsia triacanthos,) black walnut,
(juglans nigra,) elm, (ulmus americana,) dog wood,
(cornus florida,) red bud, (cercis canadensis,) mulberry, (morus rubra,) wild plum, (prunus chickasaw,)
tulip tree, (liriodendron tulipifera,) this is improperly
called *poplar* in the middle states. White oak, (quercus alba,) black oak, (quercus nigra,) swamp oak,
(quercus aquatica,) chesnut oak,(quercus prunus,)with
several other species, or varieties. Live oak, (quercus
virens,) this very useful timber is much confined to the coast, and a short distance from it. I do not
recollect seeing it in any considerable quantity in West
Florida, as far north as the boundary. Red cedar,
(juniperus virginiana,) this is likewise much confined
to the coast, and in some places very abundant. Pine,
(pinus,) broom pine, (pinus palustris,) with several
other species, or varieties ; the quantity inexhaustible.
Buck eye, (aesculus pavia,) this is sometimes con-
founded with the buck eye, (aesculus flava,) of the
Ohio ; they are not the same. Wild cherry, (prunus
virginiana,) great palmetto, or cabbage tree, (corypha
or palmitto of Walter,) cassina yapon, (ilex vomitoria,)
the black-drink used by the Creeks, and some other
                                                  Indian

Indian nations at their councils, and public meetings, is made by an infusion of the leaves of this shrub. Myrica inodora, (of Bartram,) from the berries of this shrub, the green wax used in making candles is collected: these two last are confined to the coast. Beech, (fagus ferruginea,) chesnut, (fagus americana,) chincopin, (fagus pumila,) some of them are sufficiently large in the Mississippi Territory to be split into rails. Spicewood, (laurus benzoin,) Bermudian mulberry, (callicarpa americana,) cane, (arundo gigantea of Walter,) extends through all parts of the Mississippi swamp, and occupies equally the high, as well as low land, from the Walnut-hills down the river to Point Coupee, and easterly from fifteen to twenty miles or more. The whole of that high, rich, hilly and broken tract of country, except where the farms are opened, may be considered one solid cane-brake, and is almost impenetrable; but will probably be destroyed in a few years by the cattle, hogs, and fires. Its general height is from twenty to thirty-six feet, though I have met with it on the tops of several hills forty-two feet high. The small cane, or reed, (arundo tecta of Walter,) begins to make its appearance on the boundary about twenty miles east of the Mississippi river, and with the arundo gigantea, or large cane, will be found on all the creeks and river bottoms, through to the Atlantic. The China root, (smilax China,) and passion flower, (passiflora incarnata,) are abundant in the rich grounds. The sensitive briar, (mimosa instia,) this beautiful and singular plant, is common to the poor, sandy land. Several species of that beautiful plant, the saracinia, are frequently met with in the margins of swamps, and low grounds: and three or four handsome species of the water dock, (nymphea,) poke, (phytolacca decandra,) sumack, (rhus,) several species. Along the water courses, and in the swamps where the land is good, several
species

species of well tasted grapes are found in great plenty. Many of the trees in the low grounds are loaded with a variety of vines, the most conspicuous of which are the creeper, or trumpet flower, (begnonia radicans,) and common poison vine, (rhus radicans,) misletoo, (viscum,) is in great abundance, and will be found attached to almost all kinds of trees. I have frequently observed it on peach and plum trees. In the middle states it is generally found on the common swamp gum, (nyssa integrifolia).

To those who want more information on this useful and important subject, I would recommend the perusal of Bartram's Travels, a work which contains much valuable botanical knowledge; but from some circumstances, unconnected with its real merit and design, has not met with that attention from the public, to which it is justly entitled.

Having now finished the account of our labours in establishing the southern boundary of the United States, I shall make a few observations on the prevailing diseases, that made their appearance while I was in the country which has been the subject of this journal.

The prevailing diseases on the lower part of the Ohio, on the Mississippi, and through the Floridas, are bilious fevers. They vary in their forms according to the state, or force of their remote and exciting causes: some seasons they are little more than the common intermittents, and remittents, which prevail in the middle states; but in others they are highly malignant, and approach nearly to, if not become the genuine yellow fever of the West Indies.*

P p   Although

* Gen. Sinclair who had the advantage of a medical education, and is moreover a gentleman of a discriminating mind, and distinguished talents, has assured me, " that he is well convinced the yellow fever is an endemick complaint in a large portion of our south-western country where he resided as Governor a number of years."

Although fevers are the prevailing diseases in the tract of country above mentioned, others are not uncommon, which though very different in their appearance, probably owe their origin to the same causes. In the summer of 1797, while our people were afflicted with bilious fevers, the Spanish soldiers in the same town were suffering with dysenteries, and which generally proved mortal. During the prevalence of those two diseases, our physician reported to me two cases of a genuine pleurisy, both of which yielded to bleeding. At that time, (and I yet see no reason to alter my opinion,) I supposed those different complaints had their origin from the same cause, and that their different appearance arose from accidental causes, such as difference of constitution or the manner of living. Our physician, who for nearly two months attended the Spanish soldiers, informed me that medicine had but little or no effect upon those labouring under the dysentery, and which I was afterwards informed by some intelligent Spanish gentlemen, was thought to be owing to the profuse use of stimulants, such as Cayenne pepper, by their soldiers in that country, which by its inordinate use destroyed the tone of the intestines, and rendered them insensible to the most active medicines.

It is probable that the first attack in each of those complaints was inflammatory, and had bleeding been resorted to in that stage, it would have been attended with salutary effects. The late Col. Clarke, of the Mississippi Territory was in that season attacked with a most violent fever, which in a few hours almost deprived him of his eye sight, and finding that no time was to be lost, and no medical aid to be had in his neighbourhood, he bled himself freely several times and recovered in a few days. This circumstance he has frequently mentioned to me, and attributed his recovery

to

to a paper of Dr. Rush's on the yellow fever, which he had read a short time before.

It did not appear to me during my residence in the country, that temperance by any means prevented the attacks of the fever, on the contrary the free livers frequently escape it, while the temperate suffer from it; but there is this difference to be observed, the temperate with good management generally recover, and on the contrary, the others when attacked commonly sink under the complaint in a few days. Several gentlemen of that class who were called free livers went into that country the same year I did; they escaped the fever two seasons, but sunk under it the third.

The natives, though not wholly exempted from those fevers, are much less subject to them than strangers. This no doubt arises from a very natural cause: the constitutions of the natives are accommodated to the climate from their infancy, while the constitutions of strangers being moulded to a different one, yield more readily to those diseases. For, although the human species can exist in all climates, the constitution appears to be naturally adapted to that in which the person is born, and raised, and therefore upon changing the climate, the constitution is generally found to change also, and this change, (which is called the seasoning,) is commonly effected by the prevailing endemick of the country. This change is very severe on the firm constitutions of our northern citizens, which like strong oaks in a tempest, are broken off or torn up by the roots, while weak constitutions like flexible reeds, yield to the tempest, and rise when the storm is over.

At Natchez, in the month of June 1797 we had a few cases of the fever among our people, but the complaint was not general until about the middle of July. The attacks were then severe, and one of my assistants, and several of our people were then carried off. Some

P p 2   of

of those who survived, were for several months extremely debilitated by frequent relapses, which appear to be almost unavoidable in that country : because it is to be observed, that the causes which produce a bilious fever in that climate, are of much longer continuance than in the middle and northern states, and the system consequently a longer time predisposed to yield to those causes.

As soon as our people recovered from the first attack, I had them removed about seven miles from the river in the country, and to prevent intemperance, and enforce regularity, I went and resided among them.

As those fevers frequently produce a langour, or partial lethargy which is generally removed by action, athletic exercises were encouraged, particularly playing ball, for which purpose a convenient ball-alley was prepared. The good effects of removing from the river, and the plan of exercise were soon visible in the recovery of the greater part of our people ; some however had relapses, which though generally not as severe as the first attack, they appeared to increase the difficulty of removing the complaint, and several of the cases terminated in viceral obstructions which with one exception yielded to mercurials. The unfortunate person was a Mr. Hamilton, whose case ended in a confirmed dropsy under which he sunk after we returned to Philadelphia in 1800.

During the prevalence of those fevers my own health was remarkably good, which in part I attributed to the use of some pills given to me by Dr. Rush when I left Philadelphia. I began to take them in the month of May, though very sparingly, until in July when I used them twice a week, from which I found no inconvenience,. and never lost a single meal by them; on the contrary my appetite was rather increased, and my flesh became more firm. Each of these pills was composed

posed of two grains of calomel, with half a grain of gamboge, combined by means of a little soap.

About the 20th of September the pills were exhausted, and it was the general opinion that the danger of an attack for that season was past: in conformity to this opinion I returned with our people on the 27th of the same month to the town of Natchez. I should have delayed our return for some weeks, but from a desire to be near my apparatus, and complete a course of astronomical observations which I had began soon after my arrival.

On the 7th day of October I became very much indisposed with shooting pains in my head, an oppression at my breast, but without any nausea, a pain in my bones, neck, and back, flushed countenance, with the appearance of a strong plethorick habit. These symptoms were quickly followed by a violent fever, which frequently rendered me delirious. From the strength and fullness of my pulse, affection of my head, and flushed countenance, I was of opinion that the commencement of the attack was highly inflammatory, and that bleeding would have been attended with salutary effects; but the strong prejudices against it in that part of the country prevented its being done. The fever began to abate in seven or eight days, but left me so much debilitated, that with several relapses, it was some months before my recovery was complete.

It is probable that if the pills had not been exhausted, and I had continued the use of them a few weeks longer, until the cool weather commenced, I should have escaped the attack that season.

Various theories have been devised by physicians to account for those malignant fevers which are the scourge of the human race, but the most natural appears to be that of supposing a portion of the system by some cause or other, to be rendered unfit for animal

mal life, and therefore obnoxious to the healthy part, which from a natural impulse is constantly endeavouring to expel the morbid matter, and which is probably thrown off by both the external and internal surfaces. If this theory be just, the best means of prevention appear to be gentle cathartics, and frequent cleansing the outward surface by bathing, and changing of the clothes, particularly such as come in contact with the skin. To this practice I attributed my escaping the fever during the time of its general prevalence. If the offensive matter is thrown out of the system as fast as it is generated, and removed from the surfaces, I am of the opinion that but little danger is to be apprehended; but if on the contrary, it is suffered to remain in the intestines, and on the external surface, and become entangled in foul clothes, the danger will be much increased.

The variety of diseases in our southern country is not so great as in the middle and northern states. The degree of cold in the southern states, and the Floridas, is not sufficient to make a complete change in the appearance of the prevailing diseases, or to generate those which may be considered endemick in cold countries. But it is different in the middle, and some of the northern states, which have not only a sufficient degree of heat, but such a continuance of it in some seasons, as to produce the malignant fevers of the southern states, and West Indies. The degree of cold with its continuance, is also sufficient in some winters, to produce those diseases which prevail most in cold countries, and hence a greater variety of diseases may naturally be expected.

It has been doubted by some, whether the climate of the middle, and some of the northern states, is capable of producing the malignant fevers of our southern states, and the West India islands; but those doubts would in my opinion be removed from the mind of any person, who should reside a few years in the latter, unless

unless he was previously wedded to a preconceived hypothesis, or supposed facts, and his mind entrammelled by prejudice.

A reluctance to admit truth, is little less injurious than the propagation of falshoods, and the longer we contend that the climate of the middle and some of the northern states, is incapable of generating the malignant fevers of the southern states, and West Indies, the longer we shall be in danger of suffering by those scourges; for while our measures are only taken to oppose a foreign enemy, a domestic one may begin its ravages. Experience teaches us that there are generally three things necessary to the production of the malignant southern fevers, *first* heat, *secondly* water, swamps or marshes, and *thirdly* a collection of persons. And whenever we have a long continuation of heat, aided by the miasmata from impure water, and marshes partially dry, loaded with putrid vegetables, added to a large collection of persons, each of whom by respiration is constantly rendering one gallon of air per minute unfit for the functions of animal life, we are in danger of being attacked by a malignant fever.

From the locality of those fevers in the United States, may not a conclusion be fairly drawn, that the cause, or causes, is, or are, in some degree local also? for if this were not the case, those fevers would not be confined to our large towns on the water, but extend generally over the face of the country; which is contradicted by experience. And again, if the fever had its origin from importation, why is it confined to particular places? The answer it is presumed would be, that in those places there is a greater predisposition from some exciting cause, whatever it may be, to receive the infection. Now let us see to what point this answer would conduct us. If in those places there is a greater predisposition to receive the infection, it follows, that this

predisposition

predisposition in some degree depends upon local causes: and if the causes which produce this predisposition to receive the infection, can from concurring circumstances be increased, may not a just and logical conclusion be drawn, that they may be so heightened, as to produce that species of fever which in a milder form they prepare the system to receive?

As those fevers appear evidently to depend in part upon local causes, the means of prevention will in an equal degree depend upon removing, or correcting those causes.

It is the opinion of many persons, that our large commercial cities would be materially injured, if they were thought capable of producing the malignant fevers of our southern country, and the West Indies. This opinion however plausible, certainly rests upon a slender foundation, because this opinion alone cannot prevent the recurrence of those fevers, and it must be the recurrence, whatever may be the origin, that will eventually be found injurious.

If those fevers can possibly be generated in our large commercial cities, in the middle and southern states, we may, as has already been observed, be attacked by a domestic enemy, while our measures are only taken to avoid a foreign one: And if it should be discovered that those fevers are not of domestic origin, it must be granted that from some cause or other, there is a greater predisposition to receive the infection in our large towns and villages, situated on our rivers, than in other places; an investigation of this cause would therefore be a subject of the highest importance, for in all probability the removing the cause would secure us against this scourge, so injurious to the interests, population, and happiness of our country.

On this part of the subject I should have been silent, had it not been to correct an opinion which I entertain-

ed

ed some years ago, that the climate of the middle states could not generate that species of the bilious fever commonly called the yellow fever; but from a residence of several years to the southward, where those malignant fevers frequently appear, I feel a strong conviction, that in the middle, and some of the northern states, there is both a sufficient degree of heat, and continuance of it some seasons, to generate those fevers in places situated in the neighbourhood of swamps, ponds of stagnate water, and in the midst of such filth, as will too frequently be found about large cities and towns.

The reports, with the maps of the boundary being completed on the 10th of April, we packed up our instruments and baggage, and on the 11th left Cumberland island, and sailed to the town of St. Mary's where we remained until our Commissary had finished his business at that place, which was on the 25th, when I again took the direction of the vessel, having but one sailor exclusive of two or three of our labourers who had came round Cape Florida with me. In the afternoon the wind serving, we left St. Mary's, and proceeded along the sound to the Plumb Orchard, where we were becalmed and come to an anchor.

The 26th we were becalmed great part of the forenoon, in the mean time I paid a visit to the family of the late Major General Green, who now resides on Cumberland island. Got under way about 11 o'clock A. M. and proceeded into St. Andrew's Sound, and attempted to cross the bar and put to sea; but having no pilot, and the passage appearing somewhat difficult, we returned and sailed into St. Simon's Sound, and come to an anchor.

27th. The wind serving about 8 o'clock in the morning we crossed the bar, put to sea, and laid our course for Tybee light-house. By a good observation found the latitude of the north end of St. Simon's

Q q   island

island to be about 31° 16′ 14″ N. A fresh breeze from the S. all the afternoon: about 5 o'clock P. M. spoke a schooner from Rhode-Island at anchor, she was at least 2½ leagues from land. About 9 o'clock in the evening we saw the light in the lantern of Tybee light-house. The wind almost died away, and we made but little way. A short time after midnight, the light in the lantern of the light-house went out.

28th. Very hazy in the morning, and almost calm. At 1 o'clock P. M. the mist was carried off by a smart breeze, when we found ourselves about one league from the light-house, and immediately made a signal for a pilot; but after waiting until half past 5 o'clock in the afternoon, and no pilot appearing, and the wind having become violent from the N. E. with a heavy sea, we took in the top sail, reefed the fore sail, and put to sea for fear of being driven on the coast and wrecked.

29th. Wind from the same quarter and very strong.

30th. Calm until 9 o'clock A. M. when we were favoured with a fine breeze from the S. By a good meridional observation found our latitude 31° 38′ 47″ N. Stood north until 3 o'clock P. M. when we saw the light-house: sailed to the bar, and crossed it about 6 o'clock in the evening, in company with a sloop the master of which was acquainted with the channel, and come to an anchor.

May 1st. The wind serving about 10 o'clock A. M. we sailed up to the city of Savannah, where our Commissary was employed until the 8th in settling some of his public accounts. In the mean time, the necessary arrangements were made for sending our schooner, which had been fitted up at New-Orleans, round to our newly established military post on the Mobile. Three reasons offered for this measure. *First*, the vessel was flat built, and particularly calculated for the

the coasting trade on the Gulf of Mexico. *Secondly*, the United States had no vessel for that important post, in consequence of which it was dependent on the subjects of his Catholic Majesty for the necessary supplies by water, and *thirdly*, the free navigation of the Mississippi alone had been secured by our late treaty with his Catholic Majesty, and no provision having been made for the uninterrupted use of the navigable rivers which rise in the United States, and fall into the Gulf of Mexico, between the Mississippi and East Florida. It was therefore expected, that by this measure, the free navigation of those waters would either be secured by usage to the citizens of the United States, or produce such an explanation as would effect that object.

Our Commissary having finished his business on the 8th, chartered a sloop belonging to New-York, for our passage to Philadelphia, and at 9 o'clock in the morning the pilot came on board, and we proceeded down to the light-house.

9th. Got under way at 7 o'clock in the morning, and were accompanied over the bar by the Revenue Cutter, after which she fired a salute and left us. The master of the sloop who was also the owner, had no other instruments on board than his compass, and two old Davis's quadrants, neither of which could be depended on for the latitude nearer than 15 or 20 minutes; he expressed a wish that I would make use of my instruments, and take part in the navigation of the vessel, so far as related to the courses, distances, latitude and longitude, to which I readily agreed. Our passage was a disagreeable one, owing to contrary winds, and sudden squalls; in one of which we were near losing our mast.

On the 10th we entered the Gulf Stream, and continued in it until by observation we found ourselves

north

north of Cape Hatteras, and then stood for Cape Henlopen; but the winds were so unfavourable that we did not make land until the evening of the 16th, when a pilot came on board. Early in the morning of the 17th we entered Delaware Bay, and having a good southerly breeze great part of the day, we reached Chester in the evening and come to an anchor.

18th. Got under way at 6 o'clock in the morning, the wind very light, and right a-head; come to an anchor at Fort Mifflin, and after having been examined by the Physician and Health-officer, were permitted to proceed; but the tide failing, we did not arrive at Philadelphia until 8 o'clock in the evening, when all the fatigues, hardships, and difficulties I had been exposed to during a long absence, were more than compensated by the pleasure I experienced in meeting my family in good health.

I cannot take leave of the different subjects of this journal, without acknowledging my obligations to that kind Providence, which preserved me from the dangers that have been described, and probably from many others unseen, and unknown, during a tedious absence from my family, friends, and native country; nor can I take a final view of a part of that extensive country I have traversed, without expressing the pleasure I enjoy in contemplating it, (in consequence of some late events,) as the future theatre of free governments, and of the rapid population, and national, and individual happiness that are connected with them. May the now peaceful shores of the Mississippi, never be made vocal with the noise of the implements of war, and may its waters never be dyed with human blood! ——With this wish, thanking my reader for his patience in looking over these pages, I bid him adieu.

APPENDIX.

APPENDIX.

APPENDIX.

THE following aſtronomical obſervations, &c. were made during my employ as commiſſioner for determining the ſouthern boundary of the United States. They appear in the ſame order, as publiſhed in the fifth volume, of the Tranſactions, of the American Philoſophical Society. The obſervations made at places where we were unavoidably detained, follow each other in regular ſucceſſion to preſerve uninterrupted, the order of thoſe made on the boundary. The obſervations made on the boundary, are preceded by an account of the apparatus made uſe of, a ſmall part of it was furniſhed by the Spaniſh government; and to the remainder the United States have but little claim.

The aſtronomical obſervations made at the confluence of the Miſſiſſippi, and Ohio rivers, the equal altitudes of the ſun at Natchez, with the obſervations made at New-Orleans, are entered according to the civil account, for the purpoſe of bringing the thermometrical obſervations into the journal, in the manner they are generally regiſtered.

Aſtronomical

Aftronomical, and Thermometrical Obfervations, made at the Confluence of the Miffiffippi, and Ohio Rivers.

1796.

Dec. 18th,   Arrived at the confluence of the Miffiffippi, and Ohio rivers about 2 o'clock in the afternoon.—Cloudy all day.—Thermometer 24° in the air at fun fet, and 34° in the water.

19th.   Pitched a tent, and fet the clock up in it.— Cloudy all day, except a fhort time about noon.—Thermometer by Fahrenheit's fcale 9° at fun rife, rofe to 19°; fell to 12° at fun fet, and to 11° at 9ʰ P. M.

20th.

Equal altitudes of the Sun.

A. M. 10ʰ 23′ 54″.   P. M. 1ʰ 37′ 37″.

Cloudy, except about 1½ hours before and after noon, which accounts for the equal altitudes not being taken farther from the meridian.— Cleared off in the evening.—Thermometer 11° at fun rife, rofe in the afternoon to 22°, fell to 11° at 9ʰ P. M.

Immerfion of the 3d fatellite of ♃ obferved at 9ʰ 8′ 47″ P. M. Magnifying power of the telefcope 120—♃ being very low, and attended with an uncommon tremour, which rendered the obfervation fomewhat doubtful.

21ft.   Flying clouds all day, but difappeared in the evening.—Thermometer 11° at fun rife, fell to 8° at 10ʰ A. M. rofe to 9° at noon, fell to 3° at 7ʰ P. M.

Emerfion of the 1ft fatellite of ♃ obferved at 6ʰ 56′ 0″ P. M. Atmofphere a little hazy.—Magnifying power of the telefcope 120.

The

The weather was fo intenfely cold, that although a pot of live coals was kept in the tent near the clock, the thermometer which was fixed to the cafe, fell to 4°, and the clock ftopped at 5ʰ the next morning.

22d.   Keen north wind; with fqualls of light fnow. —Clear in the evening.—Thermometer 5° below 0 at 8 o'clock A. M.—rofe to 1° above 0 at 2ʰ P. M.—fell 5° below 0 at 9ʰ P. M. —Both rivers on account of the vaft bodies of ice, thrown up in a variety of pofitions, make a romantic, and to us (on account of our boats) an alarming appearance.

23d.   Clear day. Wind from the N. W. Thermometer $7\frac{1}{2}°$ below 0 at 8ʰ A. M. 6° below 0 at 10ʰ A. M. 1° above 0 at noon, 8° at 2ʰ P. M. and at 8ʰ P. M. 7°.

24th.   Clear day. Thermometer 7° at 9ʰ A. M. —17° at 1ʰ P. M.—and 7° at 8ʰ P. M.

Traced a meridian by the circum-polar ftars.

25th.   Clear day. Thermometer 7° at fun rife, rofe in the afternoon to 17°. Applied the magnetic needle to the meridian, and found the variation to be 7° 15′ eaft.

Set up a fmall zenith fector of about 19 inches radius. Face to the eaft.

26th.   Cloudy in the afternoon. Thermometer 10° in the morning, rofe to 17°.

☉'s preceding limb on the meridian at .	11ʰ 59′ 45″
Subfequent do. at	12 2 9
Centre at	12 0 57

27th.

Dec. 27th.   Clear day. Thermometer 3° at fun rife, rofe to 33° in the afternoon.

⊙'s preceding limb on the meridian at	12ʰ	0′	33″
Subfequent do. at	12	2	57
Centre at	12	1	45

28th.   Clear day. Thermometer 8° at fun rife, rofe in the afternoon to 33°.

Equal altitudes of the Sun.
A. M. 9ʰ 40′ 2″.   P. M. 2ʰ 24′ 56″.

Emerfion of the 1ft fatellite of ♃ obferved at 8ʰ 48′ 38″ P. M. ♃ very low, the atmofphere hazy, and the belts fcarcely difcernible. Magnifying power of the telefcope 120.

29th.   Clear a fhort time about noon. Thermometer 17° at fun rife, rofe in the afternoon to 45°.

30th.   Cloudy with light fnow during the day.— Clear in the evening. Thermometer 32° in the morning, rofe to 35° in the afternoon.

31ft.   Cloudy in the evening and night. Thermometer 21° at fun rife, rofe in the afternoon to 45°.

Equal altitudes of the Sun.
A. M. 9ʰ 53′ 7″.   P. M. 2ʰ 16′ 25″.

Obferved zenith diftance of α Lyræ . 1° 37′ 23″ N.

1797.   Clear and calm in the morning, flying
Jan. 1ft. clouds in the afternoon.—From 10ʰ A. M. till noon, three fine luminous circles appeared in the atmofphere, fimilar to thofe defcribed

b   by

by Dr. Smith in his opticks*. Thermometer 21° at fun rife, rofe in the afternoon to 40°.

2d.   Cloudy with fnow the whole day.—Thermometer 16° at fun rife, rofe in the afternoon to 28°, and fell to 19° at fun fet.

3d.   Cloudy till noon, clear in the afternoon and evening. Thermometer 6° at fun rife, rofe in the afternoon to 18°, fell to 10° at 8ʰ P. M.

Obferved zenith diftance of α Cygni   .   7° 35′ 32″ N.
do.   .   .   β Andromedæ   2   25   38   s.
do.   .   .   .   β Medufæ   .   3   11   46   N.

4th.   Cloudy in the morning, the remainder of the day clear. Thermometer 12° at fun rife, rofe in the afternoon to 37°, fell to 16° at fun fet.

Equal altitudes of the Sun.
A. M. 9ʰ 26′ 36″.   P. M. 2ʰ 47′ 6.5″.

Obferved zenith diftance of α Cygni   .   7° 35′ 29″ N.

Turned the face of the Sector to the weft.

Obferved zenith diftance of β Andromedæ   2° 30′ 24″ s.
do.   .   .   β Medufæ   .   3   7   5   N.

5th.   Clear all day. Thermometer 23° at fun rife, rofe in the afternoon to 42°, fell to 30° at fun fet.

Equal altitudes of the Sun.
A. M. 9ʰ 42′ 21″.   P. M. 2ʰ 32′ 31″.

Obferved

* Book Second, Chap. 11th.

Obſerved the times, and diſtances of the ☽'s neareſt limb from that of the ☉ as follows :

	Times.			Diſtances.		
	h	'	''	o	'	''
P. M.	2	50	53	84	15	20
	2	52	56	84	16	0	Error of Sex-
	2	54	40	84	16	30	tant + 7''.
	2	58	43	84	18	20
Means	2	54	18	84	16	32

Obſerved zenith diſtance of α Lyræ	.	1° 33' 28'' N.
do. . . . α Cygni	.	7 31 19 N.
do. . . β Meduſæ		3 7 5 N.

6th.   Cloudy in the morning, clear in the after-noon.—Thermometer 24° at ſun riſe, roſe in the afternoon to 34°, fell to 12° at ſun ſet.

Obſerved zenith diſtance of β Meduſæ . 3° 7' 17'' N.

7th.   Clear day, wind N. W.—Thermometer 7° below 0 at ſun riſe, 5° below 0, at 9ʰ A. M. roſe to 19° in the afternoon, fell to 0 at ſun ſet.

Obſerved zenith diſtance of α Lyræ	.	1° 33' 37'' N.
do. . . α Cygni	.	7 31 27 N.
do. . . β Andromedæ	2	30 6 s.
do. . . β Meduſæ	.	3 7 17 N.

Turned the face of the Sector eaſt.

8th.   Clear day.   Thermometer 7° below 0 at ſun riſe, roſe in the afternoon to 29° above 0, fell to 10° at 7ʰ P. M.

Obſerved zenith diſtance of α Lyræ	.	1° 37' 40'' N.
do. . . β Andromedæ	2	25 47 s.
do. . . β Meduſæ	.	3 11 49 N.

9th.

9th.   Clear day.   Thermometer 3° below 0 at
fun rife, rofe in the afternoon to 42°, fell to
32° at fun down.

Obferved zenith diftance of *α* Lyræ   .   1° 37′ 40″ N.
    do.   .   .   *β* Andromedæ 2 25 56 s.
    do. .   .   . *β* Medufæ . 3 11 27 N.

Latitude

Latitude deduced from the Zenith Distances. Observed Zenith Distances.

Face of the Sector East.

	β Andromedæ	β Medusæ	α Lyræ	α Cygni
	° ′ ″	° ′ ″	° ′ ″	° ′ ″
1796. Dec. 31st.	· · · · · ·	· · · · · ·	1 37 23 N.	· · · · · ·
1797. Jan. 3d.	2 25 38 S.	3 11 46 N.	· · · · · ·	7 35 32 N.
4th.	· · · · · ·	· · · · · ·	· · · · · ·	7 35 29 N.
8th.	2 25 47 S.	3 11 49 N.	1 37 40 N.	· · · · · ·
9th.	2 25 56 S.	3 11 27 N.	1 37 40 N.	· · · · · ·
Means	2 25 47 S.	3 11 41 N.	1 37 34 N.	7 35 30.5 N.
4th. . . . . . Face of the Sector West.				
4th.	2 30 24 S.	3 7 5 N.	· · · · · ·	7 31 19 N.
5th.	· · · · · ·	3 7 5 N.	1 33 28 N.	· · · · · ·
6th.	· · · · · ·	3 7 17 N.	· · · · · ·	7 31 27 N.
7th.	2 30 6 S.	3 7 19 N.	1 33 37 N.	7 31 23 N.
Means	2 30 15 S.	3 7 11 N.	1 33 32.5 N.	7 35 30.5 N.
Mean. Face of the sector east . .	2 25 47 S.	3 11 41 N.	1 37 34 N.	7 33 26.7 N.
Correct observed zenith distances . .	2 28 1 S.	3 9 26 N.	1 35 33.2 N.	7 33 26.7 N.
Refractions	+ 2.5	+ 3	+ 1.5	+ 7.5
Correct zenith distances	2 28 3.5 S.	3 9 29 N.	1 35 34.7 N.	7 33 34.2 N.
Mean declinations Jan. 4th 1797	34 32 26.7 N.	40 09 55.9 N.	38 36 1.2 N.	+ 33 41.5 N.
Aberration	+ 7.2	+ 9.7	− 3.1	+ 4.3
Nutation	− 7.1	− 5.2	− 0.9	− 4.1
Correct declinations	34 32 26.8 S.	40 10 0.4 N.	38 35 57.2 N.	− 33 41.7 N.
Correct zenith distances applied . .	+2 28 3.5 S.	−3 9 29 N.	−1 35 34.7 N.	−7 33 34.2 N.
Latitudes	37 0 30.3 N.	37 0 31.4 N.	37 0 22.5 N.	7 0 7.5 N.

		o	,	,,
Latitude by	β Andromedæ .	37	o	30.3
do. .	β Medufæ . .	37	o	31.4
do. .	α Lyræ . .	37	o	22.5
do. .	α Cygni . .	37	o	7.5

Mean Latitude . . .	37	o	22.9 North.

Longitude deduced from the eclipfes of ♃'s fatellites and one lunar obfervation.

		,	,,			
1796. Dec. 20th.	Clock too faft mean time .	2	10		Daily gain.	
	Stopped on the 23d by the extreme cold.				,	,,
26th.	Clock too flow mean time .	0	38	. .	0	18.5
27th.	do.	0	19.5	. .	0	12
28th.	do.	0	7.5	. .	0	15.3
31ft.	Clock too faft mean time .	0	38.5	. .	0	4
1797. Jan. 4th.	do.	0	54.5	. .	0	7.5
5th.	do.	1	2.0	. .		

The immerfion of the 3d fatellite of ♃ was obferved on the 20th of December at 9^h 8' 47" P. M. as before noted: The clock by equal altitudes of the fun taken on that day appeared to be too faft 2' 10" mean time, and gained by fubfequent obfervations at a mean rate about 10" per diem. The clock was therefore too faft at the time of the obfervation 2' 14", the obfervation was of courfe made at 9^h 6' 37" P. M. mean time, to which add 1' 13" the equation of time, the fum 9^h 7' 50" will be the apparent time of the immerfion, which taken from 15^h 2' 34" the apparent time at Greenwich by the theory, will leave 5^h 54' 44" for the difference of meridians.

An emerfion of the firft fatellite of ♃ was obferved on the 21ft of December at 6^h 56' 00" P. M. The clock at that time by admitting the mean daily gain to be 10" was too faft 2' 25" mean time, the obfervation was therefore made at 6^h 53' 35" mean time, to which add 0' 46" the equation of time, and the fum 6^h 54' 21" will be the apparent time of the obfervation, which deducted from 12^h 49' 29" the apparent time at Greenwich by the theory, will give 5^h 55' 8" for the difference of meridians.

Another emerfion of the 1ft fatellite of ♃ was obferved on the 28th of December at 8^h 48' 38" P. M. The clock at that time was about 1" too flow mean time. The obfervation was therefore made at 8^h 48' 39" mean time, from which deduct 2' 44" the equation of time, and the remainder 8^h 45' 55" will be the apparent time of the obfervation, which deducted from 14^h 41' 53" the apparent time at Greenwich by the theory, will give 5^h 55' 58" for the difference of meridians.

On the 5th of January 1797, at 2^h 54' 18" P. M. by the clock, the diftance between the neareft limbs of the ☉ and ☽ was obferved to be 84° 16' 39" the clock at the time of obfervation was 1' 2" too faft mean time, the obfervation was therefore made at 2^h 53' 16" mean time, from which

deduct

deduct 6′ 15″ the equation of time, and the remainder 2^h 47′ 1″ will be the apparent time of the obfervation. The obferved diftance corrected for parallax refraction, &c. will anfwer to about 8^h 42′ 22″ at Greenwich, by which the difference of meridians appears to be about 5^h 55′ 21″.

By fuppofing the obfervation on the 3d fatellite of ♃, with the lunar obfervation to be equivalent to either of thofe on the 1ft fatellite, the mean longitude will be had as below.

	h	′	″
Longitude by the 3d fatellite .	5	54	44
do. by the lunar obfervation	5	55	21
Mean . . .	5	55	2.5
do. by the 1ft fatellite on the 21ft of December	5	55	8
do. by do. on the 28th of December	5	55	58
Mean . . .	5	55	22.8

= 88° 50′ 42″ weft from Greenwich, or 0^h 54′ 47.8″ = 13° 41′ 57″ weft from the city of Philadelphia.

The foregoing obfervations were made under very un-favourable circumftances, the weather intenfely cold, and not a fufficient number of tents to fecure our inftruments, and cover our men : our ftore-boat having been left behind, and was frozen up near the mouth of the Wabafh river till about the 20th of January. The fpirits in the veffel in which the plummet of the fector was fufpended were frequently congealed, and what appeared fomewhat fingular, was that the fpirits began to freeze on the out-fide of the veffel very near to the upper edge, from which it extended in prongs, like bucks-horns, and did not con-geal within till the fpirits fell about $\frac{4}{10}$ of an inch below the upper edge.—The veffel was 1$\frac{1}{2}$ inches in diame-ter.—The ice on the outfide did not appear to contain a full proportion of fpirit. Although the obfervations were made under unfavourable circumftances, I have no reafon to fuppofe them liable to any material objection, and therefore prefume that the determinations of the la-titude, and longitude, of the confluence of the two rivers are fufficiently correct for geographical purpofes, notwith-ftanding

ſtanding a difference of about 2 degrees in longitude, and 14 minutes in latitude, from Mr. Hutchins's map.

1797.
Feb. 24th.　　Arrived at Natchez.
　　27th.　　Encamped at the north end of the village.
　　28th.　　Set up the clock.
March 1ſt.　　Set up the large zenith ſector, with the face to the eaſt.

Equal altitudes of the Sun.
3d.　　A. M. 9^h 50′ 11″.　　P. M. 2^h 9′ 11″.

The obſerved times, and diſtances of the ☉'s and ☽'s neareſt limbs.

	Times.			Diſtances.		
h	′	″	°	′	″	
2	54	35*	59	46	0	
2	56	18	59	46	40	
2	59	20	59	47	0	Error of the Sextant 0″.
3	0	38	59	47	20	
3	3	53	59	47	50	
Means . 2	58	58	59	46	58	

Repeated.

h	′	″	°	′	″	
3	45	6	60	2	10	
3	48	18	60	2	30	
3	51	22	60	2	40	
3	52	45	60	3	0	Error of the Sextant 0″.
3	54	37	60	4	40	
3	56	39	60	4	50	
3	58	47	60	5	20	
4	0	34	60	5	40	
Means . 3	54	16	60	3	51	

Repeated.

* All the obſervations conneƈted *with*, or dependent upon *time*, are entered as obſerved by the clock, and will therefore require a correƈtion to reduce them to mean ſolar time, which may readily be done from the *ſtatement* of the errors of the clock, with its rate of going, to be found at the end of each courſe of obſervations.

Repeated.

h	,	,,		o	,	,,	
4	24	18		60	11	55	
4	26	15		60	12	30	
4	28	14		60	13	20	Error of the Sextant 0".
4	29	50		60	13	35	
4	32	5		60	14	10	

Means . 4 28 10   60 13 8

4th. The obferved times, and diftances of the ☉'s and ☽'s nearest limbs.

	Times.			Diftances.		
h	,	,,		o	,	,,
2	6	22		72	5	30
2	7	34		72	5	50
2	8	29		72	6	30	Error of the Sextant 0".
2	9	29		72	6	40
2	10	23		72	7	0
2	11	44		72	7	30

Means . 2 9 0   72 6 29

Repeated.

h	,	,,		o	,	,,	
4	47	45		72	57	0	
4	49	26		72	57	30	
4	51	10		72	57	40	
4	52	16		72	58	20	Error of the Sextant 0".
4	53	31		72	58	20	
4	54	30		72	58	40	
4	55	19		72	58	40	
4	56	21		72	59	0	

Means 4 52 17   72 58 9

		o	,	,,	
Obferved zenith diftance of Pollux	.	3	2	58	s.
5th. do. . . Caftor	.	0	45	56	N.
do. . . . Pollux	.	3	03	1	s.
do. . . β Tauri	.	3	7	59	s.

c   6th.

6th.   *Equal altitudes of the Sun.*
A. M. 9ʰ 37′ 57″.   P. M. 2ʰ 18′ 54″.

The obferved times, and diftances of the ☉'s and ☽'s neareft limbs.

Times.			Diftances.		
h	′	″	o	′	″
2	32	57	98	11	20
2	34	2	98	11	40
2	35	10	98	12	0
2	36	4	98	12	0
2	36	49	98	12	30
2	37	38	98	12	50
2	38	33	98	13	20

Error of the Sextant 0″

Means . 2 35 53   98 12 14

7th. Obferved zenith diftance of β Tauri .   3   7   57   s.
      do. . . . Caftor . 0   45   55   n.
      do. . . . Pollux . 3   2   58   s.

8th.   *Equal altitudes of the Sun.*
A. M. 9ʰ 23′ 42″.   P. M. 2ʰ 31′ 26″.

Obferved zenith diftance of β Tauri . 3   8   0   s.
      do. . . . Caftor . 0   45   56   n.
      do. . . . Pollux . 3   2   56

9th. Turned the face of the fector weft.

Obferved zenith diftance of Pollux . 3   4   0   s.
10th.   do. . . Caftor . 0   44   55   n.
      do. . . . Pollux . 3   3   59   s.

11th, 12th, and 13th. Cloudy with conftant, but not heavy thunder.

14th.   Cleared off very early in the morning with a violent gale of wind which blew down a number of the tents, and pufhed in the fide of the one we ufed for the obfervatory againft the clock, where it refted till the gale was over, which did not exceed 15 minutes.

Equal

Equal altitudes of the Sun.
A. M. 9ʰ 41′ 58″.   P. M. 2ʰ 7′ 36″.

	o	′	″	
Obferved zenith diftance of β Tauri .	3	8	58	s.

15th, and 16th. Cloudy with fome thunder and a little rain.

17th. Obferved zenith diftance of β Tauri . 3 8 58 s.
    do. . . . Caſtor . 0 44 57 N.
    do. . . . Pollux . 3 3 56

The obferved times, and diftances of the ☉'s and ☽'s neareſt limbs.

Times.			Diftances.		
h	′	″	o	′	″
20	57	41	109	43	40
20	59	55	109	42	30
21	1	44	109	41	20
21	2	51	109	40	30
21	4	35	109	39	30
21	5	49	109	39	00

Error of the Sextant 0″.

Means . 9 1 49   109 41 5

18th.   *Equal altitudes of the Sun.*
        A. M. 9ʰ 13′ 10″.   P. M. 2ʰ 31′ 38″.

	o	′	″	
Obferved zenith diftance of β Tauri .	3	8	54	s.

19th.   do. . . Caſtor . 0 44 50 N.
20th.   do. . . . β Tauri . 3 8 55 s.

21ſt.   Stopped the clock and fct it forward about 9 minutes.—Screwed up the pendulum bob.

Equal altitudes of the Sun.
A. M. 9ʰ 53′ 24″.   P. M. 2ʰ 3′ 43″.

C 2   The

The obferved times, and diftances of the ⊙'s and ☽'s neareft limbs.

Times.			Diftances.		
h	′	″	o	′	″
21	18	5	65	50	30
21	21	28	65	50	0
21	23	29	65	50	0
21	24	12	65	49	20	Error of the Sextant 0″.
21	25	7	65	48	40
21	26	17	65	48	0
21	29	17	65	47	30
Means	9	23	55	65	49	9

Repeated.

h	′	″	o	′	″
21	30	35	65	46	40
21	31	40	65	46	30
21	33	19	65	46	30
21	34	41	65	46	0	Error of the Sextant 0′.
21	36	10	65	45	30
21	37	43	65	45	20
21	39	14	65	45	0
Means	21	34	46	65	45	56

22d. Obferved zenith diftance of β Tauri . 3° 8′ 57″ s.

The obferved times, and diftances of the ⊙'s and ☽'s neareft limbs.

Times.			Diftances.		
h	′	″	o	′	″
21	42	32	54	49	20
21	43	35	54	48	50
21	44	28	54	48	20	Error of the Sextant 0″.
21	45	40	54	48	10
21	46	32	54	48	00
Means	21	44	33	54	48	32

23d. Obferved zenith diftance of β Tauri . 3° 8′ 56″ s.

The

The obferved times, and diftances of the ☉'s and ☽'s neareft limbs.

Times.			Diftances.		
h	'	''	o	'	''
21	21	16	43	53	10
21	23	7	43	52	40
21	24	13	43	52	20	Error of the Sextant 0''
21	25	15	43	52	10
21	26	52	43	52	00

Means . 21 24 9   43 52 28

From this time I was too much occupied in other concerns, occafioned by the different commotions in the country, to attend to a regular feries of obfervations till October; there are therefore but few entered till that time.

28th.　　　*Equal altitudes of the Sun.*
　　A. M. 9ʰ 28' 32''.　P. M. 2ʰ 26' 43''.

April 7th.　Obferved zenith diftance of Caftor　.　0° 44' 56'' N.

From this time, till the 4th of June no attention was paid to the clock, It ran down feveral times.

June 12th.　　　*Equal altitudes of the Sun.*
　　A. M. 8ʰ 58' 4''.　P. M. 3ʰ 8' 50''.

Immerfion of the 1ft fatellite of ♃ obferved at 15ʰ 28' 25''.—Belts tolerably diftinct, magnifying power of the telefcope 120.

17th.　　　*Equal altitudes of the Sun.*
　　A. M. 8ʰ 54' 41''.　P. M. 3ʰ 13' 49''.

26th.　　Clock removed from the tent, into a houfe where 1 went to refide myfelf, but on account of the ficknefs which prevailed on the river, I removed in July with my people about feven miles into the country and encamped, where

where I remained till the 27th of September, and then returned to the village of Natchez.

28th.   Cleaned the clock and fet it a-going.

Immerfion of the 1ft fatellite of ♃ obferved at 14ʰ 30′ 10″.—Belts diftinct, magnifying power 120.

29th.   *Equal altitudes of the Sun.*
                   ʰ   ′   ″   ʰ   ′   ″
         A. M. 8 53 21.5.   P. M. 3 5 17.5.
                   Doubtful 2 or 3 feconds.

30th.   *Equal altitudes of the Sun.*
         A. M. 8ʰ 59′ 44″.   P. M. 2ʰ 58′ 35″.

Immerfon of the 1ft fatellite of ♃ obferved at 8ʰ 59′ 19″. Belts diftinct, magnifying power 120.

Oct. 2d.   Prepared to obferve an eclipfe of the 4th fatellite of ♃. The fatellite was not eclipfed, neither am I convinced that it touched the fhadow of ♃, it was very diftinct, and appeared when neareft, to be its full diameter from the body of the planet.

7th.   *Equal altitudes of the Sun.*
         A. M. 9ʰ 2′ 10″.   P. M. 2ʰ 54′ 14″.

From this time, till the beginning of January following, it was with difficulty I could fit up long enough to make an obfervation, owing to a fevere fever.

18th.   *Equal altitudes of the Sun.*
         A. M. 8ʰ 58′ 41″.   P. M. 2ʰ 56′ 52″.

25th.   *Emerfion* of the 1ft fatellite of ♃ obferved at 5ʰ 55′ 12″. —Belts diftinct, magnifying power 120.

26th.   *Equal altitudes of the Sun.*
         A. M. 9ʰ 9′ 25″.   P. M. 2ʰ 47′ 5″.

Nov. 22d.   Clock ran down, wound it up, fet it a-going, and lowered the pendulum bob.

                                        24th.

24th.   *Equal altitudes of the Sun.*
A. M. 9ʰ 28′ 26″.   P. M. 2ʰ 38′ 35″.

Emerſion of the 1ſt ſatellite of ♃ obſerved at 8ʰ 7′ 33″.
—Belts diſtinct, magnifying power 120.

26th.   *Equal altitudes of the Sun.*
A. M. 9ʰ 35′ 44″.   P. M. 2ʰ 37′ 48″.

Dec. 1ſt.   Thermometer roſe to 78°.—Muſquitoes very troubleſome at night.

2d.   Thermometer 50° at ſun riſe, fell to 47°.— Cloudy.

3d.   Thermometer 22° at ſun riſe, roſe to 35°. —Snow and hail without intermiſſion till 6ʰ P. M. when it cleared away with a ſtrong N. W. wind.

Obſervations on a lunar eclipſe.

	h	′	″
Beginning	8	38	34
Beginning of total darkneſs	9	37	35
End of total darkneſs	11	18	59
End of the eclipſe	12	18	12

During the above obſervation the thermometer was at 20°.

4th.   Thermometer 18° at ſun riſe, roſe to 33″. —Mr. Dunbar's thermometer was at 17° in the morning.

Equal altitudes of the Sun.
A. M. 9ʰ 17′ 7″.   P. M. 2ʰ 57′ 35″.

5th.   Thermometer 20° at ſun riſe, roſe to 37°.
6th.   Thermometer 18° at ſun riſe, roſe to 39°.

Equal altitudes of the Sun.
h ′ ″   h ′ ″
A. M. 9 25 15.5.   P. M. 2 51 24.5.

7th.   Thermometer 30° at ſun riſe, roſe to 49°.

Emerſion

Emerſion of the 2d ſatellite of ♃ obſerved at 7ʰ 56′ 31″.—Belts diſtinct, magnifying power 120.

8th.   Thermometer 33° at ſun riſe, roſe to 51°.

Equal altitudes of the Sun.
A. M. 9ʰ 56′ 15″.   P. M. 2ʰ 22′ 19″.

9th.   Thermometer 30° at ſun riſe, roſe to 47°. —Cloudy.

10th.   Thermometer 28° at ſun riſe, roſe to 56°.

11th.   Thermometer 40° at ſun riſe, roſe to 60°.

12th.   Thermometer 52° at ſun riſe, roſe to 75°. —Cloudy part of the day.

13th.   Thermometer 60° at ſun riſe, roſe to 75°. —Flying clouds.

14th.   Thermometer 63° at ſun riſe, roſe to 75°. —It was 74° at 9ʰ in the evening, a thunder guſt at midnight.

15th.   Thermometer 46° at ſun riſe, roſe to 50°. —Flying clouds.

16th.   Thermometer 30° at ſun riſe, roſe to 51°.

Equal altitudes of the Sun.
A. M. 9ʰ 28′ 0″.   P. M. 2ʰ 58′ 15″.

17th.   Thermometer 50° at ſun riſe, roſe to 55°.

Emerſion of the 1ſt ſatellite of ♃ obſerved at 8ʰ 24′ 30″. —A little hazy, but the belts were middling diſtinct, magnifying power 120.

18th.   Thermometer 43° at ſun riſe, roſe to 54°.

Equal altitudes of the Sun.
A. M. 9ʰ 50′ 14″.   P. M. 2ʰ 38′ 8″.

19th.   Thermometer 30° at ſun riſe, roſe to 53°. —Cloudy with ſome cold rain.

20th.

20th. Thermometer 34° at fun rife, rofe to 51°.
—Cloudy with cold rain.—Cleared off at
night with a N. W. wind.

21ft. Thermometer 17½° at fun rife, rofe to 37°.

Equal altitudes of the Sun

h / "   h / "
A. M. 9 46 43.5.   P. M. 2 44 58.5.

22d. Thermometer 23° at fun rife, rofe to 41°.
—Cloudy.

23d. Thermometer 28° at fun rife, rofe to 37°.
—Flying clouds.

24th. Thermometer 41° at fun rife, rofe to 50°.

Emerfion of the 1ft fatellite of ♃ obferved at 10ʰ 21′ 1″.
—A little hazy, belts middling diftinct, magnifying power
120.

25th. Thermometer 55° at fun rife, rofe to 60°.
—Cloudy with a little rain.

26th. Thermometer 64° at fun rife, fell to 40°.
—Cloudy with a N. E. wind.

27th. Thermometer 22° at fun rife, rofe to 39°.
—Wind N. W.

28th. Thermometer 28° at fun rife, rofe to 54°.

29th. Thermometer 31° at fun rife, rofe to 52°.

30th. Thermometer 53° at fun rife, rofe to 65°.
—Heavy rain.

31ft. Thermometer 55° at fun rife, rofe to 57°.
—Heavy rain.

1798.

Jan. 1ft. Thermometer 31° at fun rife, rofe to 67°.

Equal altitudes of the Sun.
A. M. 9ʰ 50′ 10″.   P. M. 2ʰ 53′ 43″.

2d. Thermometer 48° at fun rife, rofe to 61°.
—Cloudy.

d   At

At 15 minutes after 8 o'clock A. M. ſtop-
ped the clock about 19 minutes by my watch,
and lowered the pendulum bob a ſmall matter,
but ſcarcely diſcernible with a magnifying
glaſs.

3d.   Thermometer 45° at ſun riſe, roſe to 52°.
4th.   Thermometer 47° at ſun riſe, roſe to 63°.
—Cloudy great part of the day.

Immerſion of the 3d ſatellite of ♃ }
   obſerved at   .   6ʰ 36′ 51″. } Belts diſtinct, magni-
Emerſion do. at   .   8 36 23. }   fying power 120.

5th.   Thermometer 27° at ſun riſe, roſe to 67°.

Equal altitudes of the Sun.
A. M. 9ʰ 33′ 5″.   P. M. 2ʰ 36′ 44″.

_____

6th.   Thermometer 37° at ſun riſe, roſe to 61°.
—Cloudy.
7th.   Thermometer 55° at ſun riſe, roſe to 72°.
—Rain.
8th.   Thermometer 55° at ſun riſe, roſe to 73°.

Equal altitudes of the Sun.
A. M. 9ʰ 41′ 30″.   P. M. 2ʰ 30′ 55″.

_____

Emerſion of the 2d ſatellite of ♃ obſerved at 7ʰ 22′ 12″.
—Belts diſtinct, magnifying power 120.

9th.   Thermometer 35° at ſun riſe, roſe to 62°.

Equal altitudes of the Sun.
A. M. 9ʰ 40′ 21″.   P. M. 2ʰ 32′ 52″.

_____

Emerſion of the 1ſt ſatellite of ♃ obſerved at 8ʰ 23′ 10″.
—Belts diſtinct, magnifying power 120.

10th.   Thermometer 24° at ſun riſe, roſe to 66°.
—Cloudy.

11th.

11th. Thermometer 23° at fun rife, rofe to 61°. —Cloudy with fome rain.

12th. Thermometer 27° at fun rife, rofe to 57°. —Cloudy.

13th. Thermometer 50° at fun rife, rofe to 65°. Cloudy part of the day with rain.

14th. Thermometer 62° at fun rife, fell to 55°.— Heavy rain.

15th. Thermometer 37° at fun rife, rofe to 60°.

Equal altitudes of the Sun.

h ' ''   h ' ''
A. M. 9 29 10.5.   P. M. 2 48 20.
Doubtful 3 or 4 feconds.

Emerfion of the 2d fatellite of ♃ obferved at 9h 58' 28''. —Belts obfcure, the planet and fatellites very tremulous.— Magnifying power 120.

16th. Thermometer 32° at fun rife, rofe to 69°.

Equal altitudes of the Sun.
A. M. 9h 23' 55''.   P. M. 2h 54' 20'',

Emerfion of the 1ft fatellite of ♃ obferved at 10h 19' 19'', —Belts tolerably diftinct, magnifying power 120.

17th. Thermometer 33° at fun rife, rofe to 76°.
18th. Thermometer 34° at fun rife, rofe to 64°.
19th. Thermometer 40° at fun rife, rofe to 60°. —Cloudy with fome rain.

20th. Thermometer 54° at fun rife, rofe to 71°. —Cloudy.

21ft. Thermometer 53° at fun rife, rofe to 68°. —Cloudy with rain.

22d. Thermometer 67° at fun rife, rofe to 76°. —Cleared off with a N. W. wind.

23d. Thermometer 22° at fun rife, rofe to 46°.

Equal altitudes of the Sun.
A. M. 9ʰ 13′ 47″.   P. M. 3ᵇ 8′ 2″.

The obſerved times, and diſtances of the ☉'s and ☽'s neareſt limbs.

Times.			Diſtances.			
h	′	″	o	′	″	
3	23	15	74	27	5	
3	24	36	74	27	15	
3	26	24	74	27	40	
3	27	25	74	28	0	
3	28	34	74	28	10	
3	29	34	74	28	30	Error of the Sextant 0″.
3	30	25	74	28	50	
3	31	16	74	28	55	
3	32	8	74	29	0	
3	33	4	74	29	30	
3	33	46	74	29	40	
3	34	28	74	30	00	
Means . 3	29	35	74	28	33	

The obſerved times, and diſtances of the ☽'s weſtern limb from Aldebaran.

Times.			Diſtances.			
h	′	″	o	′	″	
9	54	11	45	34	0	
9	55	14	45	33	30	
9	58	59	45	31	20	
10	0	6	45	30	40	
10	1	3	45	30	40	Error of the Sextant 0″.
10	2	5	45	30	20	
10	3	10	45	29	10	
10	4	53	45	28	0	
10	6	6	45	27	20	
Means . 10	0	39	45	30	33	

24th.   Thermometer 18° at ſun riſe, roſe to 49°. —N. W. wind.

Equal altitudes of the Sun.
A. M. 9ʰ 22′ 58″.   P. M. 2ʰ 59′ 21″.

25th.   Thermometer 48° at ſun riſe, roſe to 60°.
26th.

26th.   Thermometer 66° at fun rife, rofe to 76°.
—Cloudy.

27th.   Thermometer 49° at fun rife, rofe to 61°.

28th.   Thermometer 34° at fun rife, rofe to 63°.

Equal altitudes of the Sun.
A. M. 9ʰ 11′ 52″.   P. M. 3ʰ 11′ 51″.

29th.   Thermometer 55° at fun rife, rofe to 76°.

30th.   Thermometer 66° at fun rife, rofe to 82°.

31ft.   Thermometer 67° at fun rife, rofe to 81°.

Feb.   1ft.   Thermometer 59° at fun rife, rofe to 81°.
—Cloudy with fome rain.

2d.   Thermometer 64° at fun rife, rofe to 76°.

3d.   Thermometer 63° at fun rife, rofe to 80°.
—Cloudy.

4th.   Thermometer 66° at fun rife, rofe to 78″.
—Flying clouds.

5th.   Thermometer 55° at fun rife, rofe to 79°.

6th.   Thermometer 61° at fun rife, rofe to 71°.
—Cloudy with a little rain.

7th.   Thermometer 54° at fun rife, rofe to 80°.

Equal altitudes of the Sun.
A. M. 9ʰ 30′ 53″.   P. M. 2ʰ 53′ 48″.

8th.   Thermometer 51° at fun rife, rofe to 66°.
—Heavy rain laft night and this day.

9th.   Thermometer 33° at fun rife, rofe to 57°.
—Wind N. W.

Equal altitudes of the Sun.
A. M. 9ʰ 4′ 35″.   P. M. 3ʰ 19′ 50″.

Emerfion of the 2d fatellite of ♃ obferved at 7° 2′ 52″.
—Belts diftinct, magnifying power 120.

10th.   Thermometer 31° at fun rife, rofe to 50°.

11th.   Thermometer 55° at fun rife, rofe to 70°.

12th.

12th.   Thermometer 61° at fun rife, rofe to 78°.

Equal altitudes of the Sun.
A. M. 9ʰ 1′ 43″.   P. M. 3ʰ 22′ 28″.

13th.   Thermometer 64° at fun rife, rofe to 80°.
—Cloudy with a little rain.
14th.   Thermometer 61° at fun rife, rofe to 81°.
15th.   Thermometer 55° at fun rife, fell to 50°.
—Some rain.
16th.   Thermometer 40° at fun rife, rofe to 55°.
—Cloudy in the forenoon.

Immerfion of the 3d fatellite of ♃ obferved at 6ʰ 51′ 32″.
—Belts middling well defined, magnifying power 120.

17th.   Thermometer 30° at fun rife, rofe to 49°.
—Cloudy with a heavy rain at night.
18th.   Thermometer 50° at fun rife, rofe to 56°.
—Cloudy.
19th.   Thermometer 42° at fun rife, rofe to 55°.
—Cloudy.
20th.   Thermometer 40° at fun rife, rofe to 54°.
—Cloudy part of the day.
21ft.   Thermometer 41° at fun rife, rofe to 66°.

Equal altitudes of the Sun.
A. M. 9ʰ 39′ 19″.   P. M. 2ʰ 43′ 4″.

End of the obfervations at the Town of Natchez.

1797.   The rate of the clock's going, at the town or village of Natchez.

		′	″	Daily lofs.
Clock too flow mean time March 3d.	. . .	12	32.4	. . 11.0
do.	6th.	13	5.5	. . 10.5
do.	8th. . .	13	26.6	. . 11.2
do.	14th. .	14	33.6	. . 17.9*
do.	18th. . .	15	45.3	. . 16.3
do.	20th. .	16	18.0	

* The alteration in the going of the clock after the 14th muft have been occafioned by the tent being blown againft it, as mentioned on the 15th.
Stopped

Stopped the clock and raifed the pendulum bob.

			′	″	Daily gain.
do.	. . . .	21ft. .	.	8 40 1	″
do.	. . . .	28th.	.	7 26.2 · ·	6.6

From this time till the 4th of June the clock was but little attended to, and ran down feveral times.

			′	″	Daily lofs.
Clock too faft mean time June 12th	.	.	3	55	″
do. . . .	17th .	. .	3	40.6 · ·	2.9

June 26th.   The clock was taken down and removed into a houfe, where it was not attended to till September 28th.

			′	″	Daily gain.
Clock too faft mean time Sept. 29th.	.	.	9	30.4	″
do.	30th.	.	9	39.5 · ·	9.1
do. . .	Oct. 7th.	. .	10	47.4 · ·	9.7
do.	18th.	.	12	53.0 · ·	11.4
do. . . .	26th.	. .	14	24.3 · ·	11.4

Nov. 22d.   Clock ran down, wound it up, fet it a-going and lowered the pendulum bob.

			′	″	Daily gain.
Clock too faft mean time Nov. 24th.	.	.	16	22	″
do. . . . . ,	26th.	.	16	28 · ·	3
do. . .	Dec. 4th.	. .	16	30 · ·	0.2
do.	6th.	.	16	37 · ·	3.5
do. . . . ,	8th.	. .	16	38.5 · ·	0.7
do.	16th.	.	16	40.5 · ·	0.2
do. . . .	18th.	. .	16	44 · ·	1.7
do.	21ft.	.	16	52 · ·	2.7
do. .	1798. Jan. 1ft.	. .	17	31 · ·	3.5

1798.
Jan. 2d.   Stopped the clock about 19 minutes and lowered the pendulum bob.

			′	″	
Clock too flow mean time Jan. 5th.	.	1	21	″	
do.	8th.	. 1	20	· · 0.3 daily gain.	
do.	9th.	. 1	22	· · 2.0 daily lofs.	
				· · 1.0 do.	

do.

				ʹ	ʺ		ʺ	
do.	. . . .	15th.	.	1	28.2	. .	0.8	daily gain.
do.	. . . .	16th.	.	1	28	. .	2.3	daily lofs.
do.	. . .	23d.	.	1	44	. .	1.0	daily gain.
do.	. . .	24th.	.	1	43	. .	1.7	daily lofs.
do.	. . .	28th.	.	1	50	. .	3.5	do.
do.	. . Feb.	7th.	.	2	24.6	. .	5.5	do.
do.	. . .	9th.	.	2	35.6	. .	2.0	do.
do.	. . . .	12th.	.	2	41.6	. .	1.3	do.
do.	. . .	21ft.	.	2	53.5	. .		

1797.
The refults of the obfervations made at Natchez for the Longitude.

			h	ʹ	ʺ
March	3d.	Longitude weft from Greenwich by a lunar obfervation the ☽ from the ☉. . . .	6	6	24
		do.	6	6	41
		do.	6	5	54
	4th. .	do.	6	6	33
		do.	6	5	37
	6th. .	do.	6	4	27
	17th. .	do.	6	5	48
	21ft. .	do.	6	5	2
		do.	6	6	34
	22d. .	do.	6	5	34
	23d. .	do.	6	6	37
June	12th. .	do. by an immerfion of the 1ft fatellite of ♃	6	6	5
Sept.	28th. .	do.	6	6	23
	30th. .	do.	6	6	13
Oct.	25th. .	do. by an emerfion of do. . .	6	6	15
Nov.	24th. .	do.	6	5	58
Dec.	3d. .	by the beginning of the lunar eclipfe	6	5	36
		do. beginning of total darknefs .	6	6	6
		do. end of total darknefs . . .	6	5	29
		do. end of the eclipfe . . .	6	5	38
	7th. .	By an emerfion of the 2d fatellite of ♃	6	6	5
	17th. .	do. . . 1ft fatellite .	6	5	58
	24th. .	do. . . do. . .	6	6	12
1798. Jan.	4th.	By an immerfion of the 3d fatellite .	5	58	11
		do. emerfion do. . . .	6	0	47
		The immerfion of the fame fatellite by de Lambre's Tables }	6	2	58
		Emerfion of do. by de Lambre's Tables	6	4	57
	8th. .	Emerfion of the 2d fatellite . .	6	5	43
	9th. .	do. . 1ft . . .	6	5	57
	15th. .	do. . 2d . . .	6	5	27
	16th. .	do. . 1ft ., . .	6	5	45

			h	′	″
23d. .	By a lunar obfervation, the ☽ from the ☉.		6	4	41
	do. the ☽ from Aldebaran.		6	5	6
Feb. 9th. .	By an emerfion of the 2d fatellite		6	5	2
16th. .	By an immerfion of the 3d do.		5	59	25
	do. by de Lambre's Tables		6	3	26

The longitude of Natchez is ftated in the 4th volume of the Tranfactions of the American Philofophical Society, page 451, at 16° 15′ 46″ weft from Philadelphia, or 91° 29′ 16″ which is equal to 6ʰ 5′ 57″ weft from Greenwich.—That determination includes all the foregoing obfervations previous to the 10th of January, except the immerfion, and emerfion of the 3d fatellite* on the 4th of that month, which from the imperfection of the theory were omitted.

c Refult

---

* I have lately been furnifhed by Jofe Joaquin de Ferrer, an ingenious Spanifh gentleman, with a number of valuable aftronomical obfervations, which he has made at different places on this continent: among them there are three on the eclipfes of Jupiter's fatellites made at la Guaira, which correfpond with an equal number of mine made at Natchez.—They are the following:

	Apparent Time.		
	h	′	″
1798. ⎰ *Emerfion* of the 3d fatellite of ♃ obferv-⎱ Jan. 4th. ⎨ ed by Mr. de Ferrer at la Guaira ⎬ ⎱ Obferved at Natchez . . . ⎰	10	9	51
	8	31	51

	h	′	″
Difference of meridians , . .	1	38	0

	h	′	″
⎰ *Emerfion* of the 2d fatellite of ♃ obferv-⎱ do. 8th. ⎨ ed by Mr. de Ferrer at la Guaira ⎬ ⎱ Obferved at Natchez . . . ⎰	8	54	11
	7	15	58
Difference of meridians . . .	1	38	13

	h	′	″
⎰ *Emerfion* of the 1ft fatellite of ♃ obferv-⎱ do. 9th. ⎨ ed by Mr. de Ferrer at la Guaira ⎬ ⎱ Obferved at Natchez . . . ⎰	9	54	40
	8	16	31
Difference of meridians . . .	1	38	9
Mean	1	38	7.3

The telefcopes ufed by Mr. de Ferrer and myfelf were both acromatic, and nearly of the fame magnifying power, (that is about 120), the difference of the meridians will therefore require no correction on account of the difference of the inftruments, and may be fafely taken as above ftated: by which it appears that the town of Natchez, is 1ʰ 38′ 7″.3 or 24° 31′ 49″ weft of la Guaira.—The latitude of la Guaira as determined by Mr. de Ferrer is 10° 36′ 40″ N.

Refult of the obfervations for the latitude of Natchez.

Obferved Zenith Diftances of the following Stars.

Face of the Sector Eaft.

1797.		β Tauri.			Caftor.			Pollux.		
		o ' ''			o ' ''			o ' ''		
March 4th.		. . . .			. . . .		3 2 58		s.
5th.	3 7 59		s.	0 45 56	N.	3 3 1		
7th.	3 7 57			0 45 55		3 2 58		
8th.	3 8 0			0 45 56		3 2 56		
Means	3 7 58.7			0 45 55.9		3 2 58.2		

Face of the Sector Weft.

	β Tauri.	Caftor.	Pollux.
9th.	. . . .	. . . .	3 4 0
10th.	. . . .	0 44 55	3 3 59
14th.	3 8 58	. . . .	. . . .
17th.	3 8 58	0 44 57	3 3 56
18th.	3 8 54	. . . .	. . . .
19th.	. . . .	0 44 50	. . . .
20th.	3 8 55	. . . .	. . . .
22d.	3 8 57	. . . .	. . . .
23d.	3 8 56	. . . .	. . . .
April 7th.	. . . .	0 44 56	. . . .
Means	3 8 56.3	0 44 54.5	3 3 58.3
Means face eaft	3 7 58.7	0 45 55.9	3 2 58.2
Means	3 8 27.5	0 45 25.2	3 3 28.2
Refraƈtions	+3.1	+0.7	+3
True zenith diftance . . .	3 8 30.6	0 45 25.9	3 3 31.2

	β Tauri	Caftor	Pollux
Mean declinations March 15th.	28 25 20.3 N.	32 19 1.9 N.	28 30 10.7 N.
Aberrations	+1.7	+2.1	+0.8
Nutations	—1.0	+6.9	+3.4
Semi. ann. equations	+0.5	+0.4	+0.3
True declinations . . .	28 25 21.5	32 19 11.3	28 30 15.2
True zenith diftances applied . . .	+3 8 30.6	—0 45 25.9	+3 3 31.2
Latitudes N.	31 33 52.1	31 33 45.4	31 33 46.4

			o	'	''
Lat. by	β Tauri	. . .	31	33	52.1
do.	Caftor	. .	31	33	45.4
do.	Pollux	. .	31	33	46.4
Mean lat. N.		. .	31	33	48 nearly.

Aftronomical

Aſtronomical, and Thermometrical Obſervations, made at the City of New-Orleans on the Miſſiſſippi.

1799.

Jan. 10th.   Set up the clock, thermometer 70° in the afternoon.

   11th.   Cloudy all day, thermometer 73° in the afternoon.

   12th.   Cloudy with miſt, thermometer 72° in the morning, fell to 65° in the evening.

   13th.   Cloudy in the afternoon, thermometer 70° in the morning, fell to 64° in the evening.

   14th.   Clear, thermometer 62° in the morning, roſe to 63° in the afternoon.

Equal altitudes of the Sun.
A. M. 9^h 6′ 42″.   P. M. 2^h 53′ 3″.

Emerſion of the 1ſt ſatellite of ♃ obſerved at 6^h 10′ 37″ P. M.—Night clear, belts diſtinct, magnifying power 120.

   15th.   Clear day, thermometer 61° at ſun riſe, roſe in the afternoon to 68°.

Equal altitudes of the Sun.
A. M. 8^h 52′ 25″.   P. M. 3^h 6′ 48″.

Set up the Sector of ſix feet radius.   Face to the eaſt.

Obſervations on the paſſage of the ☽ over ♃, and three of his ſatellites.

	h	′	″	
2d. Satellite immerſed at · ·	5	35	26	
1ſt. do. · · · ·	5	41	7	
♃ began to immerſe at · ·	5	44	5	
♃ immerſed at · · ·	5	46	22	
4th. Satellite immerſed at · ·	5	53	47	P. M.
1ſt. do. emerged at · ·	7	2	0	
♃ began to emerge at · ·	7	4	42	
♃ emerged at · · ·	7	6	50	
4th. Satellite do. at · · ·	7	16	48	

The

The 3d fatellite at the time of its immerfion was obfcured by a fmall cloud, and as it emerged about the time that ♃ was ⅔ emerged, it was not attended to fo accurately, as to entitle it to a place among the obfervations.

16th.   Cloudy with rain, thermometer 62° at fun rife, fell in the afternoon to 59°.

17th.   Cloudy with rain, thermometer 58° at fun rife, rofe in the afternoon to 67°.

18th.   Cloudy, thermometer 59° in the morning, rofe in the afternoon to 61°.

19th.   Clear, thermometer 56° at fun rife, rofe in the afternoon to 66°.

Equal altitudes of the Sun.
A. M. 9ʰ 10′ 47″.   P. M. 2ʰ 46′ 10″.

			°	′	″	
Obferved zenith diftance	β Andromedæ		4	36	28	N.
do.	β Tauri	.	1	31	6	s.
do.	Caftor	.	2	22	15	N.
do.	Pollux	.	1	26	35.5	s.

20th.   Clear in the morning, cloudy in the evening, thermometer 60° at fun rife, rofe in the afternoon to 69°.

Obferved zenith diftance α Coro. Borealis   2° 32′ 52″ s.

Equal altitudes of the Sun.
h   ′   ″   h   ′   ″
A. M. 9 40 27.   P. M. 2 15 49.5.

21ft.   Cloudy all day, clear in the evening, thermometer 60° in the morning, rofe to 69° in the afternoon.

Emerfion of the 1ft fatellite of ♃ obferved at 8ʰ 2′ 9″ P. M.—Belts diftinct, magnifying power of the telefcope 120.

			°	′	″	
Obferved zenith diftance	β Tauri	.	1	31	10	s.
do.	Caftor	.	2	22	14	N.
do.	Pollux	.	1	26	31.5	s.

22d.

22d.   Clear day, thermometer 61° at fun rife, rofe in the afternoon to 72°.

Equal altitudes of the Sun.
A. M. 9^h 36′ 39″.   P. M. 2^h 18′ 18″.

		°	′	″	
Obſerved zenith diſtance	β Andromedæ	4	36	29	N.
do.	β Tauri	1	31	9	S.
do.	Caſtor	2	22	12.5	N.
do.	Pollux	1	26	35.5	S.

23d.   Clear day, thermometer 66° at fun rife, rofe in the afternoon to 74°.

		°	′	″	
Obſerved zenith diſtance	α Coro. Borealis	2	32	51	S.
do.	β Andromedæ	4	36	30	N.

Turned the face of the Sector to the weſt.

Obſerved zenith diſtance of Pollux   . 1° 28′ 16″ s.

24th.   Clear day, thermometer 68° at fun rife, rofe in the afternoon to 77°.

Obſerved zenith diſtance of α Coro. Borealis 2° 34′ 34″ s.

Equal altitudes of the Sun.
A. M. 8^h 54′ 0″.   P. M. 2^h 59′ 33″.

The equal altitudes of this day are doubtful 2 or 3 ſeconds, from the violence of the wind.

Obſerved zenith diſtance β Andromedæ   4° 34′ 49″ N.

The above zenith diſtance is doubtful, from the effect of the wind on the plumb-line.

		°	′	″	
Obſerved zenith diſtance	β Tauri	1	32	47	S.
do.	Caſtor	2	20	35	N.
do.	Pollux	1	28	17	S.

25th.   Heavy fog in the morning, thermometer 70° at 6 o'clock A. M. and 79° in the afternoon.

Obſerved

                     °   ′   ″

Observed zenith distance of β Andromedæ 4   34   46 N.

    do.   .   .   β Tauri .   1   32   50   s.

26th.   do.   .   α Coro. Borealis 2   34   31.5 s.

Clear till 9 o'clock A. M. afterwards flying clouds, thermometer 75° all last night, rose in the afternoon to 79°.

27th.   Cloudy with fine rain—the thermometer continued at 77° all last night, fell to 68° at 2ʰ P. M. The wind which had been southerly since the 10th, shifted to the north, and the mercury fell to 56° in the evening.

Feb. 6th.   *Equal altitudes of the Sun.*

             A. M. 9ʰ 18′ 44″.   P. M. 2ʰ 23′ 44″.

7th. and 8th. Heavy rain, accompanied with sharp lightning, and heavy thunder.

9th.   Clear—the thermometer 36° at sun rise, rose in the afternoon to 57°.

10th.   Clear—the thermometer 30° at sun rise, rose in the afternoon to 60°.

Emersion of the 2d satellite of ♃ observed at 9ʰ 10′ 26″. —Very clear, belts distinct, magnifying power of the telescope 120.

11th.   Clear—the thermometer 31° at sun rise, rose in the afternoon to 65°.

12th.   Clear—hoar frost—thermometer 38° at sun rise, rose in the afternoon to 71°.

17th.   Clear—the thermometer 59° at sun rise, rose in the afternoon to 74°.

Equal altitudes of the Sun.

A. M. 9ʰ 33′ 16″.   P. M. 1ʰ 57′ 33″.

Latitude

Latitude of the City of New-Orleans deduced from the Zenith Distance.

Face of the Sector East.

1799.	δ Andromedæ	β Tauri	Castor	Pollux	α Coro. Borealis.
	o ′ ″	o ′ ″	o ′ ″	o ′ ″	o ′ ″
Jan. 19th	4 36 23 N.	1 31 6 S.	2 22 15 N.	1 26 35.5 S.	· · · · · ·
20th	· · · ·	· · · ·	· · · ·	· · · ·	2 32 52 S.
21st	· · · ·	1 31 10 S.	· · · ·	· · · ·	· · · ·
22d	4 36 29 N.	1 31 9 S.	2 22 14 N.	1 26 34 S.	· · · ·
23d	4 36 30 N.	· · · ·	2 22 12.5 N.	1 26 35.5 S.	2 32 51 S.
Means	4 36 29 N.	1 31 8.3 S.	2 22 13.8 N.	1 26 34.2 S.	2 32 51.5 S.

Face of the Sector West.

	δ Andromedæ	β Tauri	Castor	Pollux	α Coro. Borealis.
24th	4 34 49 N.	1 32 47 S.	2 20 35 N.	1 28 16 S.	2 34 34 S.
25th	4 34 46 E.	1 32 50 S.	· · · ·	1 28 17 S.	· · · ·
26th	· · · ·	· · · ·	· · · ·	· · · ·	2 34 31.5 S.
Means	4 34 47.5 N.	1 32 48.5 S.	2 20 35 N.	1 28 16.5 S.	2 34 32.7 S.
Means face west	4 36 29 N.	1 31 8.3 S.	2 22 13.8 N.	1 26 34.2 S.	2 32 51.5 S.
Means	4 35 38.2 N.	1 31 58.4 S.	2 21 24.4 N.	1 27 25.3 S.	2 33 42.1 S.
Refractions	+ 4.5	+ 1.5	+ 2.3	+ 1.5	+ 2.5
Correct zenith distances	4 35 42.7 N.	1 31 59.9 S.	2 21 26.7 N.	1 27 26.8 S.	2 33 44.6 S.
Mean declinations, 23d Jan. 1799.	34 33 63 N.	28 25 23 N.	32 18 49 N.	28 29 53.2 N.	27 23 59.5 N.
Aberrations	+ 7.0	+ 2.5	− 1.6	− 2.4	− 11.3
Nutations	− 3.8	+ 4.6	+ 7.6	+ 7.5	− 1.2
True declinations	34 33 10 N.	28 25 30.1 N.	32 18 55 N.	28 29 58.3 N.	27 23 47 N.
Correct zenith distances applied	−4 35 42.7 N.	+1 31 59.9 S.	−2 21 26.7 N.	+1 27 26.8 S.	+2 33 44.6 S.
Latitudes	29 57 27.3 N.	29 57 30.0 N.	29 57 29.3 N.	29 57 25.1 N.	29 57 31.6 N.

Latitude

		o	′	″
Latitude by β Andromedæ .		29	57	27.3
do. . β Tauri . .		29	57	30.0
do. . Caſtor . .		29	57	29.3
do. . Pollux . .		29	57	25.1
do. . α Coro. Borealis .		29	57	31.6
Mean Latitude north . .		29	57	28.7

The above determination differs but 16″.3 from the latitude of New-Orleans as ſtated in the requiſite tables, and which may have ariſen from the obſervations being made in different parts of the city.

Longitude of the city of New-Orleans, deduced from the eclipſes of ♃'s ſatellites.

1799.		′	″	Daily loſs.	
				′	″
Jan. 14th. Clock too flow mean time .		9	56	. . 0	37
15th. . . . do. . . .		10	33	. . 0	36.5
19th. . . . do. . . .		12	59	. . 0	38
20th. . . . do. . . .		13	37	. . 0	36
22d. . . . do. . . .		14	49	. . 0	36
24th. . . . do. . . .		16	1	. . 0	36
Feb. 6th. . . . do. . . .		24	27	. . 0	38
17th. . . . do. . . .		29	6	. . 0	25.4

From the 24th of January, till I left New-Orleans, I was engaged in decking, and rigging a ſchooner, to tranſport our baggage, apparatus, and proviſions along the coaſt, and therefore unable to attend conſtantly to the going of the clock, which was ſet up in a place much expoſed, and probably the caſe was by ſome accident ſhifted a ſmall matter between the 6th, and 17th of February, from the poſition it had when ſet up : This appears likely from the rate of the clock's going during that interval.

An emerſion of the 1ſt ſatellite of ♃ was obſerved on the 14th of January at 6^h 10′ 37″ P. M.—the clock was then too flow mean time 10′ 05″, the obſervation was therefore made at 6^h 20′ 42″ mean time, from which deduct 9′ 48″ the equation of time, and the remainder 6^h 10′ 54″ will be the apparent time, which deducted from 12^h 12′ 19″ the apparent time at Greenwich by the theory, the remainder 6^h 1′ 25″ will be the difference of meridians.

An emerſion of the 1ſt ſatellite of ♃ was obſerved on the 21ſt of January at 8^h 2′ 9″ P. M. The clock at the time of obſervation was 14′ 34″ too flow mean time, the obſervation was of courſe made at 8^h 16′ 43″ mean time, from which deduct 12′ 0″ the equation of time, and the remainder 8^h 4′ 43″ will be the apparent time of the obſervation, which deducted from 14^h 5′ 43″, the apparent time at Greenwich by the theory, the remainder 6^h 1′ 00″ will be the difference of meridians.

On

On the 10th of February at 9ʰ 10′ 26″ P. M. an emerſion of the 2d ſatellite of ♃ was obſerved, the clock was then 26′ 26″ too ſlow mean time, the obſervation was therefore made at 9ʰ 36′ 52″ mean time, from which deduct 14′ 38″ the equation of time, and the remainder 9ʰ 22′ 14″ will be the apparent time of the obſervation, which taken from 15ʰ 22′ 5″ the apparent time at Greenwich by the theory, the remainder 5ʰ 59′ 51″ will be the difference between the meridians.

The longitude given by the 2d ſatellite, does not appear from the theory to be entitled to more than half the weight of either of thoſe by the firſt; this being admitted, the longitude will be had as below.

		Longitude weſt.		
By the emerſion of the 1ſt ſatellite on the 14th of Jan.	. .	6ʰ	1′	25″
	. .	6	1	25
By . do. . on the 21ſt of Jan.	.	6	1	0
	.	6	1	0
By an emerſion of the 2d ſatellite on the 10th of Feb.	. .	5	59	51

Mean . . . . 6 0 56 = 90° 14′ weſt from Greenwich, or 1ʰ 0′ 21″ = 15° 5′ 15″ weſt from Philadelphia.

The longitude of the city of New-Orleans is ſet down in Robertſon's Navigation at 89° 54′ 0″ or 5ʰ 59′ 36″ weſt. In the requiſite tables at 89° 58′ 45″ or 5ʰ 59′ 55″ W. and by the French academicians* at about 90° or 6ʰ weſt from Greenwich.—The difference is not conſiderable, and perhaps the reſult of my obſervations may agree with the foregoing authorities ſtill more nearly, when compared with correſponding ones, or others made about the ſame time, at any obſervatory the longitude of which has been accurately ſettled.

The obſervations on the paſſage of the ☽ over ♃, and three of his ſatellites, before mentioned, will be reduced to apparent time, by adding 34″ to each obſervation.

Obſervations made on the tranſit of ☿ in May 1799 at Miller's place on the Coenecuch river, commonly, (though erroneouſly), called the Eſcambia, in lat. 30° 49′ 33″ N. by meaſurement, from the ſouth boundary of the United States, and due ſouth from the end of two hundred and forty-eight miles, and one hundred and eighty-ſix perches eaſt from the Miſſiſſippi, in the parallel of 31° N. lat.

May 2d. The inſtruments arrived in a boat from the head of Penſacola-Bay.

f 3d.

---

* Expoſition du calcul par de la Lande 1762.

3d.   Put up the clock and fet it to apparent time nearly.

Equal altitudes of the Sun.
3ᵈ 20ʰ 22′ 34″.   4ᵈ 3ʰ 37′ 27″.

4th.

Equal altitudes of the Sun.
4ᵈ 20ʰ 30′ 17″.   5ᵈ 3ʰ 29′ 51″.

5th.

Equal altitudes of the Sun.
5ᵈ 20ʰ 22′ 47″.   6ᵈ 3ʰ 37′ 45″.

6th.   At 19ʰ ☿ appeared beautifully defined through a mid-dling heavy fog on the face of the fun, at 21ʰ the fog dif-appeared.

	h	′	″
The internal contact at the egrefs was obferved by myfelf at	22	45	24
The external do. at	22	48	29.5

The external contact is certain within the ½ of a fecond. —Magnifying power of the telefcope 200.

	h	′	″
The internal contact at the egrefs was obferved by Capt. Stephen Minor, His Catholic Majefty's commiffioner, at	22	46	21
The external do. at	22	48	14

Magnifying power of the telefcope 35.

	h	′	″
The internal contact at the egrefs was obferved by my affiftant Mr. David Gillifpie at	22	46	21
The external do. at	22	47	59

Magnifying power of the telefcope 25.

Equal altitudes of the Sun.
6ᵈ 20ʰ 15′ 21″.   7ᵈ 3ʰ 45′ 36″.

The

The rate of the clock's* going deduced from the equal altitudes.

			′	″	Daily gain.
					′ ″
May 4th.	Clock too faft mean time	.	3	23	. . 0 11
5th.	. . do. .	. .	3	34	. . 0 17
6th.	. . do.	. .	3	51	. . 0 15
7th.	. . do. .	. .	4	6	

The clock was 4′ 5″ too faft mean time when the obfervations on the tranfit of ☿ were made, and the equation of time 3′ 44″ additive to the mean time, the difference therefore between 4′ 5″ and 3′ 44″ being deduct-ed from the obfervations will give the apparent times.

A Lunar obfervation made near the mouth of the Chatta-hocha.

It was my original intention to have taken charts of the fouthern parts of all the rivers interfected by the 31ft degree of N. lat. and falling into the gulf of Mexico be-tween the Miffiffippi, and St. Marks : But having no bu-finefs up or down the Pafkagola, (which is a large river and navigable for boats of burden many miles above the boundary), it was omitted.—The Chattahocha, or as it is fometimes called the Appalachicola, is a river of more importance than the former, and a map of it from the boundary to its mouth was a defirable object ; but owing to the precipitate manner we had to leave the country in confequence of the hoftile difpofition of the Indians, and defcending the river partly in the night, it was impoffible to take a fketch of it with any tolerable degree of accu-racy.—About 4 minutes of a degree north of the entrance of its weftern branch into St. George's Sound, I found the latitude to be about 29° 46′ 51″ N.—At the fame place

on

---

* The clock was well faftened to a poft fet 3½ feet in the ground, but being neither covered, nor furrounded by any building, and feveral hun-dreds of Indians in our camp, fome individuals of whom were frequently leaning againft the poft, (though admonifhed to the contrary), which cir-cumftance might produce a fmall irregularity in the going of the regulator.

on the bank of the weftern branch, the following obfervations were made to determine the longitude.

	Watch Nº 1.	Watch Nº 2.	Double alt. ☉'s upper limb.
	d h ′ ″	d h ′ ″	o ′ ″
1799.			
Sept.	22 20 23 17	22 20 23 38	61 3 0
	22 20 23 46	22 20 24 8	61 47 10
	22 20 24 11	22 20 24 33	61 57 30 Error of Sex-
	22 20 24 49	22 20 25 11	62 12 40 tant add 10″.
	22 20 25 19	22 20 25 41	62 24 40
	22 20 26 19	22 20 26 42	62 49 50
Means	22 20 24 37	22 20 24 59	62 2 28

The obferved times, and diftances of the ☉'s and ☽'s nearest limbs.

		Dift. of the limbs.
d h ′ ″	d h ′ ″	o ′ ″
22 21 0 8	22 21 0 34	74 45 0
22 21 0 43	22 21 1 9	74 44 30
22 21 1 24	22 21 1 49	74 44 30
22 21 1 57	22 21 2 23	74 44 20 Error of Sex-
22 21 3 20	22 21 3 49	74 44 0 tant add 10″.
22 21 4 13	22 21 4 40	74 43 50
22 21 4 38	22 21 5 6	74 43 40
Means 22 21 2 20	22 21 2 47	74 44 16

Watch Nº 1.	Watch Nº 2.	Double alt. ☉'s upper limb.
d h ′ ″	d h ′ ″	o ′ ″
22 21 7 58	22 21 8 26	79 14 0
22 21 8 35	22 21 9 3	79 27 30 Error of Sex-
22 21 9 8	22 21 9 37	79 40 30 tant add 10″.
22 21 10 1	22 21 10 30	80 1 0
Means 22 21 8 55	22 21 9 24	79 35 45

The firft and third fets of obfervations were made to determine the error of the watches and their rate of going. By the firft fet of obfervations watch Nº. 1 appeared to be too flow 13″ and Nº. 2 too faft 9″. By the third fet made about 44¼ minutes after the firft, the watch Nº. 1 was too flow 23′ and Nº. 2 too faft 6″—hence Nº. 1 loft 10″ in 44¼ minutes and Nº. 2 loft 3″ nearly in fame time. The errors of the watches reduced to the time of the lunar obfervation and applied to it will give 22ᵈ 21ʰ 2′ 41″

for

for the correct apparent time. The longitude of the place of observation was estimated at 5^h 39′ west from Greenwich. From the latitude of the place, the apparent time of the observation, and the estimated longitude, the true altitude of the ☽'s centre comes out 64° 53′ 52″ and that of the ☉'s 38° 14′ 50″—from which the longitude will be had as follows:

		°	′	″			
☽'s true altitude	. . . .	64	53	52			
☉'s do. , . . .	38	14	50			
Difference true altitudes . . .	26	39	2			
☽'s apparent altitude . . .	64	29	58			
☉'s . do. . . .	38	15	56			
Difference apparent altitudes . .	26	14	2			
Apparent diſt. ☽'s and ☉'s centres .	75	16	4			
Sum	101	30	6			
Difference	49	2	2			
½ Sum	50	45	3	S	9.8889664
¼ Difference	24	31	1	.	S	9.6180087
☽'s apparent altitude . . .	64	29	58	co. ar	c. S	0.3660068
☽'s true altitude . . .	64	53	52	.	.	S	9.6276060
☉'s apparent altitude . . .	38	15	56	co. ar	c. S	0.1050480
☉'s true altitude . . .	38	14	50	.	.	S	9.8950616

$$2 \,)\, 39.5006973$$

Difference true altitudes	. .	26	39	2	. .	19.7503487
¼ Difference true altitudes	. .	13	19	31	. .	S 9.3626315
		67	43	46	. .	T^t 10.3877172
		67	43	46	. .	c. S 9.5786170
		37	27	22.5	. .	S 9.7840145
				2		

True diſtance	74	54	45.0
Diſt. at Greenwich at noon the 23^d 0^h	76	14	17
Do. . . . 23	3	74	45	57

| Difference between the 1ſt and 2d . | 1 | 19 | 32 | P. L. 3547 |
| Do. between the 2d and 3d . | 1 | 28 | 20 | P. L. 3091 |

$$0456 = 2^h\ 42'\ 4''$$
which

which added to 23 days will give for the time at Greenwich 23^d $2^h \cdot 42'$ $4''$
from which deduct the apparent time of the obfervation   22   21   2   41

Longitude of the place of obfervation weft   .   .   0   5   39   23

The above determination of the geographical pofition of the place of obfervation, is probably as correct, if not more fo, than in our beft charts. From this example it may be feen with what eafe, both the latitudes, and longitudes of places may be determined on land for common geographical purpofes with a good fextant, a well made watch with feconds, and the artificial horizon, the whole of which may be packed up in a box of 12 inches in length, 8 in width, and 4 in depth.

Philadelphia, Sept. 23d, 1800.

DEAR SIR,

IT is with real pleafure, that I embrace this opportunity of addreffing to you the following
aftronomical, and mifcellaneous obfervations, made on
the boundary between the United States, and His Catholic Majefty.

So far as this addrefs can be confidered as a mark of
refpect, you are entitled to it from the fervices you have
rendered this country, in the uniform attention, and the
judicious manner, in which you have difcharged the
laborious duties, of profeffor of the mathematicks in the
univerfity of Pennfylvania : But exclufive of this, you
are entitled to it from me in a more particular manner,
as the preceptor of my youth, and at all times fince, my
difinterefted friend.

I feel a confidence that any errors, or inaccuracies, which
may be found in the following work, will not only meet
with your indulgence, but with that of every other perfon
of fcience, acquainted with the difficulties under which
I laboured.—To William Dunbar, Efq. of the Miffiffippi
Territory I feel myfelf under the greateft obligations,
for his affiftance during the fhort time he was with us;
his extenfive fcientific acquirements, added to a fingular
facility in making mathematical calculations, would have
reduced my labour, to a mere amufement, if he had
continued.—To my affiftants Meffrs. Gillefpie, Ellicott,
junr. and Walker, the former of whom acted as furveyor, I have likewife to acknowledge my obligations,
for the promptitude with which they executed the orders,
they

they received, and the aid they gave me in making the obfervations.

I am with fincere efteem,

Your friend, &c.

AND^{W.} ELLICOTT.

Mr. ROBERT PATTERSON,
 V. P. American Philofo-
 phical Society.

___

*An Account of the Apparatus ufed on the Boundary be-
tween the United States and His Catholic Majefty.*

On behalf of the United States we had,

1ftly, One zenith fector of nearly fix feet radius fimilar to the one made by Mr. Graham for Dr. Bradley and Mr. Molyneux, with which the aberration of the ftars, and nutation of the earth's axis were difcovered, and the quantities determined.

2dly, Another zenith fector of 19 inches radius to be ufed when the utmoft accuracy was not neceffary, and where the tranfportation of the large one could not be effected without great expenfe and difficulty. Thefe inftruments were principally executed by my late worthy, and ingenious friend Mr. Rittenhoufe, except fome additions which I have made myfelf. The plumb lines of both fectors are fufpended from a notch above the axis of the inftruments, in the manner defcribed by the Rev. Dr. Mafkelyne the prefent Aftronomer Royal at Greenwich, in the introduction to the firft volume of his Aftronomical Obfervations. A particular defcription of thofe inftruments is rendered unneceffary, by being accurately done in a number of fcientific works, particularly by M. de Maupertuis in his account of the meafurement of a degree of the meridian under the arctic circle. The fector is of all inftruments the beft calculated for meafuring zenith diftances which come within its arch. The

large

large one above mentioned extends to 5 degrees north, and fouth of the zenith, and the fmall one to between 8 and 9 degrees. Stars when fo near the zenith are infenfibly affected by the different refractive powers of the atmofphere arifing from its different degrees of denfity, add to this that the error of the vifual axis is completely corrected by taking the zenith diftances of the ftars with the plane, or face of the inftrument both eaft and weft.

3dly. A large acromatic telefcope made by Mr. Dolland of London, which exclufive of a terreftrial eye piece which magnifies about 60 times has three other eye pieces for celeftial purpofes, the magnifying powers are 120, 200, and 300, the firft I generally ufed. This inftrument for producing a well defined clear image is exceeded but by few reflectors.

4thly. A tranfit and equal altitude inftrument, which I conftructed and executed in the year 1789, and ufed in running the weftern boundary of the ftate of New York, and afterwards in running the boundaries of the diftrict of Columbia, and the principal avenues in the city of Wafhington. It is mentioned in the 4th Vol. of the Tranfactions of the American Philofophical Society, No. 6. page 49.

5thly. Two acromatic telefcopes for taking fignals with fliding tubes, one of them drew out to upwards of 4 feet, and the other to about 15 inches,—the latter for its length is remarkably good, it fhews the fatellites of Jupiter very diftinctly.

6thly. A regulator which I executed in the year 1784.

7thly. An inftrument of 8 inches radius for taking horizontal angles, made by the late Mr. George Adams of London, and fimilar to the one defcribed by M. de Maupertuis in the work already mentioned.

8thly. Three brafs fextants; one of them executed by Mr. Ramfden in a fuperior ftyle. It is 7 inches radius, and by the vernier divides to 20 feconds, which may be

g   again

again fubdivided with eafe by the eye, aided with the microfcope. This fextant I ufed in taking all the lunar diftances.

9thly. A furveying compafs made by Mr. Benjamin Rittenhoufe upon the neweft, and moft approved plan.

10thly. Two excellent ftop watches, with fecond hands, to be ufed if any accident fhould happen to the regulator, or at places to which it could not be taken.

11thly. Two excellent cafes of drawing, and plotting inftruments.

12thly. Two copper lanterns to be ufed in tracing meridians, and giving the direction of lines when determined in the night by celeftial obfervation. Thofe lanterns had four fides, each fide about $4\frac{1}{2}$ inches wide, and 8 inches high: in the front of each is a flit, or aperture of about 5 inches in length, and 3 tenths of an inch in breadth; through which a lighted candle is to be feen in the night. To render this flit, or aperture more confpicuous in day-light, a flip of white paper was fometimes faftened to the copper on each fide of it, and at others a piece of white paper was placed behind the lantern, which rendered the aperture very diftinct, when the door which is on the oppofite fide to the aperture was opened. L. L. L. Plate 1. are different views of the lanterns.

13thly. An apparatus to fecure the water in ufing the artificial horizon againft the effects of the wind: As an accurate knowledge of the time, is of the utmoft confequence in aftronomy, it is abfolutely neceffary that the obfervations for that purpofe be made with certainty. On this account I fhall be more particular in defcribing the method I have purfued for fifteen years, without finding it liable to any objection of weight. It is well known that equal altitudes of the fun, or ftars, afford the readieft method of obtaining the time for occafional purpofes, and at land thofe equal altitudes muft be taken from an artificial horizon if a quadrant, or fextant be ufed. It is therefore

therefore neceſſary that the water, or any other fluid made uſe of ſhould be entirely free from any undulation both fore, and afternoon, when the obſervations are made, which will not be the caſe if the ſurface is expoſed even to a very light breeze, to effect this purpoſe I have made uſe of the following apparatus, viz.

Plate I. Fig. 1. repreſents a tin cup, about 2 inches deep, 5 inches long, and 3 wide; it is well to have the bottom made heavy by fitting ſome lead in it. This cup is to be filled with water and the wind kept from it by covering it with the roof (Fig. 2.) the ends, and lower parts of which are made of tin, and the principal part of the ſides, or inclined planes are of talc or iſinglaſs; which ſhould be of a good quality, and rendered ſufficiently thin by ſeparating, and taking off a number of laminæ with the point of a penknife. The lower part of the roof ſhould be ſo conſtructed, as to go down into the cup about 3 tenths of an inch. The degree of inclination of the planes, forming the two ſides of the roof is of little importance. The planes of the one I have always uſed ſtand nearly at right angles to each other. The lower part of the roof ſhould go eaſily into the cup, becauſe it ſometimes happens that the evaporation from the water, will be ſo abundant as to cover the iſinglaſs, and render the image of the ſun which is reflected from the water obſcure: In that caſe the roof muſt be removed a few ſeconds of time, and the particles of water on the iſinglaſs will diſappear. As the iſinglaſs when properly reduced will be very thin, and conſequently tender and delicate, it is neceſſary that it ſhould be defended againſt accidents when not in uſe, for this purpoſe a caſe of tin ſuch as repreſented by Fig. 3. will be found convenient. The equal altitudes in the following work, with a few exceptions, were taken with ſextants, ſometimes by three perſons following each other as quick as poſſible, the

correſponding

corresponding forenoon, and afternoon obfervations, were added up in feparate fums, and divided by the number of terms for the means, by which they were reduced to a fingle expreffion, as entered in the journal or diary. The three fextants gave nine obfervations, and it frequently happened that the extremes of the nine obfervations, did not differ more than 1 or $1\frac{1}{2}$ feconds. After the forenoon obfervations were made, the fextants were carefully laid away, care being taken not to touch the indexes till the afternoon obfervations were completed.

14thly. Two two-pole chains of the common conftruction.

The apparatus on the Spanifh fide was much lefs confiderable : It confifted of the following inftruments.

1ft. An excellent fextant, which graduated by the vernier to 10 feconds : It was prefented by William Dunbar, Efq. to Governor Gayofo, after my arrival in that country.

2dly. An aftronomical circle executed by Mr. Traughton of London, for the above mentioned William Dunbar, and fold by him to Governor Gayofo to be ufed on the boundary.   This inftrument is in itfelf a portable obfervatory, and executed in a mafterly manner ;—the different circles are by the vernier divided into 5 feconds, and may very eafily by the eye, aided with the microfcope be again fubdivided.   The graduations appear to be perfect, fo far as human dexterity extends.   This inftrument was fent away a few days before the Indians made an attack upon us at the mouth of Flint River.

3dly. An old furveying compafs very flightly made, and was for a fhort time accommodated with a wooden fight, which was done (with confiderable dexterity) by Mr. Patrick Taggert, a deputy furveyor on the Spanifh fide, who was very ufeful in every ftage of the bufinefs.

Obfervations

Obfervations made with the fix-feet Zenith Sector on Union Hill near the Miffiffippi river, for determining the firft point in the boundary between the United States, and His Catholic Majefty's provinces of Eaft and Weft Floridas.

Face of the Sector Weft.

1798.				o	′	″	
May 6th.	Obferved zenith diftance of	α Andromedæ	3	2	11	s.
	do. . . .	Caftor .	1	18	33.5	N.
	do. . . .	Pollux .	2	30	19	s.
7th. . .	do.	α Andromedæ	3	2	12.8	s.
	do. . . .	Caftor .	1	18	33.3	N.
	do. . . .	Pollux .	2	30	19.5	s.
	do. . . .	β Pegafi .	4	1	15	s.
8th. . .	do.	α Andromedæ	3	2	12.6	s.
	do. . . .	Pollux .	2	30	18.6	s.
	do. . . .	β Pegafi .	4	1	13.5	s.
	do. . . .	α Coro. Borealis	3	36	28.8	s.
9th. . .	do. . . .	Caftor .	1	18	33.2	N.
	do. . . .	β Pegafi .	4	1	16.3	s.
	do. . . .	α Coro. Borealis	3	36	26.2	s.

Face of the Sector Eaft

				o	′	″	
10th.	Obferved zenith diftance of	β Pegafi .	3	59	37.5	s.
11th. . .	do. . .	α Coro. Borealis	3	34	44	s.
12th. . .	do. . . .	α Andromedæ	3	0	32	s.
	do. . . .	Caftor .	1	20	10	N.
	do. . . .	Pollux .	2	28	38	s.
	do. . . .	α Coro. Borealis	3	34	46	s.
13th. . .	do. . . .	α Andromedæ	3	0	31	s.
	do. . . .	Caftor .	1	20	8.8	N.
	do. . . .	Pollux .	2	28	38	s.
	do. . .	β Pegafi .	3	59	40.5	N.
14th. . .	do. . . .	α Andromedæ	3	0	34	s.
	do. . .	α Coro. Borealis	3	34	47	s.
15th. . .	do. . . .	α Andromedæ	3	0	35	s.
	do. . .	Caftor .	1	20	12	N.
	do. . .	Pollux .	2	28	40	s.
16th. . .	do. . .	β Pegafi .	3	59	40	s.

Refult

Result of the foregoing Observations.

Face of the Sector West.

The foregoing Observed Zenith Distances when arranged stand as below.

1798.	α Andromedæ	Castor	Pollux	β Pegali	α Coro. Borealis.
May 6th.	3 2 11 s.	1 18 35.5 N.	2 30 19 s.	....	....
7th.	3 2 12.8	1 18 33.3	2 30 19.5	4 1 15 s.	....
8th.	3 2 12.6	....	2 30 18.6	4 1 13.5	3 36 28.8 s.
9th.	....	1 18 33.2	....	4 1 16.3	3 36 26.2
Means	3 2 12.1 s.	1 18 33.3 N.	2 30 19.1 s.	4 1 14.9 s.	3 36 27.5 s.

Face of the Sector East.

1798.	α Andromedæ	Castor	Pollux	β Pegali	α Coro. Borealis.
10th.	....	....	....	3 59 37.5 s.	....
11th.	....	....	....	....	3 34 44
12th.	3 0 32 s.	1 20 10 N.	2 28 38 s.	....	3 34 46
13th.	3 0 31	1 20 8.8	2 28 38	3 59 40.5	....
14th.	3 0 34	....	....	....	3 34 47
15th.	3 0 35	1 20 12	2 28 40	....	....
16th.	....	....	....	3 59 40	....
Means	3 0 33 s.	1 20 10.3 N.	2 28 38.7 s.	3 59 39.3 s.	3 34 45.7 s.
Means face of the Sector west	3 2 12.1 s.	1 18 33.3 N.	2 30 19.1 s.	4 1 14.9 s.	3 36 27.5 s.
Correct observed zenith distances	3 1 22.5 s.	1 19 21.8 N.	2 29 28.9 s.	4 0 27.1 s.	3 35 36.6 s.
Refractions	+ 3.0	+ 1.3	+ 2.5	+ 4	+ 3.5
True zenith distances	3 1 25.5 s.	1 19 23.1 N.	2 29 31.4 s.	4 0 31.1 s.	3 35 40.1 s.
Mean declination, on the 10th May	27 58 38 N.	32 18 54.4 N.	28 30 1.6 N.	26 59 26.5 N.	27 24 8.2 N.
Aberrations	— 13.2	+ 4.4	+ 3.5	— 12.7	— 4.4
Nutations	— 4.1	+ 8.7	+ 8.7	— 6.1	+ 0.8
Semi. ann. equations	— 0.5	....	....	— 0.5	+ 0.4
True declinations	27 58 20.2 N.	32 19 7.5 N.	28 30 13.8 N.	26 59 7.2 N.	27 24 5 N.
True zenith distances applied	+3 1 25.5 s.	—1 19 23.1 N.	+2 29 31.4 s.	+4 0 31.1 s.	+3 35 40.1 s.
Latitudes	30 59 45.7 N.	30 59 44.4 N.	30 59 45.2 N.	30 59 38.3 N.	30 59 45.1 N.

Latitude

			o	′	″
Latitude by	α Andromedæ	.	30	59	45.7
do.	.	Caftor	.	.	30	59	44.4
do.	.	Pollux	.	.	30	59	45.2
do.	.	β Pegafi	.	.	30	59	38.3
do.	.	α Coro. Borealis	.	30	59	45.1
Mean Latitude north	.	.	30	59	43.74

From the refult of the above obfervations it appears that the obfervatory was 16″.26 or about one thoufand, fix hundred and forty-four feet and eight-tenths of a foot Englifh meafure too far fouth, which diftance was laid off to the north on a meridional line drawn from the obfervatory O to the point A, (fee Plate I. Fig. 4.). The point A is in a deep hollow, or chafm. —From the point A a vifta was opened both to the eaft and weft, and as near at right angles to the meridian as poffible : but the point A being too low for doing it with certainty, the elevated pofition B eaft from A, and diftant thirty-four perches, was pitched upon as the moft proper place for commencing our operations. The tranfit inftrument was accordingly put up at B, and the perpendicular or vertical fibre of the telefcope, was brought to defcribe the prime vertical by taking equal altitudes of Arcturus. —This was effected in the following manner : a piece of timber T, flatted on the upper fide, was placed at the point C, diftant from B feventy-one perches, and at right angles to the vifta ; on this piece of timber at U, one of the copper lanterns already defcribed was placed on the 18th in the af-ternoon ; the tranfit inftrument being previoufly adjufted, and the vertical fibre which was a fingle thread of fpider's web, being brought to bifect the aperture in the front of the lantern — A few minutes before the ftar in its afcent was expected to appear in the field of the telefcope, it was elevated about forty-one and an half degrees : immediately upon the ftar's making its appearance, the horizontal fibre of the telefcope was brought to bifect it, and kept upon it by gradually elevating the inftrument until the ftar arrived at the interfection of the fibres, at that inftant the elevating arc was faftened, and afterwards the clamp of the perpendicular axis was loofened. On the morning of the 19th, the level of the inftrument was carefully examined and adjufted. A fhort time before the ftar was expected to appear in the field of the telefcope, in its defcent, the telefcope was directed weft : as foon as the ftar appeared in the field, the clamp was faftened and the vertical fibre brought to bifect the ftar, and kept upon it by the fcrews which direct the arm of the clamp until it arrived at the interfection of the fibres.—The elevating arc was then loofened, and the telefcope taken out of the Y's and reverfed ; a lighted candle having been previoufly put into another lantern fimilar to the firft, and placed on the fame piece of timber. The aperture of the fecond lan-tern was brought into the direction of the vertical fibre (which fuppofe to be at n) by an affiftant at C, who received the neceffary fignals for that purpofe from the obferver at B.—In the forenoon of the fame day the diftance between the apertures of the two lanterns was carefully bifected,

which

which fuppofe to be at S. The firft lantern was then removed and the aperture brought to coincide with the point of bifection. In the afternoon of the fame day, the vertical fibre of the telefcope being brought to bifect the aperture of the lantern at S, Arcturus was again obferved in its afcent, and the morning following in its defcent.—The inftrument was reverfed as in the firft cafe, and the aperture of the fecond lantern which was now put on the flatted piece of timber V, placed about 18 inches below the firft, and brought truly into the direction of the vertical fibre by an affiftant.— The candle in the firft lantern at S was then lighted, and the flames of both were bifected by the vertical fibre. Being by this obfervation convinced, that the telefcope moved accurately in the prime vertical, the line was then opened weft with that direction, the diftance of two hundred and thirty-five perches to high water mark : as the inftrument then defcribed the prime vertical, the offset into the parallel of latitude, (which became a tangent to the arc), was laid off to the north, being two and an half inches, where a hewn poft was fet up and furrounded by a mound of earth.—At S, the tangent of an angle of 2' 36" 45''' having BC for its bafe was laid off to the north by meafuring from the middle of the aperture of the lantern, the diftance of 10.68 inches, at the termination which fuppofe to be at r, a fine mark was placed, which the verticle fibre was brought to bifect. —This mark gave the direction of an arc, which continued the diftance of ten miles, would again interfect the parallel of latitude, which would then become a chord to the arc, and the offsets be to the fouth, and fall within the vifta we were opening : by taking fo fmall an arc, the trouble and expence of opening two lines through one of the moft impenetrable countries in the world was avoided.

At the termination of the firft mile ⎱ Ft. In.
which was 85 perches eaft of the tranfit ⎰ 1   0   was laid off to the fouth.
ftation at B an offset of

At the termination of the fecond mile	4	5	.	do.
do. . of the third .	7	0	.	do.
do. . of the fourth .	8	9	.	do.
do. . of the fifth .	9	9	.	do.
do. . of the fixth .	9	11	.	do.
do. . of the feventh .	9	4	.	do.
do. . of the eighth .	8	8	.	do.
do. . of the ninth .	5	9	.	do.
do. . of the tenth .	2	9	.	do.

On the 17th of July, we moved our camp to Big Bayou Sara, about 37" north of the parallel of 31° and 9.6 perches eaft of the ten mile poft. On the 19th fet up the clock, and prepared to obferve fuch of the eclipfes of ♃'s fatellites as fhould be vifible while we continued at that ftation.

Aug.

Aug. 2d.

Equal altitudes of the Sun. [*]
A. M. 8ʰ 9′ 35″.   P. M. 3ʰ 46′ 56″.

Prepared to obſerve an immerſion of the 1ſt ſatellite of ♃.—At 13ʰ 43′ a ſmall cloud began to obſcure the moon, but ♃ and his ſatellites continued very bright till about 13ʰ 44′ 26″ when the 1ſt ſatellite began to loſe its luſtre; At 13ʰ 44′ 35″ the cloud which appeared over the moon, extended itſelf almoſt inſtantaneouſly over the whole hemiſphere, and obſcured the ſtars and planets.

5th.

Equal altitudes of the Sun.
A. M. 8ʰ 6′ 41″.   P. M. 3ʰ 48′ 19″.

8th.

Equal altitudes of the Sun.
A. M. 7ʰ 57′ 19″.   P. M. 3ʰ 56′ 2″.

9th. *Emerſion* of the 2d ſatellite of ♃ obſerved at 13ʰ 13′ 9″. The planet and his ſatellites middling bright. Magnifying power of the teleſcope 120.

On the 6th and 9th of this month, at the diſtance of 9 miles and ninety perches from the firſt tranſit ſtation B, and diſtant from the point D Plate II. 10 miles and 5 perches, equal altitudes of α Delphini were taken in the ſame manner, as already related with Arcturus, to determine the direction of our arc, which on a baſe of 212.5 perches, was 31 inches ſouth of the prime vertical, which is equal to an angle of 2′ 31″ 6‴.—This angle ought to have been but 2′ 13″ 59‴, the difference 0′ 17″ 7‴ was therefore the error of the arc to the ſouth. Now ſuppoſe this error to have been gradually accumulating, which is very probable, it would at the diſtance of 9 miles and 90 perches, (the ſpace between the tranſit ſtations), have carried the arc about 2 feet too far to the ſouth: But the tranſit at the diſtance of 9 miles and 90 perches from the firſt ſtation, ought to have been 2 feet and 7 inches north of the parallel, the difference therefore of 7 inches is the diſtance of the tranſit to the north of the parallel at its ſecond ſtation, and which is included in the offsets for the ſecond arc to the termination of 18 miles, and 118 perches from the point D.—On the 9th another arc for 10 miles was laid off, making an angle of 2′ 36″ 45‴ with the prime vertical. The baſe was 212.5 perches eaſt, and the perpendicular 32 inches north from the aperture of the lantern.

12th.

Equal altitudes of the Sun.
A. M. 8ʰ 6′ 48″.   P. M. 3ʰ 47′ 7″.

h   **15th.**

---

[*] The equal altitudes of the ſun, and his paſſage over the meridian with the thermometrical obſervations when they occur, are entered according to the civil account, the others according to the mode of aſtronomers.

15th.   *Equal altitudes of the Sun.*
A. M. 8^h 32′ 55″   P. M. 3^h 15′ 55″

16th. *Immersion* of the 2d satellite of ♃ }
    observed at   }   13^h 22′ 45″
Emersion   .   do.   .   .   15   48   16
The night clear, Belts distinct, magnifying power 120.

17th.   *Equal altitudes of the Sun.*
A. M. 8^h 14′ 57″   P. M. 3^h 32′ 27″

23d.   *Equal altitudes of the Sun.*
A. M. 8^h 23′ 8″.   P. M. 3^h 19′ 54″.

Immersion of the 2d satellite of ♃ observed at 15^h 58′ 25″.
Belts distinct, magnifying power 120.

30th.   *Equal altitudes of the Sun.*
A. M. 8^h 22′ 40″.   P. M. 3^h 14′ 34″.

31st.   Clock ran down in the morning, wound
it up and set it a-going, and took the following

Equal altitudes of the Sun.
A. M. 9 42 22.5.   P. M. 2 26 11.

Sept. 1st.   *Equal altitudes of the Sun.*
A. M. 8^h 28′ 47″.   P. M. 3^h 38′ 54″.

Immersion of the 1st satellite of ♃ observed at 15^h 58′ 50″.
Belts very distinct, magnifying power 120.

2d.   *Equal altitudes of the Sun.*
A. M. 8^h 29′ 15″.   P. M. 3^h 37′ 32″.

This was the last observation made at Bayou
Sara.

Result

Refult of the equal altitudes of the Sun taken at Bayou Sara.

			′	″	Daily lofs. ″
Clock too flow mean time Aug.	2d.	. .	7	28.3	. . 9.8
do.	5th.	.	7	57.6	. . 9.2
do.	8th.	. .	8	25.1	. . 9.1
do.	12th.	.	9	1.7	. . 9.1
do.	15th.	. .	9	31.0	. . 9.5
do.	17th.	.	9	49.4	. . 9.2
do.	23d.	. .	10	33.9	. . 7.4
do.	30th.	. .	11	27.5	. . 7.7

Clock ran down early in the morning of the 31ft, wound it and fet it a-going.

			′	″	Daily lofs. ″
Clock too faft mean time Aug.	31ft.	. .	4	30	. . 6.7
do.	Sept. 1ft.	. .	4	23.3	. 7.6
do.	2d.	.	4	15.7	

Longitude deduced from the eclipfes of Jupiter's fatellites, obferevd at Bayou Sara.

Auguft	9th.	Emerfion of the 2d fatellite	6ʰ	3′	17″	
	16th.	Immerfion of . do.	6	3	3	Weft from Greenwich.
		Emerfion of . do.	6	3	58	
	23d.	Immerfion . do.	6	4	27	
Sept.	1ft.	Immerfion of the 1ft do.	6	5	21	

When the firft point of latitude was determined on the Miffiffippi, the annual inundation prevented our approaching the banks of the river : But on the 28th of July, the waters having fubfided it was mutually agreed that William Dunbar, Efq. his Catholic Majefty's aftronomical commif-fioner, fhould proceed to the point D at high water mark, and extend the line from that point to the eaftern bank of the river aforefaid, which he completed on the 18th of Auguft, and whofe report is in the following words.

" On the 28th of July, the line then approaching the 10th mile, and learning that the waters of the inundation were retired within the banks of the Miffiffippi, fo that the lands were become fufficiently dry to give firm footing to the labourers, the aftronomer for IIis Catholic Majefty taking upon himfelf the extending of the line through the river low ground to the eaftern margin of the Miffiffippi. The party allotted for this fervice did accordingly encamp at the point D, pufhing the line forward in continuation of the tangent commencing at the point B. Judging the prefent a con-venient pofition for verifying the direction of the line, the aftronomer for His Catholic Majefty eftablifhed his obfervatory near the point D, and made the following obfervations with the circular inftrument* placed in the direction of the tangent, viz.

h 2 " On

---

* The aftronomical circle already mentioned.

" On the aftronomical 15th of Auguft were taken equal altitudes of the ftar τ Pe afi the eaftern obfervatory* being made precifely on the vertical arc correfponding to the line, and the fecond to the weftward being completed, and the circle with its telefcope reverfed, the axis of the inftrument was found to make an angle to the fouth of 20″ with the lantern placed carefully in the direction of the line, and confequently the direction of the line at the obfervatory is 10″ to the north of eaft. The diftance of the obfervatory from the point B is 3430 French feet,† therefore by calculation the line paffing through the obfervatory makes an angle of 21″ 41‴ northerly with due eaft : But by obfervation this angle is only 10′, hence it would appear that the line inclines too much to the fouth by the quantity of 11″ 41‴, which in running 100 miles would caufe a deviation of nearly 28 French feet. So fmall a difference between the two fets of obfervations may well arife from the imperfection of inftruments, combined with the unavoidable errors of obfervation.

" The line being extended to the margin of the Miffiffippi on the 17th of Auguft, the meafurement from the point D was found to be 2 miles and 180 perches Englifh meafure, or 2111.42 French toifes. At the diftance of 1 and 2 miles at the points x and y, were erected fquare pofts furrounded by mounds of earth, and at the diftance of 88 French feet from the margin of the river, and in the parallel of latitude was erected a fquare poft 10 feet high furrounded by a mound of eight feet in height. On this poft is infcribed on the fouth fide a crown with the letter R underneath ; on the north U. S. and the weft fronting the river, Agofto 18th, 1798. Lat. 31° N. In erecting the mile pofts, due regard was paid to the quantity of the offsets to the north of the tangent, and are by calculation as follows,

Mounds.	Diftance from the point B. French Meafure.			Diftance from the point B. Englifh Meafure.			Offsets Englifh Meafure			Offsets French Meafure.		
	Toifes.	Feet.	Tenths.	Miles.	Perches.	Feet.	Feet.	Inches.	Tenths.	Feet.	Inches.	Lines.
D	602	3.	2	0	234	0	0	2.6		0	2.5	
x	1426	2.	0	1	234	0	1	2.4		1	1.6	
y	2250	1.	8	2	234	0	2	11.86		2	9.7	
z	2690	0.	7	3	88	4	4	3.6		4	0.4″	

On Monday the 20th of Auguft, the aftronomer for His Catholic Majefty returned with his party to camp at Bayou Sara.

On

---

* The point B.
† Mr. Dunbar's obfervatory, was a fhort diftance eaft of the point D, which is at the foot of a fteep hill.

On the firſt day of September following, William Dunbar, Eſq. after making the foregoing report declined any further ſervice and returned home.

Sept. 3d. Moved our camp to Thompſon's creek, diſtant from the point D at high water mark 18.75 miles.

4th. Cleaned the clock, and ſet it up againſt the ſtump of a tree, which was left high, and prepared for that purpoſe.

7th. *Equal altitudes of the Sun.*

A. M. 8 25 42 5.   P. M. 3 33 19.

8th. *Equal altitudes of the Sun.*

A. M. 8 18 16.5   P. M. 3 40 29.

9th. *Equal altitudes of the Sun.*
A. M. 8^h 22' 50''   P. M. 3^h 35' 28''.

10th. *Equal altitudes of the Sun*
A. M. 8^h 21' 27''.   P. M. 3^h 36' 28''.

Immerſion of the 2d ſatellite of ♃ obſerved at 10^h 45' 8'''
do. . 1ſt. . do. . 12 19 11
The night remarkably fine, belts very diſtinct, magnifying power 120.

11th. *Equal altitudes of the Sun.*
A. M. 8^h 28' 9''.   P. M. 3^h 29' 20''.

12th. *Equal altitudes of the Sun.*
A. M. 8^h 18' 12''.   P. M. 3^h 38' 45''.

13th. *Equal altitudes of the Sun.*

A. M. 8 12 38.5.   P. M. 3 43 51.

16th.

16th.

Equal altitudes of the Sun.

h ' ''   h ' ''

A. M. 8 18 13.5.   P. M. 3 36 44.5.

17th.

Equal altitudes of the Sun.

h ' ''   h ' ''

A. M. 8 47 33.   P. M. 3 6 57.5.

Immerſion of the 2d ſatellite of ♃ obſerved at 13ʰ 23' 35''
do.   .   1ſt   .   do.   .   14 14   1
Night clear, belts diſtinct, magnifying power 120.

19th.

Equal altitudes of the Sun.

h ' ''   h ' ''

A. M. 9 3 50.5.   P. M. 2 49 39.5

23d.

Equal altitudes of the Sun.
A. M. 9ʰ 4' 3''.   P. M. 2ʰ 47' 37''.

24th.

Equal altitudes of the Sun.

h ' ''   h ' ''

A. M. 8 49 57.   P. M. 3 1 23.5.

Immerſion of the 2d ſatellite of ♃ obſerved at 16ʰ 2' 1''
do.   .   1ſt   .   do.   .   16 8 40
Night clear, belts diſtinct, magnifying power 120.

25th.

Equal altitudes of the Sun.

h ' ''   h ' ''

A. M. 8 46 32.5.   P. M. 3 4 22.5.

26th.

Equal altitudes of the Sun.
A. M. 8ʰ 44' 54''.   P. M. 3ʰ 5' 41''.

Immerſion of the 1ſt ſatellite of ♃ obſerved at 10ʰ 37' 10''
do.   .   3d   .   do.   .   11 28 32
Emerſion   do.   .   do.   .   13 15 40
Night fine, belts diſtinct, magnifying power 120.

The

The arc being now extended to the weſt ſide of Thompſon's creek, the following offsets into the parallel of latitude were laid off, viz.

			F.	In.	
At the termination of the 11th mile an offset of	4	2	to the ſouth
do.	12	do.	6	11	do.
do.	13	do.	8	11	do.
do.	14	do.	10	2	do.
do.	15	do.	10	7	do.
do.	16	do.	10	3	do.
do.	17	do.	9	0	do.
do.	18	do.	7	0	do.

Took equal altitudes of τ Pegaſi, to determine the direction of our arc, which at the diſtance of 206 perches eaſt from the tranſit, was 19.35 inches ſouth of the prime vertical, which ſubtends an angle of 1′ 40″ 48‴. The tranſit was 8 miles and 118 perches eaſt from its ſecond ſtation, which diſtance ſhould have given an angle of 1′ 44″ 52‴, hence it appears, that the arc was directed too far north by 4″ 4‴ on a ſuppoſition that this was gradually accumulating, the tranſit was too far north by 6.8 inches, which is accounted for in the offsets for the 19th, 20th, and 21ſt miles.

27th.   Re-examined the direction of our arc by taking equal altitudes of the ſame ſtar, the coincidence was leſs than $1\frac{1}{2}$″ which was probably occaſioned by an imperfection inſeparable from obſervations: this ſmall difference was biſected and the diſtance of 20.8 inches was laid off from the point of biſection to the ſouth, and the arc continued through its termination as in the former caſes.

29th. Clock ran down in the night.
30th. Wound up the clock and ſet it a-going.

Oct. 7th.   *Equal altitudes of the Sun.*
A. M. 8ʰ 36′ 1″.   P. M. 3ʰ 21′ 44″.

19th.   *Equal altitudes of the Sun.*
A. M. 8ʰ 27′ 29″.   P. M. 3ʰ 27′ 50″.

Immerſion of the 1ſt ſatellite of ♃ obſerved at 10ʰ 55′ 31‴
do.   2d   do.   13 21 15
Night very fine, belts diſtinct, magnifying power 120.
20th.

20th.   *Equal altitudes of the Sun.*

h   */*   *//*   h   */*   *//*

A. M. 9 30 6.5.   P. M. 2 25 5.

End of the aftronomical obfervations made at Thompfon's creek.

The following offsets complete the work done with the Tranfit inftrument, viz.

					F.	In.	
At the termination of the 19th mile an offset of					4	3	was laid off to the S.
do.	.	20	.	do.	1	2	do.
do.	.	21	.	do.	3	1	to the North.

Refult of the equal altitudes of the Sun taken at Thompfon's creek.

					/	*//*	Daily gain.
Clock too faft mean time Sept.			7th.	.	2	1.8	doubtful 13 0 *(")*
do.	.	.	. 8th.	.	2	14.8	6.5
do.	.	.	. 9th.	.	2	21.3	8.8
do.	.	.	. 10th.	.	2	30.1	7.8
do.	.	.	. 11th.	.	2	37.9	4.7
do.	.	.	. 12th.	.	2	42.6	7.4
do.	.	.	. 13th.	.	2	50.0	5.7
do.	.	.	. 16th.	.	3	7.2	7.0
do.	.	.	. 17th.	.	3	14.2	5.9
do.	.	.	. 19th.	.	3	26.1	7.1
do.	.	.	. 23d.	.	3	54.7	11.1
do.	.	.	. 24th.	.	4	5.8*	8.4
do.	.	.	. 25th.	.	4	13.2	11.7
do.	.	.	. 26th.	.	4	24.9	

Clock ran down on the 29th, was fet a-going on the 30th.

					/	*I*	Daily gain.
Clock too faft mean time Oct. 6th.		.		⟶	11	14.1	*("")*
do.	.	.	7th.	.	11	23.4	9.3
do.	.	.	19th.	.	12	53	7.5
do.	.	.	20th.	.	12	58.5	5.5
							Longitude

---

* The night preceding this obfervation, the tent in which the clock was placed was blown down and lodged on the clock till morning, when it was removed.

Longitude deduced from the eclipfes of ♃'s fatellites obferved at Thom-
fon's Creek.

					h	′	″	
Sept. 10th.	*Immerfion* of the 2d fatellite				6	4	14	} Longitude weft from Greenwich.
	do.	.	1ft	do.	6	5	8	
17th.	do.	.	2d	do.	6	3	58	
	do.	.	1ft	do.	6	4	45	
24th.	do.	.	2d	do.	6	3	50	
	do.	.	1ft	do.	6	4	37	
	do.	.	1ft	do.	6	4	41	
26th.	do.	.	3d do. { by de Lam-bre's Tables. }		6	3	4	
	Emerfion	.	do. do.	do.	6	6	48	
Oct. 19th.	*Immerfion*	.	1ft	do.	6	4	49	
	do.	.	2d	do.	6	4	52	

At the end of the 21ft mile in the line, the land became of a more inferior quality, from which we concluded to purfue a lefs fcientific but a more expeditious method, until the goodnefs of the foil would juftify a greater
degree of accuracy : Agreeably to this conclufion, we had
a line traced eaft with a furveying compafs, from the end
of the 21ft mile, from high water mark on the Miffiffippi, to the eaft fide of Pearl or Half-way river, the
diftance being 85 miles and 194 perches, at the end of
which the following obfervations were made.

Nov. 19th.   Put up the clock and fet it to apparent time
nearly.

20th.   *Equal altitudes of the Sun.*
                A. M. 9^h 22′ 40″.   P. M. 2^h 37′ 30″.

       Emerfion of the 1ft fatellite of ♃ obferved at 9^h 43′ 30″.
—Belts diftinct, magnifying power 120.

21ft.   *Equal altitudes of the Sun.*
                A. M. 9^h 33′ 19″.   P. M. 2^h 27′ 6″.

22d.   *Equal altitudes of the Sun.*
                A. M. 9^h 38′ 34″.   P. M. 2^h 22′ 9″.

i   Obfervations

Obfervations on a Lunar Eclipfe.

At 17ʰ 10′ the ☽'s limb entered the penumbra, but was not indented till 17ʰ 11′ 34″.—The earth's fhadow was not well defined, and the atmofphere fmoky.— The ☽ was obfcured by clouds at 17ʰ 25′.—Magnifying power of the telefcope about 60.

25th.

Equal altitudes of the Sun.
A. M. 9ʰ 34′ 39″.   P. M. 2ʰ 27′ 19″.

28th.

Equal altitudes of the Sun.
A. M. 9ʰ 18′ 42″.   P. M. 2ʰ 44′ 55″.

30th.

Equal altitudes of the Sun.
A. M. 9ʰ 17′ 11″.   P. M. 2ʰ 44′ 18″.

The fmall zenith fector arrived, which we agreed to ufe for the determination of this point in the line.—The large one having been fent by water by the way of New-Orleans, and we were uncertain when it would come to hand.

Thermometer 84°.

Dec. 1ft.   Polifhed the reflectors of the eye-piece, of the telefcope of the fmall zenith fector, and fet it up

With the face to the Weft.

Cloudy.—Thermometer 60° at fun rife, rofe to 83°.

2d.   Cloudy.—Thermometer 64° at fun rife, rofe to 84°.

3d.

Equal altitudes of the Sun.
h   ′   ″   h   ′   ″
A. M. 9 34 8.5.   P. M. 2 31 45.5.

Thermo-

Thermometer 54° at fun rife, rofe to 70°.

			o	'	"	
Obferved zenith diftance	α Lyræ	.	7	34	10	N.
do.	. .	β Pegafi	4	2	22	s.
do.	. .	α Andromedæ	3	3	19	s.
do.	. .	β Andromedæ	3	30	47	N.
do.	. .	β Tauri	2	36	46	s.
do.	. .	Caftor	1	16	38	N.
do.	. .	Pollux	2	32	3	's.

4th.
Equal altitudes of the Sun.
A. M. 9ʰ 30' 11".   P. M. 2ʰ 36' 26".

Thermometer 28° at fun rife, rofe 50°.

			o	'	"	
Obferved zenith diftance of	α Lyræ	.	7	34	9	N.
do.	. .	β Pegafi	4	2	22	s.
do.	. .	α Andromedæ	3	3	18	s.
do.	. .	β Andromedæ	3	30	45	N.
do.	. .	β Tauri	2	36	37.5	s.
do.	. .	Caftor	1	16	38	N.
do.	. .	Pollux	2	32	8	s.

Emerfion of the 1ft fatellite of ♃ obferved at 13ʰ 32' 35".
—Night clear, belts diftinct, magnifying power 120.

5th.
Equal altitudes of the Sun.
A. M. 9ʰ 40' 59".   P. M. 2ʰ 36' 35".

Face of the Sector Eaft.

Thermometer 26° at fun rife, rofe to 45°
in the afternoon, and to 60° after night.

Obferved zenith diftance of α Andromedæ 2° 59' 0" s.
The ftar was feen but a few times during the obfervation
between the clouds as they paffed.

6th.   Cloudy with fome rain in the morning,
and fo dark that we had to breakfaft by candle light at 8ʰ A. M.

     7th.

7th.   Cloudy with fome rain.—Thermometer
55° at fun rife, rofe to 70°.

8th.   The clouds blew off a few minutes, when
the following obfervation was made.

Obferved zenith diftance of α Andromedæ 2° 59′ 6″ s.

Immediately after the above obfervation was made, the
hemifphere was covered with dark clouds, which were attended with rain, fharp lightning, and heavy thunder till
the next morning.

Thermometer 60° at fun rife, rofe to 82°.

				°	′	″	
9th.	Obferved zenith diftance of	α Lyræ	.	7	38	0	N.
	do. . .	β Pegafi	.	3	58	16	s.
	do. . .	α Andromedæ		2	59	8	s.
	do. . .	β Andromedæ		3	35	11	N.

Cloudy the remainder of the night.
Thermometer 51° at fun rife, fell to 31° in
the evening.

10th.   *Equal altitudes of the Sun.*
        A. M. 8ʰ 20′ 21″.   P. M. 3ʰ 50′ 33″.

_____

			°	′	″	
Obferved zenith diftance of	α Lyræ	.	7	38	1	N.
do. . .	β Pegafi	.	3	58	19	s.
do. . .	α Andromedæ		2	59	9	s.
do. . .	β Tauri	.	2	52	32	s.

Juft before the obfervation on α Andromedæ was made,
a cloud appeared above the horizon and about 30° fouth
of weft: From this cloud a number of ftreamers iffued
fimilar to an Aurora borealis, but much whiter.—One of
them paffed above the fouthern horizon, and terminated
in the weft fhoulder of Orion; another paffed over Mars
and Jupiter, and extended almoft to the eaftern horizon;
a third paffed through the northern part of Andromedæ,
and a fourth through Urfa Minor.—Thefe ftreamers in a
few

few minutes broke into very minute clouds which moved with great rapidity towards the eaſt, and in leſs than fifteen minutes extended over the whole hemiſphere.— The ſtars appeared and diſappeared almoſt inſtantly; I ſuppoſe that α Andromedæ not leſs than thirty times during the obſervation; ε Andromedæ was likewiſe ſeen, but it appeared and diſappeared too rapidly to be obſerved with any degree of certainty. β Tauri was ſeen almoſt as frequently as β Andromedæ, but the obſervation neverthelefs appeared to be correct. Before Caſtor and Pollux came to the meridian, the clouds became heavy and dark, and obſcured all the ſtars for the remainder of the night. This phenomenon was not attended with any wind.

Thermometer 31° at ſun riſe, roſe to 45°.

11th.   *Equal altitudes of the Sun.*

	h	′	″		h	′	″
A. M.	8	37	12.5.	P. M.	3	34	22.

			°	′	″	
Obſerved zenith diſtance of	α Lyræ	.	7	38	1	N.
do.	.	.	β Pegaſi	.	3	58	18	s.
do.	.	.	α Andromedæ	2	59	2	s.
do.	.	.	β Andromedæ	3	35	7	N.
do.	.	.	β Tauri	.	2	32	28	s.
do.	.	.	Caſtor	.	1	20	59	N.
do.	.	.	Pollux	.	2	27	58	s.

Emerſion of the 1ſt ſatellite of ♃ obſerved at 15ʰ 26′ 34″. —The planet was low and tremulous, the belts middling diſtinct, magnifying power of the teleſcope 120.

Thermometer during the three laſt obſervations at 21°.

12th.   Cloudy all day.
13th.   Cloudy till evening.

Obſerved

		°	′	″	
Obferved zenith diftance of β Pegafi	.	3	58	13	s.
do. . . β Andromedæ		3	35	4	N.
do. . . β Tauri	.	2	32	34	s.
do. . . . Caftor	.	1	21	4	N.
do. . . Pollux	.	2	27	58	s.

Emerfion of the 1ft fatellite of ♃ obferved at 9^h 54′ 2″. The night clear, belts very diftinct, magnifying power 120.

Thermometer 22° at fun rife, rofe to 57°.

14th. *Immerfion* of the 3d fatellite of ♃ obferved at 7^h 44′ 6″. —The belts very diftinct, and the fatellites remarkably bright, magnifying power 120.

Thermometer 31° at fun rife, rofe to 61°.

15th.   *Equal altitudes of the Sun.*
          A. M. 8^h 20′ 34″.   P. M. 3^h 52′ 42″.

Emerfion of the 2d fatellite of ♃ obferved at 12^h 50′ 19″. —Belts diftinct, magnifying power 120.

End of the obfervations made at Pearl river.

Rate of the clock's going deduced from the equal altitudes of the Sun.

			′	″		″	
Clock too faft mean time Nov. 20th.			14	8.6	.	8.5	daily lofs.
do. . . 21ft.			14	0.1	.	8.2	do.
do. . . 22d.			13	51.9	.	5.2	do.
do. . . 25th.			13	36.3	.	4.0	do.
do. . . 28th.			13	24.3	.	9.1	do.
do. . . 30th.			13	6	.	9.7	do.
do. . Dec. 3d.			12	37.1	.	3.5	do.
do. . . 4th.			12	33.6	.	2.9	daily gain.
do. . . 5th.*			12	36.5	.	7.1	daily lofs.
do. . . 10th.			12	1	.	8.4	do.
do. . . 11th.			11	52.7	.	16.4	do.
do. . . 15th.			10	47.1	.		
							Refult

---

* Till this time the clock was left expofed, and people frequently leaning againft the poft to which it was faftened, and the poft ftanding in fand, no better place to be had.

Refult of the obfervations for the longitude.

Nov.	20th.	*Emerfion* of the 1ft fatellite of ♃				6	0	24	⎫
Dec.	4th.	.	do.	.	.	.	5	58	58	⎪
	11th.	.	do.	.	.	.	5	59	8	⎪
	13th.	.	do.	.	.	.	5	59	53	⎪

14th. *Immerfion* of the 3d do. by ⎱
     do Lambre's Tables. ⎰   5   59   45

15th. *Emerfion* of the 2d do.   .   5   59   5 ⎰ Weft from
                                                         ·Greenwich.

By the lunar eclipfe November 22d.

If the ☽'s firft touching the penumbra be ⎱
confidered as the beginning, the longitude will be ⎰ 5   59   38

If the ☽'s being indented be taken for the ⎱
beginning, the longitude will be ⎰ 6   1   12

Refult

Result of the observations for the latitude.

The foregoing observed Zenith Distances when arranged stand as below.

Face of the Sector West.

	α Lyræ. N.	β Pegasi.	α Andromedæ. S.	β Andromedæ. N.	β Tauri. S.	Castor. N.	Pollux. S.
December 3d	7 34 10	4 2 22	3 3 19	3 30 47	2 36 46	1 16 38	2 32 3
4th.	7 34 9	4 2 22	3 3 18	3 30 45	2 36 37.5	1 16 38	2 32 8
Means . .	7 34 9.5	4 2 22	3 3 18.5	3 30 46	2 36 41.7	1 16 38	2 32 5.5

Face of the Sector East.

	α Lyræ.	β Pegasi.	α Andromedæ.	β Andromedæ.	β Tauri.	Castor.	Pollux.
5th.	·	·	2 59 0	·	·	·	·
8th.	·	·	2 59 6	·	·	·	·
9th.	7 38 0	3 58 16	2 59 8	3 35 11	2 32 32	1 20 59	2 27 58
10th.	7 38 1	3 58 19	2 59 9	·	2 32 28	·	·
11th.	7 38 1	3 58 18	2 59 2	3 35 7	2 32 34	1 21 4	2 27 58
13th.	·	3 58 13	·	3 35 4	·	·	·
Means . . .	7 38 0.7	3 58 16.5	2 59 5	3 35 7	2 32 31	1 21 1.5	2 27 58
Means face west .	7 34 9.5	4 2 22	3 3 18.5	3 30 46	2 36 41.7	1 16 38	2 32 5.5
True observed zenith distances	7 36 5.1	4 0 19.2	3 1 11.7	3 32 56.5	2 34 36.3	1 18 49.7	2 30 1.7
Refractions	+ 7.5	+ 4	+ 3	+ 3.5	+ 2.5	+ 1.2	+ 2.5
Correct zenith distances . . .	7 36 12.6	4 0 23.2	3 1 14.7	3 33 0	2 34 38.8	1 18 50.9	2 30 4.2
Mean declinations to the 9th .	38 36 11.1 N.	26 59 32.9 N.	27 58 41.6 N.	34 33 4.0 N.	28 25 19.4 N.	32 18 46.5 N.	28 29 57.4 N.
Aberrations	+ 5.7	+ 10.6	+ 10.7	+ 11.5	+ 1.5	- 4.0	- 3.8
Nutations	- 6.4	- 7.0	- 5.7	- 4	+ 4.5	+ 7.3	+ 7.5
True declinations	38 36 10.4	26 59 36.5	27 58 46.6	34 33 11.5	28 25 25.4	32 18 49.8	28 30 1.1
Correct zenith distances . . .	-7 36 12.6	+4 0 23.2	+3 1 14.7	-3 33 0	+2 34 38.8	-1 18 50.9	+2 30 4.2
Latitudes	30 59 57.8 N.	30 59 59.7 N.	31 0 1.3 N.	31 0 11.5 N.	31 0 4.2 N.	30 59 58.9 N.	31 0 5.2 N.

Latitude

			o	′	″
Latitude by	α Lyræ	. .	30	59	57.8
do.	β Pegaſi	. .	30	59	59.7
do.	α Andromedæ	.	31	0	1.3
do.	β Andromedæ	.	31	0	11.5
do.	β Tauri	. .	31	0	4.2
do.	Caſtor	.	30	59	58.9
do.	Pollux	.	31	0	5.2
Mean latitude North		. .	31	0	2.7

From the above reſult for the latitude, it appears that the obſervatory was too far north by 2″.7 or about 272 feet, and the guide or compaſs line being 68.8 feet ſouth of the obſervatory, it appears that the guide or compaſs line oppoſite to the obſervatory was too far north by 213.2 feet. This correction of 213.2 feet was carefully laid off to the ſouth, and the guide, or compaſs line corrected back to the 21ſt mile, by laying off to the ſouth from the end of each mile a proportional part of the 213.2 feet —For a chart of this part of the boundary ſee Plate III.* From the termination of the 213.2 feet, another guide or compaſs line was carried eaſt 99 miles, and 194 perches, to the weſtern bank of the Mobile, or Tombecby river, where the following obſervations were made.

1799.

March 18th.   Put up the clock and ſet it to apparent time nearly.

Set up the large Sector with the Face to the Eaſt.

19th.   Cloudy with heavy rain at night.

20th.   Flying clouds great part of the day, heavy rain in the afternoon, and evening, attended with ſharp lightning, and remarkably loud thunder.

21ſt.   Cloudy all day with a little rain and ſtrong north wind, cleared off about midnight with a violent wind from the N. W.

Obſerved zenith diſtance of α Coro. Borealis 3° 36′ 55″ s.

The above obſervation is doubtful owing to the violence of the wind which affected the plumb-line.

* The offsets were too ſmall to be laid down on the chart.

k

22d.

22d.   *Equal altitudes of the Sun.*
                A. M. 8ʰ 56′ 16″.   P. M. 3ʰ 3′ 13″.

Obſerved zenith diſtance of β Tauri   .   2° 35′ 0″.5 s.
    do.   .   .   α Coro. Borealis 3 36 53   s.

Thermometer 40° at ſun riſe, roſe to 51°.

23d.   *Equal altitudes of the Sun.*
                A. M. 8ʰ 44′ 36″.   P. M. 3ʰ 13′ 23″.

                                           o   ′   ″
Obſerved zenith diſtance   β Tauri   .   2 34 59.5 s.
    do.   .   .   Caſtor   .   1 18 26.7 N.
    do.   .   .   Pollux   .   2 30 29   s.
    do.   .   α Coro. Borealis 3 36 55   s.

Set up the tranſit and equal altitude inſtrument, and took
the greateſt elongation of α Urſæ Minor. Weſt.

Thermometer 39° at ſun riſe, roſe to 67°
in the afternoon.

24th.   *Equal altitudes of the Sun.*
                A. M. 9ʰ 29′ 0″   P. M. 2ʰ 28′ 2″

Took the greateſt elongation of α Urſæ Minor. Weſt, which
did not differ perceptibly from the obſervation of yeſterday.

Obſerved zenith diſtance of   Caſtor   1° 18′ 28″.8 N.
    do.   .   .   Pollux   2 30 30   s.

Took the greateſt elongation of α Urſæ Minor. Eaſt.
The obſervations on α Urſæ Minor. were made for the
purpoſe of tracing a meridian, a particular account of which
will cloſe the work done at this ſtation.

Thermometer 39° at ſun riſe, roſe to 59°.

25th.   *Equal altitudes of the Sun.*
                A. M. 9ʰ 0′ 21″.   P. M. 2ʰ 55′ 49″.

Obſerved zenith diſtance of   β Tauri   2° 34′ 57″.5 s.
                                                Took

Took the greateſt elongation of α Urſæ Minor. Weſt.

Obſerved zenith diſtance of	Caſtor	1° 18′ 27″.5 N.
do.	Pollux	2 30 26 s.

Took the greateſt elongation of α Urſæ Minor. Eaſt.

Thermometer 40° at ſun riſe.

26th.   Set the clock two minutes forward, and raiſed the pendulum bob.

Turned the face of the Sector Weſt.

Equal altitudes of the Sun.
A. M. 9ʰ 3′ 52″.   P. M. 2ʰ 55′ 26″.5.

Traced a meridian by biſecting the angle, formed by the greateſt elongations of α Urſæ Minor. Eaſt, and Weſt.

	° ′ ″	
⊙'s preceding limb on the meridian at	11 58 26*	A. M.
Subſequent do.	0 0 34	P. M.
Centre at	11 59 30	A. M.

	h ′ ″
Sirius paſſed the firſt fibre of the tranſit inſtrument at	6 11 41
The meridian at	6 12 29
The third fibre at	6 13 24

		h ′ ″	
27th.	⊙'s preceding limb on the meridian at	11 58 15	A. M.
	Subſequent do.	12 0 23	P. M.
	Centre at	11 59 19	A. M.

Obſerved zenith diſtance of β Tauri 2° 36′ 38″.5 s.

k 2

Sirius

---

* The Sun's paſſage over the meridian when it occurs, is entered according to the civil account.

		h	′	″
Sirius paſſed the firſt fibre of the tranſit inſtrument at	.	6	7	52
The meridian　at	.	6	8	41
The third fibre　at	.	6	9	36

			h	′	″	
Obſerved zenith diſtance of	Caſtor	.	1	16	47.4	N.
do.	.	Pollux	.	2	32	3	s.
do.	.	α Coro. Borealis	3	38	25	s.

Thermometer 41° in the morning, raiſed to 67°.

28th. ☉'s preceding limb on the meridian at　11 58　5.5 A. M.
　　　　Subſequent　do.　.　.　12　0　14　P. M.

　　　　Centre　.　.　.　.　11　59　9.7 A. M.

		h	′	″
Sirius paſſed the firſt fibre of the tranſit inſtrument at	.	6	4	6
The meridian　at	.	6	4	55
The third fibre　at	.	6	5	51

Obſerved zenith diſtance of　Caſtor　1° 16′ 48″.6 N.
　　　　do.　.　.　Pollux　2　32　5　s.

Thermometer 49° at ſun riſe.

29th. ☉'s preceding limb on the meridian at　11 57 59　A. M.
　　　　Subſequent　do.　.　.　.　12　0　7　P. M.

　　　　Centre　do.　.　.　.　11　59　3　A. M.

Obſerved zenith diſtance of　Caſtor　1° 16′ 50″.5
　　　　do.　.　.　Pollux　2　32　3

Thermometer 51° at ſun riſe, roſe to 73°.
30th.　Cloudy with rain.

31ſt. ☉'s preceding limb on the meridian at　11 57 41　A. M.
　　　　Subſequent　do.　.　.　.　11　59　50　A. M.

　　　　Centre　do.　.　.　.　11　58　45.5 A. M.

Obſerved

Obferved zenith diſtance of   β Tauri 2° 36′ 37″.7

		h	′	″
Sirius paſſed the firſt fibre of the tranſit inſtrument at	.	5	52	50
The meridian at	.	5	53	39
The third fibre at	.	5	54	34

		o	′	″	
Obferved zenith diſtance of	Caſtor .	1	16	50	N.
do. .	Pollux .	2	32	1	S.
do. .	α Coro. Borealis	3	38	25.7	S.

Thermometer 84° at 4 o'clock P. M.

April 1ſt. ☉'s preceding limb on the meridian at   11 57 31 A. M.
Subfequent do.   . . . 11 59 40 A. M.

Centre   do.   . . . 11 58 35.5 A. M.

Cloudy in the afternoon attended with ſharp lightning, heavy thunder, and a great fall of rain.

2d. Sirius paſſed the firſt fibre of the tranſit inſtrument at   . 5 45 19
The meridian   at   . 5 46 8
The third fibre at   . 5 47 2

Obferved zenith diſtance of α Coro. Borealis 3° 38′ 27″.5 s.

3d. ☉'s preceding limb on the meridian at 11 57 15 A. M.
Subfequent do.   . . . 11 59 24 A. M.

Centre   do.   . . . 11 58 19 A. M.

♀ paſſed the meridian at   . 1ʰ 24′ 32″ centrum.

Obferved zenith diſtance of   β Tauri 2° 36′ 38″.7 s.

Sirius paſſed the firſt fibre of the tranſit inſtrument at   . 5 41 33
The meridian   at   . 5 42 22
The third fibre at   . 5 43 17

4th.

		h	′	″	
4th. ☉'s preceding limb on the meridian at		11	57	9	A. M.
Subfequent do. . . .		11	59	18	A. M.
Centre do. . . .		11	58	13.5	A. M.

5th.   Cloudy all day.

		h	′	″	
6th. ☉'s fubfequent limb on the meridian at		11	59	10	A. M.
Deduct the paffage of the femi diameter —			1	4.5	
Centre on the meridian at .		11	58	5.5	A. M.

♀ paffed the meridian at   .   1ʰ 27′ 30″ Centrum.

		h	′	″
Sirius paffed the firft fibre of the tranfit inftrument at .		5	30	22
The meridian at .		5	31	11
The third fibre at .		5	32	6

		h	′	″	
7th. ☉'s preceding limb on the meridian at		11	56	55	A. M.
Subfequent do. . .		11	59	5	A. M.
Centre . do. . .		11	58	0	A. M.

		h	′	′
Sirius on the firft fibre of the tranfit inftrument at		5	26	39
The meridian at .		5	27	27
The third fibre at .		5	28	23

8th.   Cloudy with a little rain in the evening. Thermometer 39° in the morning.

                                       Obferved

Obſerved the times, and diſtances, of the neareſt limbs of the ⊙ and ☽ as below.

h	′	″	°	′	″	
22	51	25	48	2	0	
22	52	27	48	2	20	
22	53	27	48	2	10	Add 7″ for the error
22	54	12	48	3	0	of the Sextant.
22	54	55	48	3	20	
22	55	43	48	4	0	

Means 22 53 41   48 2 53

Taken again as follows.

h	′	″	°	′	″	
23	34	21	48	18	10	
23	35	48	48	18	40	
23	37	1	48	19	20	Add 7″ for the error
23	37	49	48	19	40	of the Sextant.
23	38	30	48	20	10	
23	39	15	48	20	20	

Means 23 37 7   48 19 23

9th. O's preceding limb on the meridian at 11ʰ 56′ 47″ A. M.
  Subſequent . do. . 11 58 56 A. M.

  Centre at . . 11 57 51.5 A. M.

♀ paſſed the meridian at . 1ʰ 30′ 38″ Centrum.

Equal altitudes of the Sun.
A. M. 8ʰ 47′ 50″.   P. M. 3ʰ 8′ 9″.

		h	′	″
Sirius paſſed the firſt fibre of the tranſit inſtrument	.	5	19	12
The meridian at	.	5	20	1
The third fibre at	.	5	20	56

10th.

10th.   Took down and packed up the inftruments.

During my employ on the boundary I made it a point to multiply my aftronomical obfervations as much as poffible when it did not interfere with my other bufinefs: in this I had two views ; *firft*, becaufe obfervations accurately made never become obfolete, and may at fome future day be found effentially ufeful, and *fecondly*, to determine by experiment, what reliance might be placed in obfervations made at temporary ftations, without any of the conveniences annexed to permanent obfervatories.—— The meridian being traced upon accurate principles, furnifhed an opportunity of comparing equal altitudes of the fun, with the tranfits of his centre over the meridian. The foregoing obfervations made at this ftation, furnifh the two following comparifons.

On the 26th of March the ⊙'s centre paffed the ⎱   11ʰ 59′ 30″ A. M.
   meridian at ⎰

Equal altitudes of the ⊙ on that day.

	h ′ ″	h ′ ″
	A. M. 9 3 52.	P. M. 2 55 26.5
Add		12
		14 55 26.5
Deduct forenoon's obfervation		9 3 52
		2) 5 51 34.5
Half		2 55 47.2
Add forenoon's obfervation		9 3 52
		11 59 39.2
Deduct for change of ⊙'s declination . .		— 9.6

⊙'s centre paffed the meridian by equal altitudes   11 59 29.6
Which differs but 4/10ths of a fecond from his paffage over the meridian by obfervation.

On the 9th of April the ⊙'s centre paffed the ⎱   11ʰ 57′ 51″.5 A. M.
   meridian at ⎰

Equal

Equal altitudes of the Sun on that day.

	h	′	″		h	′	″
A. M.	8	47	50.	P. M.	3	8	9
Add					12		

	h	′	″
	1ʃ	8	9
Deduct forenoon's obfervation	8	47	50

	h	′	″
	2) 6	20	19

	h	′	″
Half	3	10	9.5
Add the forenoon's obfervation . . .	8	47	50

	h	′	″
	11	57	59.5
Deduct for change of the ⊙'s declination .	—		8.6

	h	′	″
⊙'s centre paffed the meridian by equal altitudes at	11	57	50.9

Which differs from the obferved time but $\frac{6}{10}$ths of a fecond.

The paffage of the ftars over the meridian afford an eafy, and accurate method of determining the rate of the going of a clock, as is well known to all aftronomers; and when the right afcenfion of a ftar is well fettled, the error of a clock can be determined by it with great precifion,—as for example, take the paffage of Sirius on the 27th of March.

	h	′	″
Right afcenfion of Sirius the beginning of 1800 accord-⎫ ing to De Zach* ⎬	6	36	19.9
Deduct ann. preceffion for one year	—		2.6

	h	′	″
Right afcenfion the beginning of 1799 . . .	6	36	17.3
Aberration and preceffion on the 27th of March .	+		0.6
Nutation . do.	—		0.7

	h	′	″
True right afcenfion of Sirius	6	36	17.2
⊙'s right afcenfion by the Nautical Almanac at the time⎫ Sirius paffed the meridian, deduct ⎬	0	26	53.5

	h	′	″
Sirius paffed the meridian apparent time at . . .	6	9	23.7
Do. . . by obfervation . . .	6	8	41

	h	′	″
Clock too flow apparent time	0	0	42.7

1

⊙'s centre

---

* Vide Obfervationibus Aftronomicis Annis 1787, 1788, 1789, 1790.

	h	ı	ʺ
☉'s centre paſſed the meridian on the 27th of March at	11	59	19 A. M.
Equation of time $+ 5' 20''.8$	12	5	20.8

Clock too ſlow mean time	0	6	1.8
By the paſſage of Sirius over the meridian on the 27th and 28th the clock gained on mean ſolar time, about 10ʺ per diem, which is equal to about 2ʺ.5 when Sirius was obſerved, which is to be deducted	—		2.5

Clock too ſlow mean time when Sirius paſſed the meridian	0	5	59.3
Equation of time . . do. . .	0	5	16.1

Clock too ſlow apparent time, which differs but ½ a ſecond from the error given by Sirius	0	0	43.2

The neareſt diſtances of the limbs of the ☉, and ☽, were taken twice at this ſtation, (as entered in the journal), and may ſerve as examples of the accuracy of that method of determining the longitude.—As their altitudes were not taken at the time of the obſervations, they were determined by calculation: The latitude and time being known from obſervation, and the declinations deduced from the Nautical Almanac upon a ſuppoſition that the longitude was about 5 hours, and 52 minutes, weſt from Greenwich.—The method of calculating an altitude; the latitude, time, and declination being given, may be found in moſt books of ſpherical trigonometry, and a very eaſy one, particularly adapted to this purpoſe, in the requiſite tables problems 5, 6 and 7; but to prevent any errors which might ariſe from this ſource, and affect the determination of the longitude, I would recommend that the altitudes be determined both ways, as checks upon each other.—Either of the methods bring out the true altitude of the ☉'s, or ☽'s centre; but as the apparent is generally wanted, it will be had by ſubſtracting the parallax in altitude, and adding the refraction.

	h	ı	ʺ
The firſt obſervation was made by the clock April 8th at .	22	53	41
Clock too ſlow apparent time		2	6

The apparent time of the obſervation was therefore at .	22	55	47

	°	ı	ʺ
Obſerved diſtance of the limbs . .	48	2	53
☉'s ſemi-diameter	+ 16	0	
☽'s do.	+ 14	59	
Error of the Sextant	+ 0	7	
☽'s increaſed ſemi-diameter for her altitude	+ 0	8	

Obſerved diſtance of the centres . .	48	34	7

☉'s true

	o	′	″				
☉'s true altitude	62	19	20				
☽'s do.	33	55	58				
Difference true altitudes	28	23	22				
☉'s apparent altitude	62	19	48				
☽'s . do.	33	11	25				
Difference apparent altitudes	29	8	23				
Obferved diftance of the centres	48	34	7				
Sum	77	42	30				
Difference	19	25	44				
½ Sum	38	51	15		S	9.7975032
½ Difference	9	42	52		S	9.2272126
☽'s apparent altitude	33	11	25	co. ar.	c. S	0.0773486
☽'s true altitude	33	55	58		c. S	9.9189175
☉'s apparent altitude	62	19	48	co. ar.	c. S	0.3331280
☉'s true altitude	62	19	20		c. S	9.6669844

			2)	39.0210943
Difference true altitudes	28 23 22			19.5105471
½ Difference	14 11 41		S	9.3895525
Tangent				10.1209940
Correfponding c. S	(To be deducted from the 2d line above increafed by 10.)			9.7806675
	23 58 29.5 / 2		S	9.6088850

	o	′	″		
True diftance		47	56	59	
Diſt. at Greenwich 9ᵈ 3ʰ		47	6	51	
Do. . 9 6		48	30	30	
Difference between 1ſt and 2d		0	50	8	P. L. 5551
Do. between 2d and 3d		1	23	39	P. L. 3328

				h	′ ″
Add			2223 =	1	47 46
				9ᵈ 3	0 0
Time at Greenwich				9	4 47 46
Time of the obfervation on the Mobile				8	22 55 47
Longitude weſt from Greenwich				0	5 51 59

l 2

The

The second observation was made April 8th by the clock at $\quad$ 23^h 37' 7"
Clock too flow apparent time $\quad$. $\quad$. $\quad$. $\quad$. $\quad$. $\qquad$ 2 $\quad$ 7

The apparent time of the observation was therefore at $\quad$. $\qquad$ 23 $\quad$ 39 $\quad$ 14

	°	'	"
Observed distance of the limbs . . .	48	19	23
☉'s semi-diameter	+ 16	0	
☽'s semi-diameter	+ 14	59	
Error of the Sextant	+ 0	7	
☽'s increased semi-diameter from her altitude	+ 0	10	

Observed distance of the centres $\quad$. $\quad$. $\quad$. $\qquad$ 48 50 39

	°	'	"
☉'s true altitude . . .	66	6	20
☽'s do.	42	54	46

Difference true altitudes $\quad$. $\quad$. $\qquad$ 23 21 34

☉'s apparent altitude . . .	66	16	42
☽'s . do.	42	15	7

Difference apparent altitudes $\quad$. $\quad$. $\quad$ 24 $\quad$ 1 $\quad$ 35
Observed distance of the centres $\quad$. $\quad$ 48 $\quad$ 50 $\quad$ 39

	° ' "			
Sum	72 52 14			
Difference	24 49 4			
½ Sum	36 26 7	. .	S	9.7737238
½ Difference	12 24 32	.	S	9.3322098
☽'s apparent altitude . .	42 15 7	co. ar.	c. S	0.1306537
☽'s true altitude . . .	42 54 46	.	c. S	9.8647430
☉'s apparent altitude . .	66 16 42	co. ar.	c. S	0.3954564
☉'s true altitude . . .	66 16 20	.	c. S	9.6046490

$\qquad$ 2)39.1014357

Difference true altitudes $\quad$. $\quad$. $\quad$ 23 21 34 $\qquad$ 19.5507178

½ Difference $\quad$. $\quad$. $\quad$. $\quad$ 11 40 47 $\quad$. $\quad$. $\quad$ S $\quad$ 9.3062979

Tangent $\quad$. $\qquad$ 10.2444199

Corresponding log. cosine $\qquad$ (To be deducted from the 2d line above increased by 10.) $\qquad$ 9.6945605

$\qquad$ 24 8 34.5 $\quad$. $\qquad$ S $\quad$ 9.6117374
$\qquad$ 2

		°	'	"
True distance		48	17	9
Distance at Greenwich 9^d 3^h	.	47	6	51
do. . . 9 6	.	48	30	30

$\qquad$ **Difference**

Difference between 1ft and 2d   .   1 10 18 P. L. 4083
do.   2d and 3d   .   1 23 39 P. L. 3328

	h	'	"
$\dfrac{755}{9^d}$ =	2	31	16

Add   3

	h	'	"
Time at Greenwich	9	5	31 16
Time of the obfervation on Mobile	8	23	39 14
Longitude weft from Greenwich	0	5	52 2
do. by the firft obfervation	0	5	51 59
Mean	0	5	52 0.5

	h	'	"	
The longitude of our camp on Thompfon's creek by the mean of five immerfions of ♃'s firft fatellite was	6	4	48	West from Greenwich.
The diftance from Thomfon's creek on the parallel of 31°, to the obfervatory on the Mobile was by meafurement 184.46 miles eaft, which in time is equal to	— 0	12	17	
Longitude of the camp on the Mobile .	5	52	31	
do. by the two lunar obfervations .	5	52	0.5	
Difference	0	0	30.5	

Refult

Refult of the Obfervations made on the Mobile river for afcertaining the Latitude.

The Zenith Diftances ftand as below.

Face of the Sector Eaft.

	β Tauri. ° ′ ″	Caftor. ° ′ ″	Pollux. ° ′ ″	α Coro. Borealis. ° ′ ″
March 21ft.	. . . .	. . . .	. . . .	3 36 55 s.
22d.	2 35 0.5 s.	1 18 26.7 N.	2 30 29 s.	3 36 53
23d.	2 34 59.5	1 18 28.8	2 30 30	3 36 55
24th.	2 34 57.5	1 18 27.5	2 30 26	. . . .
25th.	. . . .	. . . .	. . . .	. . . .
Means	2 34 59.2	1 18 27.5	2 30 28	3 36 54.3

Face of the Sector Weft.

	β Tauri.	Caftor.	Pollux.	α Coro. Borealis.
27th.	2 36 38.5	1 16 47.4	2 32 3	3 38 25
28th.	. . . .	1 16 48.6	2 32 5	. . . .
29th.	. . . .	1 16 50.5	2 32 3	. . . .
31ft.	2 36 37.7	1 16 50	2 32 1	3 38 25
April 2d.	. . . .	. . . .	. . . .	. . . .
3d.	2 36 38.7	. . . .	. . . .	3 38 27.5
Means	2 36 38.3	1 16 49.1	2 32 3	3 38 26.1
Means with the face eaft	2 34 59.2	1 18 27.5	2 30 28	3 36 54.3
Means	2 35 48.7	1 17 38.3	2 31 15.5	3 37 40.2
Refractions	+ 2.5	+ 1.3	+ 2.5	+ 3.6
Correct zenith diftances	2 35 51.2	1 17 39.6	2 31 18	3 37 43.8
Mean declinations to the 26th March	28 25 28.6 N.	32 18 48.3 N.	28 29 54.6 N.	27 23 57.6 N.
Aberrations	+ 1.3	+ 2.8	+ 1.3	— 13.3
Nutations	+ 5	+ 7.5	+ 7.9	— 1.6
Semi. ann. equations	+ 0.4	+ 0.5	+ 0.5	+ 0.3
True declinations	28 25 35.3	32 18 59.1	28 30 4.8	27 23 42.4
Correct zenith diftances applied	+2 35 51.2	—1 17 39.6	+2 31 18	+3 37 43.8
Latitudes	31 1 26.5 N.	31 1 19.5 N.	31 1 22.8 N.	31 1 26.2 N.

		o	′	″
Latitude by β Tauri	. .	31	1	26.5
do. by Caftor	. .	31	1	19.5
do. . Pollux	. .	31	1	22.8
do. by α Coro. Borealis	.	31	1	26.2
Mean Latitude north	. .	31	1	23.7

From the refult of the above obfervations, the compafs line was too far north by 1′ 23″.7, or 518.55 perches, which diftance was carefully laid off to the fouth, and a ftone fet up at the termination, marked on the north fide U. S. Lat. 31° 1799,—and on the fouth fide DOMINOS de S. M. C. CAROLUS IV. Lat. 31° 1799.—From this ftone, the line was corrected back as in the foregoing cafe, agreeably to plate IV.

On our arrival at the end of the compafs line on the Mobile river, one ferious difficulty prefented itfelf, that was the continuation of the line through the fwamp, which is at all times almoft impenetrable ; but at that feafon of the year abfolutely fo : being wholly inundated :—But fortunately we found in the neighbourhood of our camp a fmall hill, the fummit of which was juft elevated above the tops of the trees in the fwamp. From the top of this hill, we could plainly difcover the pine trees on the high land, on the eaft fide. Upon afcertaining this fact, we fent a party through to the other fide, (along the water courfes, by which the fwamp is interfected in various directions), with orders to make a large fire in the night with light-wood ; the fame was likewife to be done on the hill before mentioned, to obtain nearly the direction from one place to the other.— The atmofphere was too much filled with fmoke, to difcern a flag, or other fignal,—the woods being on fire on both fides of the fwamp.—It happened unfortunately that the day before our fires were to be lighted, the fires in the woods had extended over almoft the whole of the highlands, on both fides of the fwamp ; by which fo many dead trees were fet on fire, that there was no poffibility of difcriminating between them, and our fires.—It was then agreed that the parties fhould light up, and extinguifh their fires a certain number of times ; making ftated intervals.—This fucceeded fo well, that we became certain of not taking a wrong fire in determining the angles.—Contrary to our expectation, a heavy rain fell on the fame night, a fhort time after we had finifhed the experiment, and extinguifhed all the fires in the woods.—The ftorm cleared off with a ftrong north-weft wind, which carried off all the fmoke, and enabled us to determine the angles in the day, by erecting fignals, which was accomplifhed on the fecond day of April.—This work was connected with the obfervatory in the following manner. At the obfervatory A (fee Fig. G, plate V.) a meridional line was traced, by taking the greateft elongations of α Urfæ Minoris, both eaft, and weft, with the tranfit and equal altitude inftrument :—equal diftances were carefully meafured in each direction, and a fine mark placed at the termination of each meafurement,—the diftance between thofe marks was accurately bifected, and a fine mark placed at the point of bifection for the meridian.

meridian. The fame operation was performed a fecond time, and although the difference in the refults, appeared too trifling to need any attention, it was neverthelefs bifected, and that point of bifection taken for the meridian,—which is defignated by A E and terminated by a parallel of latitude drawn through B.—From the point A, a vifta was opened to the fummit of the hill at B : from B, to C, another vifta was opened, which formed the bafe : the bafe was too fhort if it could have been avoided ; but the hill would not admit of its being any longer.—D the fignal on the eaft fide of the fwamp.—The angles were meafured on the horizontal arc of the aftronomical circle already mentioned.—This inftrument by means of a vernier is graduated to 5″, which by the help of a microfcope may be eafily fubdivided by the eye, into $1\frac{1}{2}$, or 2 feconds.—The meafurements, and angles ftand as below.

$$AB = 310.8 \text{ perches.}$$
$$BC = 70.356 \text{ perches.}$$

⟅ BAE =	37°	58′	48″
⟅ ABD =	57	43	21
⟅ BCD =	139	23	58
⟅ DBC =	39	47	1
⟅ CDB =	0	49	1

From thefe data, AE is found to be equal to 244.9 perches, BE to 191.26 perches, BD to 3211.65 perches, EF to 2987.44 perches, and DF to 316.7 perches. DB being confidered as an arc of a great circle, forming with the prime vertical an angle of 5° 42′ 9″ to the north, being the excefs of the angles BAE, and ABD above 90.—From the refult of the obfervations for the latitude, the obfervatory appeared to be too far north by 518.55 perches, which is defignated by AH. It therefore follows, that the fignal at D, was too far north by the fum of the diftances DF, EA and AH, which is equal to 1080.15 perches : this diftance was meafured due fouth from the point D, and would interfect the paralell of 31°, at the end of 215 miles and 169.6 perches from high water mark on the Miffiffippi.

___

From the termination of the above mentioned 1080.15 perches, another guide, or compafs line was continued eaft, to the eaft fide of the Coenecuch ; but the termination of the compafs line, not being in a proper place for a courfe of obfervations, the obfervatory was erected north of it, in the meridian of the termination of the 257th mile; where the following obfervations were made.

1799.

1799.

May 9th.   The inftruments arrived, fet up the clock, and both fectors, the fmall one was ufed by the commiffioner for His Catholic Majefty, at this ftation, on the Chatahocha river, the mouth of Flint river, and at our ftation up the St. Mary's.

Faces of the Sectors to the Eaft.

				o	′	″	
9th.	Obferved zenith diftance of		ε Bootes .	3	4	8	s.
	do. . . .		α Coro. Borealis	3	35	53	s.
	do.	Small fector	α Lyræ .	7	36	43	N.
10th. . .	do. . .		ε Bootes .	3	4	9.5	s.
	do.	Small fector	. do. .	3	3	20	s.
	do. . . .		α Coro. Borealis	3	35	55	s.
	do.	Small fector	α Lyræ .	7	36	48	N.
	do. . .		β Pegafi .	4	0	12	s.
11th. . .	do. . . .		Caftor .	1	19	12	N.
	do. . . .		Pollux .	2	29	41	s.
	do. . .		ε Bootes .	3	4	6.5	s.
	do.	Small fector .	do. .	3	3	8	s.
	do. . .		α Coro. Borealis	3	35	52	s.
	do.	Small fector .	do. .	3	35	9	s.
	do.	Small fector	α Lyræ .	7	37	1	N.
	do. . .		α Andromedæ	3	0	59.5	s.
12th.	do. . . .		Pollux .	2	29	43	s.
	do.	Small fector	ε Bootes .	3	3	21	s.
	do.	Small fector	α Coro. Borealis	3	35	7	s.
	do.	Small fector	α Lyræ .	7	36	52	N.

13th.   Turned the face of the Small Sector Weft.

Cloudy with rain.

14th.   Cloudy all day with heavy fhowers of rain.
15th.   Cloudy with rain till after dark, then clear.

			o	′	″	
Obferved zenith diftance of	ε Bootes .	fmall fector	3	6	47	s.
do. .	α Coro. Borealis	fmall fector	3	38	34	s.
do. .	α Lyræ .	fmall fector	7	33	30	N.

16th.   Cloudy with heavy fhowers of rain great part of the day.

		star	°	′	″	
	Obferved zenith diftance of	α Andromedæ	3	0	58.5	s.
17th.	do. . . .	Caftor .	1	19	20	N.
	do. . . .	Pollux .	2	29	45	s.
	do. Small fector	ι Bootes .	3	6	58	s.
	do. Small fector	α Coro. Borealis	3	38	34	s.
	do. . .	β Pegafi .	4	0	13	s.

Face of the large Sector Weft.

		star	°	′	″	
	do. . . .	α Andromedæ	3	2	41.5	s.
18th. . .	do. . . .	Caftor .	1	17	30.5	N.
	do. . . .	Pollux .	2	31	24	s.
	do. . . .	ι Bootes .	3	5	48.5	s.
	do. Small fector	do. .	3	6	45	s.
	do. . . .	α Coro. Borealis	3	37	27.7	s.
	do. Small fector .	do. .	3	38	22	s.
	do. . do. .	α Lyræ .	7	33	30	N.
	do. . . .	β Pegafi .	4	1	52.5	s.
	do. . . .	α Andromedæ	3	2	40	s.
19th. . .	do. . . .	Caftor .	1	17	29.5	N.
	do. . . .	Pollux .	2	31	25	s.
	do. . . .	ι Bootes .	3	5	47.5	s.
	do. . . .	α Coro. Borealis	3	37	31.8	s.
	do. . . .	β Pegafi .	4	1	52.5	s.
	do. . . .	α Andromedæ	3	2	41.5	s.
20th. . .	do. . . .	Caftor .	1	17	27	N.
	do. . . .	Pollux .	2	31	26	s.
	do. . . .	ι Bootes .	3	5	48	s.
	do. . . .	α Coro. Borealis	3	7	29.7	s.
	do. . . .	β Pegafi .	4	1	54	s.
	do. Small fector	α Lyræ .	7	33	40	N.

At this ftation, no obfervations but for the determination of the latitude were made,—the eclipfes of Jupiter's fatellites not being vifible, the planet being too near the fun.—The clock was put up to advertife us of the time a ftar would appear in the field of the telefcopes, which is at all times of importance; but at this place particularly fo, on account of the flies, and mufquitoes, which were fo numerous, and troublefome, that an obfervation which would not require more than one minute, could not be made without great pain.

Refult

Result of the Observations made with the large Sector on the Coeneuch, to determine the Latitude.

The Zenith distances stand as below.

Face of the Sector East.

	Castor.	Pollux.	ε Bootes.	α Coro. Borealis.	β Pegasi.	α Andromedæ.
	° ′ ″	° ′ ″	° ′ ″	° ′ ″	° ′ ″	° ′ ″
May 9th	. . . .	. . . .	3 4 8 S.	3 35 53.5 S.	. . . .	. . . .
10th	. . . .	. . . .	3 4 9.5	3 35 55	. . . .	. . . .
11th	1 19 12 N.	2 29 41 S.	3 4 6.5	3 35 52	4 0 12 S.	3 0 59.5 S
12th	. . . .	2 29 43	. . . .	. . . .	. . . .	. . . .
16th	. . . .	. . . .	. . . .	. . . .	. . . .	3 0 58.5
17th	1 19 10	2 29 45	. . . .	. . . .	4 0 13	. . . .
Means	1 19 11	2 29 43	3 4 8	3 35 53.5	4 0 12.5	3 0 59

Face of the Sector West.

	Castor.	Pollux.	ε Bootes.	α Coro. Borealis.	β Pegasi.	α Andromedæ.
18th	1 17 30.5	2 31 24	3 5 48.5	3 37 27.7	4 1 52.5	3 2 41.5
19th	1 17 29.5	2 31 25	3 5 47.5	3 37 31.8	4 1 52.5	3 2 40
20th	1 17 27	2 31 26	3 5 48	3 37 29.7	4 1 54	3 2 41.5
Means	1 17 29	2 31 25	3 5 48	3 37 29.7	4 1 53	3 2 41
Means face east	1 19 11	2 29 43	3 4 8	3 35 53.5	4 0 12.5	3 0 59
Means	1 18 20	2 30 34	3 4 58	3 36 41.6	4 1 2.7	3 1 50
Refractions	+ 1.3	+ 2.5	+ 3	+ 3.5	+ 4	+ 3
Correct zenith distances	1 18 21.3	2 30 36.5	3 5 1	3 36 45.1	4 1 6.7	3 1 53
Mean declinations to the 15th.	32 18 47.5 N.	28 30 49.7 N.	27 55 38 N.	27 23 54.1 N.	26 59 58 N.	27 59 3.5 N.
Aberrations	+ 4.4	+ 3.6	— 0.7	— 3.2	— 12.5	— 11.7
Nutations	+ 8.0	+ 8.2	— 0.7	— 2.1	— 6.7	— 5.0
Semi-annual equations	0.0	0.0	+ 0.4	+ 0.4	— 0.5	— 0.4
True declinations	32 18 59.9	28 30 1.5	27 55 37	27 23 49.2	26 59 32.3	27 58 46.4
True zenith distances applied	—1 18 21.3	+2 30 36.5	+3 5 1	+3 36 45.1	+4 1 6.7	+3 1 53
Latitudes	31 0 38.6	31 0 38	31 0 38	31 0 34.3	31 0 39	31 0 39.4

m 2

		°	′	″
Latitude by	Caſtor . .	31	0	38.6
do.	Pollux . .	31	0	38.0
do.	₤ Bootes . .	31	0	38.0
do.	α Coro. Borealis .	31	0	34.3
do.	β Pegaſi . .	31	0	39.0
do.	α Andromedæ .	31	0	39.4
Mean Latitude north	.	31	0	37.9

Reſult of the Obſervations made with the ſmall Sector on the Coenecuch to determine the Latitude.

The Zenith diſtances ſtand as below.

Face of the Sector Eaſt.

	₤ Bootes.			α Coro. Borealis.			α Lyræ.		
	°	′	″	°	′	″	°	′	″
May 9th.							7	36	43 N.
10th.	3	3	20 S.	3	35	2 S.	7	36	48
11th.	3	3	8	3	35	9	7	31	1
12th.	3	3	21	3	35	7	7	36	52
Means	3	3	16	3	35	6	7	36	51

Face of the Sector Weſt.

15th.	3	6	47	3	38	34	7	33	30
17th.	3	6	58	3	38	34			
18th.	3	6	45	3	38	22	7	33	20
20th.							7	33	40
Means	3	6	50	3	38	30	7	33	30
Means face eaſt	3	3	16	3	35	6	7	36	51
Means	3	5	3	3	36	48	7	35	10.5
Refractions	+		3	+		3.5	+		7.5
Correct zenith diſtances . . .	3	5	6	3	36	51.5	7	35	18

Mean declinations May 15th. . .	27	55	38 N.	27	23	54.1 N.	38	36	11 N.
Aberrations	—		0.7	—		3.2	—		11.5
Nutations	—		0.7	—		2.1	—		7.0
Semi-annual equations . . .	+		0.4	+		0.4	+		0.2
True declinations . . .	27	55	37	27	23	49.2	38	35	52.7
Zenith diſtances applied . . .	+3	5	6	+3	36	51.5	—7	35	18
Latitudes	31	0	43	31	0	40.7	31	0	34.7

Latitude

		o	′	″
Latitude by ε Bootis	.	31	0	43
do. . α Coro. Borealis		31	0	40.7
do. . α Lyræ	.	31	0	34.7
Mean Latitude North	.	31	0	39.5

The difference of the refults given by the two inftruments appears to be 1″.6; but the radius of the large fector, being more than three times that of the fmall one, it may fairly be confidered at leaft three times as accurate; and as double the number of ftars were taken with the large one, it is on that account entitled to double the accuracy :—hence if to five times the latitude given by the large fector, the latitude given by the fmall one be added, and the fum divided by fix, the quotient 30° 0′ 38″.1 will be the latitude in which each inftrument has its due weight; from which it follows, that the obfervatory was too far north by 38″.1, or 3853.8 feet; but the end of the guide line was 3617.8 feet fouth of the obfervatory,—hence the end of the guide line was too far north by 236 feet, which was carefully laid off to the fouth, and the guide line corrected back as in the former cafes agreeably to Plate V. From the termination of the meafurement another guide, or compafs line was carried on to the weft fide of the Chatahocha, or Apalachicola river the diftance of 381 miles, and 7 perches, eaft of high water mark on the Miffiffippi.

At the termination of the compafs, or guide line on the Chatahocha, or Apalachicola river, the following obfervations were made.

July 25th. Arrived at the end of the guide line, in a heavy fhower of rain.

26th. Cloudy with rain all day.

27th. Cleaned, and fet up the clock.—Cloudy with rain.

28th. Cloudy with rain all day.—Thermometer 82° in the morning, fell to 80° at 10 o'clock A. M.

29th. Thermometer 74° in the morning. Thick fog. Thermometer 84° in the afternoon.

Put up both Sectors, with their Faces to the Eaft.

30th. Thermometer 74° in the morning, rofe to 87°.

Obferved

	o	,	"	
Obferved zenith diftance of α Coro. Borealis	3	36	11	s.
do. α Andromedæ	3	1	18.6	s.
do. β Andromedæ	3	32	48	N.
do. fmall fector do	3	34	1.5	N.
do. Caftor	1	18	38.5	N.
do. Pollux	2	30	13	s.

31ft.

Equal altitudes of the Sun.
A. M. 8ʰ 44' 49".   P. M. 3ʰ 16' 15".

———————————

	o	,	"	
Obferved zenith diftance of α Coro. Borealis	3	36	8.5	s.
do. α Andromedæ	3	1	21	s.

Immerfion of the 3d fatellite of ♃ obferved at 16ʰ 8' 18".
—Belts diftinct, magnifying power 120.

	o	,	"	
Obferved zenith diftance of β Andromedæ	3	32	49.5	N.
do. fmall fector do.	3	33	58.5	N.
do. β Tauri	2	34	46.5	N.
do. Caftor	1	18	41	N.
do. Pollux	2	30	10	s.

Thermometer 74° at fun rife, rofe to 86°.

Aug. 1ft.   Thermometer 84° all laft night.—Heavy rain about 1 o'clock in the morning, cleared off before 3 o'clock.

	o	,	"	
Obferved zenith diftance of β Pegafi	4	0	26	s.
do. fmall fector do.	3	59	9	s.
do. α Andromedæ	3	1	22.5	s.
do. fmall fector	3	0	19	s.

The above two obfervations are doubtful, the ftar not being feen more than 3" through the clouds.

Thermometer rofe to 88°, frequent light fhowers.

2d.   Thermometer 74° all laft night, rofe to 84°.—Showery with thunder great part of the day.

Equal

Equal altitudes of the Sun.
A. M. 9ʰ 30′ 13″.   P. M. 2ʰ 9′ 50″.

Obſerved zenith diſtance of α Lyræ (ſmall ſector) 7° 37′ 30″ N.

3d.   Thermometer 75° all laſt night, roſe to 85°.—Clouds flying with great rapidity the fore part of the day from the N. W. cleared off in the afternoon.

			o	′	″	
Obſerved zenith diſtance of	α Coro. Borealis	3	36	7.5	s.
do.	ſmall ſector	α Lyræ	.	7	37	36	N.
do.	.	.	.	β Pegaſi	.	4	0	25	s.
do.	ſmall ſector	do.	.	3	59	3	s.

The obſervations on β Pegaſi are doubtful, the ſtar was diſcerned for a few ſeconds only between the clouds as they paſſed by.

Cloudy the remainder of the night.—At 21ʰ the clouds diſappeared, at 22ʰ 15′ the ſky was fine, at 22ʰ 20′ I prepared to obſerve the zenith diſtance of Caſtor, but in leſs than 2 minutes, an extenſive cloud formed in the zenith, with ſeveral others to the northward, they all diſappeared in about 5 minutes but the obſervation was loſt.

Obſerved zenith diſtance of Pollux   .   2° 30′ 14″ s.

4th.   Thermometer 73° all laſt night, roſe to 87° in the afternoon.

			o	′	″	
Obſerved zenith diſtance of	α Coro. Borealis	3	36	8.5	s.
do. (ſmall ſector)	α Lyræ	.	7	37	12	N.
do.	.	.	β Pegaſi	.	4	0	28	s.
do.	ſmall ſector	do.	.	3	59	12	s.
do.	ſmall ſector	α Andromedæ	3	0	28	s.
do.	.	.	β Andromedæ	3	32	49	N.
do.	ſmall ſector	do.	.	3	34	7.5	N.
do.	.	.	β Tauri	.	2	34	47.5	s.
do.	.	.	Caſtor	.	1	18	36.4	N.
do.	.	.	Pollux	.	2	30	12	s.

5th.

5th.   Thermometer 72° all laft night, rofe to 84°.

Face of the large Sector Weft.

			°	′	″	
Obferved zenith diftance of	α Lyræ	(fmall fector)	7	37	36	N.
do.	.	β Pegafi	do.	3	59	24	S.
do.	.	α Andromedæ	do.	3	0	16	S.
do.	.	β Andromedæ	do.	3	34	1	N.

6th.   Thermometer 71° all night, rofe to 79°.
—Cloudy all day, clear in the evening.

Face of the fmall Sector Weft.

			°	′	″	
Obferved zenith diftance of	β Pegafi	.	4	2	9	S.
do. fmall fector	do.	.	4	3	36	S.
do. .	α Andromedæ		3	3	5.5	S.
do. fmall fector	do.	.	3	4	30	S.
do. .	β Andromedæ		3	31	5	N.
do. fmall fector	do.	.	3	29	30	N.
do. .	Pollux	.	2	30	0.5	S.

7th.   Thermometer 70° all night, rofe to 82°.
—Cloudy part of the forenoon and rain in
the evening.

Obferved zenith diftance of β Pegafi   .   4° 2′ 7″.5 s.

At 14^h the ftars were inftantly covered by
clouds, which were followed by heavy rain.

8th.   Thermometer 70° all night, rofe to 79°.
—Heavy rain till 7 o'clock in the evening,
cleared off at 8^h P. M.

			°	′	″	
Obferved zenith diftance	β Pegafi	.	4	2	6.5	S.
do. fmall fector	do.	.	4	3	21	S.
do. .	α Andromedæ		3	3	4.5	S.
do. fmall fector	do.	.	3	4	15	S.
do. .	β Andromedæ		3	31	5.5	N.
do. fmall fector	do.	.	3	30	01	

Auguft

Aug. 9th.   Thermometer 70° in the morning, rofe to 75°.—Heavy rain all the forenoon, cleared off at noon.—Thunder-guft in the afternoon, clear in the evening.

			o	′	″	
Obſerved zenith diſtance of	α Lyræ	(ſmall fector)	7	32	45	N.
do. . .	β Pegaſi	do.	4	3	22.5	s.
do. . .	α Andromedæ	do.	3	3	4.5	s.
do. ſmall fector	do. .	.	3	4	27	s.
do. . .	β Andromedæ	.	3	31	7.5	N.
do. ſmall fector	do. .	.	3	29	31	N.

At 19^h 20′ a cloud formed in the zenith which in a few minutes extended in a belt almoſt to the eaſtern and weſtern horizon, at 20^h it diſappeared, by this circumſtance the obſervation on β Tauri was loſt.

		o	′	″	
Obſerved zenith diſtance of Caſtor	.	1	16	57.5	N.
do. . . Pollux	.	2	31	58.5	s.

The obſervations on Caſtor, and Pollux are ſomewhat doubtful, each of them being ſeen but once, and that for a few ſeconds only between the clouds which moved with great rapidity from the weſt, to the eaſt.

10th.   Thermometer 70° all laſt night, raiſed to 81°.—Rain at noon.

At 5^h 55′ prepared to obſerve the zenith diſtance of α Coro. Borealis,—in two minutes a ſpace of ſeveral degrees about the zenith was obſcured by a cloud from the weſt, at 6^h 6′ the ſky was ſufficiently clear but the ſtar had paſſed the field of the inſtrument.

		o	′	″	
Obſerved zenith diſtance of α Lyræ (ſmall fector)		7	33	4.5	N.
do. . . β Pegaſi	do.	4	3	31.5	s.

Cloudy the remainder of the 24 hours.

n   11th.

11th.   Thermometer 74° all laft night, rofe to 86°.—Cloudy with thunder from 3ʰ P. M. till fome time in the night.

12th.   Thermometer 76° at day light, rofe to 85°. —Beautiful fky till 7ʰ A. M. when it became very cloudy from the N. W.—heavy rain from 1 o'clock P. M. till 9 o'clock A. M. of the

13th.   Thermometer 72° at fun rife, rofe to 81°. —Clear a fhort time about 9ʰ A. M.—Cloudy with frequent fhowers of rain the remainder of the day.

14th.   Thermometer 74° at fun rife, rofe to 82°.

			°	′	″	
Obferved zenith diftance of	α Coro. Borealis		3	37	56	s.
do.	fmall fector	α Lyræ	7	33	1.5	N.
do.		Pollux	2	32	0.5	s.

It was too hazy to difcover Caftor, and Pollux was fcarcely difcernible.

15th.   Thermometer 74° at fun rife, rofe to 87°. —Fog during the morning.

			°	′	″	
Obferved zenith diftance of	α Coro. Borealis		3	37	56.5	s.
do.	fmall fector	α Lyræ	7	33	4.5	
do.		β Tauri	2	36	32	s.
do.		Caftor	1	16	54	N.

The obfervation on Caftor is very doubtful being not feen more than 3″ between the clouds.

Obferved zenith diftance of   Pollux   .   2° 32′ 1″.5

16th.   Thermometer 78° at fun rife, rofe to 88°. —Thunder-guft in the afternoon.—Cloudy with rain the remainder of the 24 hours.

17th.

17th.   Thermometer 73° at fun rife, rofe to 87°.
—Cloudy all day and night.

Obferved zenith diftance of β Tauri   .   2° 36′ 33″ s.

18th.   Thermometer 70° at fun rife, rofe to 81°.

Obferved zenith diftance of α Coro. Borealis 3° 37′ 59″.5 s.

Cloudy during the night.
19th.   Thermometer 70° at fun rife, rofe to 74°.
—Showery all the afternoon.

Obferved zenith diftance of β Tauri   2° 36′ 30″.5 s.

After this obfervation it was cloudy the remainder of the day.
20th.   Thermometer 71° at fun rife, rofe to 80°.
—The morning remarkably fine and clear,
wind from the eaft,—at 9ʰ A. M. it almoft
inftantly became cloudy from the fouth, and
between noon and 1 o'clock, a guft of rain
accompanied with large hail ftones from the
S. W. paffed about four miles to the north
of our camp.
    End of the obfervations made on the Cha-
tahocha.

		h	′	″	Daily lofs.
Clock too flow mean time July 31ft.	.	0	5	22	″
do. . .	Aug. 2d.	.	0	5	46	. . 12

Longitude weft from Greenwich by the immerfion of the 3d fatellite of
♃ on the 31ft of July 5ʰ 37′ 59″.

Refult

Result of the Observations made with the Large Sector on the Chatalocha, for the determination of the latitude.

The Zenith Distances when arranged stand as below.

Face of the Sector East.

	β Andromedæ. ° ′ ″	β Tauri. ° ′ ″	Castor. ° ′ ″	Pollux. ° ′ ″	α Coro. Borealis. ° ′ ″	β Pegasi. ° ′ ″	α Andromedæ. ° ′ ″
July 30th	3 32 48 N.	2 34 45.5 s.	1 18 35.5 N.	2 30 13 s.	3 36 11 s.		3 1 18.6 s.
31st	3 32 49.5	2 34 46.5	1 18 41	2 30 10	3 36 8.5		3 1 21
August 1st						4 0 26 s.	3 1 22.8
3d			1 18 36.4	2 30 14	3 36 7.5	4 0 25	
4th	3 32 49.5	2 34 47.5		2 30 12	3 36 8.5	4 0 28	
Means	3 32 49	2 34 46.5	1 18 38	2 30 12.2	3 36 8.9	4 0 26.3	3 1 20.8

Face of the Sector West.

	β Andromedæ. ° ′ ″	β Tauri. ° ′ ″	Castor. ° ′ ″	Pollux. ° ′ ″	α Coro. Borealis. ° ′ ″	β Pegasi. ° ′ ″	α Andromedæ. ° ′ ″
6th	3 31 5			2 32 0.5		4 2 9	3 3 5.5
7th						4 2 7.5	3 3 3.5
8th	3 31 5.5			2 31 58.5		4 2 7.5	3 3 45
9th	3 31 7.5		1 16 57.5	2 32 0.5			
14th				2 32 1.5	3 37 56		
15th		2 36 32	1 16 54		3 37 56.5		
17th		2 36 33					
18th					3 37 59.5		
19th		2 36 30					
Means	3 31 6	2 36 31.7	1 16 55.7	2 32 0.5	3 37 57.3	4 2 8	3 3 4.5
Means face east	3 32 49	2 34 46.5	1 18 38	2 30 12.2	3 36 8.9	4 0 26.3	3 1 20.8
Means	3 31 57.5	2 35 39.1	1 17 46.8	2 31 6.3	3 37 3.1	4 1 17.1	3 2 12.6
Refractions	+ 3.5	+ 2.6	+ 1.3	+ 2.5	+ 3.6	+ 4.0	+ 3.0
True zenith distances	3 32 1.0	2 35 41.7	1 17 48.1	2 31 8.8	3 37 6.7	4 1 21.1	3 2 15.6

Mean

	β Andromedæ.	β Tauri.	Castor.	Pollux.	α Coro. Borealis.	β Pegasi.	α Andromedæ.
	° ′ ″	° ′ ″	° ′ ″	° ′ ″	° ′ ″	° ′ ″	° ′ ″
Mean declinations Aug. 8th.	34 33 17.2 N.	28 25 28.9 N.	32 18 51.3 N.	28 29 30 N.	27 23 53.5 N.	26 59 50.3 N.	27 59 7 N.
Aberrations	— 5.0	— 2.4	+ 0.8	+ 3.2	+ 13.7	+ 0.5	— 7.2
Nutations	— 2.7	+ 6.0	+ 8.4	+ 9.1	— 2.7	+ 6.5	+ 4.7
Semi. ann. equations . .	+ 0.4	— 0.4	— 0.4	— 0.3	0.0	+ 0.4	+ 0.4
True declinations . . .	34 33 9.9	28 25 32.1	32 19 0.1	28 30 2.0	27 24 4.5	26 59 44.7	27 58 55.6
True zenith distances applied	—3 32 1	+2 35 41.7	—1 17 48.1	+2 31 8.8	+3 37 6.7	+4 1 21.1	+3 2 15.6
Latitudes	31 1 8.9 N.	31 1 13.8 N.	31 1 12	31 1 10.8 N.	31 1 11.2 N.	31 1 5.8 N.	31 1 11.2 N.

		° ′ ″
Latitude by	β Andromedæ	31 1 8.9
do.	β Tauri	31 1 13.8
do.	Castor	31 1 12
do.	Pollux	31 1 10.8
do.	α Coro. Borealis	31 1 11.2
do.	β Pegafi	31 1 5.8
do.	α Andromedæ	31 1 11.2
Mean latitude north		31 1 10.5

Refult

Result of the Observations made with the Small Sector on the Chatahocha, for the determination of the Latitude.

The Zenith Distances stand as below.

Face of the Sector East.

	β Andromedæ.	α Lyræ.	β Pegasi.	α Andromedæ.
	° ′ ″	° ′ ″	° ′ ″	° ′ ″
July 30th	3 34 1.5 N.			
31st	3 33 58.5			
August 1st		7 37 30 N.	3 59 9 s.	3 0 19 s.
2d		7 37 36		
3d		7 37 12	3 59 12	
4th	3 34 7.5	7 37 36	3 59 24	3 0 28
5th	3 34 1.5			3 0 16
Means	3 34 2.2	7 37 28.5	3 59 15	3 0 21

Face of the Sector West.

	β Andromedæ.	α Lyræ.	β Pegasi.	α Andromedæ.
6th	3 29 30		4 3 36	3 4 30
8th	3 30 1		4 3 21	3 4 15
9th	3 29 31		4 3 22	3 4 27
10th		7 32 45	4 3 31.5	
14th		7 33 4.5		
15th		7 33 1.5		
		7 33 4.5		
Means	3 29 41	7 32 58.9	4 3 27.0	3 4 24
Means face east	3 34 2.2	7 37 28.5	3 59 15	3 0 21
Means	3 31 51.6	7 35 13.7	4 1 21.3	3 2 22.5
Refraction	+ 3.5	+ 7.6	+ 4.0	+ 3
True zenith distance	3 31 55.1	7 35 21.3	4 1 25.3	3 2 25.5
Mean declination August 8th	34 33 17.2 N.	38 36 9.2 N.	26 59 50.3 N.	27 59 7 N.
Aberrations	— 5.0	+ 11.5	+ 0.5	— 7.2
Nutations	— 2.7	— 7.8	— 6.5	— 4.7
Semi-annual equations	+ 0.4	0.0	+ 0.4	+ 0.4
True declinations	34 33 9.9	38 36 12.9	26 59 44.7	27 58 55.5
True zenith distances applied	—3 31 55.1	—7 35 21.3	+4 1 25.3	+3 2 25.5
Latitudes	31 1 14.8	31 0 51.6	31 1 10.0	31 1 21.0

Latitude

								°	′	″
Latitude by	β Andromedæ	.		.		.	.	31	1	14.8
do.	α Lyræ	.	.		.		.	31	0	51.6
do.	β Pegaſi	.	.		.	.		31	1	10.0
do.	α Andromedæ	.		.		.		31	1	21.0

Mean latitude north	.	.	.	.		31	1	0.1

From the foregoing determinations it appears that the latitude given by
the large ſector, exceeds that given by the ſmall one, 1″.1 ; but as the reſult given by the large one, all circumſtances brought into view, may be
conſidered five times as accurate as that by the ſmall one : If therefore to
five times the latitude given by the large ſector, the latitude by the ſmall
one be added, and the ſum divided by ſix, the quotient 31° 1′ 10″ may
be taken as the true latitude of the obſervatory ; which exceeds the parallel of 31° by 1′ 10″, or about 7110.5 feet, which diſtance was carefully
laid off to the ſouth, and the line correčted back as heretofore agreeably to
plate VI.—From the end of the laſt mentioned correction, a map, or chart
of the river Chattahocha, or Apalachicola, was taken to the mouth of Flint
river (ſee Plate Nº VII.) but the mouth of Flint river not being a proper
place for a courſe of obſervations, we encamped on a commanding eminence where the following obſervations were made.

Aug. 23d.　　Thermometer 91° in the afternoon.

　　24th.　　Set up the clock, and equal altitude inſtru-
　　　　　ment.—Thermometer 75° at ſun riſe, roſe to
　　　　　91°.

　　　　　Began the obſervatory.

　25th.　　　　　*Equal altitudes of the Sun.*
　　　　A. M. 8ʰ 35′ 23″.　　P. M. 3ʰ 22′ 14″.

　　　　Thermometer 74° at ſun riſe, roſe to 88°.
　　　—Finiſhed the obſervatory and ſet up

　　Both Sečtors, with their faces to the Eaſt.

　　　Shower between 12 and 1 o'clock, cleared
　　off in a ſhort time, cloudy in the evening.

　Obſerved zenith diſtance of Caſtor　.　1° 37′ 42″ N.

　　　　　　　26th.

26th.   *Equal altitudes of the Sun.*
           A. M. 9ʰ 27' 28".   P. M. 2ʰ 29' 34".

Thermometer 76° at ſun riſe, roſe to 85°.
—Shower of rain at noon, cloudy at 3 o'clock
P. M. followed by a heavy rain.   During this
long continuation of rainy weather, the winds
have been very light, and ſcarcely perceptible
even when the clouds moved with prodigious
rapidity.   The winds have occupied no particular portion of the horizon, but have come
from all quarters, and that in a ſmall portion
of time.—The nights have generally been
fairer than the days.

			°	′	″	
Obſerved zenith diſtance of Caſtor	.		1	37	43	N.
do.	.	Pollux	.	2	11	7	s.

27th.   Thermometer 74° at ſun riſe, roſe to 96°.

                     Equal altitudes of the Sun.
           A. M. 8ʰ 6' 14".   P. M. 3ʰ 50' 8".

			°	′	″	
Obſerved zenith diſtance of	α Lyræ (ſmall ſector)		7	56	18	N.
do.	.	β Pegaſi	.	3	41	11.3	s.
do.	ſmall ſector	do.	.	3	40	0	s.
do.	.	α Andromedæ	.	2	42	8	s.
do.	ſmall ſector	do.	.	2	40	51	s.
do.	.	β Andromedæ	.	3	52	1.5	N.
do.	ſmall ſector	do.	.	3	52	53	N.
do.	.	β Tauri	.	2	15	37	s.
do.	.	Caſtor	.	1	37	44	N.
do.	.	Pollux	.	2	11	8	s.

28th.   Thermometer 74° at ſun riſe, roſe to 96°.

                     Equal altitudes of the Sun.
           A. M. 8ʰ 26' 6".   P. M. 3ʰ 29' 42".

                                             At

At half paſt 4 o'clock P. M. the ſky to the north loſt its fine blue, and became of a whitiſh brown, which in a ſhort time extended over the whole hemiſphere, and broke into ſmall clouds.—The evening was very diſtreſſing, the atmoſphere hazy, and ſuffocating, and not a breath of air perceptible till about 8 o'clock P. M. when we had a light breeze from the eaſt, which cleared, and corrected the atmoſphere.

			°	′	″	
Obſerved zenith diſtance of	β Pegaſi	.	3	41	13	s.
do.	ſmall ſector	do.	3	40	42	s.
do.	. . .	α Andromedæ	2	42	8.5	s.
do.	ſmall ſector	do.	2	41	0	s.
do.	. . .	β Andromedæ	3	52	2.5	n.
do.	ſmall ſector	do.	3	53	11	n.

29th.   Fog in the morning, ſucceeded by flying clouds.—Thermometer 80° all laſt night— roſe to 93°.

Obſerved zenith diſtance of α Coro. Borealis   3° 17′ 4″ s.

Turned the face of the large Sector to the Weſt.

Obſerved zenith diſtance of α Lyræ (ſmall ſector) 7° 56′ 6″ n.

Turned the face of the ſmall Sector to the Weſt.

			°	′	″	
Obſerved zenith diſtance of	β Tauri	.	2	17	17.5	s.
do.	. .	Caſtor	.	1	36	0	n.
do.	. .	Pollux	.	2	12	49	s.

30th.   Thermometer 74° at ſun riſe, roſe to 95°.

o   Obſerved

			°	′	″	
Obſerved zenith diſtance of	α Coro. Borealis		3	18	45.5	s.
do.	ſmall ſector	α Lyræ .	7	53	9	n.
do. . .	. β Pegaſi .		3	42	51	s.
do.	ſmall ſector	do. .	3	43	46	s.
do. . .	α Andromedæ		2	43	46	s.
do.	ſmall ſector	do. .	2	44	48	s.
do. . .	β Andromedæ		3	50	22	n.
do.	ſmall ſector	do. .	3	49	39	n.
do. . .	β Tauri .		2	17	16	s.
do. . .	Caſtor .		1	36	3.5	n.
do. . .	Pollux .		2	12	47	s.

31ſt.   Thermometer 76° at ſun riſe, roſe to 93°.

			°	′	″	
Obſerved zenith diſtance of	α Coro. Borealis		3	18	46	s.
do.	ſmall ſector	α Lyræ .	7	52	55	n.
do. . .	β Pegaſi .		3	42	51	s.
do.	ſmall ſector	do. . .	3	43	33	s.
do. . .	α Andromedæ .		2	43	44.5	s.
do.	ſmall ſector	do. . .	2	44	38	s.
do. . .	β Andromedæ .		3	50	23	n.
do.	ſmall ſector	do. . .	3	49	26	n.
do. . .	β Tauri . .		2	17	17	s.
do. . .	Pollux .		2	12	47	s.

Sept. 1ſt.   Thermometer 74° at ſun riſe, roſe to 94°.

Equal altitudes of the Sun.
A. M. 8^h 18′ 37″.   P. M. 3^h 34′ 41″.

		°	′	″	
Obſerved zenith diſtance of	α Lyræ (ſmall ſector)	7	52	42	n.
do. . .	β Pegaſi do.	3	43	28	s.
do. . .	α Andromedæ do.	2	44	38	s.
do. . .	β Andromedæ do.	3	49	16	n.
do. . .	Caſtor . .	1	36	3.5	n.

2d.   Thermometer 75° at ſun riſe, roſe to 90°.

Equal altitudes of the Sun.
A. M. 8^h 27′ 24″.   P. M. 3^h 25′ 20″.

Cloudy part of the afternoon.

3d.

3d.　　Thermometer 73° at fun rife, rofe to 91°.
—Cloudy great part of the day and night.

4th.　　Thermometer 76° at fun rife, rofe to 89°.
—Cloudy all the afternoon and night.

5th.　　Thermometer 74° at fun rife, rofe to 87°.
—Several fhowers of rain in the courfe of the day.

Between 13, and 14 hours, traced a meridian by γ Caffiopeæ, and ε Urfæ Minoris.

Emerfion of the 3d fatellite of ♃ obferved at 14ʰ 40′ 35″. —a little foggy, but the belts were pretty diftinct, magnifying power of the telefcope 120.

	h	′	″
Sirius paffed the firft fibre of the tranfit inftrument at	19	30	8
The meridian at	19	31	2
The third fibre at	19	31	52

6th.　　Thermometer 73° at fun rife, rofe to 89°.
—A fine clear morning, the fky remarkably blue.

	h	′	″	
☉'s preceding limb on the meridian at	11	54	8	A. M
Subfequent do. at	11	56	17	A. M.
Centre at	11	55	12.5	A. M.

When the above obfervation was made, the tremor was fo exceffive that there was no poffibility of bifecting the meridional mark with precifion, nor of examining the line of collimation with the neceffary accuracy.—Thunder-guft in the afternoon.

Immerfion of the 1ft fatellite of ♃ obferved at 14ʰ 15′ 7″ —Belts diftinct, magnifying power 120.

	○	′	″
Sirius paffed the firft fibre of the tranfit inftrument at	19	26	11
The meridian at	19	27	6
The third fibre at	19	27	56

7th.

7th.   Thermometer 73° at fun rife, rofe to 86°.
—Heavy fhower at day break, cloudy great
part of the day with a little rain.

		h	'	''
♂ Draconis paffed the meridian at . .		8	1	9
α Aquilæ do. . at . .		8	29	36

8th.   Thermometer 73° at fun rife, rofe to 87°.
—Shower at day break.
About 8 o'clock this morning the minute
hand of the clock was moved by an imperti-
nent young Indian.   The glafs having been
unfortunately broken by which the hands
were left expofed.—The clock was then fet
by my watch.

	h	'	''	
⊙'s preceding limb on the meridian at	11	53	27	A. M.
Subfequent do. at . . .	11	55	35	A. M.
Centre at	11	54	31	A. M.

Shower in the afternoon.

		h	'	''
♂ Draconis paffed the meridian at	.	7	57	10
☽'s weftern limb on the meridian at	.	8	0	34
α Aquilæ on the meridian at .	.	8	25	36

The obferved times, and diftances of the ☽'s weftern limb from Antares.

h	'	''	o	'	''	
8	41	14	39	51	0	
8	42	28	39	51	20	
8	43	42	39	52	0	Error of the Sextant
8	44	28	39	52	20	add 11″.
8	45	39	39	52	30	
8	46	54	39	52	50	
Means 8	44	4	39	52	0	

The

The obferved times, and diftances of the ☽'s weftern limb from Fomalhaut.

h	'	''	o	'	''	
8	59	5	45	18	0	
8	59	51	45	17	40	
9	0	31	45	17	20	
9	1	18	45	17	10	Error of the Sextant
9	2	9	45	17	0	add 11''.
9	3	5	45	16	40	
9	3	53	45	16	30	
9	4	43	45	16	0	
Means 9	1	49	45	17	2	

9th.   Thermometer 74° at fun rife, rofe to 90°.
—Thick fog till 8ʰ A. M.

	h	'	''	
☉'s preceding limb on the meridian at	11	53	6	A. M.
Subfequent do. at . .	11	55	16	A. M.
Centre at . • .	11	54	11	A. M.

♀'s weftern limb on the meridian at   .   •   2ʰ 13' 45''

Equal altitudes of the Sun.
A. M. 8ʰ 10' 23''.   P. M. 3ʰ 37' 26''.
Thefe equal altitudes are doubtful 3 or 4 feconds from fog and clouds.

The obferved times, and diftances of the ☽'s weftern limb from Antares.

h	'	''	o	'	''	
6	49	30	52	26	20	
6	51	11	52	27	0	
6	52	12	52	27	20	
6	52	58	52	28	0	Error of the Sextant
6	53	36	52	28	20	add 8''.
6	54	31	52	28	20	
6	55	37	52	28	30	
Means 6	52	48	52	27	41	

The

The obſerved times, and diſtances of the ☽ 's weſtern limb α Aries.

h	′	″		°	′	″	
8	31	55		95	30	20	
8	32	55		95	30	0	
8	33	45		95	29	40	
8	35	7		95	29	20	Error of the Sextant
8	36	4		95	29	0	add 8″.
8	36	53		95	29	0	
8	37	59		95	28	40	
Means 8	34	57		95	29	26	

☽ 's weſtern limb on the meridian at   8ʰ 56′ 20″

**10th.   Thermometer 71° at ſun riſe, roſe to 82°.
—Foggy.**

	h	′	″
Sirius on the firſt fibre of the tranſit inſtrument at	19	11	16
The meridian at	19	12	9
The third fibre at	19	13	0

11th.   Thermometer 74° at ſun riſe, roſe to 91°.

Note.   The obſervation on Sirius muſt have been entered wrong, or the clock moved about 45″ forward during my abſence yeſterday.

Cloudy all the afternoon with a little rain.

	h	′	″
Immerſion of the 2d ſatellite of ♃ obſerved at	13	12	0
Emerſion of do. at . . .	15	40	32

—Night clear, belts diſtinct, magnifying power 120.

	h	′	″
Sirius paſſed the firſt fibre of the tranſit inſtrument at } .	19	7	16
The meridian at	19	8	10
The third fibre at	19	9	1

**12th.   Thermometer 74° at ſun riſe, roſe to 89°.
Thunder-guſt at noon.**

Equal.

Equal altitudes of the Sun.
A. M. 8ʰ 23′ 0″.   P. M. 3ʰ 24′ 37″.

Thefe equal altitudes are doubtful 6 or 7 feconds, on account of clouds which have intervened every afternoon fince the 7th.

	h	′	″
♂ Draconis paffed the firft fibre of the tranfit inftrument at .	7	40	11
The meridian at	7	42	15
The third fibre at	7	44	26

	h	′	″
α Aquilæ paffed the firft fibre of the tranfit inftrument at .	8	9	50
The meridian at	8	10	41
The third fibre at	8	11	30

Immerfion of the 3d fatellite of ♃ obferved at 16ʰ 6′ 50″.—The night remarkably clear and fine, and I do not remember ever to have feen the fatellites, and belts, more beautifully defined.—Magnifying power 120.

	h	′	″
Sirius paffed the firft fibre of the tranfit inftrument at .	19	3	19
The meridian at	19	4	13
The third fibre at	19	5	3

13th. Thermometer 76° at fun rife, rofe to 91°.

	h	′	″
☉'s preceding limb on the meridian at	11	52	28 A. M.
Subfequent do. at . .	11	54	36 A. M.
Centre at . . .	11	53	32 A. M.

Equal altitudes of the Sun.
A. M. 8ʰ 9′ 48″.   P. M. 3ʰ 36′ 56″.

	h	′	″
♂ Draconis paffed the firft fibre of the tranfit inftrument at } .	7	36	12
The meridian at	7	38	16
The third fibre at . . .	7	40	28

	h	′	″
α Aquilæ paffed the firft fibre of the tranfit inftrument at } .	8	5	52
The meridian at . . .	8	6	43
The third fibre at . . .	8	7	32

Immerfion

Immerſion of the 1ſt ſatellite of ♃ obſerved at 16ʰ 9′ 20″.
—Belts middling diſtinct, magnifying power 120.—The ſatellite diſappeared uncommonly quick after it began to loſe
its luſtre.

	o	′	″
Sirius paſſed the firſt fibre of the tranſit inſtrument at	18	59	20
The meridian at	19	0	15
The third fibre at	19	1	6

14th. Thermometer 74° at ſun riſe, roſe to 91°.
—Cloudy part of the afternoon.

♀'s weſtern limb on the meridian at . 2ʰ 2′ 45″

Equal altitudes of the Sun.
A. M. 8ʰ 21′ 22″.   P. M. 3ʰ 24′ 38″.

	o	′	″
Sirius paſſed the firſt fibre of the tranſit inſtrument at	18	55	25
The meridian at	18	56	19
The third fibre at	18	57	9

15th. Thermometer 72° at ſun riſe, roſe to 92°.

	o	′	″
☉'s preceding limb on the meridian at	11	51	47 A. M.
Subſequent do. at . .	11	53	55 A. M.
Centre at . . .	11	52	51 A. M.

Note. Before the above obſervation was made, upon examining the tranſit inſtrument I found the ſcrew which ſcrews
the perpendicular axis was ſlackened, which probably in
ſome degree affected the preceding obſervation upon
Sirius.

	h	′	″
♀'s weſtern limb upon the meridian at . .	2	0	2

Sirius paſſed the firſt fibre of the tranſit inſtrument at	18	51	31
The meridian at	18	52	25
The third fibre at	18	53	15

16th. Thermometer 76° at ſun riſe, roſe to 96°.
—Cloudy part of the afternoon.

☉'s pre-

	h	′	″
⊙'s preceding limb on the meridian at	11	51	26 A. M.
Subfequent do. at	11	53	34 A. M.
Centre at	11	52	30 A. M.

	h	′	″
Sirius on the firſt fibre of the tranfit inſtrument at	18	47	38
The meridian at	18	48	31
The third fibre at	18	49	22

End of the obfervations made at this ſtation.

Examination of the meridian by the tranfits of ♂ Draconis, and α Aquilæ.

	h	′	″
Mean A. R. ♂ Draconis in time to the beginning of 1799.	19	12	27.9
Aberration and preceffion, Sept. 7th.		+	1.8
Nutation do.		—	0.3
True A. R. ♂ Draconis	19	12	29.4

Mean A. R. α Aquilæ in time to the beginning of 1799	19	40	58.1
Aberration and preceffion, Sept. 7th.		+	0.8
Nutation do.		—	0.7
True A. R. α Aquilæ	19	41	0.2
True A. R. ♂ Draconis	19	12	29.4
Difference	0	28	30.8
In 28′ 30″ fidereal time gains 4″.6 on mean folar time, which is therefore to be deducted		—	4.6
Difference in mean folar time	0	28	26.2
Obferved difference in mean folar time on the 7th.	0	28	27
Error of the meridian to the eaſt	0	0	0.8
Difference in A. R. between ♂ Draconis, and α Aquilæ on the 8th, mean folar time	0	28	26.2
Obferved difference on the 8th	0	28	26.0
Error of the meridian weſt	0	0	0.2

P   Difference

	h	'	"
Difference in A. R. between ♂ Draconis and α Aquilæ on } the 12th, mean folar time	o	28	26.5
Obferved difference on the 12th.	o	28	26
Error of the meridian to the weſt	o	o	0.5

	h	'	"
Difference in A. R. between ♂ Draconis, and ϖ Aquilæ on } the 13th, mean folar time	o	28	26.5
Obferved difference on the 13th	o	28	27.0
Error of the.meridian to the eaſt	o	o	0.5

Thofe ſtars being well ſituated to deteƈt any error in the meridian, and as the error comes within the probable error of taking an obfervation, it may be confidered fufficiently correƈt.

Examination of the meridian by the equal altitudes* and tranſit of the ☉'s centre on the 13th of September.

Equal altitudes of the Sun on that day.

	h	'	"		h	'	"
A. M.	8	9	48.	P. M.	3	36	56
Add					12		
					15	36	56
Deduƈt forenoon's obfervation . . .					—8	9	48
Divide by				2)	7	27	8
Half					3	43	34
Add forenoon's obfervation . . .					8	9	48
					11	53	22
Add equation for changes of the ☉'s declination .					+		9.6
☉'s centre on the meridian by equal altitudes at					11	53	31.6
☉'s centre on the meridian by obfervation at .				,	11	53	32.0
Difference to the weſt					o	o	0.4

The

---

* The equal altitudes before this day were taken with the equal altitude inſtrument. The cup for holding the water with the roof, for making an artificial horizon being ſtolen by the Indians, and not returned till the 12th. By a conſtant praƈtice of 16 years I find the equal altitudes taken from the artificial horizon rather more accurate, than when taken with the equal altitude inſtrument.

The difference by the above obfervation likewife comes within the probable error of making an obfervation.

The rate of the clock's going at this ftation.

			′	″	daily lofs.	
Clock too flow mean time Aug.	25th.		2	47.5	″	
do.	26th.		2	49.4	1.9	
do.	27th.		2	50.9	1.5	
do.	28th.		2	51.0	0.1	By equal alti-
do.	Sept. 1ft.		2	53.0	2.0	tudes of the ☉.
					daily gain.	
do.	2d.		2	51.4	1.6	
					0.4	
do.	6th.		2	51		By tranfits of
do.	8th.		2	51	0.0	the ☉'s centre
					daily lofs.	over the meri-
do.	9th.		2	51.2	0.2	dian.

On the 10th. between 10ʰ A. M. and 6ʰ P. M. the clock was altered
about 45″ forward by accident, or otherwife.

			′	″	daily lofs.	
Clock too flow mean time	13th.		2	7.4	″	By the tranfit of the ☉'s centre
					1	over the meridian.
do.	14th.		2	8.4	daily gain.	By equal altitudes of the ☉.
do.	15th.		2	6.0	2.4	By the tranfits of the ☉'s centre
do.	16th.		2	6.0	0.0	over the meridian.

Longitude of our obfervatory as deduced from the eclipfes of ♃ fatellites
and Lunar obfervations.

		h	′	″	
Sept. 5th.	By an Emerfion of the 3d fatellite	5	38	58	
6th.	Immerfion of the 1ft do.	5	39	18	
8th.	☽'s diftance from Antares	5	36	56	
	do. from Fomalhaut	5	38	30	
9th.	do. from Antares	5	37	39	Weft from
	do. from α Aries	5	38	8	Greenwich.
11th.	Immerfion of the 2d fatellite	5	37	29	
	Emerfion do.	5	36	35	
12th.	Immerfion of the 3d do.	5	37	3	
13th.	do. 1ft do.	5	39	20	

Refult

Result of the Observations made with the large Sector, at our station near the mouth of Flint River, to determine the Latitude.

The Zenith distances stand as below.

Face of the Sector East.

	β Andromedæ.	β Tauri.	Castor.	Pollux.	α Coro. Borealis.	β Pegaſi.	α Andromedæ.
August 25th	. . . .	. . . .	1 37 42 N.	2 11 7 s.	. . . .	. . . .	. . . .
26th	. . . .	. . . .	1 37 43	2 11 8	. . . .	. . . .	. . . .
27th	3 52 1.5 N.	2 15 37 s.	1 37 44	. . . .	. . . .	3 41 11.3 s.	2 42 8 s.
28th	3 52 2.5	. . . .	. . . .	. . . .	. . . .	3 41 13	2 42 8.5
29th	. . . .	. . . .	. . . .	. . . .	3 17 4 s.	. . . .	. . . .
Means	3 52 2	2 15 37	1 37 43	2 11 7.5	3 17 4	3 41 12.1	2 42 8.2

Face of the Sector Weſt.

	β Andromedæ.	β Tauri.	Castor.	Pollux.	α Coro. Borealis.	β Pegaſi.	α Andromedæ.
30th	3 50 22	2 17 17.5	1 36 0	2 12 49	3 18 46	3 42 51	2 43 46
31ſt	3 50 23	2 17 16	1 36 3.5	2 12 47	3 18 46	3 42 51	2 43 44
Sept. 1ſt	. . . .	2 17 17	1 36 3.5	2 12 47	. . . .	. . . .	. . . .
Means	3 50 22.5	2 17 16.8	1 36 2.3	2 12 47.7	3 18 46	3 42 51	2 43 45
Means face eaſt	3 52 2	2 15 37	1 37 43	2 11 7.5	3 17 4	3 41 12.1	2 42 8.2
Means	3 51 12.2	2 16 26.9	1 36 52.6	2 11 57.6	3 17 55	3 42 1.5	2 42 56.6
Refractions	+ 3.8	+ 2.3	+ 1.6	+ 2.2	+ 3.3	+ 3.7	+ 2.7
True zenith diſtances	3 51 16.0	2 16 29.2	1 36 54.2	2 11 59.8	3 17 58.3	3 42 5.2	2 42 59.3

Mean

	β Andromedæ.	β Tauri.	Castor.	Pollux.	α Coro. Borealis.	β Pegasi.	α Andromedæ.
	° ′ ″	° ′ ″	° ′ ″	° ′ ″	° ′ ″	° ′ ″	° ′ ″
Mean declinations Aug. 28th.	34 33 18.2 N	28 25 29.1 N	32 18 51 N	28 29 56.6 N	27 23 52.1 N	26 59 21.3 N	27 59 8.1 N
Aberrations	− 1.1	− 2.2	− 0.7	+ 0.5	+ 14.8	+ 4.8	+ 2.5
Nutations	− 2.6	+ 6.8	+ 8.4	+ 8.5	− 2.9	− 6.4	− 4.6
Semi-annual equations . . .	+ 0.4	− 0.4	+ 0.2	+ 0.1	− 0.5	+ 0.2	+ 0.4
True declinations . . .	34 33 14.9	28 25 33.5	32 18 58.9	28 30 5.7	27 24 4.2	26 59 29.9	27 59 6.4
True zenith distances applied . .	−3 51 16	+2 16 29.2	−1 36 54.2	+2 11 59.8	+3 17 58.3	+3 42 5.2	+2 42 59.3
Latitudes N.	30 41 58.9	30 42 2.7	30 42 4.7	30 42 5.5	30 42 2.5	30 41 55.1	30 42 5.7

	° ′ ″
Latitude by β Andromedæ .	30 41 58.9
do. . β Tauri .	30 42 2.7
do. . Castor .	30 42 4.7
do. . Pollux .	30 42 5.5
do. . α Coro. Borealis .	30 42 2.5
do. . β Pegasi .	30 41 55.1
do. . α Andromedæ .	30 42 5.7
Mean Latitude north .	30 42 2.2

Result

Result of the Observations made with the small Sector, at our station near the mouth of Flint River, to determine the Latitude.

The Zenith Distances arranged stand as below.

Face of the Sector East.

	β Andromedæ.	α Lyræ.	β Pegasi.	α Andromedæ.
	° ′ ″	° ′ ″	° ′ ″	° ′ ″
Aug. 27th	3 52 53 N.	7 56 18 N.	3 40 0 S.	2 40 51 S.
28th	3 53 11	....	3 40 42	2 41 0
29th	....	7 56 6	....	....
Means	3 53 2	7 56 12	3 40 ,21	2 40 55.5

Face of the Sector West.

	β Andromedæ.	α Lyræ.	β Pegasi.	α Andromedæ.
30th	3 49 39	7 53 9	3 43 46	2 44 48
31st	3 49 26	7 52 55	3 43 33	2 44 38
Sept. 1st	3 49 16	7 52 42	3 43 28	2 44 38
Means	3 49 27	7 52 55.3	3 43 36	2 44 41
Means face east	3 53 2	7 56 12	3 40 21	2 40 55.5
Means	3 51 14.5	7 54 33	3 41 58.5	2 42 48.2
Refractions	+ 3.8	+ 7.9	+ 3.7	+ 2.7
True zenith distances	3 51 18.3	7 54 40.9	3 42 2.2	2 42 50.9
Mean declinations August 28th	34 33 18.2 N.	38 36 12.9 N.	26 59 51.3 N.	27 59 8.1 N.
Aberrations	— 1.1	+ 15.2	+ 4.8	+ 2.5
Nutations	— 2.6	— 7.8	— 6.4	— 4.6
Semi. ann. equations	+ 0.4	— 0.3	+ 0.2	+ 0.4
True declinations	34 33 14.9	38 36 20.3	26 59 49.9	27 59 6.4
True zenith distances applied	—3 51 18.3	—7 54 40.9	+3 42 2.2	+2 42 50.9
Latitudes N.	30 41 56.6	30 41 39.4	30 41 52.1	30 41 57.3

Latitude

		°	′	″
Latitude by β Andromedæ	.	30	41	56.6
do. α Lyræ	.	30	41	39.4
do. β Pegafi	,	30	41	52.1
do. α Andromedæ	.	30	41	57.3
Mean Latitude North	.	30	41	51.3

From the refult of the foregoing obfervations, the latitude of our obfervatory by the large fector, comes out 30° 42′ 2″.2 N. and by the fmall one 30° 41′ 51″.3 N. By proceeding as in the former cafes where both fectors were ufed, and the due weight given each, the latitude appears to be 30° 42′ 0″.4, which we took for the true latitude of the obfervatory.

The ground about the mouth of Flint river not being fit for encamping on, in confequence thereof, we pitched on the nearest commanding eminence, from which with the leaft labour in falling the timber, the junction of the rivers might be difcovered: In order to connect our work with the junction of the rivers, the following method was purfued. From the obfervatory A (fee Fig. G, Plate VII.) a vifta was opened to give us a view of the point of land B, between the rivers. The angle which the line A B made with the meridian AN, we had to determine by meafurement, the aftronomical circle which was admirably calculated for that purpofe, was fent away a few days before (we were compelled by the Indians to leave the country) on account of its weight, as I was informed by the commiffioner for His Catholic Majefty! To find the value of this angle, the triangle ANC was formed on the ground.—AN a portion of the meridian was equal to 396.125 feet, AC, a portion of the line in the direction of the junction of the rivers was equal to 496.623 feet, and NC the fide oppofite to the required angle, was equal to 336.583 feet*—the fides being given, the angle CAN comes out to the nearest fecond 45° 10′ 19″ weft of north. The diftance from A to B was found by meafurement to be 369 perches, from which by the folution of a plane right-angled triangle, the difference of latitude will be found to be 260.14 perches, or about 42″.4, which added to the latitude of the obfervatory will give 30° 42′ 42″.8 for the latitude of the junction of the rivers.—The fides of the triangle, with the points of interfection were formed with the utmoft accuracy by the tranfit inftrument.

On the 17th day of September, at the time we were preparing to extend the line from the mouth of Flint river to the fource of the St. Mary's, the hoftile difpofition

---

* The three decimal places annexed to the feet arofe from taking the means of many meafurements made on each line.

fition of the Indians, and an attempt to plunder our camp, compelled us to relinquifh our defign, and leave the country. On the 9th day of December following we met at the town of St. Mary's, and took into confideration the further profecution of our bufinefs, and came to a conclufion,—that we could not attempt with any probability of fuccefs, more than to determine the fource of the St. Mary's, with its geographical pofition, until the waters fhould fubfide, and the fwamps be dried by the fummer heats, which could not be expected in lefs than eight months, added to an oppofition we had a right to look for from the Indians.—In order to determine the geographical pofition of the river St. Mary's, we erected an obfervatqry at Point Peter, near the mouth of the river, as a given point; from whence the latitude, and longitude of the fource of the river might be determined by meafurement, if we fhould fail, either in carrying on our apparatus, or in obtaining a fufficient number of obfervations for that purpofe.

At Point Peter the following obfervations were made.

Dec. 14th.   Set up the clock.

15th.   Cloudy.

16th.   Set up the fmall Sector with the face to the Eaft.

Thermometer 51° at fun rife, rofe to 67°.

Equal altitudes of the Sun.
A. M. 9^h 14' 59".   P. M. 2^h 41' 7".

Thefe equal altitudes are doubtful a few feconds, but not more than 4.

Cloudy

Cloudy all the afternoon after 3^h P. M. and continued fo all night.

17th.   Fog in the morning, cloudy all day.—Thermometer $57°$ at fun rife, rofe to $70°$. Heavy rain at night.

18th.   Thermometer $56°$ at fun rife, rofe to $64°$. —Fine rain in the morning. Strong wind from the N. E.—Cloudy with rain all the afternoon and night.

19th.   Thermometer $55°$ at fun rife, rofe to $69°$. —Heavy fog early in the morning.—Flying clouds all day and rain in the evening.

20th.   Thermometer $60°$ at fun rife, fell to $58°$. —Cloudy all day, fine rain in the morning and a heavy rain at night.

21ft.   Thermometer $59°$ at fun rife, fell to $54°$ in the afternoon, cloudy with heavy rain moft of the day.—Wind from the N. W. in the evening.

22d.   Thermometer $54°$ at fun rife, rofe to $55°$. —Cloudy early in the morning and in the evening.

Obferved zenith diftance of α Lyrœ   7° 55′ 37″ N.

Equal altitudes of the Sun.
A. M. 9^h 1′ 32″.   P. M. 3^h 7′ 28″.

23d.   Thermometer $54°$ at fun rife, rofe to $56°$. —Cloudy all laft night and this day with fine rain, wind S. W. cleared off in the evening with a N. W. wind.

		°	′	″	
Obferved zenith diftance of	β Tauri	2	15	3	s.
do.	Caftor	1	38	12	N.
do.	Pollux	2	10	38	s.

q   *Emerfion*

Emerſion of the 1ſt ſatellite of ♃ obſerved at 15ʰ 40′ 51ʺ.
Night clear, belts diſtinct, magnifying power 120.

24th.   Thermometer 34° at ſun riſe, roſe to 54°.

Obſerved zenith diſtance of α Lyræ . 7° 55′ 37″ N.

Equal altitudes of the Sun.
A. M. 9ʰ 22′ 17ʺ.   P. M. 2ʰ 50′ 12″.

			°	′	″
Obſerved zenith diſtance of	α Andromedæ		2	44	22 s.
do.	.	. β Andromedæ	3	53	16 N.
do.	.	. β Tauri .	2	14	51 s.
do.	.	. Caſtor .	1	38	20 N.

25th.   Thermometer 30° at ſun riſe, roſe to 51°.

Obſerved zenith diſtance of α Lyræ . 7° 55′ 46″ N.

Equal altitudes of the Sun.
A. M. 9ʰ 20′ 21″.   P. M. 2ʰ 53′ 50″.

Obſerved zenith diſtance of α Andromedæ   2° 41′ 16″ s.
    do. . . β Andromedæ   3 53 16 N.

Emerſion of the 1ſt ſatellite of ♃ obſerved at 10ʰ 9′ 50″.
Night clear, belts diſtinct, magnifying power 120.

Obſerved zenith diſtance of Pollux . 2° 10′ 34″ s.

26th.   Thermometer 41° at ſun riſe, roſe to 49°.
—Cloudy all day and night.

Turned the face of the Sector Weſt.

27th.   Thermometer 50° at ſun riſe, roſe to 64°.

Obſerved zenith diſtance of   α Lyræ . 7° 48′ 25″.

Equal altitudes of the Sun.
A. M. 9ʰ 19′ 51″.   P. M. 2ʰ 57′ 42″.

Obſerved

Obſerved zenith diſtance of ⍺ Andromedæ . 2° 48′ 37″ s.
do. . . β Andromedæ . 3 45 48 N.

Emerſion of the 2d ſatellite of ♃ obſerved at 7ʰ 16′ 0″.
—Belts diſtinct, magnifying power 120.

			°	′	″
Obſerved zenith diſtance of	β Tauri	.	2	22	20 s.
do.	. .	Caſtor	.	1	30	52 N.
do.	. .	Pollux	.	2	17	57 s.
do.	. .	⍺ Lyræ*	.	7	48	24 N.

28th. Thermometer roſe to 80°.—Cloudy in the morning.—Wind S. E.

Obſerved zenith diſtance of ⍺ Andromedæ 2° 48′ 33″ s.
do. . . β Andromedæ 3 45 50 N.

29th. Thermometer 67° at ſun riſe, fell to 63° in the afternoon.—Heavy rain great part of the day.—At 10 o'clock P. M. wind ſhifted to the S. W. and blew with great violence,—became clear at ſhort intervals.

			°	′	″
Obſerved zenith diſtance of	β Tauri	.	2	22	21 s.
do.	. .	Caſtor	.	1	31	0 N.
do.	. .	Pollux	.	2	17	59 s.

30th. Thermometer 54° at ſun riſe, fell to 44° in the afternoon, and to 33° at 7ʰ P. M.— Strong N. W. wind with flying clouds.

In the evening finiſhed our meridian by circum-polar ſtars, this work was begun on the evening of the 29th.

31ſt. Thermometer 25° at ſun riſe, roſe to 44°.

q 2 *Equal*

---

* On the meridian twice this day from ſidereal time gaining on mean ſolar time.

Equal altitudes of the Sun.
A. M. 9^h 41' 37".   P. M. 2^h 42' 19".

γ Caſſiopeæ paſſed the meridian at   .   6^h 11' 37"
Pole ſtar at   6   19   8

1800.

Jan. 1ſt.   Thermometer 28° at ſun riſe, roſe to 54°. —Wind N. E. ſcattering clouds from the S. E.

Emerſion of the 1ſt ſatellite of ♃ obſerved at 12^h 6' 43". —Belts diſtinct, magnifying power 120.

An immerſion of the 4th ſatellite is entered in the Nautical Almanac to happen at Greenwich at 17^h 18' 30", and the emerſion at 18^h 44' 22". As the immerſion was to happen but 1' 32" from the emerſion of the 1ſt ſatellite, it was a favourable opportunity to make both obſervations at one ſetting. At 12^h I placed myſelf at the teleſcope, and as ſoon as I had adjuſted the inſtrument to my eye, I thought the 4th ſatellite had loſt ſome of its luſtre. After noting the emerſion of the 1ſt ſatellite, I again applied myſelf to the inſtrument, but the 4th ſatellite ſtill continued viſible, and had altered but very little ſince I firſt obſerved it; it was very diſtinct at 12^h 42', and at 13^h had nearly if not quite recovered its luſtre.

2d.   Thermometer 54° all day.—Heavy rain, wind N. E. till evening, ſhifted to the N. W. in the night when it became clear.

3d.   Thermometer 39° at ſun riſe, roſe to 53°.

Equal altitudes of the Sun.
A. M. 9^h 27' 30".   P. M. 3^h 1' 18".

Emerſion of the 1ſt ſatellite of ♃ obſerved at 6^h 35' 39". —Belts diſtinct, and the planet and ſatellites remarkably well defined, magnifying power 120.

Emerſion of the 2d ſatellite of ♃ obſerved at 9^h 55' 59". —Belts and ſatellites very diſtinct, magnifying power 120.

4th.   Thermometer 36° at ſun riſe, roſe to 54°.

Equal

Equal altitudes of the Sun.
A. M. 9ʰ 48′ 45″.   P. M. 2ʰ 41′ 38″.

5th.   Thermometer 36° at fun rife.—Cloudy all day.
6th.   Thermometer 34° at fun rife, rofe to 61°.

Equal altitudes of the Sun.
A. M. 9ʰ 30′ 21″.   P. M. 3ʰ 9′ 3″.

7th.   Thermometer 38° at fun rife.—Cloudy all day.
8th.   Thermometer 40° at fun rife, rofe to 48°.

Emerfion of the 1ft fatellite of ♃ obferved at 14ʰ 3′ 12″ —Hazy, neither ♃ nor his fatellites well defined, magnifying power 120.

9th.   Thermometer 38° at fun rife, rofe to 42°. —Fine rain part of the day, and rain with hail during the night—wind N. E.
10th.   Thermometer 37° at fun rife, rofe to 40°. —Snow and hail the whole day ! which continued till 10 o'clock in the evening, when the thermometer fell to 32°, the wind fhifted to N. W. and it became clear at midnight.
11th.   Thermometer 28° at fun rife, rofe to 40°. —Snow five inches deep.

Equal altitudes of the Sun.
A. M. 9ʰ 36′ 25″   P. M. 3ʰ 4′ 24″.

12th.   Thermometer 34° at fun rife, rofe to 67°. —Cloudy great part of the day.
13th.   Thermometer 46° at fun rife, rofe to 57°. —Cloudy all day.

14th.

14th.   Thermometer 40° at fun rife, rofe to 62°.
—Cloudy.

15th.   Thermometer 42° at fun rife, rofe to 61°.
—Cloudy in the evening.

Equal altitudes of the Sun.
A. M. 9^h 49' 22''.   P. M. 2^h 57' 0''.

16th.   Thermometer 45° at fun rife, rofe to 67°.
17th.   Thermometer 64° at fun rife, fell to 42°
in the evening, cloudy in the morning, light
fhower at 11^h A. M. cleared off at noon with
a moft violent wind from the weft, which
fhifted to the N. W. in the evening.

The obferved times, and diftances, of the ☉'s and ☽'s neareft limbs.

h	'	''	°	'	''	
20	40	4	86	23	50	
20	41	23	86	23	40	
20	42	7	86	23	10	
20	42	52	86	22	40	Error of the Sex-
20	43	34	86	22	30	tant add 8''.
20	44	10	86	22	00	
20	44	48	86	21	55	
20	45	30	86	21	30	
Means 20	43	3	86	22	39	

Repeated.

h	'	''	°	'	''	
21	1	29	86	16	0	
21	1	58	86	15	50	
21	2	35	86	15	30	Error of the Sextant
21	3	7	86	15	30	add 8''.
21	3	41	86	15	0	
21	4	13	86	14	40	
Means 21	2	50	86	15	25	

18th.

18th.   Thermometer 38° at sun rise, rose to 58°.

Equal altitudes of the Sun.
A. M. 9^h 45' 10".   P. M. 3^h 5' 8".

At 6^h prepared to observe the eclipse of ♃'s 4th satellite. —At about 6^h 20' the satellite began to lose its lustre, which gradually diminished till about 6^h 46',—from that time it was not discernible with a magnifying power of 50, but distinct with 120.—at 7^h 23' 47" it was evidently more bright, and at 7^h 35' had almost recovered its usual brightness.

The observed times, and distances of the ⊙'s and ☽'s nearest limbs.

h	'	"		°	'	"	
20	46	32		73	9	30	
20	47	35		73	9	0	
20	48	12		73	8	50	
20	48	44		73	8	30	
20	49	20		73	8	15	
20	50	6		73	8	0	Error of the Sextant
20	50	43		73	7	40	add 8".
20	51	18		73	7	30	
20	51	51		73	7	20	
20	52	25		73	7	15	
20	53	0		73	6	0	
Means 20	49	59		73	8	10	

Repeated.

h	'	"		°	'	"	
21	15	29		72	59	20	
21	16	33		72	59	00	
21	17	9		72	58	50	
21	17	52		72	58	40	
21	18	32		72	58	20	Error of the Sex-
21	19	9		72	58	00	tant add 8".
21	19	40		72	57	40	
21	20	22		72	57	30	
21	20	54		72	57	20	
21	21	20		72	57	0	
Means 21	18	42		72	58	10	

19th.

19th.   Thermometer 37° at fun rife, rofe to 54°.

Equal altitudes of the Sun.
A. M. 10^h 1′ 6″.   P. M. 2^h 50′ 21″.

Thefe equal altitudes are doubtful 2 or 3 feconds but not
more, from the violence of the wind.

Rate of the clock's going at Point Peter.

1799.					′	″	Daily gain.
Clock too faft mean time		Dec.	16th.	.	3	41.2	″
do.	.	.	22d.	.	5	17.6	. . 19.4
do.	.	.	24th.	.	6	1.1	. . 21.7
do.	.	.	25th.	.	6	21.7	. . 20 6
do.	.	.	27th.	.	7	2 4	. . 20.3
do.	.	.	31ft.	.	8	16.0	. . 18.4
1800. do.	.	Jan.	3d.	.	9	16.0	. . 20.1
do.	.	.	4th.	.	9	35.9	. . 19.6
do.	.	.	6th.	.	10	15.3	. . 19.7
do.	.	.	11th.	.	11	49.8	. . 18.9
do.	.	.	15th.	.	13	7.0	. . 19.3
do.	.	.	18th.	.	14	4.9	. . 19.3
do.	.	.	19th.	.	14	23.7	. . 18.3

Refult of the Obfervations for the Longitude.

1799.				h	′	″	
By an emerfion of the 1ft fatellite of ♃ on Dec. 23d.			.	5	26	27	
25th.	do.	.	.	5	26	37	
27th.	2d. do.	.		5	25	27	
1800. Jan. 1ft.	1ft. do.	.	.	5	26	27	
3d.	do.	.	.	5	26	45	Weft from
do.	2d. do.	.	.	5	25	47	Greenwich.
17th.	By a lunar obfervation			5	26	56	
do.	.	.	do.	5	27	3	
18th.	.	.	do.	5	25	42	
do.	.	.	do.	5	26	3	

Refult

Result of the Observations made at Point Peter to determine the Latitude.

The Zenith distances stand as below.

Face of the Sector East.

1799.	β Andromedæ ° ′ ″	β Tauri ° ′ ″	Castor ° ′ ″	Pollux ° ′ ″	α Lyræ ° ′ ″	α Andromedæ ° ′ ″
Dec. 22d	. . . .	. . . .	. . . .	. . . .	. . . .	. . . .
23d	. . . .	2 15 3 S.	1 38 12 N.	2 10 38 S.	7 55 37 N.	. . . .
24th	3 53 16 N.	2 14 51	1 38 20	. . . .	7 55 37	2 41 22 S.
25th	3 53 16	. . . .	1 18 16	2 10 34	7 55 46	2 41 16
Means	3 53 16	2 14 57	1 18 16	2 10 36	7 55 40	2 41 19
Face of the Sector West.						
27th	3 45 48	2 22 20	1 30 52	2 17 57	7 48 25	2 48 37
28th	3 45 51	. . . .	. . . .	. . . .	7 48 24	2 48 33
29th	. . . .	2 22 21	1 31 0	2 17 59	. . . .	. . . .
Means	3 45 49.5	2 22 20.5	1 30 56	2 17 58	7 48 24.5	2 48 35
Means face east	3 53 16	2 14 57	1 18 16	2 10 36	7 55 40	2 41 19
Means	3 49 32.7	2 18 38.7	1 34 36	2 14 17	7 52 2.2	2 44 57
Refractions	+ 3.8	+ 2.3	+ 1.6	+ 2.2	+ 7.9	+ 2.7
True zenith distances	3 49 36.5	2 18 41	1 34 37.6	2 14 19.2	7 52 10.1	2 44 59.7
Mean declinations Dec. 25th	34 33 26 N.	28 25 28 N.	32 18 47 N.	28 29 47 N.	38 36 15 N.	27 59 13 N.
Aberrations	+ 10.8	+ 2	− 3.4	− 3.4	+ 1	+ 9
Nutations	− 1.7	+ 7	+ 8.6	+ 8.7	− 3	− 3.4
True declinations	34 33 35.1	28 25 37	32 18 52.2	28 29 52.3	38 36 8	27 59 18.6
True zenith distances applied	−3 49 36.5	+2 18 41	−1 34 37.6	+2 14 19.2	−7 52 10.1	+2 44 59.7
Latitudes N.	30 43 58.6	30 44 18	30 44 14.6	30 44 11.5	30 43 57.9	30 44 18.3

Latitude

			o	′	″
Latitude by	β Andromedæ	.	30	43	58.6
do.	β Tauri	. .	30	44	18
do.	Castor	. .	30	44	14.6
do.	Pollux	. .	30	44	11.5
do.	α Lyræ	. .	30	43	57.9
do.	α Andromedæ	. .	30	44	18.3
Mean Latitude north		.	30	44	9.8*

Examination of the meridian by the transit of γ Cassiopeæ and α Ursæ Minoris or the Pole star.

	o	′	″
Mean A. R. γ Cassiopeæ Dec. 31st 1799 . .	11	11	11.3
Aberration	—		1.3
Nutation	—		23.3
True A. R. γ Cassiopeæ	11	10	46.7

	o	′	″
Mean A. R. Pole star Dec. 31st 1799 . .	13	6	47.0
Aberration	+		36.0
Nutation	—	4	30
True A. R. Pole star	13	2	53
do. γ Cassiopeæ	11	10	46.7
Difference	1	52	6.3

	′	″
The above difference is nearly, in mean solar time equal to .	7	27
Observed difference on the 31st of Dec. . . .	7	31
Difference	0	4

The difference between the calculated, and observed time, is so small, that it is scarcely sufficient with the very best instrument to be perceptible in the motion of the Pole star. The meridian may therefore be considered as sufficiently accurate for the following purpose.

In

* Although this result is deduced from observations made with the small sector only, it may be considered as sufficiently accurate for the nicest geographical purposes.

In order to determine the exact positions of the flag staff in the fort at Point Peter, the south end of Cumberland Island, and the north end of Amelia Island, the meridian was extended south from the observatory the distance of 99.12 perches.

	°	′	″	
From the observatory the bearing of the flag staff in the fort was	S. 22	23	00	E.
From do. to a signal on the north end of Amelia Island	S. 64	33	00	E.
From do. to do. on the south end of Cumberland Island	S. 65	30	30	E.
From the south end of the base the bearing of the flag staff in the fort was	S. 42	19	30	E.
From do. to the signal on the north end of Amelia Island	S. 66	33	00	E.
From do. to do. on the south end of Cumberland Island	S. 72	2	30	E.

From these data by plain trigonometry the distance from the observatory to the flag staff in the fort comes out — 195.7 —

From do. to the signal on the north end of Amelia Island — 1421.9 — Perches.

From do. to do. on the south end of Cumberland Island — 828.7 —

		°	′	″
Diff. of latitude between the observatory and flag staff		0	0	29.5
do.	signal on Amelia Island	0	1	45.7
do.	do. on Cumberland Island	0	0	56.0

		°	′	″	
The latitude of the flag staff is therefore		30	43	49.3	
do.	north end of Amelia Island	30	42	24.1	North.
do.	south end of Cumberland	30	43	13.8	

From which it appears that the junction of the Chatahocha, or Apalachicola, and Flint Rivers, and the entrance between Cumberland, and Amelia Islands into the sound, are precisely in the same parallel of latitude.

The angles were taken with the instrument already mentioned, made by Mr George Adams.

1800.

Feb. 6th.   Ascended the St. Mary's as high as it was navigable for canoes.*

r 2   7th.

---

* We ascended the river with as little loading and baggage as possible. —I even left my hat and thermometer.

7th.   Sent out a party to difcover the fource of the river or its communication with Okefonoke fwamp.   Set up the clock.

8th.   Cloudy with heavy rain.

9th.

Equal altitudes of the Sun.
A. M. 9^h 2′ 46″.   P. M. 2^h 53′ 18″.

10th.   Cloudy all day with an appearance of rain.

11th.   Shower at day break—Cloudy all day with cold N. wind.

12th.   Smart froft, cold all day, and cloudy in the evening.

Equal altitudes of the Sun.
A. M. 8^h 46′ 1″.   P. M. 3^h 10′ 15″.

The telefcope and tranfit inftrument arrived.

13th.   Very cloudy, and cold in the morning :—heavy rain all the afternoon and night.

14th.   Cloudy with fine rain in the forenoon : cleared off in the afternoon with a N. W. wind.

Set up both Sectors with the faces to the Eaft.

			o	′	″	
Obferved zenith diftance of β Tauri (fmall fector)			1	52	31	s.
do.	. .	Caftor .	1	58	6	N.
do.	fmall fector	do. . .	2	1	3	N.
do.	. .	Pollux . .	1	50	49	s.
do.	fmall fector	do. . .	1	47	49	s.
do.	fmall fector	α Coro. Borealis .	2	54	26	s.

15th.   Very cool, ftrong wind from the N. W.

Obferved zenith diftance of β Andromedæ   4° 12′ 38″ N.

Equal

Equal altitudes of the Sun.
A. M. 8ʰ 54′ 45″. P. M. 3ʰ 1′ 24″.

Thefe equal altitudes are doubtful a few feconds (from the violence of the wind) but not more than four.

			°	′	″	
Obferved zenith diftance of	β Tauri		1	55	13	s.
do.	fmall fector	do.	1	52	35	s.
do.		Caftor	1	58	10	n.
do.		Pollux	1	50	46	s.
do.		α Coro. Borealis	2	57	16	s.
do.	fmall fector	do.	2	54	34	s.

The obferved times, and diftances, of the ☉'s and ☽'s neareft limbs.

h	′	″	°	′	″	
19	48	31	90	56	30	
19	49	35	90	56	00	
19	50	28	90	55	40	
19	51	8	90	55	30	Error of the Sextant add 5″.
19	51	42	90	55	20	
19	52	9	90	55	0	
19	52	34	90	54	50	
19	53	6	90	54	20	
Means 19	51	9	90	55	24	

16th. *Equal altitudes of the Sun.*
A. M. 9ʰ 2′ 32″. P. M. 2ʰ 53′ 29″.

Thefe equal altitudes are doubtful 2 or 3 feconds from the interference of clouds.

			°	′	″	
Obferved zenith diftance of	β Tauri	.	1	55	9	s.
do.	fmall fector	do.	1	52	36	s.
do.		Caftor	1	58	7	n.
do.	fmall fector	do.	2	0	51	n.
do.		Pollux	1	50	50	s.
do.	fmall fector	do.	1	47	36	s.

Emerfion of the 1ft fatellite of ♃ obferved at 12ʰ 5′ 40″. Night very fine, belts diftinct, magnifying power 120.

Obferved

Obferved zenith diftance of α Coro. Borealis   2° 57′ 19″ s.
    do.   fmall fector   do.   .   2 54 29 s.

17th.   Cloudy in the morning and continued fo at times all day.

Equal altitudes of the Sun.
A. M. 9ʰ 24′ 49″.   P. M. 2ʰ 31′ 3″.

The above equal altitudes are doubtful 2 or 3 feconds on account of the clouds.

Hazy all the evening.

Obferved zenith diftance of Caftor   .   1° 58′ 9″ N.
    do.   .   .   Pollux   .   1 50 50 s.

Between 14 and 15 hours traced a meridian by ε Urfæ Majoris and the Pole ftar.

Obferved zenith diftance of α Lyræ (fmall fector) 8° 17′ 8″ N.

The obferved times, and diftances, of the ☉'s and ☽'s neareft limbs.

h	′	″	°	′	″	
19	53	40	64	40	00	
19	54	14	64	39	50	
19	54	43	64	39	40	
19	55	22	64	39	30	
19	56	1	64	39	20	
19	56	26	64	39	00	Error of the Sex-
19	56	49	64	38	50	tant add 5″.
19	57	21	64	38	40	
19	57	59	64	38	40	
19	58	38	64	38	30	
19	59	10	64	38	20	
Means 19	56	24	64	39	7	

18th.   ☉'s preceding limb on the meridian at   11 56 35 A. M.
    Subfequent   do.   at   .   .   11 58 48 A. M.

    Centre   do.   at   .   .   11 57 41 A. M.

Obferved

Obferved zenith diftance of β Andromedæ 4° 12′ 39″ N.

Equal altitudes of the Sun.
A. M. 8ʰ 57′ 23″.　　P. M. 2ʰ 58′ 20″.

Turned the Face of the fmall Sector Weft.

Cloudy at times all the afternoon and night.

Obferved zenith diftance of Caftor (fmall fector) 1° 53′ 40″ N.

The obferved times, and diftances, of the ☉'s and ☽'s neareft limbs.

h	′	″	°	′	″	
20	0	7	51	39	30	
20	0	43	51	39	20	
20	1	22	51	39	10	
20	2	15	51	39	0	
20	3	6	51	38	50	Error of the Sex-
20	3	42	51	38	40	tant add 5″.
20	4	27	51	38	20	
20	4	59	51	38	0	
20	5	37	51	37	50	
20	6	14	51	37	40	
Means 20	3	15	51	38	38	

☽'s Subfequent limb on the meridian at　.　20ʰ 38′ 00″.

The obferved times, and diftances, of the ☉'s and ☽'s neareft limbs.

h	′	″	°	′	″	
20	37	42	51	28	30	
20	39	14	51	27	50	
20	39	50	51	27	40	
20	40	20	51	27	30	Error of the Sex-
20	41	2	51	27	20	tant add 5″.
20	41	29	51	27	00	
20	41	59	51	26	50	
20	42	30	51	26	40	
Means 20	40	31	51	27	25	

♀ paffed

♀ paſſed the meridian at   21ʰ 11′ 32″ centrum.

19th.   Smart froſt this morning, very cloudy at noon, clear at 2ʰ P. M.

Equal altitudes of the Sun.
A. M. 8ʰ 48′ 44″.   P. M. 3ʰ 6′ 49″.

Turned the Face of the large Sector Weſt.

				°	′	″	
Obſerved zenith diſtance of	β Tauri	.	1	56	56	s.
do. ſmall ſector	do.	.	1	59	6	s.
do.	Caſtor	•	1	56	17	N.
do. ſmall ſector	do.	.	1	53	33	N.
do.	Pollux	.	1	52	37	s.
do. ſmall ſector	do.	.	1	55	20	s.
do.	α Coro. Borealis	2	59	9	s.
do. ſmall ſector	do.	.	3	1	42	s.

Night cold, ſharp froſt, and water froze within 9 feet of our fires.

			ʰ	′	″	
♀ paſſed the meridian at	.	.	21	12	38	centrum.
☽ 's ſubsequent limb paſſed the meridian at			21	28	16.5	

20th.   ☉ 's preceding limb on the meridian at 11 56 25 A. M.
Subsequent   do.   at   .   11 58 38 A. M.

Centre at   .   .   .   11 57 31.5 A. M.

Obſerved zenith diſtance of β Andromedæ 4° 10′ 50″ N.

Equal altitudes of the Sun.
A. M. 8ʰ 30′ 55″.   P. M. 3ʰ 24′ 29″.

			°	′	″	
Obſerved zenith diſtance of	β Tauri	.	1	56	56	s.
do.	Caſtor	.	1	56	19	N.
do. ſmall ſector	do.	.	1	53	46	N.
do.	Pollux	.	1	52	35	s.
do.	α Coro. Borealis	2	59	8	s.
do. ſmall ſector	do.	.	3	1	42	s.

Cold

Cold for this climate, at 7ʰ P. M. linen
that was waſhed, and left out to dry, was
frozen ſtiff, and ice nearly ⅛th of an inch
thick was formed within 9 feet of our fires,
which were large, and kept up all night.

Obſerved zenith diſtance of α Lyræ (ſmall ſector) 8° 10′ 58″.

	h	′	″
♀ paſſed the meridian at ₑ	21	13	48 centrum.

☽ 's ſubſequent limb on the meridian at 22 25 8

21ſt. ☉'s preceding limb on the meridian at 11 56 20.5 A. M.
Subſequent do. at . . 11 58 33 A. M.
_____
Centre at . . . . 11 57 26.7 A. M.

Equal altitudes of the Sun.
A. M. 8ʰ 50′ 59″. P. M. 3ʰ 4′ 18″.

			°	′	″	
Obſerved zenith diſtance of	β Andromedæ		4	10	49	N.
do.	. .	β Tauri .	1	56	56	s.
do.	ſmall ſector	do. .	1	59	27	s.
do.	. .	Caſtor .	1	56	19	N.
do.	ſmall ſector	do. .	1	53	40	N.
do.	. .	Pollux .	1	52	37	s.
do.	ſmall ſector	do. .	1	55	48	u.

	h	′	″
♀ paſſed the meridian at	21	15	0 centrum.

22d. ☉'s preceding limb on the } 11 56 18 A. M. } tremulous.
meridian at
Subſequent do. at 11 58 38 A. M.
_____
Centre at . . 11 57 24 A. M.

Equal altitudes of the Sun.
A. M. 8ʰ 53′ 59″. P. M. 3ʰ 1′ 9″.

♀ paſſed the meridian at . 21ʰ 16′ 13″.5 centrum.

s

23d.

23d. Very warm.

Equal altitudes of the Sun.
A. M. 9ʰ 25′ 41″. P. M. 2ʰ 29′ 19″.

♀ paſſed the meridian at . 21ʰ 17′ 22″ centrum.

24th. ☉'s preceding limb on the meridian at 11 56 10 A. M.
Subſequent do. at . . 11 58 21 A. M.

Centre at . . . . 11 57 15.5 A. M.

Equal altitudes of the Sun.
A. M. 8ʰ 41′ 37″. P. M. 3ʰ 13′ 18″.

Immerſion of the 3d ſatellite of ♃ obſerved at 11ʰ 45′ 38″.
—Belts diſtinct, magnifying power of the teleſcope 120.

♀ paſſed the meridian . 21ʰ 18′ 30″ centrum.

Very hazy, the planet at times not viſible.

25th. ☉'s preceding limb on the meridian at 11 56 6 A. M.
Subſequent do. at . . 11 58 16 A. M.

Centre at . . . . 11 57 11 A. M.

Equal altitudes of the Sun.
A. M. 8ʰ 48′ 13″. P. M. 3ʰ 6′ 32″.

Emerſion of the 1ſt ſatellite of ♃ obſerved at 8ʰ 30′ 26″.
A little hazy, but the belts were middling well defined,
magnifying power 120.

End of the aſtronomical obſervations at this ſtation.

Rate

Rate of the Clock's going up the St. Mary's.

1800.

				′	″	Daily gain.
Clock too flow mean time	Feb.	9th.	.	16	48.5	″
do.	.	12th.	.	16	39.5	. . 3
do.	.	15th.	.	16	35.6	. . 1.3
do.	.	16th,	.	16	35.7	. . 0
do.	.	18th.	.	16	34.8	. . 0.4
do.	.	19th.	.	16	34.1	. . 0.7
do.	.	20th.	.	16	32.2	. . 1.9
do.	.	21ſt.	.	16	28.7	. . 3.5
do.	.	22d.	.	16	24.5	. . 4.2
do.	.	23d.	.	16	20.7	. . 3.8
do.	.	24th.	.	16	15.2	. . 5.5
do.	.	25th.	.	16	10.2	. . 5.2

Note, In the above ſtatement, where the equal altitudes, and the paſſage of the ☉ over the meridian have not given the ſame error, a mean has been taken, however the difference in all caſes was ſo ſmall, that it might ariſe from a want of perfection in making the obſervations themſelves.

Reſult of the obſervations made up the St. Mary's for determining the longitude.

		h	′	″	
Feb. 15th.	By the ☽'s diſtance from the ☉	5	29	18	
16th	*Emerſion* of the 1ſt ſatellite of ♃	5	29	7	
17th.	By the ☽'s diſtance from the ☉	5	29	55	
	do. . . .	5	30	18	Weſt from
18th.	. do. . . .	5	30	10	Greenwich.
	do. . .	5	29	16	
24th.	*Immerſion* of the 3d ſatellite of ♃	5	27	58	
25th.	*Emerſion* of the 1ſt do. .	5	28	53	

Reſult

Result of the Observations made with the large Sector, up the St. Mary's, to determine the Latitude.

The Zenith Distances stand as below.

Face of the Sector East.

1800.	β Andromedæ.			β Tauri.			Castor.			Pollux.			α Coro. Borealis.		
	°	′	″	°	′	″	°	′	″	°	′	″	°	′	″
February 14th	. . .			. . .			1	58	6 N.	1	50	49 S.	. . .		
15th	4	12	38 N.	1	55	13 S.	1	58	10	1	50	46	2	57	16 S.
16th	. . .			1	55	9	1	58	7	1	50	50	2	57	19
17th	4	12	39	. . .			1	58	9	1	50	50	. . .		
18th	. . .			. . .			. . .			. . .			. . .		
Means	4	12	38.5	1	55	11	1	58	8	1	50	48.7	2	57	17.5

Face of the Sector West.

19th	. . .			1	56	56	1	56	16	1	52	37	2	59	9
20th	4	10	50	1	56	56	1	56	19	1	52	35	2	59	8
21st	4	10	49	1	56	56	1	56	19	1	52	37	. . .		
Means	4	10	49.5	1	56	56	1	56	18	1	52	36.3	2	59	8.5
Means face east	4	12	38.5	1	55	11	1	58	8	1	50	48.7	2	57	17.5
Means	4	11	44	1	56	3.5	1	57	13	1	51	42.5	2	58	13
Refractions		+	4.2		+	2		+	2		+	1.9		+	3
True zenith distances	4	11	48.2	1	56	5.5	1	57	15	1	51	44.4	2	58	16

	β Andromedæ.	β Tauri.	Castor.	Pollux.	α Coro. Borealis.
	° ′ ″	° ′ ″	° ′ ″	° ′ ″	° ′ ″
Mean declinations on the 18th.	34 33 28 N.	28 25 28 N.	32 18 44 N.	28 29 46 N.	27 23 47 N.
Aberrations	+ 2.1	+ 2.3	+ 0.3	− 0.9	− 14.7
Nutations	− 1.4	+ 7.3	+ 9.0	+ 9.0	− 4.1
Semi-annual equations	− 0.4	+ 0.3	+ 0.1	+ 0.0	− 0.4
True declinations	34 33 28.3	28 25 37.9	32 18 53.4	28 29 54.1	27 23 27.8
True zenith distances applied	−4 11 48.2	+1 56 5.5	−1 57 15	+1 51 44.4	+2 58 16
Latitudes N.	30 21 40.1 N.	30 21 43.4 N.	30 21 38.4 N.	30 21 38.5 N.	30 21 43.8 N.

	° ′ ″
Latitude by β Andromedæ	30 21 40.1
do. β Tauri	30 21 43.4
do. Castor	30 21 38.4
do. Pollux	30 21 38.5
do. α Coro. Borealis	30 21 43.8
Mean Latitude North.	30 21 40.8

Result.

Result of the Observations made with the Small Sector, up the St. Mary's, to determine the Latitude.

The Zenith Distances when arranged stand as below.

Face of the Sector East.

1800. Feb.	β Tauri.	Castor.	Pollux.	α Coro. Borealis.	α Lyræ.
	° ′ ″	° ′ ″	° ′ ″	° ′ ″	° ′ ″
14th.	1 52 31 S.	2 1 3 N.	1 47 49 S.	2 54 26 S.	. . .
15th.	1 52 35	. . .	. . .	2 54 34	. . .
16th.	1 52 36	2 0 51	1 47 36	2 54 29	. . .
17th.	. . .	. . .	. . .	. . .	8 17 8 N.
Means	1 52 34	2 0 57	1 47 42.5	2 54 29.7	8 17 8

Face of the Sector West.

	β Tauri.	Castor.	Pollux.	α Coro. Borealis.	α Lyræ.
18th.	. . .	1 53 40	1 55 20	. . .	. . .
19th.	1 59 6	1 53 33	. . .	3 1 42	. . .
20th.	. . .	1 53 46	. . .	3 1 37	8 10 58
21st.	1 59 27	1 53 40	1 55 48	. . .	. . .
Means	1 59 16.5	1 53 39.7	1 55 34	3 1 39.5	8 10 58
Means face east	1 52 34	2 0 57	1 47 42.5	2 54 29.7	8 17 8
Means	1 55 55.2	1 57 18.3	1 51 38.2	2 58 4.6	8 14 3
Refractions	+ 1.9	+ 2	+ 1.9	+ 3	+ 8.2
True zenith distances	1 55 57.1	1 57 20.3	1 51 40.1	2 58 7.6	8 14 11.2
Mean declinations Feb. 18th.	28 25 28 N.	32 18 44 N.	28 29 46 N.	27 23 47 N.	38 36 15.5
Aberrations	+ 2.3	+ 0.3	— 0.9	— 14.7	— 14.8
Nutations	+ 7.3	+ 9.0	+ 9.0	— 4.1	— 8.6
Semi. ann. equations	+ 0.3	+ 0.1	0.0	— 0.4	— 0.1
True declinations	28 25 37.9	32 18 53.4	28 29 54.1	27 23 27.8	38 35 52.0
True zenith distances applied	+1 55 57.1	—1 57 20.3	+1 51 40.1	+2 58 7.6	—8 14 11.2
Latitudes N.	30 21 35.0 N.	30 21 33.1 N.	30 21 34.2 N.	30 21 35.4 N.	30 21 40.8 N.

Latitude

		°	′	″
Latitude by β Tauri	. . . . .	30	21	35.0
do. Caſtor	. . . . .	30	21	33.1
do. Pollux	. . . . .	30	21	34.2
do. α Coro. Borealis	. . . .	30	21	35.4
do. α Lyræ	. . . . .	30	21	40.8
Mean latitude north	. . . .	30	21	35.7

The ſame number of ſtars were taken with each ſector; but the large one from the length of its radius, being at leaſt three times as accurate as the ſmall one, the latitude by the large one, was multiplied by three, and the latitude by the ſmall one added to that product, and the ſum divided by four, the quotient 30° 21′ 39″.5 was taken for the true latitude of the obſervatory.

This being the higheſt point to which we could aſcend the river, and the country ſo covered with water, that it was impoſſible with our few remaining broken down pack horſes to convey our apparatus by land to the ſource of the river: we therefore had to determine the geographical poſition of its ſource by a traverſe; the courſes of which are as follows: viz. beginning at the obſervatory A, (Plate VIII.) where a hewn poſt was ſet up and ſurrounded by a large mound of earth, from thence N. 10° 1′ W. 4435.6 perches, thence S. 85° 14′ W. 115.6 perches, thence north 44.8 perches at the end of which a hewn poſt was ſet up, and ſurrounded by a mound of earth B.—Theſe courſes when tabled will ſtand as below.

Courſes.	N.	S.	E.	W.
N. 10° 1′ W. 4435.6 pˢ.	4360	. . . .	. . . .	771.2
S. 85° 14′ W. 115.6 pˢ.	. . . .	9.6	. . . .	115.2
N. 44.8 pˢ.	44.8	. . . .	. . . .	. . . .
	4412.8	9.6	. . . .	886.4
	— 9.6	. . . .	. . . .	. . . .
	4403.2	. . . .	. . . .	886.4

The laſt mentioned mound of earth was thrown up on the margin of the Okefonoke ſwamp, and as near to it as any permanent mark could be placed on account of the water.

From Plate VIII. upon which the above traverſe is laid down, it may be ſeen that the river St. Mary's is formed by the water draining out of the Okefonoke ſwamp along ſeveral marſhes, or ſmall ſwamps, which join into one, and form, or conſtitute the main branch or body of the river. The principal, or largeſt of thoſe ſwamps, or drains, is the moſt eaſterly one, and in which the current is the moſt viſible. This marſh, or drain is croſſed by the laſt courſe of the traverſe, which terminates at the mound B. From this mound north-eaſterly into the ſwamp, the water has but little, if any perceptible current. The ſource of the river is therefore in an indeterminate

determinate space; and no specific point could be fixed on, as the swamp is at all times almost impenetrable, and at this season of the year absolutely so without immense labour, and expence. It was therefore agreed that the termination of a line, supposed to be drawn N. 45°, E. 640 perches from the mound B, should be taken as a point to, or near which, a line should be drawn from the mouth of Flint river; which line when drawn, should be final, and considered as the permanent boundary between the United States and His Catholic Majesty, provided it passed not less, than one mile north of the mound B: but if upon experiment, it should be found to pass within less than one mile north of the said mound, it should then be corrected to carry it to that distance. To obtain as near as possible the course of the said line, with the distance between the points to be joined, the following materials deduced from our previous operations were used. The longitudes made use of are from measurements, compounded with the eclipses of the 1st satellite of Jupiter.

The longitude of the observatory near the mouth of Flint river by the eclipses of the 1st satellite of ♃ is 5^h 39' 19" west from Greenwich. The longitude of our station on Thompson's Creek, by a mean of five good observations is 6^h 4' 48" west from Greenwich. From Thompson's Creek to the Flint river observatory, the distance is 371.21 miles, which in the parallel of 31° is equal to 24' 57" in time, which deducted from the longitude at Thomson's Creek, will leave 5^h 39' 51" for the longitude of the observatory near the mouth of Flint river; which disagrees with the longitude by observation 32" in time. Measurements when accurately executed, in a known parallel of latitude, are generally preferable to observations for distances, not exceeding 100 miles: yet in this case, the measurement is not entitled to that weight, being done in haste, with a common chain, through thickets, swamps, and ponds, where pins of more than ordinary lengths had to be made use of, which involved an unsurmountable source of error: but not in so considerable a degree as to justify its rejection. It was therefore concluded, that if to twice the longitude of the observatory near the mouth of Flint river, the longitude by measurement from Thompson's Creek be added, and the sum divided by three, the quotient 5^h 39' 30" would be the longitude of the observatory near the mouth of Flint river, as correctly as it could be had from our materials: But the mouth of Flint river was found by measurement to be 260 perches, equal in time to 3".3 west from the observatory; which added to the above determination, the decimal .3 being rejected, as unimportant, when errors much larger are unavoidable, will give 5^h 39' 33" for the longitude of the mouth of Flint river.—The latitude has already been settled at 30° 42' 42".8.

The longitude of the observatory at A, up the St. Mary's by observation is 5^h 29'. The longitude of the observatory at Point Peter by four good observations is 5^h 26' 34": the difference of longitude by observation is 2' 26".—The difference of longitude between the observatories, by a traverse taken for that purpose, was 37.45 miles which is equal to 2' 32". The traverse being made under very unfavourable circumstances, and consisted of an uncommon number of courses, owing to the swamps, and ponds, (with which the country abounds), being full of water, and impassable:

paffable : the mean 2′ 29″ was therefore taken for the difference of longitude, which added to 5ʰ 26′ 34″ the longitude of Point Peter will give 5ʰ 29′ 3″ for the longitude of the obfervatory at A.—The difference of latitude between A, and the mound B, has been fhewn to be 4403.2 perches, and the difference of longitude 886.4 perches weft : thence to the end of the line fuppofed to be drawn N. 45 E. 640 perches from the mound B, the difference of latitude will be 452.5 perches ; which added to the difference of latitude between A, and B, will give 4855.7 perches, or 13′ 8″.5 nearly, which added to 30° 21′ 39″.5 the latitude of A, will give 30° 34′ 48″ for the latitude of the termination of the line fuppofed to be drawn from B.—From the obfervatory at A, to the mound B, the difference of longitude by meafurement has been ftated at 886.4 perches weft, from thence to the termination of the line fuppofed to be drawn from B, the difference of longitude is 452.5 perches eaft, which deducted from the wefting, will leave 433.9 perches weft, which is equal to about 6″ in time, and when added to 5ʰ 29′ 3″ the longitude at A will give 5ʰ 29′ 9″ for the longitude of the termination of the line fuppofed to be drawn as above ; which deducted from the longitude of the mouth of Flint river, will leave 10′ 24″ for the difference of longitude between the points.

There are now given

The latitude of the mouth of Flint river = . . 30° 42′ 42″.8

The latitude of the termination of the line fuppofed to be drawn from B $\Big\}$ = 30 34 48

The difference of longitude between the mouth of Flint river, and the termination of the line fuppofed to be drawn from B $\Big\}$ = 0ʰ 10′ 24″ = 2° 36′

To find the courfe, and diftance between the given points, that is, between the mouth of Flint river, and the termination of the line fuppofed to be drawn from B, which is done as follows :

In the fpherical triangle DEF, let DE reprefent the co. latitude of the mouth of Flint river = 59° 17′ 17″.2. FE the co. latitude of the termination of the line fuppofed to be drawn from B = 59° 25′ 12″, and the included angle DEF 2° 36′, being the difference of longitude between the given points.

For

For the required fide.

			°	′	″				
Included angle	.	.	2	36	0				
Half	.	.	1	18	0	.	.	S	8.3557835
Diff. of the fides	.	.	0	7	54.8				
Half	.	.	0	3	57.4	co. ar.		S	3.9389855
DE	.	.	59	17	17.2	.	. $\frac{1}{2}$ S		4.9671851
FE	.	.	59	25	12	.	. $\frac{1}{2}$ S		4.9674813
			89	39	44	. Tangent			12.2294354
			89	39	44	co. ar.		S	0.0000075
$\frac{1}{2}$ Diff. of the fides	.		0	3	57.4	.	.	S	6.0610145
			1	7	6.5			S	8.2904574
					2				

DF   2   14   13 = 155.2 miles nearly.

For the angles.

			°	′	″				
FE	.	.	.	.	59	25	12		
DE	.	.	.		59	17	17.2		
Sum	.	.	.	.	118	42	29.2		
Diff.	.	.	.		0	7	54.8		
$\frac{1}{2}$ Sum	.	.		59	21	14.6	co. ar.	S	0.0653339
$\frac{1}{2}$ Diff.	.	.		0	3	57.4	.	. S	7.0610145
Included angle	.	.		2	36	0			
$\frac{1}{2}$ Included angle	.		1	18	0.0		. c. Tang^t.		11.6441047
$\frac{1}{2}$ Diff. of the angles	.		3	22	24		. Tang^t.		8.7704531

$\frac{1}{2}$ Sum of the fides	.		59	21	14.6	co. ar.	c. S	0.2926586
$\frac{1}{2}$ Diff. of the fides	.		0	3	57.4	.	c. S	9.9999997
$\frac{1}{2}$ Included angle	.	.	1	18	0	.	c. Tang^t.	11.6441047
$\frac{1}{2}$ Sum of the angles	.	89	20	14	.	.	.	11.9367630
$\frac{1}{2}$ Diff. of the angles	.	3	22	24				
Greater angle	.	.	92	42	38			
Leffer angle	.	.	85	57	50			

From

From which it follows, that an arc of a great circle making an angle with the meridian at the mouth of Flint river from the fouth, towards the eaft of 87° 17′ 22″, being the fupplement of the angle EDF, will ftrike the termination of the line fuppofed to be drawn from B; provided the diftance be as before ftated. But if the diftance between the points, fhould either exceed the diftance deduced from the previous operations feven miles, or fall fhort of it an equal number, the line will neverthelefs pafs within half a mile of the termination of the fuppofed line, and therefore fall within the fpace of uncertainty as to the real fource of the river.

If a common furveying compafs fhould be ufed, the before mentioned angle of 87° 17′ 22″ muft be diminifhed at the rate of about 1′ 32″ for every three miles, to compenfate for the difference of 1° 19′ 32″ between the fupplemental angle already mentioned, and the angle DFE, to produce as near a coincidence as poffible with the arc of a great circle.

After erecting the mound B, we defcended the river, and encamped on the fouth end of Cumberland Ifland,* to prepare the report of our proceedings to both nations, and make our arrangements for leaving the country. At that encampment the following obfervations were made.

1800.

March 6th. Unloaded the veffel, encamped and fet up the clock.

  7th. Cloudy and very cold.

  8th. Stormy with cold rain.

  9th. Storm continues.

  10th. Violent wind, and heavy rain.

  11th. Cloudy in the morning, ftrong N. wind and fine rain.—Thermometer 49° in the morning, rofe to 57°.

  12th. Clear,—thermometer 47° in the morning, rofe to 70°.

Equal altitudes of the Sun.
A. M. 8ʰ 53′ 50″. P. M. 3ʰ 6′ 55″.

  13th. Thermometer 47° in the morning, rofe to 76°.

t 2   *Emerfion*

* The moft fouthern inclination of the United States on the Atlantic ocean.

Emerſion of the 1ſt ſatellite of ♃ obſerved at 6ʰ 58ʹ 49ʺ. —Evening very clear, the belts diſtinct, magnifying power 120.

14th.   Thermometer 49° at ſun riſe, roſe to 78°.

Equal altitudes of the Sun.
A. M. 8ʰ 54ʹ 6ʺ.   P. M. 3ʰ 5ʹ 57ʺ.

15th.   Thermometer 51° at ſun riſe, roſe to 84°.

Emerſion of the 2d ſatellite of ♃ obſerved at 11ʰ 54ʹ 41ʺ. —The planet was low and uncommonly tremulous—the belts indiſtinct, magnifying power 120.

16th.   Thermometer 57° at ſun riſe, roſe to 81°.

Equal altitudes of the Sun.
A. M. 9ʰ 5ʹ 0ʺ.   P. M. 2ʰ 54ʹ 30ʺ.

17th.   Thermometer 60° at ſun riſe, roſe to 81°.

Equal altitudes of the Sun.
A. M. 9ʰ 7ʹ 24ʺ.   P. M. 2ʰ 51ʹ 57ʺ.

The obſerved times, and diſtances, of the ☉'s and ☽'s neareſt limbs.

	h	′	″		o	′	″	
	19	45	15		82	10	20	
	19	45	59		82	10	0	
	19	46	38		82	9	50	Add for the error of
	19	47	15		82	9	30	the Sextant 7″.
	19	47	51		82	9	20	
	19	48	30		82	9	00	
Means	19	46	55		82	9	40	

Repeated.

Repeated.

h	'	''	o	'	''	
20	15	10	82	0	30	
20	15	51	82	0	10	
20	16	22	82	0	0	
20	16	49	81	59	50	
20	17	29	81	59	40	Add for the error of
20	18	4	81	59	30	the Sextant 7''.
20	18	33	81	59	20	
20	19	2	81	59	10	
20	19	35	81	59	0	
Means 20	17	26	81	59	41	

18th.   Thermometer 62° at fun rife, rofe to 81°.
—Cloudy with thunder great part of the day
attended with a little rain.

19th.   Thermometer 61° at fun rife, rofe to 86°.
—Cloudy part of the day.

The obferved times, and diftances, of the ☉'s and ☽'s neareft limbs.

h	'	''	o	'	''	
20	14	6	56	37	00	
20	14	45	56	36	50	
20	15	44	56	36	40	
20	16	33	56	36	30	Add for the error of
20	17	11	56	36	20	the Sextant 7''.
20	17	55	56	36	20	
20	18	28	56	36	00	
Means 20	16	23	56	36	31	

20th.   Thermometer 65° at fun rife, rofe to 82°.

Equal altitudes of the Sun.
A. M. 8^h 44' 35''.   P. M. 3^h 13' 53''.

A thick

A thick fog towards evening from the S. E.
—very cloudy at night.

21ft.   Thermometer 63° in the morning, rose to
79°.

22d.   Thermometer 60° at sun rise, rose to 84°.

Equal altitudes of the Sun.
A. M. 8ʰ 50′ 17″.   P. M. 3ʰ 7′ 53″.
Doubtful 3 or 4 seconds.

23d.   Thermometer 61° at sun rise, rose to 62°.
—Cloudy great part of the day with a violent
wind from the S. E.

24th.   Thermometer 58° in the morning, fell to
56° in the afternoon, rain with a strong wind
from the S. E.

25th.   Thermometer 56° at sun rise, rose to 70°.
—Flying clouds great part of the day.

Emersion of the 3d satellite of ♃ observed at 7ʰ 1′ 3″.—
Belts pretty distinct, magnifying power 120.

Discovered that the clock was considerably out of beat,
owing to the post to which it was fastened being moved by
people inadvertently leaning against it in the tent:—The
post being planted in loose sand, no better foundation to be
had.

26th.   Thermometer 50° at sun rise, rose to 60°.

Equal altitudes of the Sun.
A. M. 8ʰ 44′ 23″.   P. M. 3ʰ 13′ 0″.

Emersion of the 4th satellite of ♃ observed at 8ʰ 8′ 57″.
—Evening remarkably fine; magnifying power 200.—Although the satellite was too visible to be mistaken at the
time above noted, it certainly had not fully recovered its
lustre

luftre at 8^h 35′, it emerged clofe to the 2d fatellite, which gave me an excellent opportunity of judging of its brightnefs.

27th.　Thermometer 54° at fun rife, rofe to 68°.

Equal altitudes of the Sun.
A. M. 8^h 39′ 41″.　P. M. 3^h 17′ 35″.

Emerfion of the 1ft fatellite of ♃ obferved at 10^h 53′ 10″. —The planet very tremulous, and the belts fcarcely difcernible—magnifying power 120.

28th.　Thermometer 61° at fun rife, rofe to 76°. —Cloudy in the afternoon.

29th.　Thermometer 63° at fun rife, rofe to 81°. —Thunder and rain in the morning.

Equal altitudes of the Sun.
A. M. 8^h 42′ 54″.　P. M. 3^h 14′ 0″.

30th.　Thermometer 50° at fun rife, rofe to 75°.

Equal altitudes of the Sun.
A. M. 8^h 39′ 12″.　P. M. 3^h 17′ 30″.

The obferved times, and diftances, of the ☉'s and ☽'s neareft limbs.

h	′	″	o	′	″	
22	58	33	69	48	00	
23	59	25	69	48	10	
23	0	8	69	48	30	
23	0	49	69	48	50	Add for the error of
23	1	26	69	49	15	the Sextant 7″.
23	2	12	69	49	40	
23	3	3	69	50	10	
Means 23	0	48	69	48	56	

31ft.

31ft. Thermometer 53° at fun rife, rofe to 86°.
April 1ft. Thermometer 57° at fun rife, rofe to 87°.

Equal altitudes of the Sun.
A. M. 8ʰ 53′ 46″.   P. M. 3ʰ 2′ 57″.
Doubtful feveral feconds on account of clouds.

Immerfion of the 3d fatellite of ♃ obferved at 8ʰ 1′ 17″.
—The evening very fine, and the fatellite loft its luftre, and difappeared more gradually than I ever faw it before, —Magnifying power 120.

Emerfion of the fame fatellite obferved at 11ʰ 5′ 19″.
—The planet was low, and tremulous, and the belts very indiftinct, magnifying power as above.

2d.   Thermometer 61° at fun rife.

Emerfion of the 2d fatellite of ♃ obferved at 6ʰ 30′ 51″.
—The belts were well defined, but the fun having been fet about 15 minutes and the day light being very ftrong, on which account the obferved time might be diminifhed 10 or 15 feconds with propriety, magnifying power 120.

3d.   Thermometer 66° at fun rife, rofe to 78°.
—Cloudy all day with heavy rain, and thunder at night.

4th.   Thermometer 63° at fun rife, rofe to 82°.
—Cloudy all the forenoon.

5th.   Thermometer 64° at fun rife, rofe to 84°.

Equal altitudes of the Sun.
A. M. 8ʰ 39′ 11″.   P. M. 3ʰ 17′ 27″.

Emerfion of the 1ft fatellite of ♃ obferved at 7ʰ 13′ 19″.
—Belts well defined, magnifying power 120.

6th.   Thermometer 61° at fun rife, rofe to 85°.

Equal

Equal altitudes of the Sun.
A. M. 8^h 40′ 57″.   P. M. 3^h 15′ 48″.

7th.   Thermometer 62° at fun rife, rofe to 83°.
8th.   Thermometer 65° at fun rife, rofe to 85°.
9th.   Thermometer 70° at fun rife, rofe to 90°.

Equal altitudes of the Sun.
A. M. 8^h 23′ 52″.   P. M. 3^h 32′ 58″.

Emerſion of the 2d ſatellite of ♃ obſerved at 9^h 9′ 28″.
—A little hazy, magnifying power 120.

10th.   Thermometer 62° at fun rife, rofe to 87°.

Equal altitudes of the Sun.
A. M. 8^h 57′ 6″.   P. M. 2^h 59′ 48″.

Took down and packed up the inſtruments.

Rate of the Clock's going at the ſouth end of Cumberland Iſland.

				′	″	Daily gain.
Clock too flow mean time	March	12th.	.	9	44.3	″
do.	. .	14th.	.	9	31.6	6.3
do.	. .	16th.	.	9	13.0	9.3
do.	. .	17th.	.	8	59.6	13.4
do.	. .	20th.	.	8	32.1	9 2
do.	. .	22d.	.	8	4.4	13.9
do.	. .	26th.	.	7	13.7	12.7
do.	. .	27th.	.	6	58.7	15.0
do.	. .	29th.	.	6	32 2	13.2
do.	. .	30th.	.	6	19.7	12.5
do.	. April	1ſt.	.	5	42.7	18.5
do.	. .	5th.	.	4	32.2	17.6
do.	. .	6th.	.	4	13.2	19.0
do.	. .	9th.	.	3	16.4	18.9
do.	. .	10th.	.	2	56.9	19 5

Refults of the obfervations, made for the longitude, at the fouth end of · Cumberland Ifland.

			h	′	″	
March	13th.	*Emerfion* of the 1ft fatellite of ♃	5	26	29	
	15th.	do. . 2d . .	5	26	33	
	17th.	By a lunar obfervation .	5	26	59	
	17th.	do. . . .	5	26	25	
	19th.	do. . . .	5	27	25	
	25th.	*Emerfion* of the 3d fatellite of ♃	5	26	14	
	26th.	do. of the 4th do. by ⎫ the Nautical Almanac ⎬	5	51	48	Weft from
		By de Lambre's Tables .	5	27	37	Greenwich.
	27th.	*Emerfion* of the 1ft fatellite of ♃	5	25	43	
	30th.	By a lunar obfervation .	5	26	6	
April	1ft.	*Immerfion* of the 3d fatellite of ♃	5	24	6	
		Emerfion do. . .	5	26	0	
	2d.	*Emerfion* of the 2d fatellite of ♃	5	26	49	
	5th.	do. . 1ft do. .	5	26	40	
	9th.	do. . 2d do. .	5	26	57	

By a mean of the 3 eclipfes of the 1ft fatellite of ♃, the longitude of the fouth end of Cumberland ifland comes out 5^h 26′ 17″ weft from Greenwich : By a traverfe from the obfervatory at Point Peter acrofs the found, the difference of longitude between that ftation, and the fouth end of Cumberland ifland is 10″ nearly, which added to the longitude above, will give 5^h 26′ 27″ for the longitude of Point Peter; which is 7″ lefs than by obfervation. But as there were more obfervations on the eclipfes of the 1ft fatellite taken at Point Peter, and a better agreement, that determination is entitled to the moft weight.—If therefore 2″ be deduɛted from the longitude of the obfervatory at Point Peter as determined by obfervation, and 5″ added to the longitude of the fouth end of Cumberland ifland as deduced from obfervation, the longitudes will ftand as below.

	h	′	″	
Longitude of the S. end of Cumberland ifland	5	26	22	Weft from
Longitude of the obfervatory at Point Peter .	5	26	32	Greenwich.

Thefe longitudes are probably as correɛt as they can be had by obfervations, the refult of which depends upon a theory not yet abfolutely perfeɛt : but thefe, with other deduɛtions of a like nature in the foregoing work, may be further correɛted when compared with correfponding obfervations, or others made about the fame time, at obfervatories whofe pofitions have been accurately fettled. The latitude of the fouth end of Cumberland Ifland has already been ftated at 30° 43′ 13″.8 N.

The

The obfervations being now brought to a clofe, I have only to add, that they were made, and regiftered with fidelity, and correctly copied from the original entries in my journal, without a fingle alteration.—The errors of the clock, with its rate of going, as entered at the end of each courfe of obfervations, may readily be examined by the equal altitudes and other obfervations made for that purpofe: and for fear miftakes might happen, in reducing the obferved *time* of an obfervation for the longitude, to either mean, or apparent, the original *entry as noted at the clock*, has in all cafes been retained ;—fo that any refult, which depends upon an accurate knowledge of the time, may be re-examined, and corrected if found erroneous.

It is prefumed, that no apology will be neceffary, for any fmall inaccuracies which may be difcovered in the aftronomical obfervations, when it is confidered that they were made at temporary ftations, and the apparatus frequently expofed to the weather, for want of tents, and other covering ; and almoft as frequently fo injured by the tranfportation from one place, to another, through the wildernefs, that if I had not been in the habit of conftructing, and making inftruments for my own ufe, our bufinefs muft have been feveral times fufpended, till the repairs could have been made in Europe.

THE END.

FOLIO OF PLATES AND CHARTS

Plate A.

Lon West from Philad.

Lon West from Philad.

CINCINNATI
NEWPORT
COLUMBIA
Deer Cr.
Crawfish Cr.
Licking R.
Mill Cr.
Little Miami R.

VIRGINIA MILITARY LANDS

This is not from actual Survey but supposed to be tolerably correct

LIMESTONE

KENTUCKY

OHIO RIVER

Sciota R.
Little Sciota
Pine or Platte Cr.
French Settlem.t
Little Sandy R.
Little Sandy R.
12 Pole Cr.
Guyandot
Sandy R.

CHILICOTHA DISTRICT

15 A Elliott del.

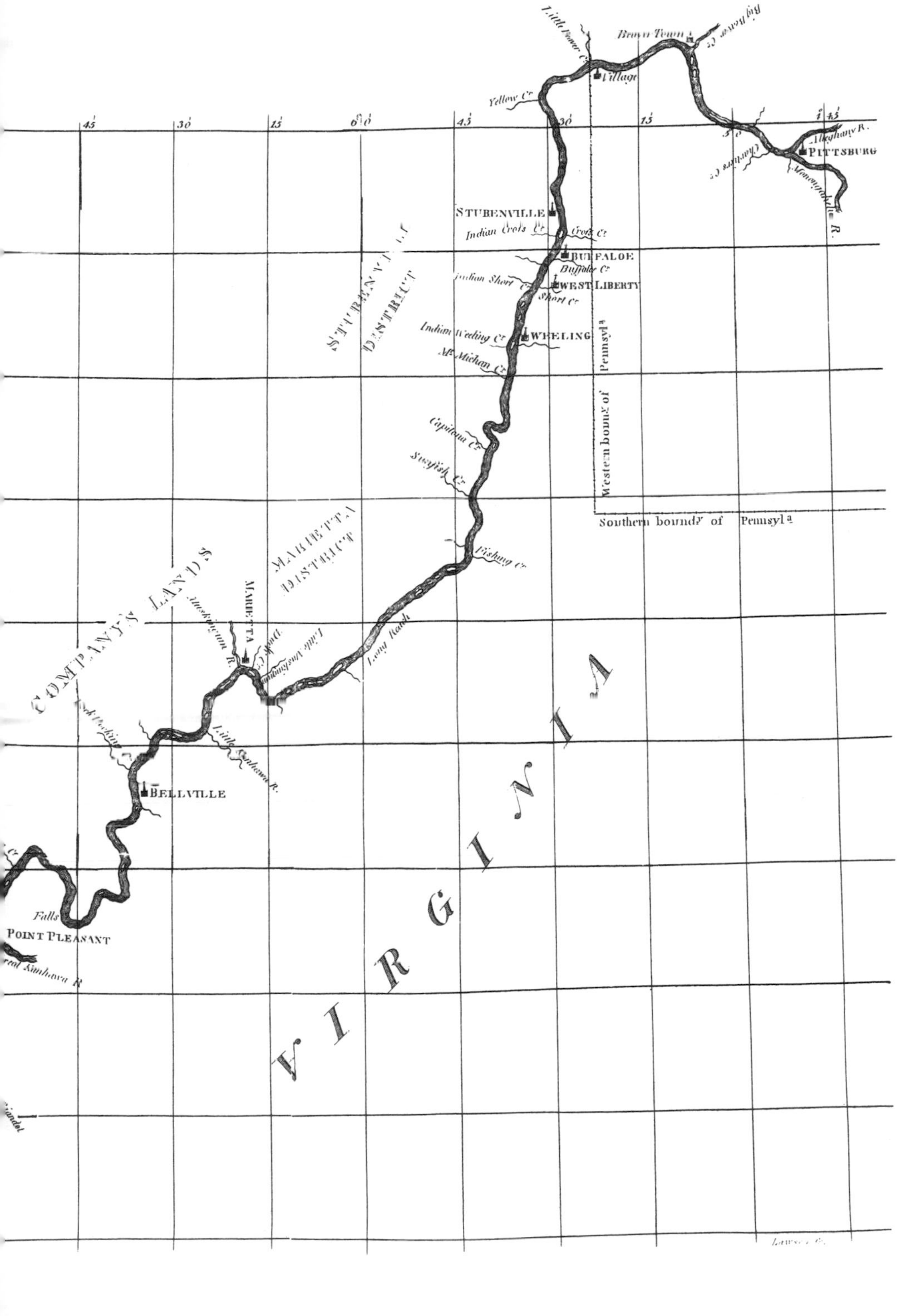

45
30
15
60
45
30
15
45
STUBENVILLE DISTRICT
MARIETTA DISTRICT
COMPANY'S LANDS
VIRGINIA
Little Beaver Cr.
Beaver Town
Big Beaver Cr.
Yellow Cr.
Village
Alleghany R.
PITTSBURG
Chartiers Cr.
Monongahela R.
STUBENVILLE
Indian Crols Cr.
Crols Cr.
BUFFALOE
Buffaloe Cr.
Indian Short Cr.
WEST LIBERTY
Short Cr.
Indian Weeling Cr.
WEELING
Mc Michan Cr.
Capitena Cr.
Sunfish Cr.
Fishing Cr.
Long Reach
Western boundy of Pennsyla
Southern boundy of Pennsyla
MARIETTA
Muskingum R.
Little Muskingum
Little Kanhawa R.
BELLVILLE
Falls
POINT PLEASANT
Great Kanhawa R.

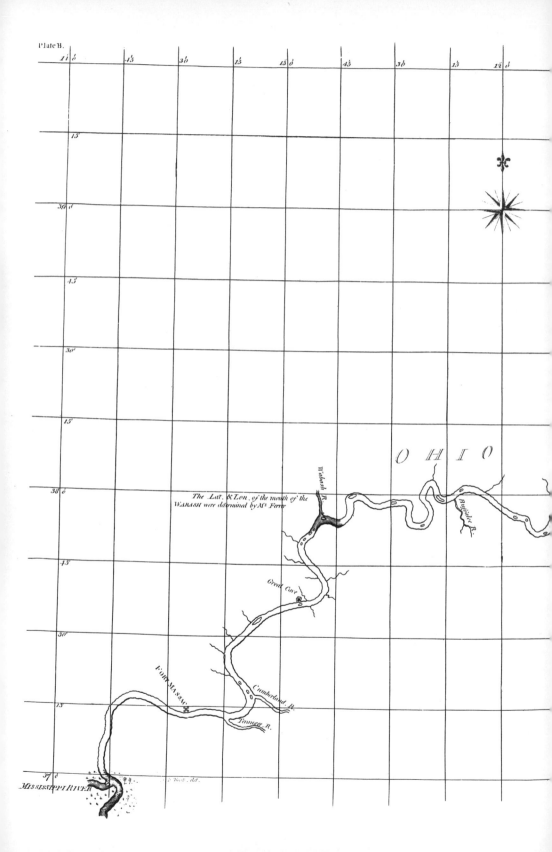

Plate B.

The Lat. & Lon. of the mouth of the
WABASH were determined by Mr Ferrer

O H I O

Wabash R.

Bright's R.

Great Cave

Fort Massac

Cumberland R.

Tenness R.

MISSISSIPPI RIVER

30 | 15 | 11 0 | 45 | 30 | 15 | 16 0 | 45 | 30

CINCINNATI

Great Miami R.

Tanner's Cᵏ

Laughery's Cᵏ

Gunpowder Cᵏ

Big Bone Cᵏ

Indian boundary Line

FORT WILLIAM

Kentucky R.

I V E R

Rapids of Ohio

The Lat. & Lon. of the RAPIDS were
determined by Mʳ Farrer

Bear Grass Cᵏ
LOUISVILLE

The unshaded part of the River is not from actual Survey

Lewson fc

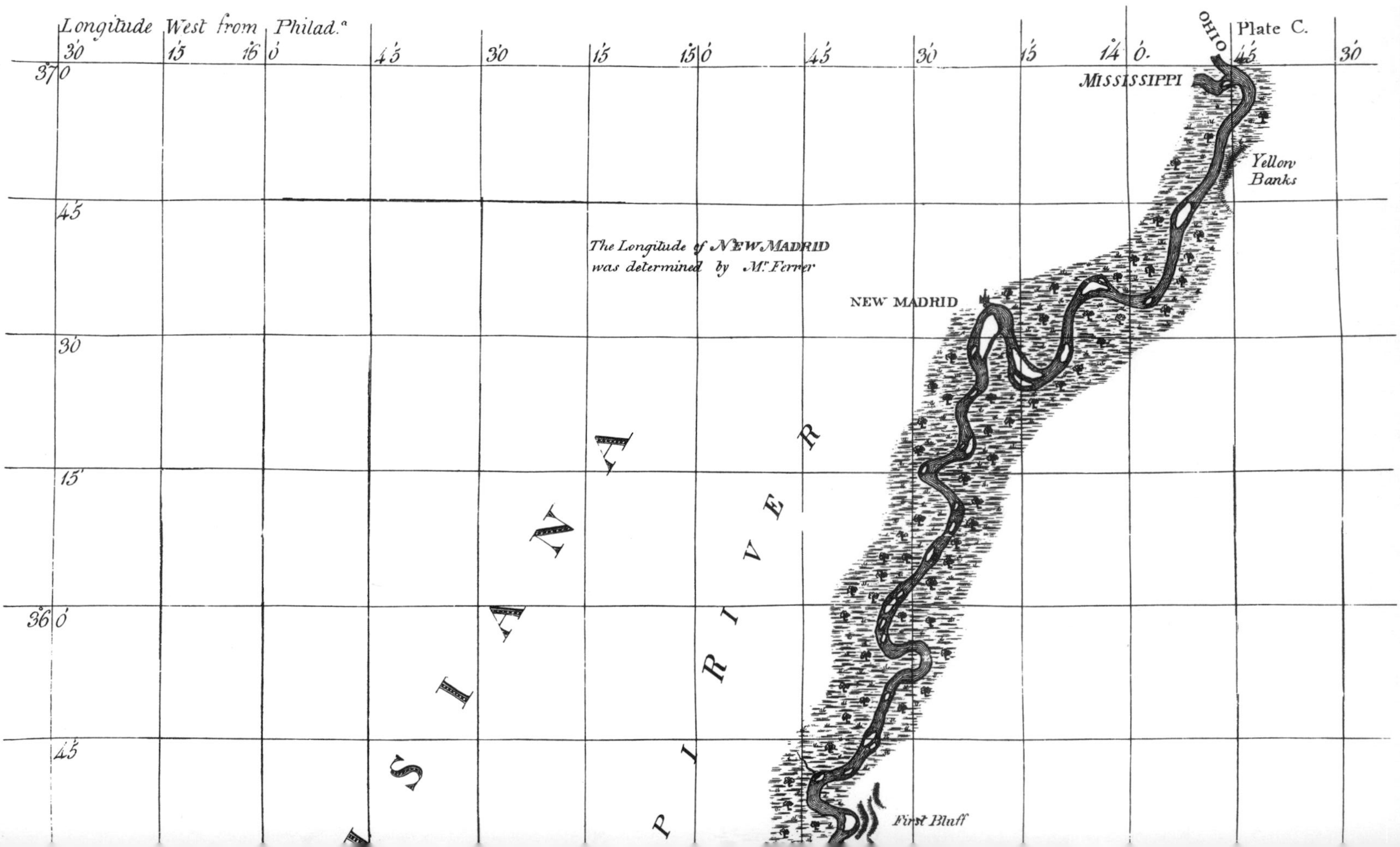

Plate C.

Longitude West from Philad.ᵃ

OHIO

Yellow Banks

MISSISSIPPI

NEW MADRID

Fort Bluff

The Longitude of NEW MADRID was determined by Mr Ferrer.

LOUISIANA

RIVER

Third Bluff

Wolf Run

Fort

Chickasaw Bluffs

St. Francis

White River

Arkansas R.

L O U I S I S S I P P I

The Latitude & Longitude of the Arkansas
were determined by Mr. Ferrer.

15

350

45

30

15

34 0

Jones fc.

Andw Ellicott del

Longitude west from Philad.ª

15   30   45   150   15   30   45

L'ISIANA

R I V E R

Arkansas Riv.

Yazous Riv.

34° 0'

45'
30'
15'
330
45'
30'

Southern Boundary of the United States

And.ᵂ Elliott de.

For the Map of the Mississippi from the boundary to the Gulf of Mexico, see chart

d Walnut Hill's HILLS was determined by Mᵣ Ferrer.

MISSISSIPPI

LO

Big Black

Bayou Pierre

Cole's Creek

NATCHEZ FORT

Sandy Cr.

St Catherine

White Cliffs

Homochitto

Buffaloe

Loftus Heights

FORT ADAMS

Williams Bayou

Red River

15'

32 0'

45'

30'

15'

31 0'

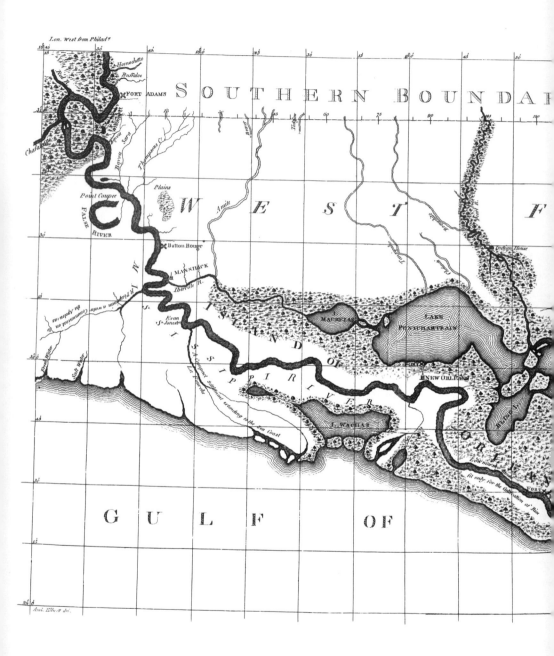

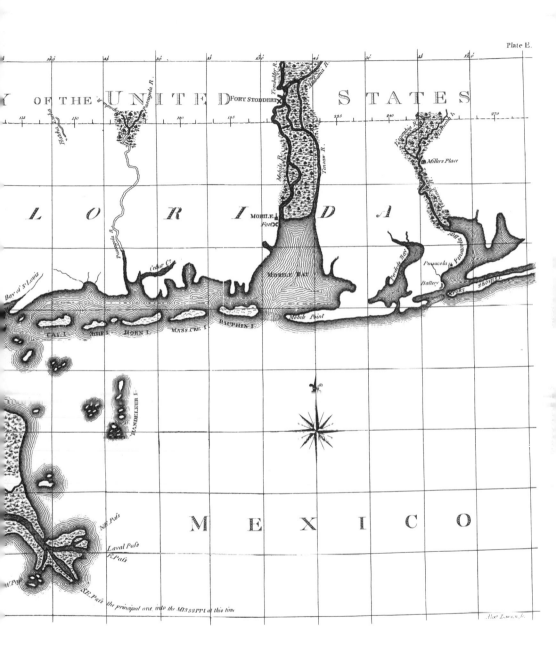

Plate E.

Y OF THE UNITED STATES
FORT STODDERT

L O R I D A

MOBILE
Fort

MOBILE BAY

MEXICO

Lon West from Philad.

SOUTHERN BOUNDARY OF THE UNITED STATES

White Creek &c.
Yellow Water
Small Lake
Choctaw R.

S. ROSE'S BAY

S. ROSE'S I.

Indian Village

High Bluff

Great Bend

The Seminoles have several
Villages above the Great bend

Flint R.

SOUTHER

E

W. Appapados
Fort

Old Tower

Chockley R.

APALACH
BAY

G U L F OF M E X I C O

S. GEORGE'S SOUND

CAPE S. BLASS

S. George's I.

This Island is not laid down
on any Chart before published

Elliott del.

On the East end of this Island, his
Britanic Majesty's Schooner the FOX
Commanded by Lieut Woobridge of the
Royal Navy, was cast away on the 17th
Sept. 1799, Mr Bowles (commonly called
Genl Bowles) and Suite were on Board.

OUNDARY OF THE UNITED STATES

AST FLORIDA

Okifonoke Swamp

The Dimensions of the Okefonoke
Swamp are yet but little known tho
Certainly much less than have generally
been Supposed

St. Mary's R.

ATLANTIC OCEAN

COLERAIN FORT

St. MARYS

Little St. Mary's

REFERENCES
A. The source of the River St Marys
B. Fort on point Peter
C. Cumberland Island
D. Amelia Island

E. Spanish Fort on Amelia Island

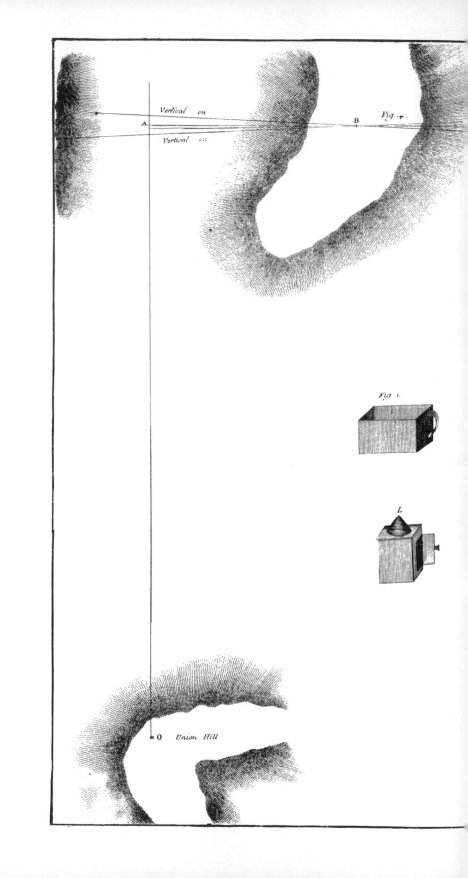

Vertical on

A   B   *Fig. 4.*

Vertical on

Fig. 1.

L

O   *Union Hill*

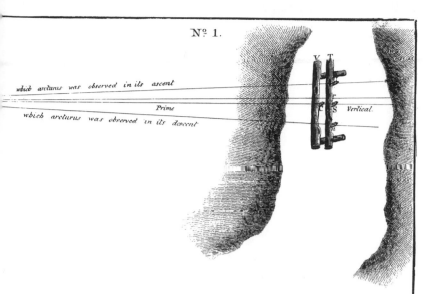

which arcturus was observed in its ascent

Prime   Vertical.

which arcturus was observed in its descent

Fig. 2.

Fig. 3.

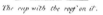

The cup with the roof on it.

L

L

Engrav'd by B.Jones.

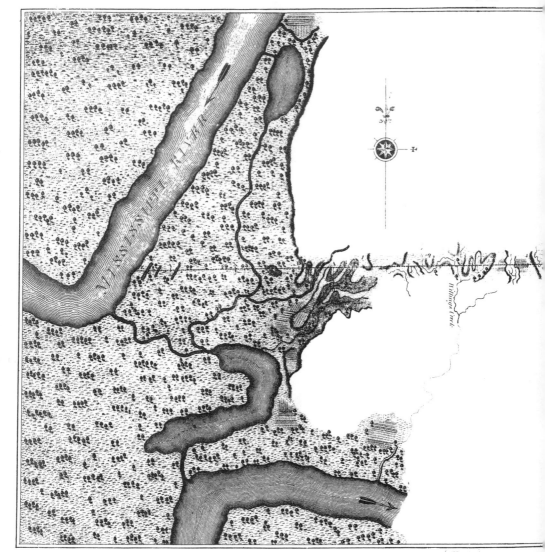

Note. In order to render the beginning, and references, more conspicuous, all the work on
this Plate, from the Mississippi, to the 3ᵈ mile east, from high water mark, is
laid down by a scale of 1 mile to an inch: —the remainder of the boundary is all laid
down by a scale of half a mile to an inch.

22 23 24 25 26 27 28 29 30 31

0.14. 0.28. 0.43. 0.57. 0.76. 0.86. 1. 1.11. 1.29. 1.11.

N.E. branch of Thompsons Cr.

Conodo

45 46 47 48 49 50 51 52

3.45. 3.60. 3.74. 3.89. 4.3. 4.18. 4.32. 4.46.

Little

River

66 65 66 67 68 69 70 71 72 73

6.19. 6.34. 6.48. 6.63. 6.77. 6.91. 7.6. 7.10. 7.25. 7.19.

Tanodyrator

85 86 87 88 89 90 91 92 93 94 95

9.22. 9.37. 9.51. 9.65. 9.80. 9.94. 10.9. 10.23. 10.37. 10.52. 10.66.

latitude were too small to be laid down on this part of the boundary.

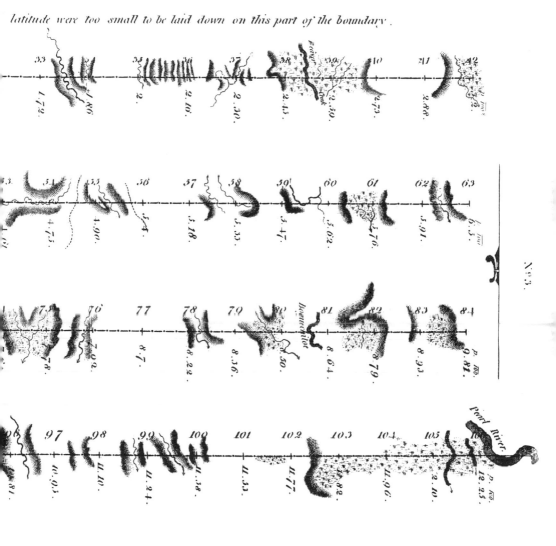

No. 3.

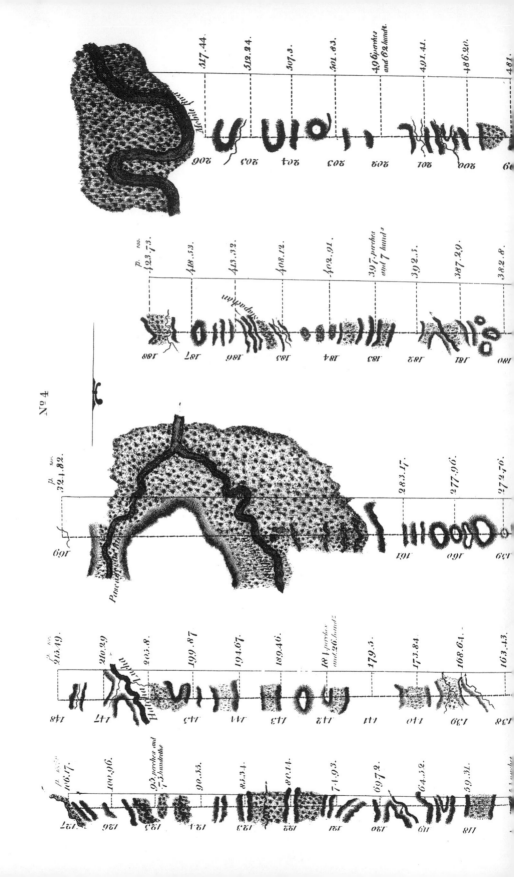

Nº 4

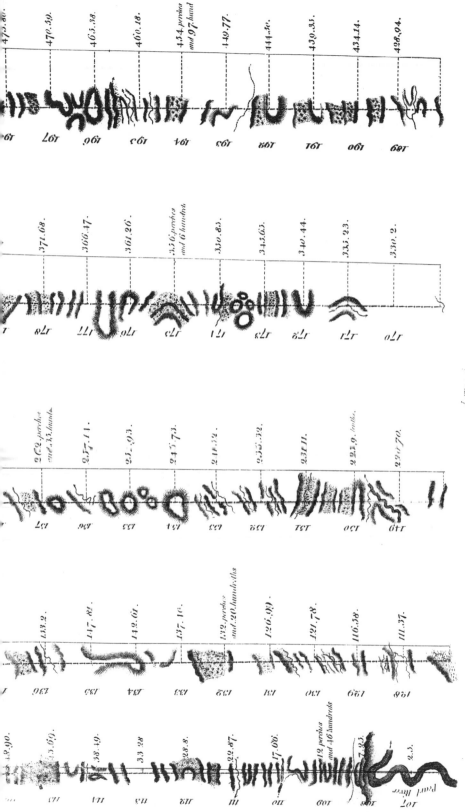

475.86. 470.59. 465.38. 460.18. 454.perches and 97 hund 449.77. 444.56. 439.35. 434.14. 428.04.

197. 196. 195. 194. 193. 192. 191. 190. 189.

371.68. 366.47. 361.26. 356.perches and 6 hundth 350.85. 345.65. 340.44. 335.23. 330.2.

179. 178. 177. 176. 175. 174. 173. 172. 171. 170.

2.62.perches and 83.hundth 257.41. 252.93. 247.73. 242.52. 237.32. 231.11. 225.9.perbs. 220.70.

137. 136. 135. 134. 133. 132. 131. 130. 140.

153.2. 147.81. 142.61. 137.10. 132.perches and 20.hundredths 126.99. 121.78. 116.58. 111.37.

136. 135. 134. 133. 132. 131. 130. 129. 128.

48.90. 43.69. 38.49. 33.28. 28.8. 22.87. 17.66. 12.perches and 46.hundreds 7.85. 2.5.

117. 116. 115. 114. 113. 112. 111. 110. 109. 108. 107.

Pearl River

Lower A.

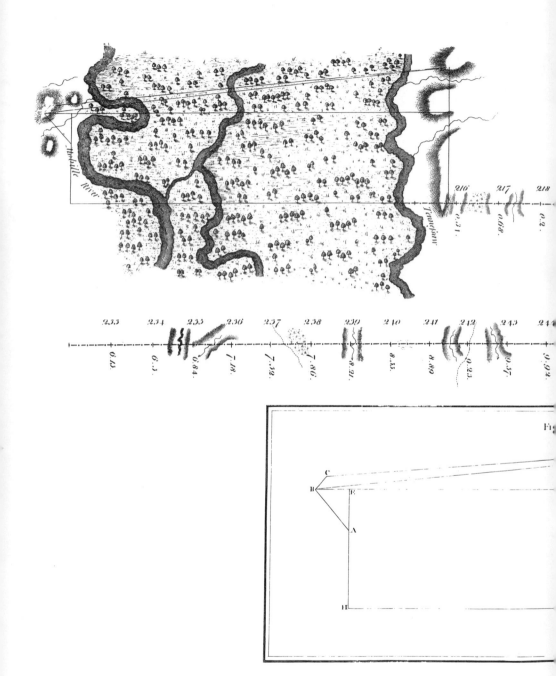

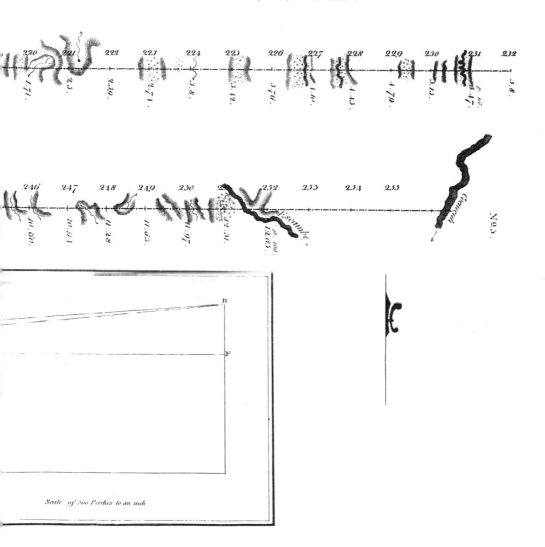

Note. The offsets between the guide line and parrallel of latitude were too small to be laid down on this part of the boundary.

Scale of 500 Perches to an inch

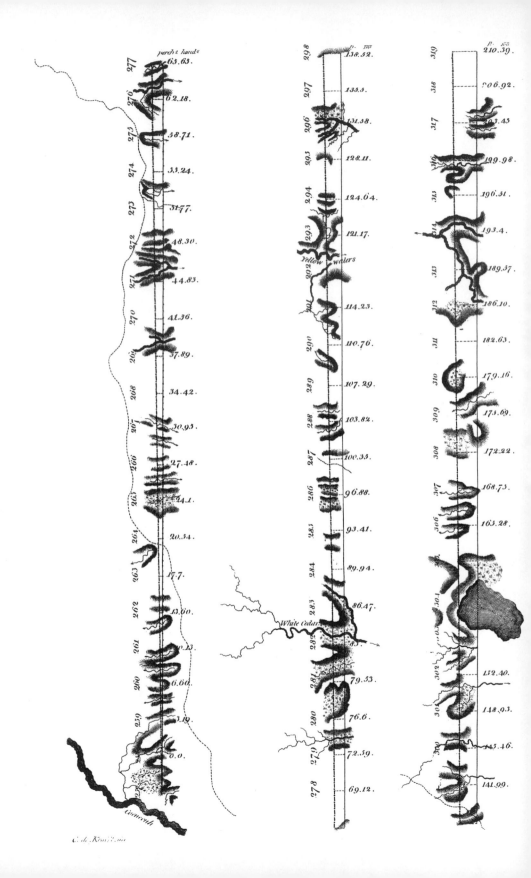

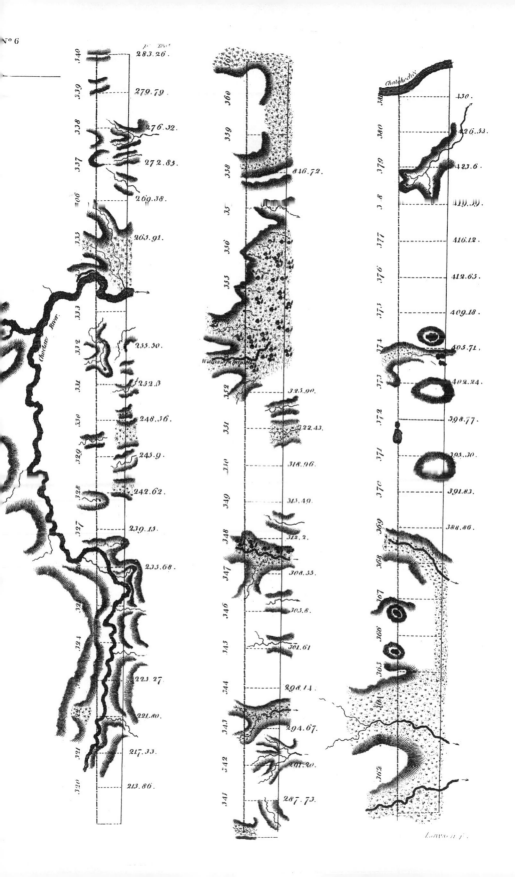

Column 1 (left):

340 — 283.26.
349 — 279.79.
348 — 276.32.
347 — 272.85.
346 — 269.38.
333 — 265.91.
333 —
Ocalaw Rivr.
332 — 255.50.
331 — 252.3
330 — 248.56.
329 — 245.9.
328 — 242.62.
327 — 239.15.
326 — 235.68.
325 —
324 —
323 — 225.27.
322 — 221.80.
321 — 217.33.
320 — 213.86.

Column 2 (center):

361 —
360 —
339 —
338 — 846.72.
35 —
336 —
335 —
Wilsons Branch
332 —
351 — 325.90.
350 — 322.43.
350 — 318.96.
349 — 315.49.
348 — 312.2.
347 — 308.55.
346 — 305.8.
345 — 301.61.
344 — 298.14.
343 — 294.67.
342 — 291.20.
341 — 287.73.

Column 3 (right):

Chatahochii
380 — 430.
380 — 426.53.
379 — 423.6.
3 8 — 419.99.
377 — 416.12.
376 — 412.65.
375 — 409.18.
374 — 405.71.
373 — 402.24.
372 — 398.77.
371 — 395.30.
370 — 391.83.
369 — 388.86.
368 —
367 —
366 —
365 —
364 —
363 —
362 —

Lawson F.

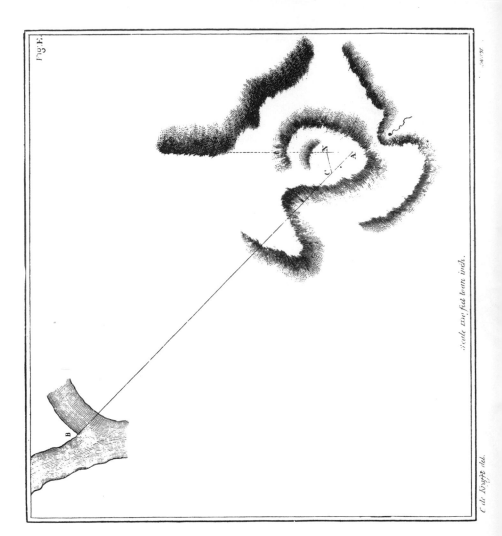

Scale nine feet loan inch.

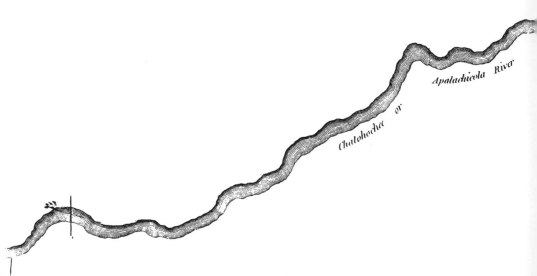

Chatohochee or Apalachicola River

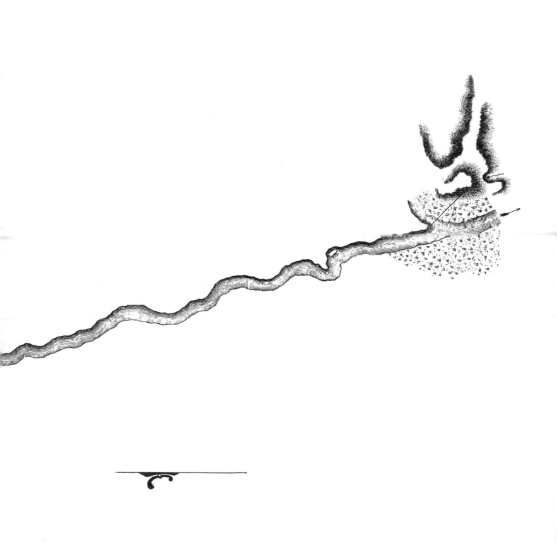

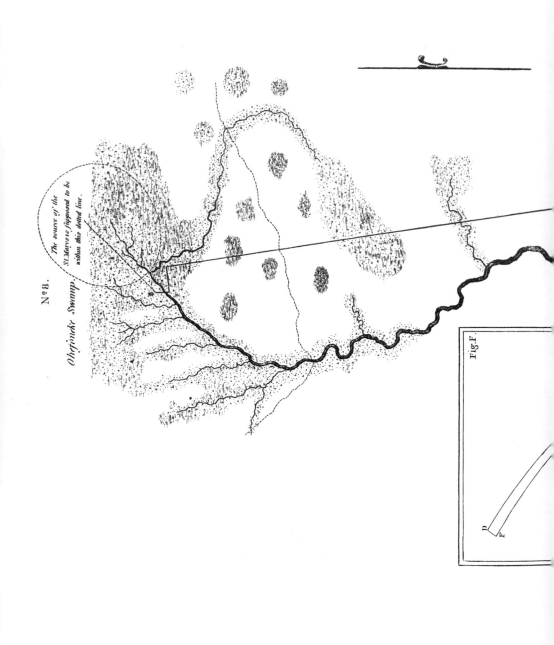

N°8.

Okefinoke Swamp.

The source of the
St. Marys is supposed to be
within this dotted line.

Fig. F.

D
F

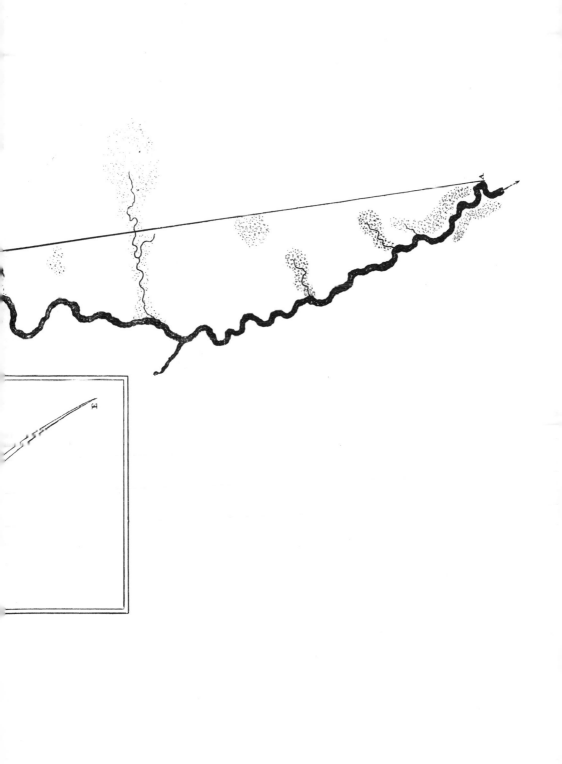